MW00826679

Soviet Adventures in the Land of the Capitalists

In 1935, two Soviet satirists, Ilya Ilf and Evgeny Petrov, undertook a 10,000-mile American road trip from New York to Hollywood and back accompanied only by their guide and chauffeur, a gregarious Russian Jewish immigrant and his American-born, Russian-speaking wife. They immortalized their journey in a popular travelogue that condemned American inequality and racism even as it marveled at American modernity and efficiency.

Lisa Kirschenbaum reconstructs the epic journey of the two Soviet funnymen and their encounters with a vast cast of characters, ranging from famous authors, artists, poets, and filmmakers to unemployed hitchhikers and revolutionaries. Using the authors' notes, US and Russian archives, and even FBI files, she reveals the role of ordinary individuals in shaping foreign relations as Ilf, Petrov, and the immigrants, communists, and fellow travelers who served as their hosts, guides, and translators became creative actors in cultural exchange between the two countries.

Lisa A. Kirschenbaum is an award-winning author whose research explores how individuals navigated the traumas of the twentieth century. Her books include *Small Comrades: Revolutionizing Childhood in Soviet Russia, 1917–1932* (2000), *The Legacy of the Siege of Leningrad, 1941–1995* (2006), and *International Communism and the Spanish Civil War* (2015).

Soviet Adventures in the Land of the Capitalists

Ilf and Petrov's American Road Trip

Lisa A. Kirschenbaum

West Chester University

CAMBRIDGE
UNIVERSITY PRESS

Shaftesbury Road, Cambridge CB2 8EA, United Kingdom

One Liberty Plaza, 20th Floor, New York, NY 10006, USA

477 Williamstown Road, Port Melbourne, VIC 3207, Australia

314–321, 3rd Floor, Plot 3, Splendor Forum, Jasola District Centre,
New Delhi – 110025, India

103 Penang Road, #05-06/07, Visioncrest Commercial, Singapore 238467

Cambridge University Press is part of Cambridge University Press & Assessment,
a department of the University of Cambridge.

We share the University's mission to contribute to society through the pursuit of
education, learning and research at the highest international levels of excellence.

www.cambridge.org
Information on this title: www.cambridge.org/9781316518465

DOI: 10.1017/9781009008914

First published 2024

Printed in the United Kingdom by CPI Group Ltd, Croydon CR0 4YY

A catalogue record for this publication is available from the British Library

Library of Congress Cataloging-in-Publication Data
Names: Kirschenbaum, Lisa A., 1965- author.
Title: Soviet adventures in the land of the capitalists : Ilf and Petrov's American
    road trip / Lisa Kirschenbaum, West Chester University, Pennsylvania.
Description: Cambridge ; New York : Cambridge University Press, 2024. |
    Includes bibliographical references and index.
Identifiers: LCCN 2023032720 (print) | LCCN 2023032721 (ebook) |
    ISBN 9781316518465 (hardback) | ISBN 9781009009232 (paperback) |
    ISBN 9781009008914 (ebook)
Subjects: LCSH: United States–Description and travel. | Il'f, Il͡ia, 1897-1937–
    Travel–United States. | Petrov, Evgeniĭ, 1903-1942–Travel–United States. |
    Automobile travel–United States–History–20th century. | United States–
    Social life and customs–1918-1945. | Soviet Union–Relations–United States. |
    United States–Relations–Soviet Union. | Il'f, Il͡ia, 1897-1937. Odnoėtazhnai͡a
    Amerika.
Classification: LCC E169 .I283 2024 (print) | LCC E169 (ebook) |
    DDC 917.304/917–dc23/eng/20230814
LC record available at https://lccn.loc.gov/2023032720
LC ebook record available at https://lccn.loc.gov/2023032721

ISBN 978-1-316-51846-5 Hardback

For my family

Contents

Figures

Acknowledgments

It is my pleasure to acknowledge the many institutions, colleagues, friends, and strangers across the continent who made this road trip possible. At every stop along the way, I was fortunate to receive the generous assistance of archivists, librarians, and curators. I thank Barbara Bair at the Library of Congress; David Langbart at the National Archives, College Park; Leah Early at the Jewish Historical Society of Greater Hartford; Diane Bird at the Laboratory of Anthropology; Nancy Brown-Martinez at the Center for Southwestern Research in Albuquerque; Christy Schoedinger Coleman and Nikki Donner at Fechin House in Taos; Tiane Marie at the Boulder City/ Hoover Dam Museum; Tami J. Suzuki at the San Francisco History Center; Cody White at the National Archives, Denver; and Louise Hilton at the Academy of Motion Picture Arts and Sciences Margaret Herrick Library.

I am indebted to the colleagues near and far who responded to my queries with warmth, suggestions, documents, and encouragement: Flannery Burke, Daniel Daniloff, David Evans, Milla Fedorava, Earl Ganz, Fran Hirsch, Nicholas Kupensky, Alice Nakhimovsky, Carl Note, Benjamin Sawyer, Marsha Siefert, Marshall Trimble, José Vergara, and Francis Wyman. A special thank you to Erika Wolf, who offered crucial feedback and help with the photographs. I am grateful to all those who read and responded to my work in progress: the press's anonymous readers, Choi Chatterjee, Deborah Field, Steven Kim, Ali Kocho-Williams, Elizabeth McGuire, Hank Reichman, Barbara Walker; and the editors of the (forthcoming) *Anti-Atlas* – Michal Murawski, Wendy Bracewell, and Tim Beasley-Murray. I benefitted from the opportunity to participate in *Kritika*'s "Eurasians Abroad" workshop and the Higher School of Economics' conference, "Soviet Encounters with West and East." As always, Diane Kirschenbaum eagerly read and discussed each chapter of "our book." Nancy Wingfield read everything I sent her and provided much wise counsel and encouragement. Bob

Weinberg read the entire manuscript with great attention and wry humor, and it is much the better for it.

Grants from the Kennan Institute, West Chester University, the WCU College of Arts and Humanities, and the Pennsylvania State System of Higher Education funded research travel and, when Covid-19 made travel impossible, defrayed costs for duplication services.

It has been a joy to work with everyone at Cambridge University Press. I thank Michael Watson for his enthusiasm for the project.

Since making the first long summer drive with my parents and brothers so many years ago, I have been fortunate to have the best of traveling companions. I thank my family for all their love and support, and especially John for making the journey with me.

Note on Transliteration and Translation

The pages that follow mix two systems of transliteration. In the notes, I use the Library of Congress system without diacritical marks. In the text, I follow common English usage and omit soft signs – so Il'ia Il'f and Evgenii Petrov become Ilya Ilf and Evgeny Petrov.

Ilf and Petrov often incorporated transliterated English words and phrases into their Russian text. To communicate their efforts to replicate the sound of American speech, I transliterate, rather than translate these. Where the meaning may be unclear, I provide a translation in brackets.

In retracing Ilf and Petrov's road trip, I used both the 1937 edition of their book *Odnoetazhnaia Amerika* (One-Story America) and Charles Malamuth's 1937 English translation, *Little Golden America*. If the translation is my own, I cite *Odnoetazhnaia Amerika* (as OA) in the notes. If I quote Malamuth's translation with no or minor alterations, I cite it first (as LGA) in the notes. I likewise drew on the serialized photo essay Ilf and Petrov published in the journal *Ogonek*, as well as Anne Fisher's translation, *Ilf and Petrov's American Road Trip*, edited by Erika Wolf. When I use the translation, I cite it (as ART) in the footnote. Unless indicated, all other translations are my own.

The title *Odnoetazhnaia Amerika*, literally "One-Story America," defies elegant English translation. I have rendered it as *Low-Rise America* to avoid the double meaning of "story" in English.

Abbreviations

ART   Erika Wolf, ed., *Ilf and Petrov's American Road Trip: The 1935 Travelogue of Two Soviet Writers Ilya Ilf and Evgeny Petrov*, trans. Anne O. Fisher (New York: Cabinet Books, 2007).

FRUS   United States Department of State, *Foreign Relations of the United States: The Soviet Union, 1933–1939* (Washington, DC: US Government Printing Office, 1933–1939).

LGA   Il'ia Il'f and Evgenii Petrov, *Little Golden America: Two Famous Soviet Humorists Survey the United States*, trans. Charles Malamuth (New York: Farrar and Rinehart, 1937).

NACP   National Archives, College Park, Maryland

NYT   *New York Times*

OA   Il'ia Il'f and Evgenii Petrov, *Odnoetazhnaia Amerika* (Moscow: Khudozhestvennaia literatura, 1937).

PIA   Il'ia Il'f and Evgenii Petrov, *Odnoetazhnaia Amerika: Pis'ma iz Ameriki*, ed. A. I. Il'f (Moscow: Tekst, 2003).

ZK   Il'ia Il'f, *Zapisnye knizhki, 1925–1937: Pervoe polnoe izdanie*, ed. A. I. Il'f (Moscow: Tekst, 2000).

Introduction

> We knew. There was no need to hurry. It was too soon to generalize.
> First of all, we must see as much as possible.
>
> Ilf and Petrov, *Little Golden America*

Every detail of the adventure sounds implausible. In 1935, two Soviet humorists undertook a 10,000-mile road trip from New York to Hollywood and back, accompanied only by their guide, a gregarious Russian Jewish immigrant, and chauffeur, his Russian-speaking, American-born wife. That the Soviet Union under Stalin even had humorists will come as a surprise to many. But Ilya Ilf and Evgeny Petrov were genuine Soviet funnymen, the coauthors of two beloved satirical novels, *The Twelve Chairs* (1928) and *The Little Golden Calf* (1931). Even more surprising for those looking back through the prism of Cold War hostility, neither the FBI nor the Soviet political police (the NKVD) seems to have restricted the freewheeling trip.[1]

Ilf and Petrov arrived in the United States at a moment of hopeful transition. The famine and shortages caused by the collectivization of agriculture and Stalin's crash industrialization program (the First Five-Year Plan, 1928–1932), had eased. During the "three good years" of the decade, 1934–1936, life for Soviet citizens was better if not quite, as Stalin famously asserted, more joyous.[2] The booming Soviet economy offered an optimistic contrast to the West suffering through the Great Depression. In the arts, the method of socialist realism had yet to be

---

[1] Jonathan Waterlow, "Sanctioning Laughter in Stalin's Soviet Union," *History Workshop Journal*, no. 79 (2015): 201–202; Dina Fainberg, *Cold War Correspondents: Soviet and American Reporters on the Ideological Front Lines* (Baltimore: Johns Hopkins University Press, 2021). The FBI learned of the trip in connection with an investigation of Donald Ogden Stewart and Ella Winter, who were married in 1939; "Solomon A. Trone: Internal Security – R," 19 October 1945, FBI 77-HQ-27252 (Trone FBI). In 1950, informants of "known reliability," who had known their guide Solomon Trone "intimately" between 1928 and 1934, told an FBI agent that the Soviet authorities were "highly suspicious" of him as "possibly an American Intelligence Agent," Report 20 June 1950.

[2] Sheila Fitzpatrick, *Everyday Stalinism: Ordinary Life in Extraordinary Times: Soviet Russia in the 1930s* (New York: Oxford University Press, 2000), 7.

rigidly codified. In the realm of foreign affairs, the Soviet state's 1933 establishment of diplomatic ties with the United States appeared to presage more open relations with the West. Indeed, the trip seemed designed to promote friendly cultural exchange.

By the time Ilf and Petrov published their account of their American travels, the good years had ended. The August 1936 show trial of Stalin's political opponents produced more than a dozen death sentences and a paroxysm of xenophobia. The Great Purges of 1937–1938 often targeted cultural and political elites, who accused each other of ideological failings and participation in vast and far-fetched conspiracies involving foreign intelligence agencies. Supposedly implemented to root out hidden enemies who might organize a lethal fifth column in the event of war, the purges coincided with mounting distrust of friendly, or indeed any relations with the capitalist world.

Thus, the most mindboggling feature of Ilf and Petrov's adventure is the fact that in 1937, at the height of the Stalinist terror, when any sort of connection to foreigners raised suspicions of treason or espionage, their American travelogue was published in both the Soviet Union and the United States.[3] Despite the grim political climate, their photo essay "American Photographs" and their book *Odnoetazhnaia Amerika* (Low-Rise America, literally One-Story America) reached a wide and appreciative Soviet audience. The title referred to the writers' interest in finding the "real" America of low-rise buildings beyond the skyscrapers of New York. To capitalize on the American success of *The Little Golden Calf*, the US publisher substituted *Little Golden America* for the clunky "one-story America." Under the circumstances, the American title with its golden spin on the land of capitalism was unfortunate. But it was not wholly inaccurate. The America Ilf and Petrov described was at once the spiritually impoverished antithesis of the socialist utopia under construction in the USSR and, even during the Great Depression, a phenomenally rich model of efficiency and modernity.

Taking Ilf and Petrov's adventure as a point of departure, this book tells the story of Soviet–American relations as a road trip. While there is a vast historical literature on the interwar "pilgrimage to Russia" that Michael David-Fox deems "one of the most notorious events in the political and intellectual history of the twentieth century," historians have

---

[3] Il'ia Il'f and Evgenii Petrov, *Odnoetazhnaia Amerika* (hereafter OA) (Moscow: Khudozhestvennaia literatura, 1937); *Little Golden America: Two Famous Soviet Humorists Survey the United States* (hereafter LGA), trans. Charles Malamuth (New York: Farrar and Rinehart, 1937).

paid relatively little attention to travel in the opposite direction.[4] Interwar trips to Russia came to seem particularly "notorious" because they were managed and monitored by the Soviet state with the apparent aim of persuading – if not "duping" – Western visitors, especially intellectuals, into supporting the Soviet system. Not incidentally, the state's role in cultural diplomacy has left historians a vast and centralized archive from agencies such as VOKS (the All-Union Society for Cultural Ties Abroad) that offers a window into the Soviet side of these exchanges.

By contrast, in the interwar years, the United States government had little involvement in cultural diplomacy beyond the basic regulatory task of issuing visas. For the historian, this situation offers an opportunity to push the history of cultural diplomacy beyond its traditional focus on state initiatives (such as VOKS) by exploring how a variety of nonstate actors shaped cultural relations. However, the fact that the US government did not guide or systematically track Soviet visitors also means that the archival records of their activities are fragmented and incomplete.

Retracing Ilf and Petrov's American road trip offers an innovative and fruitful means of locating the widely scattered individuals engaged in building friendly relations. To a degree unacknowledged in their published accounts, the writers relied on immigrants, communists, and fellow travelers as hosts, guides, and translators. Following the clues in their notes and letters, I identified many of these intermediaries. Their stories not only open new perspectives on Ilf and Petrov's American adventures, they also illuminate the understudied question of how Soviet travelers in the United States interacted with immigrant communities and allow us to understand how ordinary people became creative actors in cultural exchanges.

Because Ilf and Petrov were famous writers who met with prominent American authors, artists, and critics, many of their exchanges involved "culture" in the narrow sense. Investigating their adventures, I was able to flesh out cultural studies scholars' references to the transnational networks that linked Soviet and American modernists.[5]

---

[4] Michael David-Fox, *Showcasing the Great Experiment: Cultural Diplomacy and Western Visitors to the Soviet Union, 1921–1941* (New York: Oxford University Press, 2012), 1. See, for example, Sylvia R. Margulies, *The Pilgrimage to Russia: The Soviet Union and the Treatment of Foreigners, 1924–1937* (Madison: University of Wisconsin Press, 1968); Paul Hollander, *Political Pilgrims: Western Intellectuals in Search of the Good Society*, 4th ed. (New Brunswick, NJ: Transaction Publishers, 1998); Ludmila Stern, *Western Intellectuals and the Soviet Union, 1920–1940: From Red Square to the Left Bank* (New York: Routledge, 2006); Julia L. Mickenberg, *American Girls in Red Russia: Chasing the Soviet Dream* (Chicago: University of Chicago Press, 2017).

[5] Katherine M. H. Reischl, *Photographic Literacy: Cameras in the Hands of Russian Authors* (Ithaca, NY: Cornell University Press, 2018), 17; Barnaby Haran, *Watching the Red*

My reconstruction of Ilf and Petrov's encounters with American cultural producers, including the novelists John Dos Passos and Ernest Hemingway, as well as Russian and Jewish immigrants working in Hollywood, reveals the personal, multidirectional, and contingent nature of cultural exchange.

The book also examines culture in the broader sense, addressing the fundamental question of whether and how cross-cultural understanding happens. Under what conditions can interactions with other cultures and other people become mutually transforming experiences? Work on Western travelers in the Soviet Union proposes that their visits "triggered a process of intense mutual appraisal."[6] By contrast, much of the scholarship on Russian travelers in the United States suggests that such contacts produced little self-reflection, let alone transformation. The historian Meredith Roman argues that Soviet visitors were more concerned with signaling their "superior racial consciousness" than in questioning their stereotypes of African Americans as "naturally gifted dancers, musicians, and performers."[7] Literary studies of Russian American travelogues, including Ilf and Petrov's, emphasize that they relied less on "firsthand impressions" than "the framework imposed by literary tradition." Quoting Ilf and Petrov's assertion that they "glided over the country, as over the chapters of a long, entertaining novel," Milla Fedorova concludes that "the travelers read America rather than saw it." They were less interested in making discoveries than in confirming their view of their own country and themselves in the mirror of a mythical Other.[8] Without minimizing the power of the literary, ideological, and cultural preconceptions that prompted a particular "reading" of America, I focus on the complex task of translating American people,

Dawn: The American Avant-Garde and the Soviet Union (Manchester: Manchester University Press, 2016), 5.

[6] Michael David-Fox, "The Fellow Travelers Revisited: The 'Cultured West' though Soviet Eyes," *Journal of Modern History* 75 (June 2003): 301; Sheila Fitzpatrick, "Foreigners Observed: Moscow Visitors in the 1930s under the Gaze of Their Soviet Guides," *Russian History* 35 (Spring/Summer 2008): 232–33; Jessica Wardhaugh, "Europe in the Mirror of Russia: How Interwar Travels to the Soviet Union Reshaped European Perceptions of Borders, Time, and History," *Contemporary European History* 32 (2023): 97–113.

[7] Meredith L. Roman, "Forging Soviet Racial Enlightenment: Soviet Writers Condemn American Racial Mores, 1926, 1936, 1946," *Historian* 74 (Fall 2012): 528, 545.

[8] Milla Fedorova, *Yankees in Petrograd, Bolsheviks in New York: America and Americans in Russian Literary Perception* (DeKalb: Northern Illinois University Press, 2006), 7; Olga Peters Hasty and Susan Fusso, trans., eds., *America through Russian Eyes, 1874–1926* (New Haven, CT: Yale University Press, 1988); E. R. Ponomarev, "Puteshestvie v tsarstvo Koshcheia: Angliia i Amerika v sovetskoi putevoi literature 1920–1930-kh gg," *Vestnik SPBGUKU*, no. 1 (March 2012): 29–42, and no. 2 (June 2012): 26–34.

places, and practices into Soviet terms.[9] Drawing on sources from both sides, I examine specific encounters between the Soviet tourists and the "natives" as a means of assessing the process and possibility of questioning or even reshaping presuppositions about the Other.

Ilf-and-Petrov

Ilya Ilf and Evgeny Petrov shared roots in Odesa, a bustling, cosmopolitan port on the Black Sea. The only city in the empire to which Jews could move without special permission, Odesa had a reputation for rogues, wit, and irreverence.[10] Ilf, born Ilya Arnoldovich Fainzilberg in 1897, was Jewish, the son of a bank clerk. Petrov, born Evgeny Petrovich Kataev in 1903, came from more elevated circumstances as the son of a lycée teacher. He took the pen name Petrov to distinguish himself from his older brother Valentin Kataev, already an established writer. In 1923, Ilf and Petrov moved separately to Moscow, where both eventually became writers at *Gudok* (The Steam Whistle), the railway workers' newspaper that employed Kataev and other writers who became major literary figures: Isaac Babel, Mikhail Bulgakov, and Yuri Olesha.[11]

The writers began their partnership in 1927. According to Kataev, he proposed the treasure hunt story that became their first collaboration, *The Twelve Chairs*, a cross-country search for diamonds hidden in one of twelve dining room chairs dispersed by the Revolution. Ilf and Petrov, writing each sentence together, quickly finished the novel. It was an immediate success among readers, who took to its hero, the "smooth operator" Ostap Bender. Out to make a fortune in the not fully socialist Russia of the 1920s, Bender got his throat cut at the end of the story. But the con man proved so popular that Ilf and Petrov resurrected him for their second novel, *The Little Golden Calf*, which took Bender on another road trip. This time he and his sidekicks stalked an underground Soviet

---

[9] Eleonory Gilburd, *To See Paris and Die: The Soviet Lives of Western Culture* (Cambridge, MA: Belknap Press of Harvard University Press, 2018), 9–12.

[10] Jarrod Tanny, *City of Rogues and Schnorrers: Russia's Jews and the Myth of Odessa* (Bloomington: Indiana University Press, 2011); Roshanna Sylvester, *Tales of Old Odessa: Crime and Civility in a City of Thieves* (DeKalb: Northern Illinois University Press, 2005).

[11] Biographical material from Alice Nakhimovsky, "How the Soviets Solved the Jewish Question: The Il'f-Petrov Novels and Il'f's Jewish Stories," *Symposium* 53 (January 1999): 94–96; Alexandra Il'f, "Foreword," in Il'ia Il'f and Evgenii Petrov, *The Twelve Chairs: A Novel*, trans. Anne O. Fisher (Evanston, IL: Northwestern University Press, 2011), xi–xxvi; Mikhail Odesskii and David Fel'dman, "Kommentarii," in Il'ia Il'f and Evgenii Petrov, *Dvenadstat' stul'ev* (Moscow: Vagrius, 1999), 444–541.

Figure 0.1 Ilya Ilf reading the book *The 12 Chairs,* c. 1930. Eleazar Langman. Wikimedia Commons

millionaire, whose riches Bender hoped to appropriate. (Figures 0.1 and 0.2)

Thus, the writers became the much-loved single entity Ilf-and-Petrov. By the early 1990s, print runs of their novels ran to over 40 million copies.[12] In the 1930s, English translations found enthusiastic readers in the United States. When Ilf and Petrov met Upton Sinclair, he told them that "he had never laughed harder than when reading *The Little Golden Calf.*"[13] In the United States, the two writers were sometimes referred to as the "Soviet Mark Twain." They seemed to appreciate the irony of the nickname and played up their kinship with the American

[12] Lesley Milne, *How They Laughed: Zoshchenko and the Ilf–Petrov Partnership* (Birmingham: Centre for Russian and East European Studies, 2003), 127–28.

[13] Il′f, 22 December 1935, in Il′ia Il′f and Evgenii Petrov, *Odnoetazhnaia Amerika: Pis′ma iz Ameriki,* ed. A. I. Il′f (Moscow: Tekst, 2003) (hereafter PIA), 476; *Diamonds to Sit On: A Russian Comedy of Errors,* trans. Elizabeth Hill and Doris Mundie (New York: Harper & Bros., 1930); *The Little Golden Calf,* trans. Charles Malamuth (New York: Farrar and Rinehart, 1932).

Figure 0.2 Evgeny Petrov reading the English edition of *The Little Golden Calf*, c. 1930. Eleazar Langman. Wikimedia Commons.

funnyman.[14] Via an interpreter, Petrov told reporters from the *New Yorker* that "It is because life is so tragical that we write funny books." His mention of the pair's visit the previous day to the Mark Twain house in Hartford, Connecticut, prompted a grinning Ilf, the more reserved and sardonic of the two, to chime in with the assertion "that Mark Twain had a very tragical life. Dark, gloomy."[15]

[14] Erika Wolf, "Introduction," in Erika Wolf, ed., *Ilf and Petrov's American Road Trip: The 1935 Travelogue of Two Soviet Writers Ilya Ilf and Evgeny Petrov*, trans. Anne O. Fisher (New York: Cabinet Books, 2007) (hereafter ART), xiii.
[15] A. J. Liebling and Harold Ross, "Soviet Funny Men," *New Yorker*, 9 November 1935, 13.

By the time Ilf and Petrov came to America, the heyday of Soviet satire was passing.[16] When the reporters from the *New Yorker*, Harold Ross and A. J. Liebling, wondered whether the Second Five-Year Plan "had anything to say about humor," Petrov responded, "it hasn't." At the same time, Ross and Liebling reported that both authors were "somewhat concerned" by Commissar of Enlightenment Anatoly Lunacharsky's warning that at some point there would be no "imperfections" left to satirize in the Soviet Union. To the question of what the writers would do then, "Petrov said that there would always remain some material: standard stuff like mothers-in-laws." But America was a different story. In the United States they could describe "rogues, swindlers, and other raffish characters" to their hearts' content.[17]

As it turned out, Ilf and Petrov's American road trip was their last major collaboration. Ilf, whom the *New Yorker* profile described as "gaunt," was ill with tuberculosis. He died in April 1937, just as the first edition of *Low-Rise America* was published. In 1942, Petrov, working as a war correspondent, died in a plane crash. Their untimely deaths helped to shield them and their work from political attacks. Such attacks were certainly possible in the toxic atmosphere of the Stalinist purges, as the authors well understood. Nonetheless, the travelogue remained a popular Soviet guide to all things American and, with a hiatus during the so-called anti-cosmopolitan campaign of the late 1940s, widely available.[18]

Fiction and Fact

In early October 1935, Ilf and Petrov, traveling as reporters for *Pravda*, arrived in New York City in style but on a budget. They sailed from Le Havre on the *Normandie*, at the time the largest, fastest, and swankiest ship afloat. Because it was the off season, the cruise line upgraded them from tourist to first-class accommodation. In letters to their wives, Ilf and Petrov described their cabin as "luxurious," paneled in highly polished wood, with two wide wooden beds, two "huge wall closets with a million

---

[16] Annie Gérin, *Devastation and Laughter: Satire, Power, and Culture in the Early Soviet State (1920s–1930s)* (Toronto: University of Toronto Press, 2018), 185–90.

[17] Liebling and Ross, "Soviet Funny Men," 13–14; A. V. Lunacharskii, "Il'f and Petrov," 1931, http://lunacharsky.newgod.su/lib/ss-tom-2/ilf-i-petrov/ (accessed 21 August 2022).

[18] Evgenii Petrov to Charlz [Charles Malamuth], 4 June 1937; Malamuth to [John] Farrar, 7 July 1937, Charles Malamuth Papers, Columbia University Rare Books and Manuscript Library, Box 1. Wolf, "Introduction," ART, xiv; Aleksandr Etkind, *Tolkovanie puteshestvii: Rossiia i Amerika v travelogakh i intertekstakh* (Moscow: Novoe literaturnoe obozrenie, 2001); Milne, *How They Laughed*, 255–68.

hangers" for their meagre wardrobes, armchairs, and a private bath.[19] Their first night in New York, the authors paid $5 (the equivalent of about $110 in 2023) for an "old-fashioned" room at the Prince George Hotel. Conveniently located on Twenty-Eighth Street between Fifth and Madison Avenues, the hotel attracted many Soviets doing business in the United States. The next day, after meeting with the Soviet consul in New York, they moved to what Petrov described as a "very fashionable area" of Midtown Manhattan near Park Avenue, Radio City, and the Empire State Building. From their room on the twenty-seventh floor of the Shelton Hotel at Lexington and Forty-Ninth Street (three stories below Georgia O'Keeffe's 1920s studio) they had an "enchanting" view of Manhattan's "most famous skyscrapers," Brooklyn, and two bridges over the East River, which Petrov mistook for the Hudson.[20] It is not clear who picked up the bill. Ilf, who brought $999 to New York, carefully kept track of expenses down to a ten-cent cup of tea. But he did not specify the cost of the room overlooking New York.[21]

The pair's first big purchase in the United States was a "splendid typewriter" ($33), on which they immediately began documenting their journey.[22] Like many Soviet writers, Ilf and Petrov had experience as journalists, novelists, playwrights, and screenwriters. The work they produced during and after their trip to the United States attests to this flexibility. They published feuilletons in *Pravda* while still in the United States and sent numerous letters home. Ilf kept a journal and took hundreds of photographs. In 1936, *Ogonek*, something like a Soviet *Life* magazine, serialized their photo essay "American Photographs," which featured Ilf's photos and their collaborative text.[23] *Low-Rise America* itself defies classification. Literary critics have variously identified it as a book-sketch, literary reportage, a novel, a satire, a picaresque, and a travelogue.[24]

---

[19] PIA, Il'f, Petrov, 4 October 1935, 422, 425; P. de Malglaive, "French Ideas of Ship Planning and Decoration," *Journal of the Royal Society of Arts* 85 (16 April 1937): 500–520.

[20] Il'ia Il'f, *Zapisnye knizhki, 1925–1937: Pervoe polnoe izdanie*, ed. A. I. Il'f (Moscow: Tekst, 2000) (hereafter ZK), 7 October, 426; PIA, Petrov, 8 October 1935, 426, 427; Nancy J. Scott, *Georgia O'Keeffe* (London: Reaktion Books, 2015), 105–07; Bureau of Labor Statistics, CPI Inflation Calculator, www.bls.gov/data/inflation_calculator.htm (accessed 8 April 2023).

[21] ZK, 1 October, 423, 477.   [22] PIA, Il'f, 11 October 1935, 428.

[23] Karen L. Ryan, "Imagining America: Il'f and Petrov's 'Odnoetazhnaia Amerika' and Ideological Alterity," *Canadian Slavonic Papers* 44 (September–December 2002): 264–65.

[24] Ryan, "Imagining America," 263–64; Fedorova, *Yankees*, 75; Marcia Morris, "Russia: The Picaresque Repackaged," in J. A. Garrido Ardila, ed., *The Picaresque Novel in*

Clearly grounded in fact, Ilf and Petrov's literary production blurred the border between documentary and fiction. Their published work often hews closely to notes made and letters sent during the trip. My research in American archives and published sources largely corroborates their tales. Nonetheless, Ilf and Petrov took many liberties with chronology, names, and identifications. In addition to obscuring many of their contacts' roots in the Russian empire, Ilf and Petrov left quite a bit out of their published work – notably Ilf's uncles and cousins in Hartford and the writers' efforts to sell a screenplay. Such "refashioning of factual material" was common in Soviet newspaper sketches, which aimed not only or primarily to inform readers but to persuade and activate them.[25]

While Ilf and Petrov's published work left out and reworked a great deal, it was not straightforward anti-capitalist propaganda. As reporters for *Pravda*, the writers' remit was highlighting the "distance" that separated "the world of socialism" from the "the capitalist world."[26] But they were always astute observers, attuned to, and willing to include, the perspectives of people who straddled the divide between "ourselves" and the Other. Having received a $300 advance from their American publisher, which bankrolled their brand-new Ford Fordor Sedan ($260 down and $312 due in two months), Ilf and Petrov collected their impressions with the expectation that their travelogue would have audiences in both the Soviet Union and the United States.[27] Certainly, they included many condescending generalizations about Americans: they are loud and always laughing; they lack curiosity; they prefer trashy movies to good books. Yet Ilf and Petrov also found much to admire and described plenty of Americans who did not fit the stereotypes.[28] The very forms in which they told their tale – the photo documentary and the picaresque – connected them to modernist literary experiments in both the Soviet

---

Western Literature: From the Sixteenth Century to the Neopicaresque (New York: Cambridge University Press, 2015), 211–13; Mark Hale Teeter, "The Early Soviet de Tocquevilles: Method, Voice, and Social Commentary in the First Generation of Soviet Travel 'Publitsistika' (1925–1936)" (PhD diss., Georgetown University, 1987), 4–15, 263–325.

[25] Jeremy Hicks, *Dziga Vertov: Defining Documentary Film* (London: I. B. Tauris, 2007), 14 (refashioning), 9; Matthew Lenoe, *Closer to the Masses: Stalinist Culture, Social Revolution, and Soviet Newspapers* (Cambridge, MA: Harvard University Press, 2004), 26, 157, 235–36.

[26] OA, 394.

[27] ZK, 18 October 1935, 437; PIA, Il'f, 10 November 1935; Petrov, 12 November 1935, 446, 447.

[28] Maria Natarova, "Ot agitatsionnogo lozugna k khudozhestvennomu obrazu: Amerika v povesti I. Il'fa i E. Petrova 'Odnoetazhnaia Amerika,'" in *Rossiia i SShA: Formy literaturnogo dialoga* (Moscow: RGGU, 2000), 31.

Union and the capitalist West that challenged simplistic ways of seeing the world.[29]

On the Road

From their first days in New York, Ilf and Petrov started planning an American road trip. Initially, their plans were modest. In early October, Ilf wrote his wife, Maria Nikolaevna, that they would undertake a two-week trip with the Soviet consul to Chicago and Detroit, then to Canada and back to New York City.[30] Within two weeks, their plans became grander: a "colossal journey" of more than 15,000 kilometers (9,300 miles) to begin in early November. Doing some calculations in his notebook, Ilf figured the two-month journey would set them back about $2,000. Petrov sketched the proposed route for his wife, Valentina Leontevna: "New York, Buffalo, Niagara Falls, across Canada to Detroit, Chicago, Kansas City, Santa Fe, then ... to San Francisco. That's already California. Then – Los Angeles (including Hollywood), San Diego, a bit of Mexican territory, Texas, Mississippi, Florida, Washington, New York." Upon returning in January 1936, Ilf and Petrov planned to take a twelve- or fourteen-day trip by "banana boat" to Cuba and Jamaica before sailing for home via England. The eight-week road trip largely followed this ambitious itinerary; the pair decided to skip the "tropics," likely out of growing concern for Ilf's health (Figure 0.3).[31]

While working out their route, Ilf and Petrov traveled around the East Coast, visiting Washington, DC, Hartford, and the General Electric (GE) headquarters in Schenectady, New York. They made the last of these trips on 28 October 1935 with Solomon Trone, a retired engineer who had worked for GE in the Soviet Union, and his wife Florence. In early November, the Trones agreed to guide Ilf and Petrov on their journey through the "real" America of small towns and low-rise buildings.[32] Florence did the driving. In *Low-Rise America*, Ilf and Petrov turned the couple into Mr. and Mrs. Adams, retaining his connection to GE and her skill as a chauffeur.

---

[29] Erika Wolf, "The Author as Photographer: Tret′iakov's, Erenburg's, and Il′f's Images of the West," *Configurations* 18 (2010): 384; Jeff Allred, *American Modernism and Depression Documentary* (Oxford: Oxford University Press, 2009), 6–10, 21; Miriam Udel, *Never Better! The Modern Jewish Picaresque* (Ann Arbor: University of Michigan Press, 2016), xiv–xv.

[30] PIA, Il′f, 8 October 1935, 428.

[31] ZK, 18 October, 437; PIA, Petrov, 6 November 1935, 444.

[32] PIA, Il′f, 4 November 1935, 443.

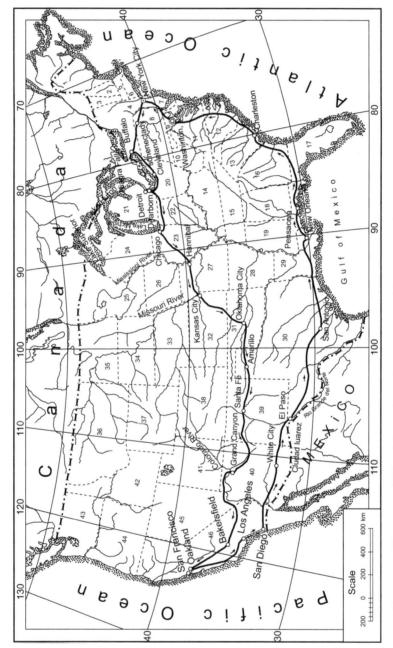

Figure 0.3 The route of Ilf and Petrov's road trip as mapped in *Low-Rise America*

Eighty-four years later, with Ilf and Petrov's copious notes as my guide, I undertook my own Soviet American road trip. Each stop along their route became a discrete research problem, and each vignette required its own, often creative, sourcing solution. I tracked down a wide range of characters who had interacted with Ilf and Petrov: diplomats, journalists, anthropologists, artists, poets, novelists, filmmakers, engineers, jokers, dockworkers, revolutionaries, and a few scoundrels. In some cases, I was able to corroborate their stories. When I found no direct trace of Ilf and Petrov's visit, I investigated their contacts' wider connections to Soviet visitors and Soviet culture. In addition to personal papers, the book makes extensive use of institutional, governmental, and corporate archives to establish the conditions under which personal and cultural exchanges occurred. The most challenging problem was finding the ordinary people with whom Ilf and Petrov interacted. I drew on community oral history projects, including a remarkable series of life history interviews collected in 1935–1936 as part of a survey of San Francisco's ethnic minorities. In addition to archival sources, I have employed published sources including newspapers, memoirs, and contemporary anthropological research to get a sense of how individuals participated in and understood cultural exchanges.

My road trip through the past begins with a review of the rules of the road and lay of the land: visa regulations, travel restrictions, and must-see attractions. But I focus on the process of travel, the planned and chance encounters that transform an itinerary into a journey. My purpose in excavating the archival traces of Ilf and Petrov's trip was less to judge their accuracy than to locate their informants' perspectives. Read against Ilf and Petrov's notes and narratives, the American stories illuminate the shared concerns as well as the preconceptions and misconceptions that shaped and sometimes limited efforts to understand the Other.

I also retraced Ilf and Petrov's road trip more literally. Following their abundant clues, I was able to rephotograph many of Ilf's subjects from virtually the same spots from which he shot them in 1935. Rephotography can be a powerful means of documenting social change. For sociologists, it involves producing photographs of a particular place, social group, or phenomenon over time and reviewing the resulting photographs for evidence of change.[33] Ilf's photographs are well suited to this technique as he was explicitly interested in documenting the social reality of the Depression. But I was less concerned with establishing what

[33] Jon H. Rieger, "Rephotography for Documenting Social Change," in Eric Margolis and Luc Pawels, eds., *The SAGE Handbook of Visual Research Methods* (Los Angeles: SAGE, 2011), 132–49.

was/is in front of the lens than what the photographer cropped. Locating Ilf's vantage point, standing almost literally in his shoes, allowed me to see how he framed his shots and constructed his view of "real America."

In undertaking my own Soviet American road trip, I tried, like Ilf and Petrov, to travel and observe unhurriedly, striving to see as much as possible. Like the Soviet visitors, I made the trip always aware of the difficulty of leaving my own world behind. For Ilf and Petrov, the American highways over which they traveled were always "in our thoughts" Soviet highways. Similarly, for the historian traveling the highways of the past, the present is never far away. The travelers' investigations of American modernity, inequality, racism, and immigration inevitably call to mind current problems. Imagining present-day landscapes as the subject of the Soviet author and photographer's gaze opens unexpected alternatives to our own ingrained ways of seeing Russia, America, and ourselves.[34]

---

[34] Fedorova, *Yankees*, 22; Tim Youngs, *The Cambridge Introduction to Travel Writing* (New York: Cambridge University Press, 2013), 163–66.

Part I

Promised Lands

In 1935, as at the time of this writing, travel from Russia to the United States required a visa. Because the US government, unlike the Soviet government, provided neither guides, translators, nor minders to visitors from the other side of the capitalist–socialist divide, the main point of contact between Soviet travelers and American officialdom was the State Department's Visa Division. Thus, I made the National Archives' campus in College Park, Maryland, the first stop on my Soviet American road trip. My goal was to try to locate Ilf and Petrov's visa applications and to investigate the process by which they and other Soviet citizens got permission to enter the United States. More broadly, I wanted to understand why, despite deep mutual suspicions that persisted even after the normalization of diplomatic relations in 1933, Soviet citizens came to the United States and why the US government let them come.

In the summer of 2018, I immersed myself in visa applications, policy guidelines, memos of discussions with Soviet diplomats, and ordinary Americans' letters to the State Department that shed light on American immigration policy in the 1930s. That same summer, an immigration crisis raged at the US–Mexico border. The photo of a two-year-old girl screaming while US immigration agents patted down her mother became the symbol of the "zero tolerance" policy that separated migrant parents from their children.[1] Unexpectedly, I heard echoes of the eighty-plus-year-old documents, with their terror of "aliens" "contaminating" the United States, in contemporary headlines. Parents crossing the southern border with their children, the president warned, "could be murderers

---

[1] Avi Selk, "The Crying Face of the US Immigration Crisis," *Washington Post*, 21 June 2018.

and thieves and so much else."[2] The attorney general pledged, "We are not going to let this country be overwhelmed."[3]

The contemporary crisis also threw into sharp relief what was unique about fears of "aliens" in the 1930s. Then, it was not only a question of the imagined dangers that immigrant Others in search of the Promised Land posed for white America.[4] In the 1930s, Americans engaged in a sometimes fierce, sometimes friendly struggle with a competing Promised Land. The speed and achievements of the Soviet industrialization drive, the official Soviet commitment to antiracism and anticolonialism, and the Soviet vision of the radiant communist future appealed to many disillusioned with capitalism and appalled by fascism. In this context, the specter of emissaries from the Soviet Union sparking a violent overthrow of the American government seemed plausible enough to influence the process for granting even nonimmigrant visas. At the same time, the US government allowed into the country a constant stream of Soviet visitors, especially engineers, who came to pick up machinery or study new techniques at American firms – even those engaged in sensitive military projects. During the Depression, such exchanges were good, if potentially dangerous, business.

Piecing together the archival evidence reveals the assumptions, regulations, exceptions, compromises, and workarounds that shaped whether and how Soviet visitors made it into the United States. The records also allow us to catch glimpses of individuals – some famous, like Ilf and Petrov, others obscure – who in coming to the United States became both subjects of surveillance and agents in the construction of friendlier relations. Ultimately, these individual stories help us to understand how, at this moment of transition in Soviet–American relations, people on both sides looked to the opposing promised land with both fear and longing.

---

[2] Marissa Lang, "Activists Plan White House Protest over Family Separations at Border," *Washington Post*, 20 June 2018.

[3] Christopher Ingraham, "Sessions Says Family Separation Is 'Necessary' to Keep the Country from Being 'Overwhelmed,'" *Washington Post – Blogs*, 18 June 2018.

[4] Steve Lopez, "A Prison in Promised Land," *Los Angeles Times*, 19 June 2018.

1   Amerikanizm

> [Henry Ford] has the close-set, prickly eyes of a peasant. As a matter of
> fact, he looks like a sharp-nosed Russian peasant, a genius inventor, who
> unexpectedly shaved off his beard and donned an English suit.
>
> Ilf and Petrov, *Low-Rise America*

As the Bolsheviks began constructing a new socialist order, they represented the United States as both a foil and a prototype of the socialist
future. The Soviet press predicted the revolutionary demise of the land of
capitalism, with its unfettered wealth, unremitting poverty, and violent
racism. But it also promoted a veritable cult of *Amerikanizm*. The
builders of socialism aimed to do more than borrow advanced
American technology; they wanted to learn American *tekhnika*. Often
translated as "technique," tekhnika conjured up uniquely American
know-how, efficiency, practicality, ingenuity, and energy.[1] In 1924,
Stalin expressed his commitment to American tekhnika in an aphorism
endlessly quoted during the industrialization drive of the next decade:
"The combination of Russian revolutionary sweep with American efficiency is the essence of Leninism in Party and state work."[2] Understood
in this way, Amerikanizm had the potential not only to speed the tempo
of work and modernize Soviet industry but also to produce a modern
socialist society and modern Soviet people. As the Austrian writer René

---

[1] Jeffrey Brooks, "The Press and Its Message: Images of America in the 1920s and 1930s,"
in Sheila Fitzpatrick, Alexander Rabinowitch, and Richard Stites, eds., *Russia in the Era of
NEP: Explorations in Soviet Society and Culture* (Bloomington: Indiana University Press,
1991), 235; Kendall E. Bailes, "The American Connection: Ideology and the Transfer of
American Technology to the Soviet Union, 1917–41," *Comparative Studies in Society and
History* 23 (January 1981): 421; Alan M. Ball, *Imagining America: Influence and Images in
Twentieth-Century Russia* (Lanham, MD: Rowman and Littlefield, 2003), 145–53.

[2] Josef Stalin, "The Foundations of Leninism," Stalin Internet Archive, www.marxists.org/
reference/archive/stalin/works/1924/foundations-leninism/ch09.htm (accessed 5 July 2021);
Hans Rogger, "*Amerikanizm* and the Economic Development of Russia," *Comparative
Studies in Society and History* 23 (July 1981): 385.

Fülop-Miller observed in the late 1920s, "industrialized America, for the Bolsheviks, became the Promised Land."[3]

Nothing more clearly captures the paradoxical nature of the Soviet cult of Amerikanizm than its worship of the archetypical capitalist Henry Ford.[4] When in the mid-1920s the American journalist Maurice Hindus returned to the Belorussian village that he had left in 1905, he was surprised to learn that America, which the Bolsheviks regarded as "the most capitalistic and most reactionary nation in the world," was "universally idolized." "Again and again," he reported, "Soviet officials would say to me that Russia's salvation lay in her ability to learn to do things in the American way, which is the best way."[5] Soviet intellectuals and technical experts revered Ford "as a guide and teacher who can show them how to obtain the best results in the quickest time with the least outlay of capital and labor." Russian peasants, enamored of their Fordson tractors, celebrated the automaker as the cleverest of inventors.[6] Ilf and Petrov's account of their brief audience with the great man in Dearborn, Michigan, quoted in the epigraph, clearly followed in this tradition. Emphasizing Ford's physical resemblance to a sharp-eyed peasant, they described one of the richest capitalists in America in homespun terms as an "amazing mechanic," who "detests Wall Street," and left them with the advice, "Don't ever get into debt, and help one another."[7] (Figure 1.1)

Overwhelmingly, the Soviet people who visited the United States in the 1930s came to study American technology.[8] In the initial period of normalized relations (the last quarter of 1933), the United States issued eighty-one visas to Soviet visitors. The most high-profile were cultural emissaries such as the ballet dancers Tatiana Vecheslova and Vachtang Chabukiani, who performed at Carnegie Hall in January 1934. The group also included a general manager of Intourist, the Soviet tourist bureau, and a handful of trade representatives, many of whom came with their wives, looking to sell everything from petroleum products to sausage casings. But the vast majority (sixty-three) were engineers and mechanics (all men), who traveled both to take delivery of already purchased

---

[3] René Fülop-Miller as quoted in Marina L. Levitana, *"Russian Americans" in Soviet Film: Cinematic Dialogues between the US and the USSR* (London: I. B. Tauris, 2015), 2.

[4] Richard Stites, *Revolutionary Dreams: Utopian Vision and Experimental Life in the Russian Revolution* (New York: Oxford University Press, 1989), 146–49.

[5] Maurice Hindus, *Broken Earth* (New York: International Publishers, 1926), 41.

[6] Maurice Hindus, "Ford Conquers Russia," *Outlook* 147 (29 June 1927): 280, 282.

[7] LGA, 102–103; OA, 135–36.

[8] A. Dana Hodgdon to Mr. Kelley, 7 July 1931, National Archives, College Park (NACP), Record Group (RG) 59, 811.111 Russian Students/20; State Department to American Consul Berlin, 21 July 1932, 811.111Russian Students/22.

Figure 1.1 Henry Ford, c. 1934. Ilf and Petrov claimed that Ford
looked like a sharp-nosed Russian peasant in an English suit.
Prints and Photographs Division, Library of Congress, LC-USZ62-78374.

equipment and to study American industry. The largest contingent,
sixteen mechanics and engineers, were headed to training courses at
the Ford Motor Company.[9]

To take advantage of the tantalizing business opportunities offered by
Soviet interest in American technology, the US government put few
restrictions on visiting engineers. After the normalization of diplomatic
relations in 1933, American officials' concerns about economic and even
military competition scarcely restricted Soviet procurement of American
equipment. The War and Navy Departments usually registered "no
objection" to the Soviet embassy's numerous requests on behalf of
Soviet engineers for permission to visit sites connected with national
security – airfields, aircraft manufacturers, munitions factories –

---

[9] "Report on Applications for Non-immigrant Visas," 5 March 1934, NACP, RG 59,
811.111 U.S.S.R./396.

provided they occurred with twenty-four or forty-eight hours' notice.[10] Commercial agreements that included the long-term placement of Soviet engineers in factories fulfilling military contracts more frequently generated a "military objection."[11] However, as a 1936 dispute over Soviet personnel at Radio Corporation of America (RCA) plants demonstrates, a "military objection" did not necessarily constitute a veto.

In the RCA case, the Navy worried that the company's plan to host forty-six Soviet engineers, physicists, technicians, and mechanics for six months at its facilities in Camden and Harrison, New Jersey, might threaten national security.[12] Admiral W. H. Standley, the acting secretary of the Navy, explained to Secretary of State Cordell Hull that the "continuous presence" of a large number of Soviet citizens "at a plant where so much confidential naval work is in progress" would likely compromise "military secrecy." At the same time, he assured Hull that the Navy was "most anxious to avoid" any interference with "business relations."[13] As a workaround, the Navy determined that the breach of "military secrecy" involved was "not vital." While refusing to "sanction the prolonged visit of Russian nationals," the Navy would permit RCA to continue work on military contracts at the plants in question.[14] RCA's lawyers rejected this solution; the company was unwilling "to violate the Navy rule" even with assurances that the Navy would not punish the violation.[15] Company officials cautioned that they might have no choice but to "terminate the stay of the Russian Nationals" despite the possible "international consequences."[16]

Anxiety about these "international consequences" pushed Hull to intervene on RCA's behalf with the secretary of the Navy. Underscoring his acknowledgment that only the Navy could make the determination of whether military secrets were safe, Hull emphasized the State Department's "desire to obviate any incident which might bring

[10] W. H. Standley to Secretary of State, 30 January 1934, NACP, RG 59, 811.20161/7; Additional cases: 2 February 1934, 811.20161/9 to 18 December 1936, 811.20161/61.
[11] Secretary of War to Secretary of State, 15 August 1935, NACP, RG 59, 811.20161/27; Department of State to the Ambassador Troyanovsky, 23 April 1937, United States Department of State, *Foreign Relations of the United States: The Soviet Union, 1933–1939* (Washington, DC: US Government Printing Office, 1933–1939) (hereafter FRUS), 470–71.
[12] J. T. Clement to Secretary of State, 10 July 1936, NACP, RG 59, 811.20161/48.
[13] W. H. Standley to Secretary of State, 18 July 1936, NACP, RG 59, 811.20161/49.
[14] J. G. Harbord, RCA to Secretary of State, 28 August 1936, NACP, RG 59, 811.20161/51.
[15] Frank W. Wozencraft to Joseph Coy Green, 29 August 1936, NACP, RG 59, 811.20161/52.
[16] J. G. Harbord, RCA to Secretary of State, 28 August 1936.

about unnecessary difficulties" with the Soviet government.[17] The Navy continued to object.[18] Only the State Department's warning that the ouster of the Soviet engineers might undermine Soviet–American relations persuaded the Navy to relent, albeit with "considerable irritation."[19] Ironically and tragically, this relatively lax American supervision of Soviet engineers in the United States ended up feeding Soviet fears of American espionage. In 1937, many of the people who had trained at RCA's plants in New Jersey were arrested at home as enemy agents.[20]

But in 1935, the year Ilf and Petrov arrived in the United States, Soviet officials were still looking for better ways to learn American tekhnika. P. A. Bogdanov, just returning from five years as a Soviet trade representative in New York City, advocated for more sustained contacts. In a series of articles on "How to Study American Technique" that ran in *Pravda* and the English-language *Moscow Daily News* in the spring and summer of 1935, Bogdanov complained that junkets to the United States had not achieved their transformative goals: "A commission comes to America to familiarize itself with a branch of production; the men inspect plants, become enraptured, give thanks; return to the Soviet Union – and that is the last of them." Instead, Bogdanov argued, the Soviets needed to set up an "organizational nucleus in America" and "permanent relations" with American research institutes and professional societies.[21] The American ambassador in Moscow, William C. Bullitt, forwarded translations of the articles to the State Department, warning that, if implemented, Bogdanov's "nucleus" could facilitate Soviet industrial espionage. The Soviets were already routinely forcing American citizens doing business in the Soviet Union "to hand over their documents, including blue prints, specifications and formulae."[22] But Bogdanov was interested in something more basic than industrial secrets. Reminding his readers that "Comrade Stalin teaches us to combine the wide Russian revolutionary élan with American business efficiency," he

---

[17] Cordell Hull to Claude A. Swanson, 31 August 1936, NACP, RG 59, 811.20161/51.
[18] Joseph C. Green to Secretary of State, 31 August 1936, NACP, RG 59, 811.20161/54; Joseph C. Green to Secretary of State, 1 September 1936, NACP, RG 59, 811.20161/55. Memorandum, Office of Arms and Munitions Control, 17 April 1937, FRUS, 470.
[19] Joseph C. Green, Memorandum, 5 September 1936, NACP, RG 59, 811.20161/58.
[20] Loren F. Jones to E. W. Engstrom, 13 July 1937, David Sarnoff Library, www.davidsarnoff.org/jones-letter01.html; Loren F. Jones to Dr. Irving Wolff, 11 March 1938, Sarnoff Library, www.davidsarnoff.org/jones-letter04.html (accessed 9 July 2021).
[21] P. A. Bogdanov, "How to Study American Technique," *Pravda*, 20 June 1935 as translated in Bullitt to Secretary of State, 22 June 1935, NACP, RG 59, 711.61/527.
[22] Bullitt to Secretary of State, 22 June 1935.

urged the acquisition of "the main elements of American business efficiency." He defined these as "the ability to solve problems in the simplest and most efficient manner, with the minimum expenditure of funds and labor and attended with the maximum effort."[23]

Bogdanov's recognition that the American "efficiency" he hoped to introduce into the Soviet Union operated by squeezing "maximum effort" out of workers highlights the central conundrum of Soviet Amerikanizm. Optimistic that American methods could be adapted to socialist conditions, Soviet observers denied any necessary connection between the capitalist system and the capitalists' tekhnika.[24] The Depression scarcely clouded Bogdanov's sunny view of the potential of American techniques and habits. He argued that even efficiencies designed to intensify the exploitation of workers "must and can be used by us ... in the interests of the toilers."[25] Once in Soviet hands, American tools would, somehow, naturally serve the workers.

Ilf and Petrov, too, operated on the assumption that American techniques could be cleanly and fully detached from American misery. Their descriptions of the Ford plant juxtaposed glowing assessments of American mechanical genius and grim reminders of the mind-numbing tedium of the assembly line. Contrasting the "excellent cheap cars" rolling off the line and driving "into freedom" with the workers "imprisoned" in the factory, they reflected that, in this case, "the triumph of tekhnika" brought only the "misfortune of man."[26] However, the obvious alienation and mistreatment of labor did not appreciably dampen their wide-eyed admiration of the colossal and efficient plant and its grandfatherly proprietor. They distinguished "our" Henry Ford, an industrial innovator and master mechanic, from the Henry Ford idolized in the United States, a merchant and millionaire. If they knew of Ford's promotion of antisemitism, they did not mention it.[27] The Soviet authors were far kinder to Ford than the American novelist John Dos Passos. His nearly contemporary thumbnail biography, "Tin Lizzie," published in the final volume of his U.S.A. trilogy, blamed Ford for the 1932 murder of four hunger marchers as they approached the River Rouge plant seeking work.[28]

On the American side, officials and corporations welcomed Soviet visitors, anticipating that Americans stood to profit from economic and

---

[23] P. A. Bogdanov, "Notes on American Business Efficiency," *Pravda*, 19 May 1935 as translated in Bullitt to Secretary of State, 22 June 1935.
[24] Stefan J. Link, *Forging Global Fordism: Nazi Germany, Soviet Russia, and the Contest over the Industrial Order* (Princeton, NJ: Princeton University Press, 2020), 82–85.
[25] Bogdanov, "How to Study."   [26] OA, 122.   [27] OA, 252; Fedorova, *Yankees*, 139.
[28] John Dos Passos, *U.S.A.* (New York: Library of America, 1996), 813.

cultural exchanges. Their calculations rested on the assumption that openness, friendly relations, and material benefits would soften the Soviet commitment to international revolution – would, in short, make the Soviet Union more like "us." Signing off on a 1937 agreement to allow the Soviet purchase of battleships and submarines, Robert F. Kelley, chief of the Division of Eastern European Affairs, explained that he expected "the evolution of the Soviet Government eventually into a purely national Government."[29] Here Americans fundamentally misunderstood Soviet enthusiasm for the "American way." The Soviet state sent engineers, and engineers of human souls, to the United States to learn how to apply American tools to the project of building a socialist state antithetical to and in competition with capitalist America.[30]

In 1933, the Soviet and American governments undertook the project of establishing friendlier relations with the goal of leveraging open exchanges to strengthen "our" side. As Ilf and Petrov's road trip illustrates, on the micro level, Soviet–American interactions relied on people able to operate across linguistic, cultural, and political borders. Officials on both sides needed, but also distrusted, even feared such people, whose loyalties might lie with the "promised land" on the other side. In the Soviet Union, these fears resulted in the devastation of people with connections abroad during the Great Purges.[31] In the United States, the government treated immigrants as potentially nefarious agents of a ruthless adversary. Ilf and Petrov seem to have had a clear sense of the fraught status of immigrants and border crossers on both sides of the ideological divide. They often identified their Russian Jewish American guides as simply "Americans." But they also recognized that "real America" and "real Americans" were deeply politicized concepts.

---

[29] Memorandum, 24 March 1937, FRUS, 466.   [30] Link, *Forging Global*, 11–13.

[31] Michael Gleb, "'Karelian Fever': The Finnish Immigrant Community during Stalin's Purges," *Europe-Asia Studies* 45 (1993): 1096–104; Sergei Zhuravlev, "American Victims of the Stalin Purges, 1930s," in Brigitte Studer and Heiko Haumann, eds., *Stalinistische Subjeckte: Individuum und System in der Sowjetunion und der Komintern, 1929–1953* (Zurich: Chronos, 2006), 397–414; Andrea Graziosi, "Foreign Workers in Soviet Russia, 1920–40: Their Experience and Their Legacy," *International Labor and Working-Class History*, no. 33 (Spring 1988): 48–49; Markku Kangaspuro, "American Finnish Emigration to Soviet Karelia: Bread, Work and Broken Dreams," *Twentieth Century Communism* 7 (November 2014): 89, 94–97; Tim Tzouliadis, *The Forsaken: An American Tragedy in Stalin's Russia* (New York: Penguin, 2009), 5; Alexey Golubev and Irina Takala, *The Search for a Socialist El Dorado: Finnish Immigration to Soviet Karelia from the United States and Canada in the 1930s* (East Lansing: Michigan State University Press, 2014), 121–55.

2   Alienism and Radicalism

>   As for communism, that is something for dirty Mexicans, Slavs, and
>   Negroes. It is no business for Americans.
>
>   Ilf and Petrov, *Little Golden America*

In *Low-Rise America*, Ilf and Petrov usually represented the Russian
(Jewish) American immigrants they chanced to meet along the way as
embodying the emptiness of American promises of plenty. One of the
most vivid of these encounters came in Schenectady. Stopping to buy
popcorn and discussing among themselves (in Russian) what this strange
food might be, Ilf and Petrov were surprised to hear the seller respond in
(according to Ilf's letter) "good Russian" that it was "ordinary corn."
As they related the story in the published work, the man proceeded to
lament his economic hardships not in "good" Russian but in a heavily
accented "Ukrainian Russian" "lavishly equipped with English words."
In the thirty years (or, as the letter specified, twenty-two years) since he
had emigrated from Volhynia in the Russian empire (now Ukraine), the
immigrant had worked in coal mines, on a farm, and at the Schenectady
Locomotive Works. Out of a job for six years, he had sold his belongings
and been evicted. Peddling popcorn, he earned "hardly enough for
deener," a meal he specified in English and that the writers transliterated
into Cyrillic.[1]

No fan of capitalism, the popcorn man had nonetheless internalized
what Ilf and Petrov astutely identified as the American strategy of dis-
paraging communism by associating it with "dirty Mexicans," Slavs,
African Americans, and, they might have added, Jews.[2] When the pair
asked why the immigrant remained in America, they learned "that this
man who had left Russia in the dim past attentively follows everything
that is said and written in Schenectady about his former homeland."

---

[1] OA, 96–97; PIA, Il'f, 29 October 1935, 442; Lioudmila Fedorova, "Found in Non-
Translation: English Language in the American Travelogues of Russian Writers
(1890–1930s)," *Literatura dvukh Amerik*, no. 6 (2019): 191–94.

[2] OA, 95; LGA, 73.

Technically speaking, his "homeland," Volhynia, had become part of the new state of Poland, which the man deemed even worse than America. But like many Jews in the United States, who often hailed from former provinces of the Russian empire that were part of newly independent states in the interwar period, when he imagined his "homeland," he looked to the Soviet Union.[3] An immigrant deeply interested in the Soviet experiment, he hesitated to trust positive reports of developments there. He told Ilf and Petrov that "they write bad things about whoever speaks for the Soviet government, *veri bed*." The American media vilified even as prominent a figure as Colonel Hugh L. Cooper, the American engineer who had designed the Muscle Shoals Dam in Alabama and the Dneprostroi Dam in Ukraine, one of the signature projects of the First Five-Year Plan. Ilf and Petrov's informant told them that when Cooper "spoke well about the Soviet government," the press dismissed him as having been paid off, noting he "Got two million" for the job.[4] Unsuccessful as an American, the poor immigrant hesitated to embrace the "un-American" Soviet alternative.

In adulterated Russian, the popcorn vendor articulated the dilemma of long-term immigrants who retained connections to the "other" side. As Ilf and Petrov told the story, the problem was political: immigrants feared that evincing any sympathy for, or even interest in, the Soviet Union would mark them as dangerous aliens. The writers sidestepped, or perhaps did not notice, the question of the self-identification of immigrants, especially those who sought to leverage their familiarity with both sides to bridge cultural and political divides. Instead of considering how their more successful immigrant contacts managed and understood their in-between status, Ilf and Petrov ignored it.

While the writers turned their Jewish Russian American guide Solomon Trone into "Mr. Adams," they completely elided another important hybrid contact, Alexander Gumberg. One of the earliest and most active of the immigrant go-betweens working to facilitate friendlier Soviet–American relations, Gumberg, among other services to Ilf and Petrov, arranged their aborted "banana boat" cruise. Yet he scarcely registers in their account.[5] Like many of the "Russian Americans" we will meet in this story, Gumberg was undeniably "Russian" in the sense

---

[3] Daniel Soyer, "Soviet Travel and the Making of an American Jewish Communist: Moissaye Olgin's Trip to Russia in 1920–1921," *American Communist History* 4 (2005): 1–20.

[4] OA, 97.

[5] Gumberg to Il'f and Petrov, 9 January 1936, Wisconsin State Historical Society, Division of Library, Archives, and Museum Collection, Alexander Gumberg Papers, New York Mss J; PH 3989, Box 8, Folder 6.

that he spoke Russian and embraced Russian culture. But he likely grew up speaking Yiddish. His hometown, Elisavetgrad (now Kropyvnytskyi, Ukraine), was in the Pale of Settlement, to which most of the empire's Jews were restricted. Both the tsarist and (after 1932) the Soviet state authorities would likely have identified this son of a rabbi as "Jewish," not Russian, on his internal passport.[6] After emigrating to the United States in 1902, Gumberg remained connected to his family in Russia and later the Soviet Union. His older brother, Veniamin, became the head of the Russian–German Trading Company. His younger brother, Sergei, had briefly emigrated to the United States, but returned in 1917 with Lev Trotsky. Known by the revolutionary name Zorin, he was an active participant in the Bolshevik seizure of power.[7]

In 1917, Alexander Gumberg, too, returned to Russia. He went not as a revolutionary, but as an observer and cultural mediator. After the February Revolution that overthrew the tsar, he interpreted Russian language and Russian politics for American journalists and nongovernment officials. On the night of the Bolshevik seizure of power in Petrograd, he accompanied John Reed, Louise Bryant, Bessie Beatty, and Albert Rhys Williams from Bolshevik party headquarters to the Winter Palace. They traveled in an open truck from which they tossed leaflets proclaiming the fall of the Provisional Government. Only Williams's and Beatty's accounts of that night acknowledge Gumberg's presence; although Bryant does mention Gumberg in other contexts, identifying him as a "Russian from America." Williams described him as "the little Russian-American, friend and pilot to so many Americans in the days of the Revolution."[8] Beatty, with a similar combination of affection and condescension, recalled him as "an odd little bundle of materialism and idealism, who had a deep love for the country of his adoption which his scoffing cynicism could not hide."[9] By contrast, Reed, who did not like Gumberg (the feeling was apparently mutual), gave his "Russian acquaintance" the pseudonym "Trusishka," or little

---

[6] Eugene M. Avrutin, *Jews and the Imperial State: Identification Politics in Tsarist Russia* (Ithaca, NY: Cornell University Press, 2010), 93–94; Sven Gunnar Simonsen, "Inheriting the Soviet Policy Toolbox: Russia' s Dilemma over Ascriptive Nationality," *Europe–Asia Studies* 51 (1999): 1069–71.

[7] James K. Libbey, *Alexander Gumberg and Soviet–American Relations: 1917–1933* (Lexington: University Press of Kentucky, 1977), 15–16, 165.

[8] Albert Rhys Williams, *Through the Russian Revolution* (New York: Boni and Liveright, 1921), 26 (quotation), 105–108; Louise Bryant, *Six Months in Red Russia: An Observer's Account of Russia before and during the Proletarian Dictatorship* (New York: George H. Doran, 1918), 150 (quotation), 83–84; Libbey, *Alexander Gumberg*, 18–19.

[9] Bessie Beatty, *The Red Heart of Russia* (New York: Century, 1918), 201 (quotation), 203–208.

coward.[10] In these sketches, Gumberg was at once "one of us" and Other. His American friends and acquaintances diminished Gumberg, who was not of notably small stature, as a "little Russian American," if not a little coward.

As in the case of less prominent mediators, Gumberg's ability to "pass" in both worlds generated praise and aroused suspicion on all sides. In 1919, at a congressional hearing on Bolshevik propaganda, one senator suggested that Gumberg was a Bolshevik agent. Raymond Robins, who as head of the Red Cross commission in Petrograd had relied on Gumberg's language skills and connections to top Bolsheviks, forcefully objected. Telling the committee that he had been advised to "ditch this little Jew," Robins instead testified "in defense of [Gumberg's] genuine, manly service,"[11] implicitly contesting racialized stereotypes of Jewish men as at once dangerous and effeminate. By the end of the decade, it was Soviet officials who distrusted Gumberg's border crossing. His business trips to the Soviet Union became "evidence" of the anti-Soviet activities of his brother Veniamin, who was arrested in 1930. Nonetheless, Gumberg remained on the executive committee of the American–Russian Chamber of Commerce. In 1933, he hosted a dinner at the Waldorf Astoria in honor of Commissar of Foreign Affairs Maxim Litvinov and the American recognition of the Soviet Union.[12]

Historians, like contemporaries, have struggled to categorize hybrid figures like Gumberg. In his history of this period, George F. Kennan noted that when Gumberg returned to Russia after the February Revolution he "availed himself ... of a Russian passport, and apparently thought of himself, in those months, as a Russian citizen." But he also reflected that "Gumberg, one feels, stood squarely between the two worlds in which his life revolved."[13] More recently, Gumberg's biographer James K. Libbey has emphasized his American characteristics. In 1902, already demonstrating an affinity for the "American tradition of independence," Gumberg, age fifteen, emigrated unaccompanied to the United States. According to Libbey, he returned to Russia in 1917 "as an American businessman," albeit one who could "exist in two dimensions."[14] In Gumberg's case, as in many others, it is not always clear

---

[10] John Reed, *Ten Days that Shook the World* (New York: Bantam, [1919] 1987), 70–71, 133–34.
[11] As quoted in George F. Kennan, *Russia Leaves the War: The Americans in Petrograd and the Bolshevik Revolution* (New York: W. W. Norton, [1958] 1984), 67.
[12] Libbey, *Alexander Gumberg*, 166–70, 175.   [13] Kennan, *Russia Leaves*, 66.
[14] Libbey, *Alexander Gumberg*, 16–18.

whether and when he considered himself Russian, Jewish, Russian American, American, all of these, or something else entirely.[15]

In the wake of the post-World War I Red Scare, such identifications mattered both personally and politically. Largely overshadowed in popular memory by the Red Scare of the 1950s, the anticommunist "hysteria" of 1919 and 1920 provided a foundation for persistent American anticommunism, transforming the Bureau of Investigation (after 1935, the FBI) into a tool of political surveillance and giving birth to the American Civil Liberties Union (ACLU).[16] At the center of the hysteria stood the Third or Communist International (Comintern). Founded in Moscow in March 1919, the self-proclaimed "general staff" of world revolution had scanty accomplishments.[17] But it effectively generated fears that a well-coordinated group of radicals at home might, like the Bolsheviks in Russia and with their assistance, overthrow the government. In the context of postwar labor and racial unrest, anticommunists confidently asserted that "radicalism," by which they might mean unionism, feminism, or civil rights activism, was the work of un-American "aliens."

Panic about a Bolshevik conspiracy spiked just before May Day 1919, when the federal government intercepted mail bombs addressed to prominent figures including John D. Rockefeller, Supreme Court Justice Oliver Wendell Holmes, Jr., and Attorney General A. Mitchell Palmer. To counter the alleged threat, the attorney general authorized the so-called Palmer Raids, in which about 10,000 people were arrested, many without warrants, and held for weeks, often without charge. Palmer characterized his targets in thinly veiled anti-Jewish language as "outcasts from the East Side of New York" allied with the "disreputable alien" Leon Bronstein, aka Trotsky, with whom they shared "the same misshapen cast of mind."[18] The crackdown resulted in the deportation of some 600 immigrants, most famously Emma Goldman, a Jewish immigrant anarchist from the former Russian empire.[19]

---

[15] Marina Mogilner, "When Race Is a Language and Empire Is a Context," *Slavic Review* 80 (Summer 2021): 210.

[16] Robert K. Murray, *Red Scare: A Study in National Hysteria, 1919–1920* (Minneapolis: University of Minnesota Press, 1955).

[17] Alexander Vatlin and Stephen A. Smith, "The Comintern," in S. A. Smith, ed., *The Oxford Handbook of the History of Communism* (New York: Oxford University Press, 2014), 187–203.

[18] Palmer quoted in John Holmes, "American Jewish Communism and Garment Unionism in the 1920s," *American Communist History* 6 (2007): 180.

[19] John F. Lyons, "Red Scare," in Thomas Riggs, ed., *St. James Encyclopedia of Popular Culture*, 2nd ed., vol. 4 (Farmington Hills, MI: St. James Press, 2013), 301–302; Regin Schmidt, *Red Scare: FBI and the Origins of Anticommunism in the United States, 1919–1943* (Copenhagen: Museum Tusculanum Press, University of Copenhagen, 2000); Theodore Kornweibel Jr., *Seeing Red: Federal Campaigns against Black Militancy,*

In the 1920s, the conviction that "undesirable aliens" were taking American jobs, committing a disproportionate number of crimes, and advocating the overthrow of the American government produced nativist immigration restrictions. Laws passed in 1921 and 1924 set quota formulas that severely limited the number of new arrivals from Southern and Eastern Europe and virtually banned migrants from Asia. No immigrant group raised greater suspicion than Jews. Albert Johnson, the congressman from Washington state who was a key sponsor of the 1921 legislation, warned that immigrants of the "Semitic race" were carriers of both "Bolshevism and typhus."[20]

The power of this association is suggested by the fact that nonimmigrants who wrote to the State Department, whether to denounce communists or to register support for the Soviet Union, made a point of highlighting their status as "real" Americans. S. E. Tull of the First Baptist Church in Middlesboro, Kentucky, who in 1935 wrote to Secretary of State Cordell Hull to urge that the United States sever diplomatic relations with the Soviet Union, recalled local efforts in 1932 to prevent an ACLU investigation into the alleged mistreatment of striking miners. He emphasized that he himself had assembled the evidence that "proved" the American Civil Liberties Union supported "all Alienism and Radicalism in the United States."[21]

On the other side, those who supported friendly relations with the Soviet Union worked to deny any hint of "alienism." When Stearns Morse, the chair of the Hanover, New Hampshire, branch of the American League against War and Fascism, wrote to the State Department to make the case for maintaining ties with the Soviet Union, he stressed that he could trace his "ancestry back to the very beginnings of New England." A professor of English at Dartmouth, Morse pointed out that he shared with many "young men of your Department ... [the] advantage of a Harvard education," a fact underlined in pencil, perhaps by one of those young men.[22]

Immigrants with potentially suspect ethnic connections often "found in anti-communism a way of demonstrating their loyalty to American

1919–1925 (Bloomington: Indiana University Press, 1998); Adam J. Hodges, "Introduction: Reassessing the Red Scare of 1919–20 at Its Centennial," *Journal of the Gilded Age and Progressive Era* 18 (2019): 3–6.

[20] Peter Schrag, *Not Fit for Our Society: Immigration and Nativism in America* (Berkeley: University of California Press, 2010), 110 (quotation), 108–21.

[21] S. E. Tull to Cordell Hull, 2 September 1935, NACP, RG 59, 711.61/546; Tom Pettey, "N. Y. Coal Field Investigators Lose in Court," *Chicago Daily Tribune*, 14 May 1932.

[22] Stearns Morse to Cordell Hull, 30 August 1935, NACP, RG 59, 711.61/545.

society and values."[23] Some proffered their residual otherness as a vital tool in ferreting out subversives. One notorious case was that of Jacob Spolansky, a Russian immigrant who built a career in both the public and private sectors uncovering the involvement of immigrants and African Americans in "unsavory radicalism."[24] As we will see, in Carmel, California, Ilf and Petrov chanced to meet another immigrant working covertly as a Red hunter.

A letter written in September 1932 by Harry Frohlich, a jeweler in Batavia, Illinois, to Secretary of State Henry L. Stimson offers a vivid illustration of how immigrants struggled to decouple ethnic otherness and un-American radicalism. Frohlich wrote to express concern about "Reds" coming to the United States to "spread propaganda." The occasion for the jeweler's foray into foreign affairs was his recent experience sailing back to the United States after visiting relatives in Galicia, which he identified as "a former Austrian province." Frohlich emphasized that he himself was an American citizen, who had arrived in the United States in 1913 and had served in the cavalry during World War I. As such, he was compelled to report that on board the ship home he had encountered "several men and a woman claiming to be American citizens, travelling back to the United States from Russia and denouncing our country, constitution, the American flag, our president and everything that is American ... in such bold terms as to make one wonder how the rascals get to be citizens." For his part, Frohlich "did not take any of them seriously" because "there are still about 100 million of us, that know what the stars and stripes stand for." Nonetheless, he wrote Stimson to "suggest that operatives be placed on all foreign vessels coming from central Europe." He further specified that these operatives "should be men that can mix with such crowd and in this way you can trace those snakes at the source of supply and if we cant [sic] jail them then at least deport them to their beautiful country of borscht and herring."[25]

More explicitly than many letter writers, Frohlich depicted immigrants as at once the source of dangerous propaganda and as key players in detecting and countering it.[26] On one hand, and quite typically, Frohlich drew a clear line between "us" and "them." The radicals he described

---

[23] Kangaspuro, "American Finnish," 85; M. Tarasovsky to Secretary of State, 2 September 1931, NACP, RG 59, 811.00B/1257; Libby Garland, "Fighting to Be Insiders: American Jewish Leaders and the Michigan Alien Registration Law of 1931," *American Jewish History* 96 (June 2010): 117–18.

[24] Nick Fischer, *Spider Web: The Birth of American Anticommunism* (Urbana: University of Illinois Press, 2016), 128–43.

[25] Harry Frolich to Henry L. Stimson, 14 September 1932, NACP, RG 59, 811.00B/1351.

[26] NACP, RG 59, 811.00B/1294, 811.00B/1265, 811.00B/1493.

claimed to be American citizens, but their powerful political, linguistic, and perhaps familial ties to Russia marked them as outsiders and made them dangerous conduits of propaganda. Underscoring the fact that he himself was a citizen and a veteran, Frohlich indignantly reported their attacks on *our* country and insisted on the need to deny *them* citizenship, to jail or deport them. With bitter irony he rejected "their beautiful country of borscht and herring." On the other hand, Frohlich admitted that he was in some ways very much like the "Russian" Americans he denounced. He, too, had linguistic and familial ties that crossed borders. Indeed, his transnational ties made him particularly adept at spotting the "snakes." The fact that he, a native of Austrian Galicia, could "mix with such crowd" suggests that these immigrants, born in the Russian empire, were Jews who spoke Yiddish and English (even if they also spoke Russian). Such kinship sat uneasily with Frohlich's need to clearly distinguish "us" and "them" and may help to explain his recourse to a culinary litmus test: An American is someone who, even if he visits relatives in Galicia, has no taste for herring. "Who," he asked Stimson, "wants to eat herring anyway?"

Such claims to insider knowledge had to overcome the strong "racial and cultural prejudices" that American officials used "to identify suspects and interpret their activities."[27] That the State Department responded noncommittally to the intelligence offered by people like Frohlich is perhaps unsurprising.[28] Given that responsibility for the regulation of immigration fell to the Department of Labor and for prosecution of subversive activities to the Department of Justice, there was not much the State Department could do in any case.[29] However, State did maintain its own networks for tracking travel between the Soviet Union and the United States.[30] In doing so, diplomats did not distinguish between those who went to the USSR for "purely" economic reasons and those who traveled as committed communists. Instead, they often assumed, as George Kennan did in a 1931 memorandum written in Berlin, that all were potential enemies, "whose allegiance in their own minds at least is to the Soviet Government and no longer to the U. S."[31]

[27] Nick Fischer, "The Founders of American Anti-communism," *American Communist History* 5 (2006): 83.
[28] Loy W. Henderson to Harry Frohlich, 21 September 1932, NACP, RG 59, 811.00B/1351; Robert F. Kelley to M. Taranovsky, 18 October 1931, 811.00B/1265.
[29] Department of State to Mr. Hodgdon, 28 July 1932, NACP, RG 59, 811.00B/1346.
[30] NACP, RG 59, 811.00B/1306, 811.00B-American Travelers, Russia/75, 811.00B/1335, 811.00B-American Travelers, Russia/120, 811.00B-American Travelers, Russia/125.
[31] Kennan as quoted in Zhuravlev, "American Victims," 405; NACP, RG 59, 811.00B/1216.

This tendency to conflate "aliens" and "radicals" complicated efforts to establish friendly relations with the Soviet Union. Those like Gumberg able to operate in both the socialist and capitalist worlds were at once critical facilitators and suspect as subversives. As the popcorn vendor from Volhynia noted, the American press said "very bad" things about anyone who spoke in favor of the Soviet Union. The kind of economic cooperation the engineer Hugh Cooper – no leftist – advocated stood to benefit both sides and was a key factor in the establishment of Soviet–American diplomatic relations in 1933.[32] But even the most potentially beneficial relations had to contend with the ingrained perception that speaking on behalf of the Soviet Union was tantamount to inciting revolutionary violence.

---

[32] Katherine A. S. Siegel, *Loans and Legitimacy: The Evolution of Soviet–American Relations, 1919–1933* (Lexington: University Press of Kentucky, 1996), 129–31, 134; Harold Dorn, "Hugh Lincoln Cooper and the First Détente," *Technology and Culture* 20 (April 1979): 338–47.

3   Pernicious Propaganda

> Revolution is a form of government abroad.
>
> Billboard seen by Ilf and Petrov in upstate New York

A key feature of American anticommunism was the conviction that communist propaganda worked. Or at least, given the right (or wrong) conditions, it could work. The assumption that words and images had the power to contaminate "us" with the virus of revolution prompted popular concern and government surveillance of seemingly harmless cultural products and cultural producers. In 1933, a Soviet pledge to cease distributing propaganda in the United States became a critical condition of normalized diplomatic relations. But far from allaying American fears, the vow generated new conflicts that on the eve of Ilf and Petrov's visit threatened to rupture Soviet–American relations.

Soviet filmmaker Sergei Eisenstein's 1930 visit to the United States, which elicited an official investigation and impassioned letters to the State Department, provides a useful indicator of the level of American anxiety about communist propaganda and propagandists. In September, the secretary of labor requested information from the State Department as part of an investigation into "a charge that one Serge Eisenstein, a citizen of Russia who was admitted to the United States on May 12, 1930 ... was engaged in radical activities in connection with the moving picture industry in Hollywood."[1] In reply, the State Department sent a four-page memorandum that included nothing more incriminating than Eisenstein's association with Sovkino, the Soviet Union's central cinema organization.

A more overheated version of the same request arrived at the State Department in November 1930 from the Beverly Hills chapter of the Daughters of the American Revolution (DAR). Writing on behalf of her DAR chapter, Julia M. Lucas asserted that she had it on "good authority"

---

[1] W. W. Husband to Henry L. Stimson, 9 September 1930, NACP, RG 59, 800.00B Eisenstein, Serge/3.

that "a Soviet agent who calls himself Eisenstein has been admitted to the United States." This Eisenstein, she continued, "poses as an artist," but his real intention was to "decry, belittle, villify [sic], the Government of the United States." In light of these facts, she wrote "to inquire whether any lawful thing can be done to forestall Eisenstein's pernicious activities, or, if possible, to send him back whence he came." She worried that if he remained in the United States, Americans would ultimately have to "fight the effects of his activities, exactly as we fight the ravages of epidemic typhoid fever." She begged Secretary of State Henry L. Stimson, "If you cannot eliminate the cause, instruct us how we can best struggle against the effects."[2] Replying on Stimson's behalf, Robert F. Kelley assured Lucas that before granting Eisenstein – or indeed any Soviet national – a visa, a "careful investigation was made" and "no evidence was found that would indicate that Mr. Eisenstein had been active in the international revolutionary movement." He tried to further calm her with the information that Eisenstein's permission to remain in the United States "will expire on December 1, 1930."[3]

In cases like Eisenstein's, anticommunists equated speech, that is disseminating "pernicious" propaganda or vilifying the American government, with subversive activity, "infecting" Americans with revolution. It was this failure to distinguish between word and deed that made not only political pamphlets but also Soviet cultural products important enough to justify careful monitoring. The consulate in Berlin regularly reported on which films Amkino, the distributor of Soviet films in the United States, purchased in Germany for export.[4] The legation in Riga sent reports on books and films from the Soviet Union being imported into the United States. These included innocuous-sounding publications such as "The Soviet Patent Law" and more political tracts such as "Where the Workers Are in Power."[5] Beginning in 1928, the London embassy provided synopses of Soviet films "considered worth keeping an eye on." These included Esfir Shub's *The Fall of the Romanov Dynasty* (1927) and Vsevolod Pudovkin's *Storm over Asia* (1928), which the embassy critic judged "a very remarkable piece of cinematography" but

[2] Julia M. Lucas to Henry L. Stimson, 1 November 1930, NACP, RG 59, 811.00B/Eisenstein, Serge/5.

[3] Robert F. Kelley to Mrs. William E. Lucas, 18 November 1930, NACP, RG 58, 811.00B/Eisenstein, Serge/6.

[4] Reports 1930–32: NACP, RG 59, 811.00B-Motion Pictures/60, 811.00B-Motion Pictures/67, 811.00B-Motion Pictures/72, 811.00B-Motion Pictures/77, 811.00B-Motion Pictures/79, 811.00B-Motion Pictures/82, 811.00B-Motion Pictures/86, 811.00B-Motion Pictures/93, 811.00B-Motion Pictures/94.

[5] Robert P. Skinner to Secretary of State, 13 May 1932, NACP, RG 59, 811.00B-International Publishers/1.

nonetheless dangerous propaganda as "it shows villainous soldierly in British uniform."[6]

The fear that these films could spark revolutionary violence emerges clearly in a March 1930 report on a screening of Ilya Trauberg's film *China Express* (the Russian title was *Goluboi ekspress*, *Blue Express*, 1929) at the Cameo Theater in Manhattan. LeRoy A. Mullen, a State Department special agent, emphasized "the particularly vicious, pernicious and revolting character of the Communist propaganda in the film," which he deemed the "sort of stuff of which riots and revolution are made." He was put off by the "lusty cheers from the audience" that accompanied scenes in which "the coolies seize a shipment of arms and kill off all the white men." Noting that the Cameo crowd was "standing room only," he concluded with the suggestion that "there should be some way for the Federal Government" to restrict the import and distribution of such films.[7]

Mullen moderated his assessment in July 1930, when he determined that few Americans were likely to see such Soviet films. He reported that *China Express* "definitely is not and has not been distributed by any concern connected with the Motion Picture Producers and Distributors of America," the industry group that in March 1930 had adopted the Production (or Hays) Code designed to foster morally upright filmmaking. (The code was loosely enforced before 1934.) The mainstream distributors, Mullen explained, "keep hands off the Russian propaganda films for two reasons: first, because they contain noxious propaganda, second, because they do not pay commercially," noting parenthetically, "I may have reversed the order in which the reasons should be stated." In any case, "these propaganda films from Russia do not go into what is technically known in the movie world as 'the sticks,' meaning any place outside of New York or possibly Chicago ... as the provincials in this country do not seem to be sufficiently interested in Bolshevik propaganda to see it."[8] However dangerous such films might be in New York, where crowds seemed receptive to Bolshevik propaganda, wholesome or isolated "provincials," Mullen concluded, were unlikely to be infected.

With no authority to censor or regulate the importation and distribution of Soviet films or books, the State Department forwarded its information on communist propaganda to other agencies. It sent synopses of

---

[6] Memorandum, 10 April 1930, NACP, RG 59, 811.00B-Motion Pictures/76.

[7] L. A. Mullen to A. R. Burr, 12 March 1930, NACP, RG 59. 811.00B-Motion Pictures/63.

[8] L. A. Mullen to R. C. Bannerman, 16 July 1930, NACP, RG 59, 811.00B-Motion Pictures/71; Thomas Doherty, *Hollywood's Censor: Joseph I. Breen and the Production Code Administration* (New York: Columbia University Press, 2007), 41–48.

Soviet films to the Treasury Department, which under the Tariff Act of
1922 had authority to "subject to censorship" all imported "photographic films."[9] In July 1930, the Smoot–Hawley Tariff Act repealed
the relevant paragraph of the 1922 Act, but Treasury assured State that it
would continue to apply censorship "as before the repeal," confident that
the new act's authorization of the censorship of "pictures" would be
construed as applying to "moving pictures."[10] Kelley at the Division of
Eastern European Affairs also forwarded information on Soviet films to
J. Edgar Hoover, the head of the Bureau of Investigation. Here the issue
was less censorship than uncovering subversive activities. For example,
Kelley called Hoover's attention to the possibility of using a 1928 documentary on the Sixth Comintern Congress to identify and perhaps investigate American participants.[11]

This sharing of information notwithstanding, the State Department
took a pragmatic approach to balancing fears of communist propaganda
and efforts to develop trade with the Soviet Union. It refrained from
endorsing the committee convened by New York Republican
Congressman Hamilton Fish, Jr. to uncover communist activities and
propaganda in the United States.[12] Asked for his advice, Kelley suggested to the undersecretary of state a carefully worded response to the
Fish Committee that took a narrow view of the problem: from the
perspective of the State Department's strictly delimited interest in the
matter – "namely, the direction and supervision of communist activities
in the United States from Moscow, – the Department does not believe
that an investigation is necessary at this time." His conclusion is perhaps
surprising given that Fish's investigation was based on documents
(ultimately revealed as forgeries) that purported to demonstrate ties
between the Communist International and Amtorg Trading
Corporation, a joint stock company chartered in New York State with a
concession from the Soviet government. In other words, Fish alleged
exactly the sort of "interference of a foreign power in our internal affairs"
that Kelley deemed the State Department's only legitimate interest in the
American communist movement.[13]   Nonetheless, Kelley, an

---

[9] O. R. Luhring to Secretary of State, 7 May 1930, 811.00B-Motion Pictures/62.

[10] "Importation of Motion Picture Films," 20 August 1931, NACP, RG 59, 811.00B-
Motion Pictures/88.

[11] Robert F. Kelley to Mr. Hoover, 23 April 1930, NACP, RG 59, 811.00B-Motion
Pictures/60A; 21 July 1930, 811.00B-Motion Pictures/71.

[12] Jack Hodgson, "From the Bronx to Stalingrad: Harry Eisman and the Young Pioneers of
America in New York City," New York History 103 (Summer 2022): 73.

[13] RFK to Mr. Cotton, 28 March 1930, NACP, RG 59, 811.00B-House Investigation/5;
Siegel, Loans and Legitimacy, 134.

anticommunist "hard-liner," was unwilling to sacrifice trade and business relations to a crusade against communist propaganda.[14]

In 1933, these economic concerns helped propel the normalization of Soviet–American relations. Americans mired in the Depression looked forward to opening new markets. So important were better relations that President Franklin D. Roosevelt agreed to postpone the question of how much of the debt cancelled by the Bolshevik government would be repaid; the issue was never resolved. For their part, the Soviets desired American technology and expertise that could aid their industrialization drive. Both sides hoped to limit Japanese expansion and militarism.[15]

The long history of American politicians and government officials equating advocacy of revolution and actual revolutionary violence made a Soviet promise to desist from distributing propaganda in the United States a requirement of recognition. In a November 1933 note to President Roosevelt, Commissar of Foreign Affairs Maxim Litvinov complied, pledging that the Soviets would "refrain from interfering in any manner in the internal affairs of the United States." This seemed to effectively bar the Soviet Union from supporting the US Communist Party or supplying communist propaganda.[16] To make sure that the Soviet Union was living up to its word, the United States continued to monitor potentially subversive books and films arriving from the Soviet Union and to track American travelers to the Soviet Union.[17]

As it turned out, the sweeping language of Litvinov's pledge obscured fundamental disagreements regarding what constituted an organization under the Soviet government's "direct or indirect control." For the Americans, this included the Comintern. Soviet authorities, by contrast, rather disingenuously maintained that the Comintern was an independent organization. When, in October 1934, the American ambassador in Moscow, William C. Bullitt, protested to Litvinov about "direction from Moscow of the activities of the Communist movement in the United States" and possible attacks on the US government at the upcoming Comintern Congress in Moscow, the commissar pled ignorance.

[14] Siegel, *Loans and Legitimacy*, 140.
[15] FRUS, 1–62; Norman E. Saul, *Friends or Foes? The United States and Soviet Russia, 1921–1941* (Lawrence: University Press of Kansas, 2006), 254–315; David Foglesong, "Rival and Parallel Missions: America and Soviet Russia, 1917–1943," in Christopher R. W. Dietrich, ed., *A Companion to U.S. Foreign Relations: Colonial Era to the Present, Volume I* (New York: John Wiley, 2020), 454.
[16] The Soviet Commissar for Foreign Affairs (Litvinov) to President Roosevelt, 16 November 1933, FRUS, 28; Malbone W. Graham, "Russian–American Relations, 1917–1933: An Interpretation," *American Political Science Review* 28 (June 1934): 405.
[17] NACP, RG 59, 811.00B/1594, 811.00B/1683, 811.00B-American Travelers, Russia/120, 811.00B-American Travelers, Russia/125.

On the eve of the 1935 gathering, Litvinov continued to insist that Bullitt knew "more about the Third International" than either he or Stalin.[18]

By the summer of 1935, both the advantages and dangers of "friendly relations" were quite clear. The United States and Soviet Union were simultaneously negotiating a trade agreement and engaged in a rancorous dispute over whether the participation of American communists in the Seventh Comintern Congress constituted a violation of the Soviet promise to refrain from anti-American propaganda.[19] At the close of the Congress, Ambassador Bullitt sent a strongly worded telegram to Secretary of State Cordell Hull describing the meeting as a "flagrant violation of Litvinov's pledge to the President." He blamed the Soviets for encouraging, if not scripting, the "numerous speeches by American delegates in which Stalin was referred to as their leader" and decried the election of Americans to the executive committee of what Bullitt called the "Communist International of Russia." Such actions, he concluded, "juridically and morally justified ... severing diplomatic relations." He proposed, however, that the question be decided "neither on emotional nor juridical grounds but on the basis of a cold appraisal of the wisest course to pursue to defend the American people from the efforts of the Soviet Government to produce bloody revolution in the United States."[20]

This alarmist tone represented a stunning shift in Bullitt's view of the Soviet Union. In 1919, Bullitt, together with the journalist Lincoln Steffens, had undertaken a failed mission to negotiate American recognition of Soviet Russia. When President Roosevelt appointed him ambassador shortly after relations were normalized in 1933, Bullitt had a reputation at home and in Moscow as a friend of the Soviet Union. By the time he left his post in 1936, constant concerns about wiretapping and surveillance had radically altered his attitude toward the Communist Party, which he described "as an institution similar to the Spanish Inquisition."[21]

---

[18] Bullitt to Secretary of State, 5 October 1934, NACP, RG 59, 811.00B/1566; Bullitt to Secretary of State, 8 July 1935, FRUS, 222, 218–68; Litvinov to A. A. Troianovskii, 14 July 1935, in B. I. Zhiliaev, ed., *Sovetsko-Amerikanskie otnosheniia, 1934–1939* (Moscow: Materik, 2003), 335.

[19] G. N. Sevast'ianov, "Obostrenie sovetsko-amerikanskikh otnoshenii letom 1935 g.: Prichiny i posledstviia," *Novoe i noveishaia istoriia*, no. 6 (1998): 19–35; FRUS, 192–218.

[20] Bullitt to Secretary of State, 21 August 1935, NACP, RG 59, 861.00-Congress, Communist International, VII/56; FRUS, 220–21, 228–44.

[21] Alexander Etkind, *The Road Not Taken: An Intellectual Biography of William C. Bullitt* (Pittsburgh: University of Pittsburgh Press, 2017), 113 (quotation), 36–40, 110–26.

The high stakes pushed Bullitt to urge maintaining diplomatic relations. He warned that if relations were severed it would be "inordinately difficult" to restore them. In any case, the United States had more to lose than the Soviet Union. Without "an official observation post" in Moscow, the United States would be unable to monitor the Soviets' "increasingly noxious activities." He thought it unlikely that the Soviet government would be similarly handicapped in the event of a rupture in relations. Unless the United States expelled both Soviet diplomats and "Soviet citizens including officials of such organizations as Amtorg and Intourist, the Soviet Government for all practical purposes would still have representation in the United States."[22] Thus, rather than severing relations or lodging a written protest, Bullitt suggested reducing the number of Soviet diplomats in the United States and rigorously vetting and limiting Soviet visitors.[23]

The combination of moral outrage and practical interests evident in Bullitt's suggestions ultimately resulted in a note from Roosevelt protesting the Congress as a "flagrant violation" of the Litvinov pledge; however, relations were not broken.[24] The president's note responded at least in part to popular fears that the Soviet Union was plotting against America. In a telegram to Bullitt, Hull informed the ambassador that the "Hearst press is continuing its endeavors to mobilize public opinion against the Soviet Union," as evidenced by the fact that "the Department has been receiving communications protesting against alleged violations of the Soviet Government's pledge."[25] One such letter, written after the president's protest by Marvin A. Harlan, the national commander of the Disabled Veterans of the World War, captures the tone of such appeals. Describing himself as convinced "beyond the shadow of a doubt" that the Kremlin aimed to "overthrow ... our government," Harlan advised that if the president's "solemn warning does not accomplish its purpose," relations should be severed "until the benighted Russian millions remove the few autocrats who have held them in serfdom and there arises a government fitted to be a part of the

[22] Bullitt to Secretary of State, 21 August 1935, NACP, RG 59, 861.00-Congress, Communist International, VII/57; FRUS, 244–68.
[23] Bullitt to Secretary of State, 5 October 1934, NACP, RG 59, 811.00B/1566; 21 August 1935, 861.00 Congress, Communist International, VII/57; Memorandum of Conversation with Soviet Ambassador Troyanovsky, 9 October 1935, 811.00B/1683; Fischer, "Founders," 87–91; FRUS, 192–267.
[24] Press Release, 25 August 1935, FRUS, 250.
[25] Secretary of State to Bullitt, 16 August 1935, FRUS, 241.

self-respecting society of nations."[26] He seemed to miss the irony that his ultimate objective was the overthrow of the Soviet government.

The Soviet government "flatly rejected" Roosevelt's protest, replying that it could take no responsibility for the actions of the ostensibly independent Comintern. Although Bullitt had not been in favor of the president's note, he now considered action imperative, lest the Soviet government "feel free in the future to behave as it pleases in its relations with us." "We will," he concluded, "never find a better moment to act against the direction of the Communist movement in the United States by the Dictator in the Kremlin."[27] In the event, Hull answered on 30 August 1935 with the stern admonition that the Soviet government could not "disclaim and avoid responsibility for the activities of the Communist International on Soviet territory." Rather than taking immediate action, the secretary of state made the vague threat that, "If the Soviet Government pursues a policy of permitting activities on its territory involving interference in the internal affairs of the United States … the friendly and official relations between the two countries cannot but be seriously impaired."[28]

If the continued flow of communist propaganda could not be allowed to derail "friendly" relations, it remained a serious concern. State Department officials worked to uncover plans for the importation of materials in English related to the Seventh Comintern Congress.[29] In addition to keeping track of Comintern publications coming into the United States, the State Department continued to treat Soviet cultural products as potential pollutants. In a May 1936 dispatch, Loy Henderson reported the importation of the movie musical *Circus* (directed by Grigory Aleksandrov, 1936). Based on the play "Under the Big Top" by Ilf, Petrov, and Petrov's brother Valentin Kataev, the movie told the story of a white American circus performer, driven out of the United States by a racist mob, who found a home for herself and her mixed-race child in the Soviet Union. Henderson noted that the "main purpose of this film, apparently, is to contrast the prejudice in the United States against the mixing of the white and black races with the alleged enlightened attitude on the subject to be found in the Soviet Union."

[26] Marvin A. Harlan to Secretary of State, 26 August 1935, NACP, RG 59, 711.61/539.

[27] Bullitt to Secretary of State, 29 August 1935, NACP, RG 59, 711.61/542; FRUS, 252–53.

[28] Department of State to Embassy, Moscow, 30 August 1935, NACP, RG 59, 711.61/542A.

[29] E. L. Packer to Secretary of State, 5 October 1935, NACP, RG 59, 711.61/566; Ray Atherton to Secretary of State, 12 December 1935, 711.61/581.

He worried that "the display of this film in its present form in the United States is likely to deepen race feelings."[30]

These concerns about pernicious propaganda and subversive activities constituted the immediate backdrop to Ilf and Petrov's fall 1935 arrival in the United States. Indeed, they encountered some echoes of these worries in the broader American landscape. They marveled, for instance, at a billboard in upstate New York that proclaimed, "Revolution is a form of government abroad." Such an emphatic protest, they concluded, surely demonstrated "that there are people who need to be persuaded that there can be no revolution in America."[31]

Historians often depict the Soviet government, which promoted the idea that writers should be "engineers of human souls," as particularly concerned with how language shaped and determined subjectivity and action. But the American government's concerns about pernicious propaganda suggest that it, too, assumed that words had the power to deform, if not engineer, souls; to infect healthy Americans with the bacillus of revolution; to incite subversive activities; or to "deepen race feelings." Thus, the State Department kept close tabs on communist political tracts entering the country. Officials also treated more subtle or entertaining propaganda as a potentially dangerous contaminant. As Ilf and Petrov found when they applied for visas, American officials exercised caution in allowing authors – even funny ones – into the United States.

---

[30] Loy Henderson to Secretary of State, 27 May 1936, NACP, RG 59, 811.00B-Motion Pictures/108.
[31] Il'ia Il'f and Evgenii Petrov, "Amerikanskie fotografii: IX: Reklama," *Ogonek*, no. 21 (30 July 1936): 15; OA, 117.

4   Two Russian Gentlemen

—You have not answered my question. I asked whether you would sympathize with any movement for the overthrow of the Government of the United States by force or violence.

—I think the question is peculiar. No.

Special interrogatory in the case of Pavel Liudvigovich Mikhalsky (aka Lapinsky),
conducted at the American consulate general in Berlin, 1 September 1932

The question "Do you believe in the overthrow of the Government of the United States by force or violence?" was a standard one asked of Soviet applicants for nonimmigrant visas to the United States. As Pavel Mikhalsky, a member of the Communist Party and correspondent for *Izvestiya*, observed in his visa interview, it is a rather "peculiar" question. Who would admit this aim to a consular official? Nonetheless, the question had to be asked and, as Mikhalsky found, answered directly. His initial response – "I shall hold myself aloof from anything which affects the internal relations of the United States" – was inadequate. The American visa process required a "No." To the follow-up question, "Do you believe in the assassination of public officials because of their political positions?" Mikhalsky answered with an emphatic, "Of course not." These denials notwithstanding, he was deemed "inadmissible to the United States" because he was a member of the Communist Party.[1] American immigration law excluded visitors "who believe in or advocate the overthrow by force or violence of the Government of the United States" or were "affiliated with any organization entertaining and teaching disbelief in or opposition to organized government."[2] American officials considered the Communist Party precisely such an organization.

---

[1] Special Interrogatory, 1 September 1932, NACP, RG 59, 811.111 Firms-Amtorg-Mikhailski Pavel Ludvigovich.

[2] "An Act to Regulate the immigration of aliens to, and the residence of aliens in the United States," Sess. II., Ch. 29, 5 February 1917, U.S. Congress, *U.S. Statutes at Large, Volume 39 – 1916, 64th Congress,* www.loc.gov/item/llsl-v39/ (accessed 9 August 2023), 874–76; "An Act to exclude and expel from the United States aliens who are members of the

Nonetheless, a month later, Mikhalsky had his visa. As in the cases of other Soviet visitors, the State Department appealed to the Department of Labor, which handled immigration, to grant "temporary admission" through the "Ninth Proviso of Section 3" of the 1917 Immigration Act. This loophole, which the State Department used widely but was loathe to publicize, made an exception for otherwise "inadmissible aliens" whose visit to the United States did not pose an immediate political danger and offered some economic or cultural benefit.[3]

Two weeks after Mikhalsky's interview, Earl L. Packer of the Division of Eastern European Affairs argued for extending the Ninth Proviso to include journalists. He noted that "the admission and courteous treatment" of correspondents might give them "a friendly feeling toward the United States" that could ultimately facilitate "further growth of business and trade relations." Packer also warned that refusing the visa "would probably cause a distinctly unfavorable reaction toward the United States in the Soviet press" and harm the position of American correspondents in the Soviet Union. Granting that it might not be wise to let a Soviet journalist attend a White House press conference, Packer did not think this possibility should "be made the basis for refusing to admit him."[4] The State Department relayed Packer's assessment to the Department of Labor, which approved Mikhalsky's temporary admission.[5] The Berlin consulate issued a visa on 3 October 1932.[6]

This willingness to welcome otherwise "inadmissible" aliens illustrates the tensions between the fear of revolutionary contamination and the desire for beneficial relations. Committed to tracking Moscow's alleged interference in American domestic politics, the State Department monitored American travelers to the Soviet Union and strictly controlled Soviet visitors to the United States. But the State Department also hoped to foster "friendly" interactions, or at least mitigate the hostility between the two states, precisely by encouraging border crossing. It thus urged the Department of Labor to issue temporary visas to some card-carrying communists.

anarchistic and similar classes," Sess. II., Ch. 186, 16 October 1918, U.S. Congress, *U.S. Statutes at Large, Volume 40 – 1919, 65th Congress,* www.loc.gov/item/llsl-v40/ (accessed 9 August 2023), 1012–13.

[3] A. Dana Hodgdon to Mr. Flournoy, 23 July 1932, NACP, RG 59, 811.00B/1345; Changes in Consular Regulations, 18 July 1931, NACP, RG 59, 811.00B/1316.

[4] E. L. Packer, "Memorandum on the visa case,"13 September 1932, NACP, RG 59, 811.111 Firms-Amtorg-Mikhalski Pavel Ludvigovich.

[5] W. W. Castle, Jr., 14 September 1932, NACP, RG 59, 811.111 Firms-Amtorg-Mikhalski Pavel Ludvigovich.

[6] Visa granted, 7 October 1932, NACP, RG 59, 811.111 Firms-Amtorg-Mikhalski Pavel Ludvigovich.

The establishment of normal diplomatic relations with the Soviet Union in 1933 did not alter US immigration law or the use of the Ninth Proviso to circumvent it. The State Department continued to routinely suggest that "politically undesirable" immigrants whose visits offered some "advantage" to the United States be admitted under the Ninth Proviso procedure.[7] The several days of delay required for the procedure was common enough for the Soviet consul general in New York to complain in 1934 that the situation tempted Soviet applicants to deny that they were party members, "but they did not like to lie."[8] The State Department explained that it was not discriminating against "Soviet nationals"; it excluded all "aliens belonging to organizations which advocate the overthrow by force of the Government."[9] Still, friendly relations were important enough for US diplomats to look for ways to defuse the situation, including simply delaying all visas for several days so as to obscure the "discrimination" against party members.[10]

When Ilf and Petrov applied for American visas in the fall of 1935, the American government viewed the Soviet funnymen, like all Soviet visitors in this period, as at once potentially important mediators of friendly relations and possible subversive agents. In their 3 September 1935 visa interviews, both Ilf and Petrov affirmed that they had no interest in violently overthrowing the US government. Neither was a party member, but both admitted to being, like all professional writers in the Soviet Union, members of the Union of Soviet Writers and the Trade Union of Workers of the Printing and Publishing Industry of the USSR.[11] Their memberships in these organizations, which the US government regarded as "affiliated" with the Communist Party, made both authors "politically undesirable" and thus "inadmissible aliens."[12]

In the case of Ilf and Petrov, as in so many others, the State Department asked the Department of Labor to authorize their "temporary admission" under the Ninth Proviso. Acknowledging that the authors fell into a politically suspect class, Ambassador Bullitt informed the State Department that he believed their admission was not "contrary to the

---

[7] Visa Division correspondence, March 1935, NACP, RG 59, 811.111 U.S.S.R./461 and March 1934, 811.111 U.S.S.R./435.

[8] Memorandum of Conversation, Tolokonsky, Packer, 11 July 1934, 811.111/U.S.S.R./412.

[9] Memorandum of Conversation, Henderson, Stolyar, 16 May 1934, NACP, RG 59, 811.111/U.S.S.R./408.

[10] J. F. Simmons to Mr. Carr, 4 March 1935, p. 4, NACP, RG 59, 811.111 U.S.S.R./461.

[11] Carol Any, *The Soviet Writers' Union and Its Leaders: Identity and Authority under Stalin* (Evanston, IL: Northwestern University Press, 2020).

[12] Special interrogatory, 3 September 1935, NACP, RG 59, 811.111 Kataev, Evgeni P.; Special interrogatory, 3 September 1935, 811.111 Fainzilberg, Ilya A.

public safety," would be "to the advantage of the public and economic interests of the United States," and was desired by the Soviet foreign office. In its appeal to the Department of Labor, the State Department bolstered Bullitt's case with a 5 September clipping from the *New York Times* that described the authors as planning to "write a book that will picture the American scene not from a harshly Communist viewpoint but as it appears to acute and unbiased observers." On 10 September 1935, the Department of Labor authorized their temporary admission.[13]

In this climate of mutual suspicion, potential Soviet visitors had to establish themselves as friendly, but not too friendly. This may explain why Ilf and Petrov denied knowing anyone in the United States, despite the fact that they had, at the very least, working relationships with their translator Charles Malamuth and their US publisher Farrar and Rinehart. Ilf also claimed that he had no relatives in the United States. The fact of the matter was that the Odesa Fainzilbergs, with the exception of Ilf's father, had emigrated to the United States at the turn of the century. In 1935, many of them, now Finesilvers, lived in Hartford.[14] These less-than-truthful answers suggest wariness of both the American and Soviet governments' concerns about blurred boundaries and dual loyalties.

Ilf and Petrov mentioned their experiences acquiring visas only in passing in their published work. When they arrived in El Paso, Texas, at the end of 1935, they hoped to spend a day in Mexico. But, they noted, they were afraid to cross the border. In their passports, they carried one-year visas issued by the American vice consul in Moscow, Ellis A. Johnson. The problem was that "every visa ends automatically as soon as you depart the country." This was the reason that earlier in the trip they had abandoned their plan to visit Canada.[15] In El Paso, the fear that they would have to pass "the rest of our days" in Juarez competed with their desire to see Mexico. In the end, an "unexpectedly benevolent" official assured them that they would be readmitted to the United States, and they made the trip.[16]

The visa situation was actually more complicated than Ilf and Petrov suggest in this vignette. In September 1935, the Department of Labor had "authorized the admission of these aliens for a temporary period not to exceed three months to study conditions in the United States for the

[13] Special interrogatory, 811.111 Fainzilberg, Ilya A.; "Russians to Visit," *New York Times* (NYT), 5 September 1935.

[14] ZK, 496nn202–203.

[15] PIA, Il'f, 8 October 1935, Petrov, 6 November 1935, Il'f, 29 December 1935, 428, 444, 483.

[16] OA, 351.

purpose of writing regarding their observations and experiences."[17] They arrived in the United States on 7 October 1935 with leave to stay until early January 1936, a little over a week after their adventures in Mexico. By that time, they were back in Washington, DC. On 9 January 1936, the Department of Labor granted an extension of their visas to 7 April 1936. In the published text, the two three-month visas became a single one-year visa. They thus downplayed the logistical annoyances facing Soviet visitors. Moreover, they described the American officials with whom they dealt, Ellis A. Johnson in Moscow and an unnamed border officer in El Paso, as nothing but helpful, even gracious.

Ilf and Petrov's account of their day trip to Juarez highlighted the unexpected ease and value of crossing borders. In their published account they described themselves as dismayed to find upon their return to El Paso an unknown border agent with an "angry face." But when he looked at their passports, the forbidding officer exclaimed, "These are the two Russian gentleman who this morning went to Mexico. ... The two Russian gentlemen may freely enter the United States."[18] At the Texas–Mexico border they were not inadmissible aliens, but gentlemen and expected guests.

The fact that the officer on duty in the morning had informed his colleague about the "Russian gentlemen" elicited from Mr. Adams, Ilf and Petrov's guide and translator, a paean to American efficiency and organization: "this is a country where you can calmly drink raw water out of a tap without catching typhoid fever – the water will always be perfect. ... This is a country where you don't have to think of how to drive by automobile from one city to another. The road will always be good." For Ilf and Petrov, the day in Mexico and the ease of their return called attention to the "good roads, good service, cleanliness, and comfort" that they had begun to take for granted in the United States. They concluded that "Sometimes, in order to know a country better, it is useful to leave it for a day."[19] Border crossing helped them to see the United States and, implicitly, the Soviet Union anew.

---

[17] NACP, RG 59, 811.111 Fainzilberg, Ilya A.   [18] OA, 357.   [19] OA, 358.

Part II

New York and the Eastern States

Before their road trip got rolling, Ilf and Petrov spent a month in and around New York City. They quickly learned, they told their readers, that the city was not quite America. Their "new friends" told them that "New York is only the bridge between Europe and America,"[1] a metaphor that chimes with their representation of the city as an oddly liminal space. Full of strange, even hellish features and characters, Ilf and Petrov's New York was also oddly familiar. The Salvation Army soup kitchen, where hungry men participated in evening and morning prayers as the price of a meal and a bed, struck them as an "American staging of Gorky's *Lower Depths.*" Amid the jumping and flashing lights of Broadway that they likened to trained circus animals, Ilf and Petrov encountered the Cameo Theater screening a familiar Soviet film.[2] Although they did not acknowledge the fact in their published texts, many of their New York friends were in fact Russian Jewish immigrants, who themselves bridged (at least) two worlds.

The traces of this most sedentary segment of Ilf and Petrov's American journey are widely scattered. Fortunately for the historian, many of the people they met were famous enough to have their personal papers preserved in various archives, and many saved evidence of their interactions with the Soviet funnymen. In a few cases, American newspapers and magazines carried stories about the visiting authors. The pair's letters home and Ilf's notebook make it possible to track their movements quite precisely. Often, I was able to locate archival or published records that offered corroboration, diverse perspectives, and sometimes wholly different accounts of the people, places, and events they described. I also spent a long afternoon circling the Empire State building, trying the patience of my traveling companion, in order to locate the spot from which Ilf photographed its facade.

[1] OA, 60.   [2] LGA, 17; OA, 16–17.

Sifting the remains of Ilf and Petrov's New York sojourn, I aimed not only to learn the details of their travels and encounters. I also wanted to answer larger questions about the possibilities and pitfalls of cultural exchange. Investigating Ilf and Petrov's encounters with renowned American artists and authors offered a way of tracing the transnational networks that connected Soviet and American cultural producers. How and what did they learn from each other? Where and why did they fail to understand one another? I was particularly interested in uncovering the role of immigrants in these networks. How did Soviet art and Russian artists become "American"? How did Ilf and Petrov make Soviet sense of American culture and American consumption?

One final note. In this part of the book, I adopt Ilf and Petrov's own mental map of America. They included Chicago among the Eastern states – something that no native Chicagoan would do. For Ilf and Petrov the city on the lake was "Eastern" because it had industry and skyscrapers. It was not part of the ostensibly more authentic low-rise America that existed somewhere out there, on the prairie, between the Mississippi River and Hollywood.

5 Extraordinary Adventures in the Land of the Capitalists

> America is not the premier of a new play, and we are not theater critics. We transferred to paper our impressions of this country.
>
> Ilf and Petrov, *Low-Rise America*

Long before they arrived, Ilf and Petrov knew what to expect in New York. They were certainly acquainted with the Russian literary convention, dating back at least to Maxim Gorky's visit in the early twentieth century, of depicting a journey to America as a descent into hell. Gorky had employed Dantesque imagery in his account of his 1906 visit to the "City of the Yellow Devil." Later travelers, notably the poets Vladimir Mayakovsky and Sergei Esenin, who toured the United States in the 1920s, and the novelist Boris Pilnyak, who in 1931 undertook his own coast-to-coast trip by automobile, were more enthusiastic than Gorky about American technical achievements. But their diverse travel accounts retained Gorky's narrative framework. They described themselves as navigating the fiery rings of American cultural vacuity, alienated labor, racism, and worship of Mammon – Gorky's yellow devil. Anticipating hell, they found it, and then trumpeted their "discovery" of America.[1]

Ilf and Petrov, too, described an American hellscape. Their New York was a melodramatic Inferno. Approaching from the sea, they saw the city's skyscrapers "rising straight out of the water like calm pillars of smoke." The subway buzzed hellishly underfoot. "The red glow of the advertisements cast an operatic light" on the steam rising from vents in the sidewalk.[2] The one-storied America they found beyond New York and Chicago was a different sort of torment, endlessly repetitious and

---

[1] Milla Fedorova, *Yankees in Petrograd, Bolsheviks in New York: America and Americans in Russian Literary Perception* (DeKalb: Northern Illinois University Press, 2006), 5–11, 101–89; Olga Peters Hasty and Susanne Fusso, "Introduction," in Olga Peters Hasty and Susan Fusso, trans., eds., *America through Russian Eyes, 1874–1926* (New Haven, CT: Yale University Press, 1988), 2–15.

[2] OA, 11, 15.

mind-numbingly provincial. As experienced visitors to the hell of small-town America, they prepared their readers for a diabolical warping of time and space: "You may drive a thousand miles, two thousand, three thousand, the natural surroundings and the climate will change, the watch will have to be moved ahead, but the little town in which you stop for the night will be exactly the same as the one that appeared before you two weeks ago."[3]

Still, the Soviet funnymen had a far lighter touch than their predecessors. They clearly saw the hellish aspects of America, but they also described it as a land in which marvels were routine. Their hotel room in New York was small, but it was "clean and comfortable." It came standard with "hot and cold water, a shower, stationery, telegraph blanks, postcards with views of the hotel, paper laundry bags, and printed laundry blanks." Sending out their dirty clothes was a pure joy, almost a miracle. Their ironed shirts came back looking "better than new ones on display in a store window." Shirts returned mended; socks darned. In America, they found, "such comforts are not at all a sign of luxury. They are standardized and accessible." Indeed, they were available even in the most remote small towns, whose similarity now seemed almost heavenly: "In all these cities you can buy the latest model automobile and electric refrigerator (the dream of newlyweds)" and "there is hot and cold water in all the taps of all the houses, and if the little town is of a slightly better grade, it has a decent hotel, where in your room you will have *three* kinds of water: hot, cold, and iced."[4]

In contrast to earlier Soviet visitors, Ilf and Petrov arrived in New York less as revolutionary scolds than as curious observers and eager adventurers. We might even say they came as lighthearted ethnographers, committed to both learning and laughing – at themselves as much as the Other.[5] Indeed, Petrov seemed to retain some of the optimism of the pair's American fieldwork. In 1939, he began writing a utopian novel, *A Journey to the Land of Communism*. In his imagination, the material reality of the Soviet Union of 1963 bore a strong resemblance to the land

[3] OA, 89; Anne Nesbet, "Skyscrapers, Consular Territory, and Hell: What Bulgakov and Eizenshtein Learned about Space from Il'f and Petrov's America," *Slavic Review* 69 (Summer 2010): 383–84, 390.

[4] LGA, 19, 70; OA, 21, 90.

[5] Malcolm Crick, "The Anthropologist as Tourist: An Identity in Question," in Marie-Francoise Lanfant, John B. Allcock, and Edward M. Bruner, eds., *International Tourism: Identity and Change* (London: SAGE, 1995), 207.

of capitalism, with its refrigerators, good roads, and smiling service, that he and Ilf traversed in 1935.[6]

Earlier Russian and Soviet travelogues provided an important, but not the only, framework for Ilf and Petrov's account of their American journey. While *Low-Rise America* can be read as a descent into hell, it can also be read as a rollicking adventure story in the vein of Lev Kuleshov's 1924 hit comedy *The Extraordinary Adventures of Mr. West in the Land of the Bolsheviks*. Kuleshov's film delivers an inverse take on the problem of bridging ideological divides. Expecting hell, Mr. West, the president of the American YMCA, arrives in Moscow with a cowboy bodyguard, Jeddy. This precaution notwithstanding, he is almost immediately kidnapped by a gang of lowlifes and former aristocrats. Bent on separating Mr. West from his dollars, the thieves play on his expectation of murderous Bolsheviks, going so far as to stage a mock trial of the visiting capitalist. In the end, a timely rescue by a real Bolshevik, a leather-jacketed secret police agent, reveals to him the "true" Land of the Bolsheviks. A grateful and newly enlightened Mr. West cables his wife to burn the New York magazines that printed lies about Bolshevism, and to hang a portrait of Lenin in his study.[7]

To tell this story of an American's enlightenment in Soviet Russia, Kuleshov appropriated and repurposed the elements of American films that so delighted Soviet audiences, effectively turning the capitalists' own tools against them.[8] Mr. West (Porfiry Podobed) himself resembled the silent film star Harold Lloyd, known for his milquetoast characters, and cowboy Jeddy (the boxer and future director Boris Barnet) channeled Douglas Fairbanks. The key features of what Kuleshov ironically called *Amerikanshchina* (usually translated as Americanitis) included gangsters and cowboys as well as the repertoire of cinematic techniques associated with Hollywood films: "continuity editing, close framing, fast cutting, chases, stunts … slapstick … and chaplinesque tricks (one of the trial 'judges' produces a bowl for ink from his sleeve and a quill pen from his collar)."[9] This sort of borrowing was the dream of Soviet Amerikanizm, the application of American technique and tempo to the building of

---

[6] Lesley Milne, *How They Laughed: Zoshchenko and the Ilf–Petrov Partnership* (Birmingham: Centre for Russian and East European Studies, 2003), 250.

[7] Rimgaila Salys, "Introduction: *The Extraordinary Adventures of Mr. West in the Land of the Bolsheviks*," in Rimgaila Salys, ed., *The Russian Cinema Reader*, vol. 1, *1908 to the Stalin Era* (Boston: Academic Studies Press, 2013), 89.

[8] Ian Christie, "Neobychainye priklucheniia Mistera Vesta v strane bol'shevikov," in Brigit Beumers, ed., *The Cinema of Russia and the Former Soviet Union* (London: Wallflower Press, 2007), 26.

[9] Salys, "Introduction," 92; D. J. Youngblood, "'Americanitis: The *Amerikanshchina* in Soviet Cinema,'" *Journal of Popular Film & Television* 19 (Winter 1992): 148–56.

socialism. In Kuleshov's case, the appropriation included the added twist of transforming both Soviet film and (fictional) American minds.

The Extraordinary Adventures of Mr. West in the Land of the Bolsheviks offered not a template for Ilf and Petrov's extraordinary adventures in the Land of the Capitalists, but an optimistic appraisal of the possibility of challenging engrained stereotypes.[10] Of course, in the film the person who abandons his erroneous preconceptions is the capitalist. The Soviet authors could hardly end their journey by burning *Pravda* and hanging a portrait of George Washington. Still, they, like Kuleshov, embraced American technique and tempo. Constrained, like previous Soviet visitors, by ideology as well as their own expectations and presuppositions, Ilf and Petrov nonetheless let their readers glimpse "us" in the Other and, with a smile, some of the Other in us.

Rather than emphasizing their ideological certainty, Ilf and Petrov lingered over the "extra-ideological realities"[11] of the American landscape and made gentle fun of themselves as eager participant observers. On their first evening in New York, on the way up to their room on the twenty-seventh floor, they learned their "first American custom": that men removed their hats when a woman entered the elevator. Several days later, riding the elevator to their publishers' office, they hastened to put their new knowledge to use "and with the expeditiousness of old experienced New Yorkers" they doffed their hats when a woman entered. But the other men in the elevator "did not follow our knightly example ... and even regarded us with curiosity." Here they were confronted with the reality that "acquaintance with the customs of a foreign country is not so easy and is almost always accompanied by confusion." It turned out, they informed their readers, "that hats should be taken off only in private and hotel elevators; whereas, in buildings where people transact *biznes* [business] one may keep one's hat on."[12] The episode can be understood as mocking American gender and business norms. But the emphasis on the (comical) limits of cross-cultural understanding blunts the critique. The pair's "self-irony" stood in sharp contrast to Mayakovsky and Pilnyak's self-seriousness. Indeed, the travelogue's lack of ideological charge disappointed some early readers, who complained that Ilf and Petrov ignored oppressed workers, the class struggle, and the influence of the American Communist Party.[13]

---

[10] Fedorova, *Yankees*, 203.

[11] Aleksandr Etkind, *Tolkovanie puteshestvii: Rossiia i Amerika v travelogakh i intertekstakh* (Moscow: Novoe literaturnoe obozrenie, 2003), 162.

[12] LGA, 19; OA, 20.   [13] PIA, 500–504; Fedorova, *Yankees*, 89, 93 (self-irony).

That Ilf and Petrov were comic writers helps to account for the striking differences in tone and substance between their jaunty narrative and the gloom, vitriol, and haughtiness of earlier Soviet American travelogues. They shared Mayakovsky and Pilnyak's disgust with American capitalism and racism, and they mocked American consumerism. But unlike their predecessors, they tried to reserve judgment. As they noted in the travelogue's penultimate chapter, they came not to criticize but to transfer their impressions to paper.[14] Here, they resembled "professional" anthropologists intent on acquiring, collating, and communicating "experiences of alterity."[15]

It is also worth considering how Ilf and Petrov's approach fit the particular moment in which they traveled. Gorky, who came to the United States to raise funds for revolutionaries in Russia and to "discredit" American democracy, recorded "ambivalent" responses to America in his letters, but in his published work engaged in "unrelieved invective."[16] Ilf and Petrov, by contrast, traveled as emissaries from a Soviet Union working to establish friendly relations with the United States. Ironically, the Soviet writers found themselves less bound by political correctness than the prerevolutionary Bolshevik. Their published work shared the inquisitive tone of their letters and Ilf's notebook.[17]

The Seventh Comintern Congress's endorsement of the Popular Front constituted another important international context of Ilf and Petrov's journey. In the summer of 1935, the United States had threatened to sever relations with the Soviet Union over the participation of American communists in the Congress. But the meeting implemented a more moderate line that required communist parties to put revolution on the back burner and focus instead on building inclusive coalitions against fascism. In October 1935, just as Ilf and Petrov arrived in New York, the Soviet ambassador, Alexander Troyanovsky, promoted the significance of the Congress's decisions. He told State Department official Earl Packer that communists were now committed to "collaboration with socialist, liberal and even bourgeois groups" in defense of democracy. According to Packer, the ambassador insisted that "the Communists are sincere in this." For his part, Packer expressed skepticism, calling the shift merely a "tactical maneuver." He predicted that "whenever it might

---

[14] OA, 401.
[15] Justin Stagl and Christopher Pinney, "Introduction: From Travel Writing to Ethnography," *History and Anthropology* 9 (1996): 121.
[16] Hasty and Fusso, "Introduction," 11.   [17] Etkind, *Tolkovanie puteshestvii*, 162.

be convenient," communists "would follow the Bolshevik example" of violent revolution.[18]

For Ilf and Petrov, however, the new line was a significant shift that authorized them to reach out to all progressive Americans. In their published work, enthusiasm for the Popular Front is associated above all with their guide Mr. Adams. Evoking the Italian attack on Ethiopia that became an early galvanizing cause of the Popular Front, Ilf and Petrov described the scene after an absent-minded Adams, intent on explaining the League of Nations to a perplexed shop owner, walked through a plate glass window: "It looked as if a heavy Caproni bomber had just dropped its entire supply of bombs earmarked for Haile Selassie."[19] This image of fascist aggression was a far cry from Mayakovsky and Pilnyak, who in line with the Comintern stance at the time of their visits and their own propensities, documented signs of imminent revolution in America.

Domestically, too, the context of Ilf and Petrov's trip differed from that of their predecessors. They were the first Soviet writers to visit the United States following the proclamation of socialist realism as the governing doctrine of Soviet art. Articulated beginning in 1932 and adopted in 1934 at the First All-Union Congress of Soviet Writers, socialist realism dictated that authors (and other cultural producers) show the world of socialism as it was becoming, describing the "reality" of the socialist future still under construction. Such art had the pedagogical function of ideological transformation. Writers became "engineers of human souls."[20]

What socialist realism implied for a description of the United States was not entirely clear. Indeed, Ilf and Petrov visited at a moment when the practice of socialist realism was still in flux. Tellingly, they alluded to the new literary dispensation only once in their published travelogue, in the context of their discussion of the American author John Dos Passos. The first two volumes of Dos Passos's *U.S.A.* trilogy had been translated into Russian, and at the time of the pair's American road trip, Soviet authors and critics were debating whether his methods could be considered a form of "revolutionary realism."[21] As we will see, Ilf and Petrov's depiction of New York implicitly put this proposition to the test.

---

[18] Memorandum of Conversation, 9 October 1935, NACP, RG 59, 811.00B/1683.

[19] OA, 209.

[20] Petre M. Petrov, *Automatic for the Masses: The Death of the Author and the Birth of Socialist Realism* (Toronto: University of Toronto Press, 2015), 200–219; Katerina Clark, *The Soviet Novel: History as Ritual* (Chicago: University of Chicago Press, 1981), 27–36.

[21] A. Yelistratova as quoted in Deming Brown, "Dos Passos in Soviet Criticism," *Comparative Literature* 5 (Autumn 1953): 332.

Finally, unlike the authors of earlier Soviet American travelogues, Ilf brought a camera. Ilf's Leica connected the pair to a large number of contemporary Soviet and American author-photographers (or author-photographer teams), who, despite the very different contexts in which they worked, embraced the photodocumentary as a means of revolutionizing artistic production. Traveling across America in a new Ford and taking photographs along the way, Ilf and Petrov applied modern technology to the task of exploring, assessing, and perhaps understanding modern America.

6   Photographing New York

> New York opened at once on several planes. The upper plane was occupied by the tops of those skyscrapers which were higher than ours. ... On the next plane, open in its entirety to our gaze, in addition to smokestacks, skylights, and tomcats one could see flat roofs on which stood small one-storied houses with gardens, skimpy trees, little brick paths, a small fountain, and even rattan chairs. ... [The elevated railway] was on the next plane of New York City. ... In order to see the last and fundamental plane, the plane of the street, one had to bend out of the window and look down at a right angle.
>
> Ilf and Petrov, *Low-Rise America*

Ilf purchased his first camera in the winter of 1929–1930, and his interest in photography quickly turned into an obsession that slowed work on *The Little Golden Calf*. Petrov, who loaned Ilf the 800 rubles for the purchase, joked that he had thereby lost both his money and his coauthor.[1] In America, however, Ilf's photographs became part of the project. He carried a lightweight Leica that, as the photographer Alexander Rodchenko noted in a 1936 article in *Sovetskoe foto*, "was created for close-ups and for capturing life on the fly." It was perfect for the streets of New York, where, Ilf marveled, everyone moved at a run, but less suited to what Rodchenko called "general views."[2] Ilf took both. On the back of a print labeled a "View of New York from the twenty-seventh floor," Petrov informed his wife that his partner "clicks the shutter all day long."[3] The photo essay "American Photographs," published in *Ogonek* in 1936, combined Ilf's photographs and their collaborative text. The eleventh and final installment focused on New York City, where the authors began and ended their trip. As originally planned, the book

---

[1] Nesbet, "Skyscrapers," 387.
[2] PIA, Il'f, 26 October 1935, 439. Rodchenko as quoted in Timothy A. Nunan, "Soviet Nationalities Policy, USSR in Construction, and Soviet Documentary Photography in Comparative Context, 1931–1937," *Ab Imperio* 2 (2010): 61n37.
[3] Nesbet, "Skyscrapers," 387.

Low-Rise America, too, included photographs, although they were omitted for reasons that remain unclear.[4]

In his letters home from New York, Ilf doubted than any photograph – or indeed any words – could provide an adequate conception of "this desperate city." Still, he tried to capture it, spending at least one day in October 1935 "walking around the city and photographing it."[5] Ilf did not record what he photographed. Instead, he focused his letter on the delay in getting his photos printed and the irony that the photographer had hardly any pictures of himself to share. But the "New York" installment of the photo essay allows us to follow Ilf around the city and get a sense of what caught his eye.[6]

The essay opened with one of the most prominent of all New York landmarks, the Empire State Building. The building had featured just a few months earlier in a photo essay in the journal *Za rubezhom* (Abroad) by another Soviet visitor to America, the architect Boris M. Yofan. Best known for designing the massive and unrealized Palace of Soviets that was to be topped with a statue of Vladimir Lenin twice the size of the Statue of Liberty, Yofan had traveled to New York in 1934 specifically to study skyscrapers.[7] In both Yofan's and Ilf and Petrov's essays, the photographs and the texts presented the towering, sleek, and majestic Empire State Building as a "supreme embodiment of technology, efficiency, and modernity." Although, as we will see, Ilf and Petrov did not ignore the fact, as architects' articles often did, that the building also stood as a symbol of capitalism.[8]

Elsewhere in New York, Ilf took notice of the city's dynamism, its crowds, its noise, and its multiple angles and "planes." Just a couple of blocks from the Empire State Building, facing south on Fifth Avenue at Thirty-Fifth Street, he captured a corner Woolworth's and an intersection choked with cars and pedestrians. On West Thirty-Second Street, he snapped the elevated tracks and crowds in front of Gimbel Brothers. At Sixtieth Street and Fifth Avenue, he took an awkwardly framed photograph of a traffic jam and a wall of skyscrapers. On Riverside Drive, Ilf shot an almost rustic scene: a half-dozen cars stopped at a light and a few pedestrians strolling and sitting in the park (Figure 6.1). From

---

[4] Erika Wolf, "Introduction," in ART, x–xi.

[5] PIA, Il'f, 8 October 1935, 427; Il'f, 26 October 1935, 439.

[6] Il'ia Il'f and Evgenii Petrov, "Amerikanskie fotografii: XI. N'iu-Iork," *Ogonek*, no. 28 (August 1936): 5–9.

[7] B. I. Iofin, "N'iu-Iorkskie neboskreby," *Za rubezhom*, no. 10 (5 April 1936): 228–29.

[8] Sona S. Hoisington, "Soviet Schizophrenia and the American Skyscraper," in Rosalind P. Blakesley and Susan Reid, eds., *Russian Art and the West: A Century of Dialogue in Painting, Architecture, and the Decorative Arts* (DeKalb: Northern Illinois University Press, 2007), 156.

Figure 6.1 Views of the city from the "New York" installment of
"American Photographs." Clockwise left to right: Fifth Avenue near the
entrance to Central Park; Riverside Park; a restaurant or nightclub
façade; a demonstration "against war and fascism" in Harlem. *Ogonek*,
no. 23 (20 April 1936): 7. Courtesy Library of Congress.

the pair's twenty-seventh-floor room in the Shelton Hotel, Ilf photographed a view of New York City that focused on the rooftops below, a glimpse of the street, and a pack of skyscrapers of varied shapes and sizes framed by a thin strip of sky.

Ilf often pointed his camera at signs and advertisements, apparently the brighter and gaudier the better. Somewhere between Midtown and Harlem, he took a closeup of part of a nightclub or restaurant marquee, capturing the word "Entertainment" in an Art Deco font beneath larger-than-life figures of two dancing couples. From an elevated platform he photographed the busy sidewalk below and a sign advertising "3 decker toasted sandwiches." On Broadway after dark, he photographed the brilliantly lit restaurants, shops, and theaters. The snapshots seemed to confess, as Ilf wrote to his wife, that he had "fallen in love with this city," despite it being "too big, too dirty, too rich and too poor."[9]

In "New York," Ilf and Petrov combined text and images to do what Ilf had suggested neither words nor photographs alone could do: capture a city that was "too" everything. If the sense of the impossibility of representing New York was born out of their personal experiences, their solution resembled that of many writers and photographers in the 1930s, who were experimenting with the hybrid documentary genre of the photo essay or photobook.[10] The photodocumentaries of the period were not simply cheaper, more widely distributed versions of the illustrated magazines that since the 1890s had combined photographs and nonfictional narratives. In the 1930s, authors and artists in the Soviet Union and the West applied the camera eye's "distinctively fragmentary mode of vision"[11] to the page.

Whether they appeared in the Soviet Union, the United States, or Weimar Germany, in state-regulated media, government reports, coffee-table books, or the political press, the photodocumentaries of the 1930s shared a reliance on montage, the juxtaposition of images and text. Authors, photographers, and author-photographers played on the paradoxical power of the photographic "fact" to appear fixed and objective, while actually being quite malleable, taking on different meanings in different contexts. Blurring the line between "art" and "life," modernist photodocumentaries used modern media not only to reveal and capture,

---

[9] PIA, Il'f, 26 October 1935, 439.
[10] Daniel H. Magilow, *The Photography of Crisis: The Photo Essays of Weimar Germany* (University Park: Pennsylvania State University Press, 2012), 6, 4.
[11] Jeff Allred, *American Modernism and Depression Documentary* (Oxford: Oxford University Press, 2000), 7, 9.

but to construct and propagate truths invisible to the human eye.[12] Complex amalgams of words and images, they "taught" viewers new ways of seeing.[13]

The widespread use of montage in the photodocumentaries of the 1930s owed much to the international circulation of photographs and films and the people who produced them. Before 1933, as we have already seen in the case of Soviet films headed to the United States, Germany served as a conduit for much of the cultural traffic between East and West. When Sergei Tretyakov, one of the first members of the Soviet avant-garde to take and publish photographs, visited Germany in 1931, he introduced audiences to the "literature of fact." Rejecting "imaginative" or "invented" literature as incapable of representing revolutionary transformation, Tretyakov favored journalism and nonfiction genres such as the memoir and the travelogue.[14] The slides and photographs he used to illustrate his lectures on the collectivization of agriculture impressed both Walter Benjamin and Berthold Brecht. In Benjamin's 1934 essay "The Author as Producer," which he planned to deliver at the Paris Institute for the Study of Fascism, he identified Tretyakov's blending of photography and text as a model for cultural producers who aimed not only to document, but to change the world.[15]

The Soviet photodocumentary also reached Germany via the communist-aligned *Arbeiter-Illustrierte-Zeitung* (Worker's Illustrated Newspaper, *A-I-Z*).[16] In 1931, *A-I-Z* published Soviet photographers Max Alpert and Arkady Shaikhet's photo essay "A Day in the Life of a Moscow Working Class Family" (later reprinted in the Soviet Union). Juxtaposing text and images, the photo series constructed a narrative that verified a revolution in everyday life – a transformation that for most

[12] Malte Hagener, *Moving Forward, Looking Back: The European Avant-garde and the Invention of Film Culture, 1919–39* (Amsterdam: Amsterdam University Press, 2007), 168–80; Patrizia Di Bello and Shamoon Zamir, "Introduction," in Patrizia Di Bello, Colette Wilson, and Shamoon Zamir, eds., *The Photobook: From Talbot to Ruscha and Beyond* (London: I. B. Tauris, 2012), 2.

[13] Allred, *American Modernism*, 6; Magilow, *Photography of Crisis*, 4; Pepper Stetler, *Stop Reading! Look!: Modern Vision and the Weimar Photographic Book* (Ann Arbor: University of Michigan Press, 2015), 9–10.

[14] Evgeny Dobrenko, "Literary Criticism and the Transformation of the Literary Field during the Cultural Revolution, 1928–1932," in Evgeny Dobrenko and Galin Tihonov, eds., *A History of Russian Literary Theory and Criticism: The Soviet Age and Beyond* (Pittsburgh: University of Pittsburgh Press, 2011), 55–56.

[15] Erika Wolf, "The Author as Photographer: Tret′iakov's, Erenburg's, and Il′f's Images of the West," *Configurations* 18 (2010): 384; Katerina Clark, *Moscow, the Fourth Rome: Stalinism, Cosmopolitanism, and the Evolution of Soviet Culture, 1931–1941* (Cambridge, MA: Harvard University Press, 2011), 43–50.

[16] Clark, *Moscow*, 66–67; Magilow, *Photography of Crisis*, 43–44.

Soviet people remained on the distant horizon.[17] Brecht, who in 1931 wrote a brief congratulatory note on the occasion of *A-I-Z*'s tenth anniversary, likely saw the Soviet photo series. It certainly fit with his praise for the radical magazine's efforts to counter the "immense quantity of images that is spewed out daily" in the popular illustrated press, which appeared "to bear the stamp of truth," but in fact served only "to obfuscate the way things are." His own suggestions for training viewers to dismantle the glossy, mystifying veneer of such photographs included re-captioning them.[18]

Even before 1933, when Hitler's rise to power cut off connections with Germany and the normalization of Soviet–American relations eased travel, connections between American and Soviet documentary photographers and filmmakers also flourished. In 1930, Margaret Bourke-White, one of the most famous photographers in the United States, traveled to the Soviet Union to photograph Soviet factories. Her warm welcome is somewhat surprising, as she was at the time "a photographer employed by industrialists who paid her handsomely to take promotional photographs for glossy magazines"[19] – that is, a producer of exactly the sort of obfuscating images that Brecht decried. But as American photographers and writers, no less than Brecht, understood, recaptioning a photograph could fundamentally reshape the story it told.[20] In her memoir, Bourke-White recalled that when she sought permission to photograph industrial sites of the First Five-Year Plan, her "pictures of American steel mills, factories, and refineries," which emphasized "the drama of the machine," immediately recommended her to her hosts. Ignoring the capitalist context in which they were produced and originally published, Soviet authorities realized that Bourke-White's photographs could illustrate their preferred narrative of Soviet industrialization as heroic reality.[21]

---

[17] Katherine M. H. Reischl, *Photographic Literacy: Cameras in the Hands of Russian Authors* (Ithaca, NY: Cornell University Press, 2018), 153–59.

[18] Carl Gelderloos, "Simply Reproducing Reality – Brecht, Benjamin, and Renger-Patzsch on Photography," *German Studies Review* 37 (October 2014): 562–64; J. J. Long, "Paratextual Profusion: Photography and Text in Bertolt Brecht's War Primer," *Poetics Today* 29 (2008): 202, 204 (quotations).

[19] Ada Ackerman, "Margaret Bourke-White and Soviet Russia," in William Benton Whisenhunt and Norman E. Saul, eds., *New Perspectives on Russian–American Relations* (New York: Routledge, 2015), 195.

[20] Leah Bendavid-Val, *Propaganda and Dreams: Photographing the 1930s in the USSR and the US* (Zurich: Edition Stemmle, 1999), 35–36.

[21] Margaret Bourke-White, *Portrait of Myself* (New York: Simon and Schuster, 1963), 70; Ackerman, "Bourke-White," 196–98; Nicholas Kupensky, "The Soviet Industrial Sublime: The Awe and Fear of Dneprostroi, 1927–1932" (PhD diss., Yale University, 2017), 178–80.

While Bourke-White tapped into the needs of Soviet propaganda, she also participated in a transnational modernist network. Before she departed for the Soviet Union, an official at the Soviet Information Bureau in Washington, DC, told the photographer that her pictures had the "Russian style," and arranged for her to meet Sergei Eisenstein, then visiting the United States. The director obligingly provided her with "letters of introduction to artists in Berlin, Paris, and Moscow, which he wrote out in his own hand in German, French, and Russian."[22] Eisenstein played a similar role for Ilf and Petrov, spending "a whole evening" equipping them with handwritten letters of introduction in English. One of this pile of letters is preserved in the archive of theater and film director Rouben Mamoulian.[23] It was a letter from the journalist Louis Fischer that introduced the writers to Bourke-White in New York. Fischer, who may not have been aware of Ilf's interest in photography, suggested (or perhaps joked) that Bourke-White might illustrate their proposed travelogue.[24]

Published in both the United States and the Soviet Union, Bourke-White's photographs of Soviet industrialization illustrate how images crossed borders and how montage could alter their meanings. As Soviet and American publications juxtaposed her photographs with different texts and images, they opened or encouraged different interpretations of the photographic "fact." Bourke-White's photograph of a tractor assembly line published in her photobook *Eyes on Russia* (1931) with the caption "The New Tractor" and in *Fortune* magazine with the caption "Tractorstroy," the name of the factory, could be read as evidence of revolutionary transformation or of business opportunities. A heavily retouched (and uncredited) version of the same photograph that appeared in *SSSR na stroike* (USSR in Construction), the most "visually pyrotechnic"[25] of the Soviet documentary magazines published in the 1930s, with the caption "Adjusting the Front Wheels of a Tractor on the Conveyor," suggested still other readings. The Soviet caption called attention to the worker's action – rather than the product or the place of production. At the same time, the retouching anonymized the

---

[22] Margaret Bourke-White, *Eyes on Russia* (New York: Simon and Schuster, 1931), 25–26, 39, 42.

[23] LGA, 35; OA, 42. Sergei Eisenstein to Mamoulian, [1935], Box 39, Folder 3, Rouben Mamoulian Papers, Manuscript Division, Library of Congress, Washington, DC.

[24] Louis Fischer to Margaret Bourke-White, 15 September 1935, Margaret Bourke-White Papers, Special Collections Research Center, Syracuse University, Syracuse, NY, Box 17. I thank Nick Kupensky for this document and information about the meeting.

[25] Nunan, "Soviet Nationalities Policy," 47; Erika Wolf, "When Photographs Speak, to Whom Do They Talk? The Origins and Audience of SSSR na stroike (USSR in Construction)," *Left History* 6 (1999): 57, 53.

brooding worker in Bourke-White's photo, unwittingly turning him into an expressionless "automaton."[26] Differently captioned, credited, and arranged, the photographs could tell distinctive stories of the production of new tractors or the production of new people.

The international circulation of illustrated books and magazines provided opportunities for photographers and filmmakers unable to travel abroad to learn about different photographic practices.[27] Publishing Bourke-White's photographs without attribution, *USSR in Construction* allowed Soviet photographers to see how she suffused her images "with dramatic light, texture, and tonality."[28] Bourke-White herself distributed her photographs in the Soviet Union through unofficial channels, sending Eisenstein a copy of *Eyes on Russia*, and sharing news of its publication with the director Vsevolod Pudovkin. She also corresponded with Tretyakov, to whom she sent a copy of *Fortune* with some of her photos from the Soviet Union.[29]

These kinds of exchanges may explain the overlaps in the subjects, if not necessarily the "visual language," of Ilf's photographs and those of "socially engaged" American photographers such as Bourke-White.[30] The resemblances could also have been a result of American borrowing from Soviet sources. Bourke-White seems to have been influenced by the Soviet photographs she saw in illustrated journals such as *Ogonek* as well as exhibition catalogs and photographic almanacs.[31] Indeed, Bourke-White emerged as a "socially engaged" photographer only in 1934, after her visits to the Soviet Union, when she covered the Dust Bowl on assignment for *Fortune* magazine.[32]

Ilya Ehrenburg's 1933 photobook *Moi Parizh* (My Paris) provided another potential source of Soviet influence on American photographers. It reached Walker Evans and Ben Shahn via the filmmaker Jay Leyda, who had studied with Eisenstein in the Soviet Union. Likely neither Evans nor Shahn, who had emigrated from the Russian empire at age eight, read the text. But the photographs impressed them both. They even took up Ehrenburg's practice of shooting with a Leica equipped

[26] Barnaby Haran, "Tractor Factory Facts: Margaret Bourke-White's Eyes on Russia and the Romance of Industry in the Five-Year Plan," *Oxford Art Journal* 38 (2015): 83–85 (automaton), 89; *USSR in Construction*, no. 10–11 (1930): 34–35; Ackerman, "Bourke-White," 200; Wolf, "When Photographs Speak," 53, 62; Kupensky, "Soviet Industrial Sublime," 188n66.
[27] Martin Parr, "Preface," in Martin Parr and Gerry Badger, *The Photobook: A History*, vol. 2 (New York: Phaidon Press, 2006), 4.
[28] Haran, "Tractor Factory," 77.   [29] Ackerman, "Bourke-White," 203–206.
[30] Reischl, *Photographic Literacy*, 17.
[31] Clark, *Moscow*, 63; Ackerman, "Bourke-White," 200–207.
[32] Kupensky, "Soviet Industrial Sublime," 158–59, 208–209.

with a side viewfinder that made it possible to photograph subjects surreptitiously.[33] Ilf, too, traveled with a small Leica (although one without a side viewfinder). His journal does not reveal whether he talked about photography when he visited Ehrenburg in Paris en route to the United States.[34]

This brief excursion into the international diffusion of photodocumentaries in the 1930s provides a framework for interpreting the photographs in Ilf and Petrov's travelogue. Rodchenko's contemporary criticism of Ilf's American photographs emphasized precisely the interplay of text and image that characterized modernist photodocumentaries. He deemed Ilf's photographs inferior to Ehrenburg's, characterizing them as lacking "the ironic, sharp eye that Ilf and Petrov possess in literature." Conceived as "documentary records," Ilf's photographs were, Rodchenko concluded, "bookkeeping," not photography. Still, he encouraged Ilf to continue working on his photography. Echoing Benjamin's call for photographers to give each picture a "caption that wrenches it from modish commerce and gives it a revolutionary use value," he urged Ilf "to take photographs with captions."[35] Given this call for captions, it is perplexing that Rodchenko focused his criticism (published in August 1936) on the photographs rather than the photo essay "American Photographs" that began appearing in *Ogonek* four months earlier.

However, if we focus on the hybrid photo essay as a whole – and not on the quality of the photographs alone – it immediately becomes clear that Ilf's photographs interacted in complex ways with the texts in which they were embedded.[36] Looking only at the photograph, Rodchenko criticized Ilf's view of the Empire State Building as both unthinking and "ultra-formalist": "If you cast a glance at a skyscraper from the window of an automobile traveling on narrow streets, whether you want to or not, you become a formalist and shoot from below to above."[37] This is a fair description of Ilf's photograph of the building that ran in the "New York" installment of "American Photographs." But what Rodchenko read as the image's unthinking "formalism" takes on new meaning when set in the context of the lengthy caption that accompanied it. The caption begins with a vision of the sublime "formal" skyscraper: "Cold, noble, and clean, it rises up like a beam of artificial ice." The tone quickly shifts from reverence to social critique, as the authors note that "Half of the floors in the Empire are empty, since due to unforeseen circumstances

[33] Reischl, *Photographic Literacy*, 179–81.   [34] ZK, 26 September [1935], 421.
[35] Benjamin as quoted in Wolf, "Author as Photographer," 384; Aleksandr Rodchenko, "Ilya Ilf's American Photographs," in ART, 149, 151–52.
[36] Reischl, *Photographic Literacy*, 171–78.   [37] Rodchenko, "Ilya Ilf's," 151–52.

the completion of its construction coincided with the beginning of the crisis." Finally, the authors shift to self-deprecation as they describe their inarticulate responses to the awe-inspiring monument to capitalist excess and failure. They confessed that "In a month and a half of life in New York, we walked past it every day, and each time we involuntarily muttered words which were as delighted as they were meaningless, things like 'Oh, the devil!' or 'Well, now!'"[38] Juxtaposed with these varied assessments of the Empire – noble, empty, delightful, meaningless – the photograph intensifies the ironies of the authors' view of New York. The caption and a retracing of Ilf's steps in New York further suggest that the photograph may not have been as slapdash as it appeared to Rodchenko. Ilf snapped the photo from the corner of Fifth Avenue and Thirty-First Street, three blocks south of the main entrance to the Empire State Building, one of the only vantage points along Fifth Avenue that allows a full view of the "artificial ice" of the building's façade (Figure 6.2).

Examined out of the context of the photo essay, the photograph of Fifth Avenue at Central Park appears to be one of the images Rodchenko had in mind when he described Ilf as shooting "in a bustling manner, in fact not thinking, not picking anything out, not emphasizing anything."[39] Ilf snapped the photograph at the entrance to the park at Sixtieth Street, a spot the authors would likely have passed on their way to the Central Park Zoo (see Figure 6.1). The scene does seem hurriedly and haphazardly framed. Ilf cut off one of the tall buildings and left much empty space in the foreground. However, as in the case of the Empire State Building, the caption suggests a clear emphasis, and the photograph adds to the humor of the narrative. Ignoring the intersection entirely, the caption instead describes the zoo. "Here," the authors explain, gesturing toward a place beyond the photograph, "children get some idea of what a cow looks like by examining a rhinoceros. Cows are rarer in New York than rhinos."[40] From the perspective of the caption, the photograph's awkward vertical composition, taking in the tall buildings and the traffic, makes more sense. The photograph materializes the unnatural environment in which a cow is rarer than a rhino. It provides the context that makes the story of the zoo both funny and sharp.

If, as Rodchenko noted with some frustration, Ilf's photographs on their own were amateurish and inexpressive, Ilf and Petrov's photo essay effectively operated according to the principle of montage or juxtaposition central to modernist documentary projects.[41] By 1936, when

---

[38] ART, 128–29.   [39] Rodchenko, "Ilya Ilf's," 151.   [40] ART, 133.
[41] Reischl, *Photographic Literacy*, 17.

Figure 6.2 Finding an unobstructed view of the Empire State Building from Fifth Avenue is not easy. South façade from Fifth Avenue and Thirty-First Street. Photo by author, 2019.

Ogonek published the photo essay, the Soviet "documentary moment" had passed, supplanted by the method of "socialist realism," which banished fractured, disorienting, and ironic perspectives.[42] Yet Ilf and Petrov's photo essay provided just such modernist vistas. Because they turned their satirical eyes on the Other, they could be understood as complying with (or at least not violating) the fundamental socialist realist dictum that literature reveal the single truth of socialist construction.

In 1937, *Low-Rise America* appeared shorn of photographs, perhaps because of Rodchenko's negative review, the changing literary environment, or an effort to cut costs.[43] Even so, the travelogue reflected the photographer's habit of fragmenting the world through the camera's eye. Ilf and Petrov's description of the panorama from their room on the twenty-seventh floor of the Shelton Hotel in Manhattan (quoted in the epigraph) reads like a storyboard for a film. They "shot" the scene from varied angles, included a series of close-ups, and described a complex montage of "planes" that constituted their view. They offered not a static postcard view of the New York City skyline, but an almost cubist cityscape, that manages to superimpose four planes at once, the precariousness of the whole procedure underscored by the image of the authors craning their necks out of the twenty-seventh-floor window. Transposing the camera's mode of vision to the page, they evoked the American modernist writer who had attracted more Soviet attention than any other and who showed the pair around New York City: John Dos Passos.

---

[42] Elizabeth Astrid Papazian, *Manufacturing Truth: The Documentary Moment in Early Soviet Culture* (DeKalb: Northern Illinois University Press, 2009), 4.
[43] Wolf, "Author as Photographer," 401–402.

7 Dos

John Dos Passos, who is even better known among us [than Ernest Hemingway] and who provoked even more discussions in connection with disputes on formalism in art, stopped by to introduce us to Hemingway.

Ilf and Petrov, "The Electric Chair," *Za rubezhom* (5 November 1936)

In the first half of the 1930s, a John Dos Passos craze gripped the Soviet intelligentsia. Translations of his novels circulated in large print runs. Young writers imitated him. In the "largest and most fundamental literary dispute that has ever arisen over an American writer," Soviet critics hotly debated whether Dos Passos should be considered a revolutionary realist or a petty-bourgeois pessimist.[1] The debate ultimately had less to do with whether Dos Passos was worth Soviet readers' time than with the future of Soviet literature itself. At a moment when the recently enshrined slogan of socialist realism was still open to some interpretation, Dos Passos offered a model for a possible socialist literature that combined a revolutionary critique of capitalism and modernist prose. His use of techniques that had parallels in Soviet avant-garde film polarized critics and underscored the local stakes.[2] When Ilf and Petrov met Dos Passos in New York City in the fall of 1935, the outcome of the debate remained uncertain.

The source of Ilf and Petrov's introduction to Dos Passos was likely Sergei Eisenstein, who had met the author during his 1928 visit to the

---

[1] Brown, "Dos Passos," 332 ("largest"), 343; E. M. Salmanova, "'Sovetskii' Dos Passos: Mif i real'nost (K istorii vospriiatiia pisatelia v Rossii)," in V. E. Bagno, P. R. Zaborov, and M. Iu. Koreneva, eds., *Nachalo veka: iz istorii mezhdunarodnykh sviazei russkoi literatury* (St. Petersburg: Nauka, 2000), 272–75.

[2] Hans Günther, "Soviet Literary Criticism and the Formulation of the Aesthetics of Socialist Realism, 1932–1940," in Evgeny Dobrenko and Galin Tihanov, eds., *A History of Russian Literary Theory and Criticism: The Soviet Age and Beyond* (Pittsburgh: University of Pittsburgh Press, 2011), 90–100; E. D. Gal'tsova, "Zapadnye pisateli-modernisty v zhurnale 'Literaturnyi kritik': Prust [Proust], Dzhois [Joyce], Dos Passos," in E. D. Gal'tsova, ed., *Postizhenie zapada: Inostrannaia kul'tura v sovetskoi literature, iskusstve i teorii, 1917–1941 gg.: Issledovaniia i arkhivnye materialy* (Moscow: IMLI RAN, 2015), 671, 674.

Soviet Union. At the time of their meeting, both Eisenstein and Dos Passos had been experimenting independently with montage – Eisenstein in the film *Battleship Potemkin* (1925) and Dos Passos in the novel *Manhattan Transfer* (1925, Russian translation 1927). Dos Passos later recalled that "We agreed thoroughly about the importance of montage."[3] By 1935, Dos Passos had seen Eisenstein's films, and drew on his theories in fashioning the complex montage of his *U.S.A.* trilogy. What Dos Passos self-mockingly called the novels' "four-way conveyer system" combined fiction, biography, memoir, and something like the Soviet "literature of fact."[4] He intercut realistic, occasionally overlapping narratives focused on a cast of twelve characters with often sardonic biographical portraits of the "great" men (and, in the final volume, one woman) who defined the era; "camera eye" interludes, cryptic, autobiographical interior monologues that refracted the panorama of *U.S.A.*; and a series of "newsreels," collages of headlines, song lyrics, political speeches, and advertising copy that evoked the wider stage on which the individual narratives played out.[5] The ambitious novels briefly made Dos Passos in the estimation of some Soviet critics "the most important contemporary writer of the non-Soviet world"[6] (Figure 7.1).

For Ilf and Petrov, Dos Passos became an important American contact. They had arrived in New York City with a suitcase full of introductions from friends and acquaintances in the Soviet Union, notably Eisenstein and the American journalists Walter Duranty and Louis Fischer. Indeed, they came with so much "recommendational merchandise" that the Soviet consul general in New York despaired of coping with it; ultimately, he came up with the solution of inviting everyone to a reception at the consulate. As Ilf and Petrov depicted it, the affair required them to stand for three hours on a second-floor landing greeting the more than 150 "spirits" conjured by the letters as they filed past

[3] John Dos Passos, *The Best Times: An Informal Memoir* (New York: New American Library, 1966), 180.

[4] Dos Passos as quoted in Michael Denning, *The Cultural Front: The Laboring of American Culture in the Twentieth Century* (New York: Verso, 1997), 170; Justin Edwards, "The Man with a Camera Eye: Cinematic Form and Hollywood Malediction in John Dos Passos's *The Big Money*," *Literature Film Quarterly* 27 (1999): 247. I thank José Vergara for calling my attention to the "quasi-factographic nature" of Dos Passos's work.

[5] Denning, *Cultural Front*, 169–70; Juan A. Suárez, "John Dos Passos's U.S.A. and Left Documentary Film in the 1930s: The Cultural Politics of 'Newsreel' and 'The Camera Eye,'" *American Studies in Scandinavia* 31 (1999): 43–66; Maddelena Mendolicchio, "La technique cinématographique dans *Manhattan Transfer*," *Roman 20–50: Revue d'Étude du Roman du XXe Siècle* 26 (1998): 157–68; Gretchen Foster, "John Dos Passos's Use of Film Technique in *Manhattan Transfer* and *The 42nd Parallel*," *Literature Film Quarterly* 4 (1986): 186–94.

[6] Brown, "Dos Passos," 334.

Figure 7.1 John Dos Passos, undated. The author was among Ilf and
Petrov's most important American contacts. CC BY-SA 3.0.
Wikimedia Commons.

toward glasses of punch and "little diplomatic sandwiches." The
unpleasant, if not hellish party became one of the inspirations, along
with an extravaganza at the American ambassador's Moscow residence,
for Satan's "great ball" in Mikhail Bulgakov's *The Master and Margarita.*[7]

Undaunted by the experience, Ilf and Petrov allowed Dos Passos and
other friends and acquaintances in New York to refill their suitcase.
Alexander Gumberg, the Jewish Russian American businessman who
had shown American journalists around revolutionary Petrograd, supplied them with formal letters of introduction to politicians and businessmen.[8] Dos Passos wrote "numerous letters" attached to an index listing
all the recipients' addresses and how they might be useful.[9] But Dos

[7] LGA, 61, 34–35; OA, 78, 42–43; Nesbet, "Skyscrapers," 382.
[8] Alexander Gumberg to Il'f and Petrov, 4 November 1935; to G. Parker Toms,
4 November 1935; to Philip F. LaFollette, n.d., Gumberg Papers, Box 8, Folder 5.
[9] LGA, 61; OA, 78; PIA, Il'f, 26 October 1935, 438.

Passos seems to have dashed off the letters and perhaps the list without making copies for himself. I have located only one of his handwritten letters, in the papers of the poet Witter Bynner.[10] Apparently Dos Passos made the introduction to Ernest Hemingway in person; neither Hemingway's nor Ilf's letter about the meeting are entirely clear on the matter.[11]

Within twelve months of Ilf and Petrov's return, in late 1936, the Soviet Dos Passos craze ended abruptly. An excerpt from the final volume of his *U.S.A.* trilogy, *The Big Money*, appeared on the cover of the journal *Za rubezhom* (Abroad) in October 1936. From an early chapter about Mary French, a middle-class young woman who becomes a labor activist, the excerpt tells the gritty and dismal story of a failed steelworkers' strike. The translator barely captured Dos Passos's distinctive voice. In line with the emerging consensus that Soviet literature should use the "language of the classics," the translator "corrected" Dos Passos's characters' slang and untangled his modernist word streams: "Get all the dope you can" became "Find out all you can," and "big black rows of smokegnarled clapboarded houses" turned into "big, black, sooty barracks."[12] While the chapter told an acceptably anti-capitalist story of American workers struggling against corrupt and debauched bosses, the book itself came dangerously close to a denunciation of American communists. Dos Passos clearly fell afoul of socialist realism's ideological strictures.[13] The novel also transgressed its emerging formal strictures, which rejected "all forms of fragmentation, episodic techniques, and montage."[14] Soon after the novel's publication, Dos Passos broke with the political left, ultimately becoming a vehement anticommunist.[15] *The Big Money* was never published in the Soviet Union.[16]

When it came out in 1937, Ilf and Petrov's *Low-Rise America* made no mention of Dos Passos. However, just five months before the book's publication, Dos Passos starred in an excerpt from the travelogue

[10] John Dos Passos to Hal Bynner, n.d., Witter Bynner Papers, Houghton Library, Harvard College Library, MS Am 1891–1891.7, bMS Am 1891 (222).

[11] Ernest Hemingway to Ivan Kashkin, 12 January 1936, in Ernest Hemingway, *Selected Letters, 1917–1961*, ed. Carlos Baker (New York: Charles Scribner's Sons, 1981), 430; PIA, Il'f, 29 October 1935, 440.

[12] Dzhon [John] Dos Passos, "Bol'shie dengi," trans. Iu. Savel'eva, *Za rubezhom*, no. 29 (15 October 1936): cover, 668; John Dos Passos, *U.S.A.* (New York: Library of America, 1996), 879, 881; Günther, "Soviet Literary Criticism," 93–97.

[13] Salmanova, "'Sovetskii' Dos Passos," 279–80; Brown, "Dos Passos," 349–50.

[14] Günther, "Soviet Literary Criticism," 100.

[15] Townsend Ludington, *John Dos Passos: A Twentieth-Century Odyssey* (New York: Carroll & Graf, 1980), 362–409; Denning, *Cultural Front*, 526n7.

[16] Brown, "Dos Passos," 349; V. A. Libman, *Amerikanskaia literatura v russkikh perevodakh i kritike: Bibliografiia, 1776–1975* (Moscow: Izdatel'stvo "Nauka," 1977), 105–106.

published in *Za rubezhom*, and his featured role survived in Charles Malamuth's English translation. Both the 1936 excerpt and the English translation of the travelogue's "Electric Chair" chapter – an account of Ilf and Petrov's visit to the Death House at Sing Sing Prison, some thirty miles north of New York City – began with Dos Passos introducing the two writers to Ernest Hemingway. With gentle irony, they hinted that Dos Passos, the more famous of the two in the Soviet Union, was at home the lesser light. The earlier version of the chapter also included a reference to Dos Passos's part in Soviet literary debates. In an aside, the authors observed that recent polemics had forever shifted the associations of the expression "soulless formalist." Previously conjuring up the figure of an officious building manager, the term now brought to mind a "writer, composer, or some other hairy servant of the Muses."[17] The excerpted chapter (and the English translation) ended with Dos Passos taking the writers to the Hollywood Restaurant, a nightclub on Broadway. The book retained the episode but omitted both Dos Passos and the pair's farewell to Dos, as Ilf and Petrov called the author, as did all his friends: "See you in Moscow."[18]

Dos Passos may have disappeared from the 1937 text, but even excised from the book, he influenced it profoundly. The deleted passages make clear that Ilf and Petrov were familiar with the debates swirling around Dos Passos. Indeed, they may have had a rooting interest in the dispute. According to Ilf's daughter, Dos Passos was the pair's "favorite author."[19] As a writer of letters of introduction, a tour guide, and a literary model, he shaped where Ilf and Petrov went, what they looked for, and how they wrote about America. The Dos Passos connection allows us to understand the genre-defying *Low-Rise America* as not only a travelogue, satire, and picaresque but also as a valedictory intervention in the debate on the possibility of socialist realism with a modernist sensibility.

Dos Passos's novels merited discussion among Soviet critics owing to their "bitter criticism of capitalism."[20] But they became readers' favorites because they offered immersive, exhilarating, often disorienting journeys into the seamy realities of American life. *Manhattan Transfer*, published in Russian translation two years after it appeared in English, tells a kaleidoscopic history of New York City from the turn of the century to the 1920s through the overlapping stories of characters ranging from immigrants to socialites. Hemingway called it a "spiritual Baedecker

---

[17] Il'ia Il'f and Evgenii Petrov, "Elektricheskii stul," *Za rubezhom*, no. 31 (5 November 1936): 716.
[18] OA, 48–49, 57–58; LGA, 39–41, 46–47; Il'f and Petrov, "Elektricheskii stul," 716–17.
[19] ZK, 497n215.   [20] Brown, "Dos Passos," 333.

[sic] to New York" and averred that Dos Passos, "alone of American writers has been able to show to Europeans the America they really find when they come here."[21]

Critical of capitalism and the exploiting classes, the first two sprawling volumes of Dos Passos's *U.S.A.* trilogy, too, met Soviet ideological requirements. Excerpts from *The 42nd Parallel* (1930) and *1919* (1932) appeared in Russian translation almost immediately. By 1936, they had gone through multiple Russian editions.[22] Yet even more than *Manhattan Transfer*, the *U.S.A.* novels, which took readers not only to New York City, but to big cities and small towns from coast to coast, provided a cinematic, boozy tour of America. At a Writers' Union meeting in 1932, Lev Nikulin, identifying Dos Passos as a "revolutionary" writer, asserted: "If I want to know and 'see' America, I read" *The 42nd Parallel* and *1919*.[23]

Introducing Dos Passos in a chapter on the electric chair, Ilf and Petrov nudged readers to recall his radical credentials. Dos Passos's vocal defense of Nicola Sacco and Bartolomeo Vanzetti, two Italian anarchists convicted of murder during the Red Scare on the flimsiest of evidence and executed in 1927, underpinned his fame in the Soviet Union. In his 1966 memoir, Dos Passos belittled this fame, noting that when he visited Moscow in 1928, he was able to leverage "the prestige I had gained in those parts through my efforts for Sacco and Vanzetti" to get a coveted ticket to the Kabuki Theater.[24] This retrospective scorn for his radical reputation understates the degree to which the execution shaped his life and his art. After writing a long pamphlet in defense of Sacco and Vanzetti, *Facing the Chair: Story of the Americanization of Two Foreignborn Workmen*, Dos Passos "went on to become the most visible radical [American] novelist" of the era. His commitment to combatting the "idiot lack of memory" that threatened the "sane awakening that followed the shock of the executions" became the starting point of his *U.S.A.* trilogy.[25]

Ilf and Petrov referenced none of this, ascribing their interest in the Death House at Sing Sing to lower literary motives: They had "heard of it since childhood," when they had followed the serialized adventures of the "two famous detectives, Nat Pinkerton and Nick Carter." Still, they titled the chapter the "Electric Chair," not "Sing Sing," although the

---

[21] Desmond Harding, *Writing the City: Urban Visions and Literary Modernism* (New York: Routledge, 2003), 176n48.
[22] Libman, *Amerikanskaia literatura*, 105–106; Brown, "Dos Passos," 334.
[23] Nikulin as quoted in Gal'tsova, "Zapadnye pisateli-modernisty," 671.
[24] Dos Passos, *Best Times*, 181.
[25] Denning, *Cultural Front*, 164, 166; John Dos Passos, "Sacco and Vanzetti," *New Masses* 3 (November 1927): 25.

prison's exotic name might have more reliably summoned nostalgic memories like those of Petrov's brother Valentin Kataev, who recalled his fondness for the forbidden Pinkerton novels and the detective who had "sent more than one villain to the electric chair of New York's Sing Sing prison."[26] Dos Passos's presence in the chapter is to some extent straightforward reporting, since he introduced the authors to Hemingway, who, through his father-in-law, a friend of the warden, obtained permission for the Soviet authors to visit the prison.[27] But the authors collapsed the timeline in order to more closely associate Dos Passos with the electric chair. Ilf's notebook and letters place their visit with Dos Passos to the Hollywood Restaurant about ten days before their visit to Sing Sing, not, as recounted in the chapter, the evening they returned from the prison.[28] Readers who knew anything about Dos Passos would have known of his association with Sacco and Vanzetti and the electric chair. Certainly, those who had followed the recent literary disputes could be counted on to make this connection. After Dos Passos's excision from the book, the only clue that Ilf and Petrov's interest in the electric chair might be linked to Sacco and Vanzetti was the parenthetical note that they had seen small groups of prisoners playing an unfamiliar ball game, which their guide explained "was an Italian game, that there are many Italians in Sing Sing."[29]

Even this truncated and indirect reminder of Dos Passos as a "revolutionary" writer – the juxtaposition of "Italians" and "electric chair" – might have been enough to encourage attentive readers to notice other ways in which Ilf and Petrov "saw" America much as Dos Passos described it. Among the most obvious features of that description is the ubiquitous cocktail party. As the critic Michael Denning observes of *U.S.A.*, "everyone parties in these books." The same could be said of *Manhattan Transfer* – Prohibition notwithstanding. The novels' "endless rounds of drinks" can be understood as an object of satire and an "emblem of ... decadence and decay." But cocktail parties function as more than mere symbols of American shortcomings; they materialize Dos Passos's vision of America itself as an endless, repetitive, vacuous, and "oppressive" search for amusement.[30]

Ilf and Petrov's impressions were not quite so bleak. But especially in their account of Manhattan – the quintessential Dos Passosian

[26] Kataev as quoted in Boris Dralyuk, *Western Crime Fiction Goes East: The Russian Pinkerton Craze, 1907–1934* (Leiden: Brill, 2012), 8–10.

[27] OA, 49; Il'f and Petrov, "Elektricheskii stul," 716; Hemingway to Kashkin, 430.

[28] PIA, Il'f, 29 October 1935 and 6 November 1935, 440, 445; ZK, 25 October and 5 November, 440, 442.

[29] LGA, 43; OA, 52.   [30] Denning, *Cultural Front*, 182–83.

location – they confirmed that cocktails made the city go round. Naturally, the meeting with Dos Passos and Hemingway happened over drinks (whiskey and water). The highballs prompted the reflection: "So far as we have been able to observe, everything in America begins with a drink." Even "literary business." At their publishers, "the cheerful, red-headed Mr. Farrar, a publisher and poet," led them to a library equipped not only with books but an icebox. "Pulling ice cubes and a variety of bottles out of the box," the publisher "asked, what kind of cocktail we preferred – Manhattan, Bacardi, or Martini? – and then began to mix with such skill that it seemed he'd never in his life published a book or written a verse, but had always worked as a barman. Americans love mixing cocktails."[31] They warned their readers – few of whom had any prospects of visiting the United States – that the first American they met would "surely invite you to a cocktail party." At the party, the unsuspecting guest would immediately receive invitations to ten more parties, where other guests would invite them out for cocktails, so that "in two days you acquire a hundred new acquaintances, and in a week several thousand," all proffering invitations to endless cocktail parties. "It is," they concluded, simply dangerous to spend a year in America."[32]

Where Ilf and Petrov most fully evoked the sights and sounds of Dos Passos's Manhattan was in their cubist descriptions of the city itself. Through their panoramas of New York City, they implicitly intervened in the debates that so divided Dos Passos's critics – was his montage too decadent, subjective, and puzzling to provide a useful model for Soviet authors? – by simply adapting his cinematic techniques to their own ends. We have already seen them leaning out of their twenty-seventh-floor window to catch a glimpse of the fundamental "plane" of the street. The night before that acrobatic adventure, they marveled at the vista from windows that looked out on three sides. They tried to capture in words a shifting view that Ilf found impossible to photograph.[33]

Nearby rose several skyscrapers. They seemed close enough to touch. You could count their lighted windows. Farther away the lights became more and more dense. Among them were especially bright ones, stretching in straight and sometimes slightly curved little chains (probably streetlights). Beyond sparkled a continuous gold dust of small lights, and then came a dark, unlit strip. (The Hudson? Or maybe the East River?) [...] Here the little red light of a cutter slowly passed down the river. A very small automobile drove down the street. Occasionally, suddenly, somewhere on the other shore of the river, a little light as tiny as a particle of dust flickered and went out. Surely one of the seven million

---

[31] OA, 48; PIA, Il'f, 26 October 1935, 439.   [32] OA, 35.
[33] Nesbet, "Skyscrapers," 387; PIA, Il'f, 8 October 1935, 428.

denizens of New York had turned off the light and gone to sleep. [...] Perhaps a lonely salesgirl had gone to sleep [...] And at this very moment, lying under two thin blankets, agitated by the steamer whistles of the Hudson, was she seeing in her dreams a million dollars?[34]

They "saw" the city that Dos Passos had primed them to see:

All night the great buildings stand quiet and empty, their million windows dark. Drooling light the ferries chew tracks across the lacquered harbor. At midnight the fourfunneled express steamers slide into the dark out of their glary berths. Bankers blearyeyed from secret conferences hear the hooting of the tugs as they are let out side doors by lightingbug watchmen; they settle grunting into the back seats of limousines, and are whisked uptown into the Forties, clinking streets of ginwhite whiskey-yellow cider-fizzling lights.[35]

To be sure, Ilf and Petrov's streetlights were "bright" not "ginwhite," and their cutter "passed" while Dos Passos's ferry "chewed" and "drooled." But the view is equally dizzying, zooming in on skyscraper windows that seemed near enough to touch, capturing a tiny particle of light on the far side of the river, suggesting 7 million perspectives on the deceptively shimmering city.

While Dos Passos's novels prepared Ilf and Petrov to see the city, the author himself made sure to show them "what occupies the average American while in your country people read books." Having told Ilf and Petrov that he was working on *The Big Money*, he wondered how it would sell: "Each of my books has a smaller print run than the one before it: *The 42nd Parallel* had a print run of twenty thousand copies; *1919*, fifteen thousand; this one will probably have ten thousand." To this lament, Ilf and Petrov replied that "ten thousand copies of his *1919* disappeared from Soviet book counters in several hours."[36] Dos Passos responded, "In your country people have been taught to read books, but with us here..." And with that he proposed an outing to the Hollywood Restaurant at Forty-Eighth and Broadway, to see a "legshow."[37]

---

[34] OA, 22–23.

[35] John Dos Passos, *Manhattan Transfer* (Boston: Houghton Mifflin, [1925] 2000), 260.

[36] These figures may overstate US sales. Virginia Spencer, *Dos Passos: A Life* (Evanston, IL: Northwestern University Press, [1984] 2004), 379–80.

[37] LGA 29; PIA, Il'f, 29 October 1935, 440; Il'f and Petrov, "Elektricheskii stul," 717; Dos Passos, *U.S.A.*, 352.

8 The Business of Pleasure

> The Zulu ceremony continued for several hours. This is pornography mechanized to such an extent that it acquires a kind of industrial-factory character. There is as little eroticism in this spectacle as in the mass production of vacuum cleaners or adding machines.
>
> Ilf and Petrov, *Low-Rise America*

The Hollywood Restaurant was the place to go in Times Square for glamour on the cheap. A huge venue accommodating 1,000 patrons for dining, dancing, and socializing, the nightclub, founded before the end of Prohibition, pioneered a business model that revived New York nightlife during the Depression. There was no cover charge, and diners brought their own alcohol. They paid as little as $1.50 for dinner and a show in the early evening or $2.00 after the theaters let out.[1]

Dos Passos, Ilf, and Petrov caught the early show, at seven o'clock. It is not clear whether they indulged in the extras – a table in front of the stage ($3.00) or ice and glasses for brown-bag booze ($1.00). The club's four nightly performances featured low-budget "novelties" such as roller skaters and contortionists, which Ilf and Petrov's account ignored. They focused on the main attraction: the nearly nude chorus girls in their late teens, chosen more for their looks than their talent.[2] Ilf and Petrov recorded that the "average New Yorker" found complete pleasure dancing to jazz, "eating a cutlet," and admiring the chorines. In their capacity as careful observers, they saw the show and ate the dinner. But they separated themselves from the natives' pleasure. "We were saddened," they concluded, "by New York's happiness."[3]

---

[1] Burton W. Peretti, *Nightclub City: Politics and Amusement in Manhattan* (Philadelphia: University of Pennsylvania Press, 2011), 113–14.

[2] PIA, Il'f, 29 October 1935, 440; Rachel Shteir, *Striptease: The Untold Story of the Girlie Show* (Oxford: Oxford University Press, 2004), 163; Lewis Erenberg, *Inventing Times Square: Commerce and Culture at the Crossroads of the World* (New York: Russell Sage, 1991), 171.

[3] OA, 58.

Dos Passos was not the only acquaintance to guide Ilf and Petrov through the American dreamworld of leisure and consumption. The "several thousand" new friends acquired at endless cocktail parties eagerly suggested what the Soviet visitors "must see" in order to really "know America." The writers' "amusements" became "most business-like," as they visited nightclubs, an auto race, the "Zulu ceremony" of a burlesque show, penny arcades, boxing and wrestling matches, a rodeo, and the New York auto show.[4]

As Ilf and Petrov investigated American amusements, back home in the USSR leisure and consumption were becoming serious matters. The completion of the First Five-Year Plan and the lifting of bread rationing coincided with a propaganda campaign celebrating the arrival of socialist abundance. In 1935, Stalin famously declared, "Life has become better, comrades. Life has become happier."[5] Soviet leaders promised consumers that they would soon find not only necessities but luxuries such as caviar, champagne, and cosmetics in Soviet shops. For the moment, only elites – party cadres, Stakhanovites (workers who overfilled their production quotas), and favored members of the intelligentsia – had regular access to such goods. Nonetheless, in the Soviet media tempting visions of "cultured" consumption displaced revolutionary appeals to asceticism and toughness. The upwardly mobile communist man of the 1930s traded his leather jacket and Nagant revolver for a suit and tie. His wife, "with her permanent wave, fur-collared coat, and stylish cloche," likewise rejected the militarized and masculinized appearance associated with earlier cohorts of Bolshevik women.[6] But in this transitional moment, understandings of what made Soviet consumers "cultured" – and how "cultured" consumption could be distinguished from capitalist excess – remained fluid.[7]

[4] LGA, 30; OA, 35, 40.

[5] Iosif Stalin, "Speech at the First All-Union Conference of Stakhanovites," 17 November 1935, Seventeen Moments in Soviet History, http://soviethistory.msu .edu/1936-2/year-of-the-stakhanovite/year-of-the-stakhanovite-texts/stalin-at-the-conference-of-stakhanovites/ (accessed 14 August 2020); Julie Hessler, *A Social History of Soviet Trade: Trade Policy, Retail Practices, and Consumption, 1917–1953* (Princeton, NJ: Princeton University Press, 2004), 201–22.

[6] Rebecca Balmas Neary, "Mothering Socialist Society: The Wife Activists' Movement and the Soviet Culture of Daily Life, 1934–41," *Russian Review* 58 (July 1999): 410 (quotation); Randi Cox, "All This Can Be Yours! Soviet Commercial Advertising and the Social Construction of Space, 1928–1956," in Evgeny Dobrenko and Eric Naiman, eds., *The Landscape of Stalinism: The Art and Ideology of Soviet Space* (Seattle: University of Washington Press, 2003), 144.

[7] Philippa Hetherington, "Dressing the Shop Window of Socialism: Gender and Consumption in the Soviet Union in the Era of 'Cultured Trade,' 1934–53," *Gender and History* 27, no. 2 (August 2015): 419–22.

The new emphasis on consumerism, increasingly understood as the domain of women, interacted with a rethinking of the state's commitment to women's emancipation.[8] Before their American adventures, Ilf and Petrov had participated in the campaign to promote the sanctity of marriage and the sentimentalization of motherhood. This was an area in which the Soviet authorities tolerated something that passed as "satire." In a piece published in *Pravda*, they pointed out that Soviet "divorce laws were not written so that a person could use marriage like a tramway, paying ten kopecks fare, enjoying the ride, and then chasing after another car."[9] In 1936, Soviet legislation that recriminalized abortion and made divorce more difficult and expensive to obtain marked the official enshrinement of motherhood as a woman's most important role and greatest joy. But even after legislating compulsory motherhood, the Stalinist state continued to employ the rhetoric of women's emancipation and to uphold the new woman, whether a young tractor driver or daring aviatrix, as a revolutionary icon.[10] Thus, Stalinist visions of appropriate gender roles – and of appropriately gendered consumption – were ambiguous. Could a good communist mother wear lipstick and the latest fashions without succumbing to petty-bourgeois materialism? What made consumption tasteful, socialist, and cultured?

Ilf and Petrov's exploration of American consumption and leisure provided them with a series of case studies that probed the line between wholesome, enriching consumption and capitalist vulgarity. They usually avoided explicit comparisons with Soviet practices, counting on readers to supply the contrast for themselves. Instead, their reports of encounters with the amusements of the "common people" highlighted what Dos Passos called the "dream" of the New York shop clerk or the crass materialism of American wives. Doing so, they had leeway to mock and criticize and, in one telling case, to make fun of themselves.

From the moment they arrived in New York City in early October 1935, Ilf and Petrov avidly sampled America's cultural offerings from high – rarely discussed in the published work – to low. Less than a week into their stay, they left the city with the Soviet consul in New York, Jean

---

[8] Cox, "All This," 147.

[9] Il'f and Petrov, "Mat'," *Pravda*, 7 June 1935; "Topics of the Times," NYT, 10 June 1935.

[10] Victoria E. Bonnell, *Iconography of Power: Soviet Political Posters under Lenin and Stalin* (Berkeley: University of California Press, 1997), 10; Susan E. Reid, "All Stalin's Women: Gender and Power in Soviet Art in the 1930s," *Slavic Review* 57 (Spring 1998): 136; Melanie Ilič, "*Traktoristka:* Representations and Realities," in Melanie Ilič, ed., *Women in the Stalin Era* (Basingstoke: Macmillan, 2001), 110–12; Choi Chatterjee, "Soviet Heroines and the Language of Modernity, 1930–39," in Ilič, ed., *Women in the Stalin Era*, 54–59.

Lvovich Arens, to see the auto races at the Danbury Fair. The lengthy account of the fair in *Low-Rise America* illustrates the typical features and the complexity of their responses to American popular culture. The three-hour drive itself was an unmitigated pleasure. This first encounter with American roads made of "concrete slabs separated by expansion joints" elicited raptures. In his notebook, Ilf gushed: "Cars roll along with merry-go-round smoothness; the road is so beautiful that I looked only at it, not paying attention to the wonderful red autumn land-scape."[11] Petrov agreed, writing, "the roads in America are mindbog-gling. You want to dance on them."[12] In the published chapter, they paid more attention to the foliage, asserting that the roads deserved a "special chapter" all to themselves, which they supplied and in which they recounted their initial wonder.[13]

After driving through the "Indian sylvan festival" of southern New England, Ilf and Petrov found themselves at a "drab provincial fair" of the sort they had read about in O. Henry's stories.[14] They surveyed agricultural exhibitions, souvenir vendors, and a carnival midway, which reminded them of home. The "openhearted, hysterical female squeal" let out as a carnival ride turned the occupants of a boat-shaped swing upside down high in the air "immediately carried us from the state of Connecticut to the state of Moscow, to the Park of Culture and Rest," better known in the West as Gorky Park.[15] Opened in 1928, the Moscow park, its pompous name notwithstanding, had become by the mid-1930s "a sort of Moscow Coney Island," a place that materialized promises of a happier life.[16] Ilf and Petrov suggested that the carnival ride united modern urban cultures across the socialist–capitalist divide. So, too, did a good clown act, which they thoroughly appreciated.

By contrast, the writers represented the auto races that brought them to the fair as a wholly alien concoction, a potent distillation of the dangers and depravities of capitalism. Not that their account of the races lacked excitement. They described red, white, and yellow cars with numbers painted on their sides "rocketing" around the track, kicking up gravel and hot sand. The audience roared. But Ilf and Petrov denied that watching five, six, even ten cars "flying" past had any appeal for them. They pronounced the whole thing "frightfully boring." Only the horror of an accident broke the tedium. Catching a glimpse of the injured driver, they

---

[11] ZK, 12 October, 430; 11 October, 433; PIA, Petrov and Il'f, 13 October, 430, 431.
[12] PIA, Petrov, 23 October, 435.   [13] OA, 35.   [14] OA, 36; LGA, 30.
[15] OA, 36; "The Danbury Fair, 1869–1981," https://connecticuthistory.org/ (accessed 26 December 2020).
[16] Walter Duranty, "The Capitals of Two Opposite Worlds," NYT, 28 August 1932.

imagined him "angry" because he had "lost the prize for which he had risked his life." Unlike the carnival rides or the clown act, the races were an "empty, gloomy, soul-draining" spectacle.[17]

Positioning themselves as cultured representatives of the Soviet intelligentsia, Ilf and Petrov characterized the penny arcades they found around Times Square and on the Lower East Side as similarly soul-draining. They marveled that people spent hours in the "solitary entertainment" of feeding coins, "without anger or delight," into pinball machines, slowly accumulating the points to claim one of the "lovely prizes" on display: a glass vase or an aluminum cocktail shaker, a table clock or a cheap fountain pen or razor. They had even less patience for the mechanized fortunetellers tempting passersby to part with their nickels. All of these "idiotic wonders," they concluded, were "disgusting" even amid the city center's "glitz and noise"; in the dark, dirty, impoverished streets of downtown they became "unbearably depressing."[18]

In *Low-Rise America*, Ilf and Petrov underscored the parallels between these mind-numbing mechanical games and the auto races by compressing the timeline and narrowing the focus. Ilf's notebook lists the episode's key words – "mech. fortuneteller. Entertainment. Stroll around the East Side. Dirt. Resourceful young people. Café Royal" – in an entry dated 21 October, nine days after their visit to the fair. But in the book, they narrate the encounter with pinball machines and the mechanized fortuneteller as the adventure that immediately followed, and was in part inspired by, the auto races.

Tellingly, they omitted in the published travelogue what was likely the most engaging, if the least "American," piece of the East Side adventure, Café Royal, a "kibitzers' hangout" on the southeast corner of Second Avenue and Twelfth Street. Renowned for its chicken paprikash, Café Royal was, according to a 1937 *New Yorker* profile, "the forum of the Jewish intelligentsia." Actors, writers, and impresarios – "everybody who is anybody in the creative Jewish world" – came to see and be seen and argue in English, Yiddish, and Yiddish-English about "the sacred cause of Art."[19] Ilf perhaps understood the conversation in Yiddish.[20] But Jewish intellectuals from the Russian empire likely spoke Russian, a marker of cultural prestige even among those who wrote in Yiddish.[21]

---

[17] OA, 37–38. [18] OA, 39, ZK, 21 October, 439.

[19] Leonard Q. Ross [Leo Rosten], "Café Royal," *New Yorker* (10 April 1937): 45; Sachar M. Pinsker, *A Rich Brew: How Cafés Created Modern Jewish Culture* (New York: New York University Press, 2018), 226–33.

[20] Nakhimovsky, "How the Soviets Solved," 101–102.

[21] Steven Cassedy, *To the Other Shore: The Russian Jewish Intellectuals Who Came to America* (Princeton, NJ: Princeton University Press, 1997), 3–14.

Interactions with the Jewish Russian American intelligentsia constituted an essential linchpin of Ilf and Petrov's sojourn in the city.[22] However, vibrant, cultured, immigrant New York had no place in their efforts to parse and judge the American business of pleasure.

Ilf and Petrov placed the climax of their sampling of "soul-draining" entertainments – their encounter with the "industrial-factory" striptease – on the same eventful day or couple of days as the fair and their visit to penny arcades. In this case, too, they condensed the timeline. A letter from Ilf indicates that they saw an "absolutely vulgar" and "therefore interesting" burlesque show on 16 October, several days before their encounter with the mechanized fortuneteller.[23] Long a part of the New York scene, burlesque was at least a notch less respectable than the leg show to which Dos Passos took the authors. It offered a variety show mix of "baggy-pants comics, slapstick, double entendres and strip tease."[24] As the Depression decimated legitimate (and more expensive) theater, producer Billy Minsky moved burlesque from the immigrant enclaves of the Lower East Side to Broadway, leasing the venerable Republic Theater on Forty-Second Street.[25] More burlesque theaters and other downscale entertainments soon followed: dance halls, peep shows, penny arcades, and no-frills cafeterias. By the mid-1930s, the area around Times Square, a five-minute walk from Ilf and Petrov's hotel, offered a "bargain-basement sexual smorgasbord." Captivated, if also somewhat appalled, by the gaudy lights, Ilf and Petrov depicted Broadway as more showy than seedy.[26]

The authors selected a very cheap entrée from the cultural buffet. Tickets for legitimate Broadway theater went as high as $8.80, while opening night tickets to the more popular musicals might set theatergoers back $75 or $100 dollars.[27] Ilf, who kept careful accounts, reported in his letter home that the pair paid thirty-five cents each for a burlesque review on Broadway. *Low-Rise America* cites the same low figure, the cost of a movie ticket.[28] This was cut-rate even for burlesque. "High class" venues, such as Minksy's Republic Theater, which featured luxurious movie palace-style interiors and ushers in fancy uniforms, charged $1.50; the most successful spot in the mid-1930s, the Irving Place Theater,

---

[22] ZK, 8–13 October, 23 October, 426–30, 433–34, 440.

[23] OA, 40; PIA, Il'f, 17 October, 434; ZK, 16 October, 436.

[24] Robert C. Allen, "'The Leg Business': Transgression and Containment in American Burlesque," *Camera Obscura*, no. 23 (May 1990): 45; Shteir, *Striptease*, 166–67.

[25] Shteir, *Striptease*, 134–39; Perretti, *Nightclub City*, 116–18; Alva Johnston, "A Tour of Minskyville," *New Yorker* (28 May 1932): 34–40.

[26] Peretti, *Nightclub City*, 102–16 (quotation); LGA, 33.

[27] Brock Pemberton, "In Re the Year 1935," NYT, 29 December 1935.

[28] PIA, Il'f, 17 October, 434; ZK, 6 October, 436.

charged $1.10. Even more modest theaters on Forty-Second Street or downtown charged fifty cents.[29] Perhaps Ilf misquoted the price. Or perhaps they really did find the bargain basement of the bargain basement.

Unsurprisingly, Ilf and Petrov judged burlesque uncultured. Their account omitted the comedians and the performers' cynicism and raunchy humor. The language barrier may have rendered the dirty jokes indecipherable. But did observers as sharp-witted as Ilf and Petrov really fail entirely to understand that the show was both a sexual display and a sendup of sex? Whatever the case, they steered clear of depicting the laughter that, as the historian Rachel Shteir argues, afforded "women more agency than other forms of popular entertainment by acknowledging their sexuality and allowing them to connect directly with the audience."[30] Instead, Ilf and Petrov portrayed the show as a disturbing parody of high culture. The performers could neither sing nor dance. The audience, the writers astutely concluded, had come "for something else." What that "something else" was became clear when the first performer began to take off her clothes and then, "with a bedroom squeal, ran into the wings." The master of ceremonies' proposition, "If you applaud harder, she'll take off something else," produced an "explosion of applause" the likes of which the most accomplished performers would never in their whole lives enjoy.[31] This sounds very much like a description of the show at the Irving Place Theater where, according to a contemporary article in *Billboard*, "The customers expect the limit and get it by applauding."[32] Of course, the ploy may have been widespread. In Ilf and Petrov's telling, the talentless stripper reappeared and "sacrificed what little was left of her garments." Ten more strippers did exactly the same, becoming graceless cogs in a pornographic machine.

Having established that striptease was not "culture" in the sense of opera or ballet, Ilf and Petrov approached it as culture in the anthropological sense, calling the show a "Zulu ceremony." The racialized metaphor can be understood as highlighting the exotic, even uncivilized nature of the spectacle. *Variety*'s Sime Silverman made a similar point with a different exoticized culture, comparing a stripper to a Polynesian icon.[33] But in Ilf and Petrov's account, the evocation of a primitive ritual sat uneasily with the depiction of striptease as modern mechanized

---

[29] Shteir, *Striptease*, 133, 136, 164; Russel Maloney, "Burlesk," *New Yorker* (8 June 1935): 15.
[30] Shteir, *Striptease*, 141; Kathleen Spies, "'Girls and Gags': Sexual Display and Humor in Reginald Marsh's Burlesque Images," *American Art* 18 (Summer 2004): 32–57.
[31] OA, 40.   [32] As quoted in Shteir, *Striptease*, 164.
[33] OA, 40; Shteir, *Striptease*, 139.

pornography. Their quasi-ethnographic description functioned less as an explanation of burlesque than as an explanation – or rationalization – of their own decision to spend "several hours" watching a show they found offensive and, even worse, dull. Like the English travel writer and anthropologist Geoffrey Gorer, who published a study of New York burlesque in 1937, they distanced themselves from the "men who go to burlesque theaters week after week, year after year." Emphasizing, like Ilf and Petrov, the show's "extra-ordinary monotony," Gorer, more forthrightly than the Soviet writers, asserted that the spectators desired not "simple entertainment" but "sexual stimulation."[34] Declaring themselves repelled and bored by the spectacle, Ilf and Petrov, like the anthropologist, positioned themselves as outsiders, who watched the show and the audience as systematic observers, not as pleasure-seekers. As in their account of the leg show, the writers emphasized that they suffered through the vulgarity in the service of scientific thoroughness.

Ilf and Petrov's reactions to the striptease and the leg show resembled those of leftist Western critics, who likewise reached for industrial metaphors when they condemned modern capitalism's commodification of the female body.[35] But they expressed less sympathy for the strippers than the chorines. In both cases, they highlighted the entertainments' machine-like qualities. However, while they depicted the strippers as gears in a pornographic apparatus, they portrayed the chorus girls as exploited assembly line workers – albeit workers whose jobs required that they appear "half naked, three-quarters naked, and nine-tenths naked." Noticing that the nightclub's proprietor, with a "passion for service," would not let the dancers "be idle," Ilf and Petrov described the young performers at the Hollywood Restaurant as disempowered women workers: "The girls ran out" again and again – "in the interval between the first and second course, before coffee, and during coffee" – with the result that they sometimes "dipped their feathers into bowls of soup or jars of mustard." In fact, the dancers may have worked seventy to eighty hours per week. Ilf and Petrov saw the results of this overwork on their faces, some of which were "blank, others pitiful, and still others hard, but all equally tired."[36] However, they failed to register that the strippers, too, were overworked; only a month before their visit, the

[34] Geoffrey Gorer, *Hot Strip Tease, and Other Notes on American Culture* (London: Cresset, 1937); Spies, "'Girls and Gags,'" 53–54.
[35] Christina Kiaer, "African Americans in Soviet Socialist Realism: The Case of Aleksandr Deineka," *Russian Review* 75 (July 2016): 419–20; Alix Beeston, "A 'Leg Show Dance' in a Skyscraper: The Sequenced Mechanics of John Dos Passos's *Manhattan Transfer*," *PMLA*, 131 (2016): 646.
[36] OA, 58, 59; LGA, 47; Shteir, *Striptease*, 158.

burlesque workers' union had staged a four-day strike in hopes of improving performers' wages and working conditions.[37]

As "chaste Soviets abroad," Ilf and Petrov appeared unable or unwilling to grant the legitimacy of women expressing (if also commodifying) their sexual agency.[38] They narrated their burlesque adventure as a moral tale in which Stalinist virtue was virtually indistinguishable from bourgeois puritanism. Representing the strippers as mass-produced and interchangeable objects of erotic consumption – the only way to tell them apart was by their hair color – Ilf and Petrov focused on the unseemly display's dangerous effects on men.[39] Their concerns about the allegedly unnatural spectacle of women articulating or embodying sexual desire sounded very much like those of the American moral reformers, who managed to get most of New York's burlesque theaters shut down in 1937. American middle-class opponents of burlesque bluntly characterized the audience as "sex crazed perverts."[40] From the Soviet perspective, the frantically applauding burlesque spectators embodied the male American consumer's irrational and sexualized desires.[41]

Applying emerging Soviet understandings of consumption and leisure to the United States, Ilf and Petrov represented American men as often succumbing to the coarse charms of popular commercial spectacles: auto races, strip shows, professional wrestling, boxing matches. At the same time, Ilf and Petrov saw elements of American vulgarity on the Soviet side of the divide. In a letter home, Ilf expressed the same criticisms of American culture as in the published work: the line about the half, three-quarters, and nine-tenths naked dancers appears verbatim. He also noted that the show reminded him of the "artistic conceptions" of the director Grigory Aleksandrov, with whom the writers were embroiled in a dispute about changes to their screenplay for the film *Circus*. Ilf and Petrov objected to the director's decision to add "large-scale dance numbers with showgirls in skimpy costumes" to their comedy. Ultimately, the funnymen had their names removed from the musical's credits.[42]

While Ilf and Petrov satirized the (American) male taste for vulgar and sexualized spectacles, they associated women with the obsessive consumption of vulgar things. This linkage of women and "rampant

---

[37] Shteir, *Striptease*, 6, 158–62.   [38] Kiaer, "African Americans," 420.   [39] OA, 40.

[40] Andrea Friedman, "'The Habitats of Sex-Crazed Perverts': Campaigns against Burlesque in Depression-Era New York City," *Journal of the History of Sexuality* 7 (October 1996): 203–38.

[41] Hessler, *Social History*, 213.

[42] Kiaer, "African Americans," 420; Richard Taylor, "The Illusion of Happiness and the Happiness of Illusion: Grigorii Aleksandrov's 'The Circus,'" *Slavonic and East European Review* 74 (October 1996): 605.

consumerism" was not "unique to the Soviet Union."[43] It was both deeply embedded in Soviet conceptions of gender and rife among American radicals. Deploring women's commodification under capitalism did not prevent men on the left, in the Soviet Union no less than the United States, from representing women, and especially spendthrift housewives, as "materialist viragoes."[44]

On the American side, what literary historian Seth Moglen calls "left misogyny" shows up with particular clarity in Dos Passos's fiction. In his sketch of the socialist Eugene Debs, the first biography in the *U.S.A.* trilogy, Dos Passos asked, where were "Debs' brothers in nineteen eighteen when Woodrow Wilson had him locked up in Atlanta for speaking against the war"? His answer shifted the blame for political docility from "the big men fond of whisky and fond of each other" to women, who subdued their husbands by playing on their desires for "a house with a porch to putter around and a fat wife to cook for them." In Dos Passos, women like the fictional Maisie, who nags Mac to give up his activism in the International Workers of the World in order to get married and settle down, appear as small-minded consumers: "Maisie read a lot of magazines and always wanted new things for the house, a pianola, or a new icebox, or a fireless cooker."[45]

Dos Passos's assumption that women lacked "revolutionary" virtues chimed with Soviet images of "real" revolutionaries as male. While Bolshevik ideology promised gender equality, Bolshevik culture associated women with the domestic sphere and intractable political "backwardness."[46] The mid-1930s campaign for "culturedness" (*kul'turnost*) featured both men and women as enlightened "new consumers." Soviet leaders themselves modeled the new image of the communist man in a tailored suit; they sponsored a "wife activist" movement that encouraged factory managers' spouses to use their homemaking skills to beautify their husbands' workplaces. Still, the fear that "backward" women would "corrupt" men with demands for frivolous goods died hard. The Soviet media simultaneously urged women to pay attention to their clothes and hairstyles and worried that women were more liable than men to cross

---

[43] Hetherington, "Dressing the Shop Window," 422.

[44] Seth Moglen, *Mourning Modernity: Literary Modernism and the Injuries of American Capitalism* (Stanford, CA: Stanford University Press, 2007), 216.

[45] Moglen, *Mourning*, 144; Dos Passos, *U.S.A.*, 31–32, 104.

[46] Anne E. Gorsuch, "'A Woman Is Not a Man': The Culture of Gender and Generation in Soviet Russia, 1921–1928," *Slavic Review* 55 (Fall 1996): 644–46; Elizabeth Wood, *The Baba and the Comrade: Gender and Politics in Revolutionary Russia* (Bloomington: Indiana University Press, 1997), 17; Lisa A. Kirschenbaum, "The Man Question: How Bolshevik Masculinity Shaped International Communism," *Socialist History* 52 (2017): 76–84.

the thin line that divided "culturedness" from "petty bourgeois vulgarity" (*meshchanstvo*).[47]

In Ilf and Petrov's telling, American women enslaved by their desire for the latest thing crossed this line. They depicted working-class women, whether exhausted chorines or heavily rouged secretaries having breakfast at a drugstore, as trapped by their longing to fulfill the American dream on the installment plan. Less charitably, the writers described American housewives as shrewish angels with the "blue eyes of a vestal virgin" and the insatiable greed of the fisherman's wife in the tale of the golden fish. The pair may well have seen thin pretty women "moaning" over the 1936 models on show at the New York auto show. To overcome a Depression-era slump in car sales, manufacturers included features expressly designed to appeal to women: automatic controls, deeper and more luxuriously upholstered seats, and roomier luggage compartments that made it "possible for women to carry apparel on long trips without wrinkling or crushing it." But Ilf and Petrov clearly invented the conversation that occurred the "night after" the auto show: She will not listen to the sensible husband who wants to get a few more years out of the Plymouth with only 20,000 miles. She wants a "golden Chrysler!"[48] (Figure 8.1).

Freely admitting their own enthusiasm for automotive marvels, Ilf and Petrov assayed a world of difference between their rational – if also comically eager – consumerism and the grasping materialism of the American wife. They "knew beforehand that we would buy the cheapest automobile to be found anywhere in the United States." And so, at the auto show, the writers enjoyed the opportunity to sit a while in a Rolls Royce they deemed "too luxurious for us." They gleefully pushed the button to reveal the Cord 810's popup headlamps. Moving among the Plymouths, Oldsmobiles, Studebakers, Hudsons, Nashes, Chevrolets, Buicks, and Cadillacs, they turned steering wheels, honked horns, and examined engines without being tempted to buy something beyond their means. As they surveyed the business of pleasure in New York, Ilf and Petrov carefully marked the differences between coarse American and cultured Soviet consumption, even as they admitted that a lack of funds held them in check.

In late October 1935, as they were preparing to leave New York, Ilf and Petrov themselves took center stage at a very businesslike

---

[47] Hetherington, "Dressing the Shop Window," 423–24, 427, 434; Sheila Fitzpatrick, *Everyday Stalinism: Ordinary Life in Extraordinary Times: Soviet Russia in the 1930s* (New York: Oxford University Press, 1999), 92, 156–59; Neary, "Mothering Socialist Society," 396–403.

[48] OA, 172–73, 37–38, 70–71; "Early Auto Show Stimulates Sales," NYT, 7 November 1935.

Figure 8.1 To sell their 1936 models, carmakers added features designed to appeal to women. New York Auto Show, November 1935, Grand Central Palace: Studebaker. Image courtesy of the AACA Library & Research Center, Hershey, PA.

amusement, a meeting of the Dutch Treat Club. Their publisher John Farrar, who was a member, likely arranged the invitation to the New York club frequented by editors, writers, illustrators, lyricists, and other literary types. The members gathered every Tuesday for, as the club's name suggested, a no-host lunch that lasted no more than hour. After all, as Ilf and Petrov noted, these were "businesspeople," who needed to be back in their offices "advancing culture or simply making money."[49] Only the guest speakers got their meals covered in exchange for a humorous, or at least brief speech.

The theme of Ilf and Petrov's speech, delivered at Farrar and Rinehart's insistence, by Ilf in Russian and Petrov in almost incomprehensible English, was the pair's quest to find "real" America.[50] They related that everywhere they went – New York City, Washington, DC,

[49] OA, 59.   [50] ZK, 28 October, 440–41; PIA, Il′f, 29 October, 441.

Figure 8.2 The louche emblem of the Dutch Treat Club, c. 1915.
Prints and Photographs Division, Library of Congress, LC-B2-2531-9.

Hartford – Americans gestured vaguely into the distance and told them that "real America" was elsewhere. They concluded with an appeal to the gathered gentlemen "to show us where America really is located, because we have come here in order to learn as much as we can about it."[51]

After their speeches, the guests received a "medal" featuring the club's emblem, which Ilf and Petrov described as portraying a "reveler in a crushed top-hat, slumbering under the club's initials."[52] The logo was somewhat more louche than they allowed. The reveler, with top hat, monocle, and cigarette holder, reclined at the bottom of a martini glass (Figure 8.2). The image was in line with an organization whose all-male membership produced an elaborate annual dinner show featuring songs and skits filled with political satire, unsubtle double entendre, and casual misogyny. (The club began admitting women in 1991, but it retains the emblem.) One wonders what Ilf and Petrov would have thought of the yearbook distributed at the April 1935 show, overflowing with images of women in various stages of undress. It included a drawing of a topless

[51] LGA, 48; OA, 60.   [52] OA, 59.

woman, her back toward the viewer, shaking her hips with the caption, "The most popular revolutionary movement of all time."[53]

In their account of the Dutch Treat Club, as in their account of the American business of pleasure more generally, Ilf and Petrov identified themselves as thorough and eager participant observers. They bravely explored all manner of entertainments and asked the natives to point them in the direction of "real" America. But the Soviet distinction between cultured and uncultured consumption remained *Low-Rise America*'s guiding star. To make the Dutch Treat Club more "business-like," Ilf and Petrov removed the martini glass from its emblem. To emphasize the soul-draining crassness of popular amusements, they deemed cars "rocketing" around a track monotonous and drained the laughter from the burlesque stage. Thus, Ilf and Petrov tried to make Soviet sense of what they saw. But their account is not wholly persuasive. The reader is left wondering whether they, too, yearned for a golden Chrysler, thrilled to speeding race cars, or enjoyed the nightlife more than they let on.

---

[53] *Revolt: The Dutch Treat Show of 1935: The Fizzles of 1935* (Privately printed, 1935), 39, Kislak Center, University of Pennsylvania; "Politics Pilloried in 'Fizzles of 1935,'" NYT, 6 April 1935; Lily Koppel, "Cultural Elite Still Does Lunch, and It's Still a Private Conversation," NYT, 19 May 2008.

9   Black New York

Father Divine explained that he was not in complete accord with communism but that he was interested in any movement that sought "to abolish racial discrimination, eradicate prejudice and establish the fundamentals which stand for the good of humanity." ... Later Father Divine claimed credit for the excellent weather...

"May Day Peaceful Here as Thousands March in Gay Mood," *New York Times*, 2 May 1935

Black New York hardly figures in *Low-Rise America*. In the published travelogue, Ilf and Petrov's big night out in the city ended with them bidding farewell to Dos Passos or, in the abridged version, confessing that New York's happiness had made them sad. But the night was young, and the pair ventured uptown to Harlem, where, as Ilf informed his wife "only Black people live."[1] They ended up at the Ubangi Club at 131st Street and Seventh Avenue. Opened in 1934, the club "traded on the taste for the exotic that tourists craved from Harlem."[2] Ilf and Petrov went to see the "Black dances," which Ilf politely described in a letter to his wife as "interesting, but very sexual." Ilf's letter offered no further details. He immediately pivoted to the coincidence that the singer Paul Robeson happened to be seated at the table alongside theirs. The detail that Robeson was "in Moscow not long ago" seemed to balance, if not entirely cancel out, the impropriety of going to a club with "very sexual" dancing.

"Very sexual" scarcely begins to cover what Ilf and Petrov likely saw at the Ubangi Club. The venue's chief attraction was the *Ubangi Club Follies'* genderfluid headliner, Gladys Bentley. When her show opened in 1934, Bentley, a 250-pound Black lesbian from Trinidad, performed in a white tux and top hat attended by a chorus line of forty to fifty "pansies" (Figure 9.1) By the time of Ilf and Petrov's visit in the fall of 1935, police pressure had forced the club to replace the "be-ribboned

---

[1] PIA, Il'f, 29 October, 440–41.
[2] James F. Wilson, *Bulldaggers, Pansies, and Chocolate Babies: Performance, Race, and Sexuality in the Harlem Renaissance* (Ann Arbor: University of Michigan Press, 2011), 178.

Figure 9.1 Blues pianist and singer Gladys Bentley in her signature white tux and top hat, c. 1940. Collection of the Smithsonian National Museum of African American History and Culture, 2011.57.25.1.

and be-rouged" men with female chorines. But the show remained notoriously risqué, if no longer quite filthy. A fan recalled that when not accompanying herself on the piano, the "huge, voluptuous, [and] chocolate colored" Bentley cruised the audience, flirting with the women and soliciting dirty lyrics for her parodies of popular songs.[3] By the end of

[3] Richard Bruce Nugent, *Gay Rebel of the Harlem Renaissance* (Durham, NC: Duke University Press, 2002), 222 (be-ribboned); George Chauncey, *Gay New York: Gender, Urban Culture, and the Making of the Gay Male World, 1890–1940* (New York: Basic Books, 1995), 252 (huge); Chad Heap, *Slumming: Sexual and Racial Encounters in American Nightlife, 1885–1940* (Chicago: University of Chicago Press, 2009), 91–94.

1935, the *Ubangi Club Follies* had made Bentley a "bona fide Harlem celebrity" known for pushing the limits of propriety as much as for her talents as a blues singer and pianist.[4]

Soviet categories and concerns suggested no obvious way to narrate this gender-bending uptown adventure. Like all Soviet visitors since the poet Vladimir Mayakovsky in the mid-1920s, Ilf and Petrov regularly condemned "backward" American racism, while touting Soviet "racial enlightenment."[5] But Soviet antiracism offered little guidance when it came to understanding or recounting the unsettling intersections of gender, sexuality, race, and pleasure the writers encountered in Harlem. Depicting the Ubangi Club show as a raucous and liberating challenge to white male heterosexual power was impossible, perhaps unthinkable. Moving toward more traditional conceptions of family and gender, the Stalinist state in 1934 had recriminalized male homosexuality.[6] Given this context, Ilf and Petrov could conceivably have used the show to demonstrate American decadence. But the need to perform racial enlightenment ruled out condemning "Black dances" as, in the words of an indignant American critic, "parading sexual perverts."[7] Even an attenuated description of the "very sexual" display threatened to feed racist stereotypes of Black people as hypersexual.

As practiced by Ilf and Petrov, "racial enlightenment" relied less on a condemnation of white savagery than a celebration of Black culture and character. Here they diverged significantly from Mayakovsky, who in *My Discovery of America* (1926) made violence the defining feature of white Americans, who "will tear off a Negro's arms and legs and roast him alive over a bonfire." By contrast, Ilf and Petrov signaled their antiracism primarily by satirizing the excuses white Americans used to justify Jim Crow and highlighting Black contributions to American culture. Writing at a moment of relatively cordial Soviet–American relations, they suggested that white Americans – potential allies in a war against racist Nazi Germany – were not beyond redemption.[8]

Nowhere was Ilf and Petrov's tendency to overlook anti-Black violence clearer than in their apparent expurgation of Ernest Hemingway's invitation to Florida. In a letter to his wife, Ilf wrote that Hemingway proposed that the writers call on him in Key West. Ilf and Petrov repeated the story in the published travelogue, adding that, although they knew their

[4] Wilson, *Bulldaggers*, 179.
[5] Roman, "Forging Soviet Racial Enlightenment," 529, 531.
[6] Dan Healey, *Homosexual Desire in Revolutionary Russia: The Regulation of Sexual and Gender Dissent* (Chicago: University of Chicago Press, 2001), 181–88.
[7] As quoted in Wilson, *Bulldaggers*, 156.
[8] Roman, "Forging Soviet Racial Enlightenment," 534–41 (quotation at 534).

schedule would not allow it, they promised with reckless optimism to visit Hemingway to "go fishing and have a really serious talk on literature."[9] In his own letter to his Russian translator Ivan Kashkin, Hemingway recalled a far more inflammatory offer. Nonchalantly repeating a racist slur, Hemingway reported that he had "promised to let them shoot a n----- or to shoot a n----- for them if they had moral scruples and one of them asked if we could have the n----- roasted so he evidently didn't take the offer seriously. Or is he maybe a cannibal."[10]

The Soviet authors perhaps did not understand that Hemingway employed a powerful and dehumanizing epithet. Russian speakers in this period might have taken the slur, a near homophone of the Russian *negr*, as carrying a neutral connotation akin to the contemporary American usage of "Negro."[11] But it is also possible that they caught the insult; in his 1932 study of American "people and mores," the anthropologist Vladimir Bogoraz included it in his catalog of pejorative "national names" applied to Black people.[12] In any case, if Hemingway is to be believed, the Soviet authors (or at least one of them) got the "joke" that the business of American pleasure rested on violently enforced racialized (and implicitly gendered) hierarchies.[13] They even evoked, consciously or not, Mayakovsky's image of roasting a Black man. Cleaning up Hemingway's proposition in their published and unpublished work, Ilf and Petrov concealed the literary icon's casual racism.

Ilf and Petrov not only declined to out Hemingway as a racist. They ignored or perhaps failed to understand the insight he crudely offered into the connections between pleasure and white male violence. They came to the United States ready to deplore capitalism's oppression of both women and African Americans. Translating Soviet rhetoric into the American context, they described the nine-tenths naked chorines as exploited laborers. They were prepared to depict African Americans in Soviet terms as an oppressed "national minority" subject to the irrational "chauvinism" of their white neighbors.[14] But Soviet ideology did not understand "white chauvinism," the American party's version of "national chauvinism," and "male chauvinism," a term popularized by American women communists,

---

[9] PIA, Il'f, 29 October1935, 440; OA, 49; LGA, 40.   [10] Hemingway to Kashkin, 430.

[11] Kiaer, "African Americans," 404n3; Maria Radchenko, "Odnazhdy vstretilis' Il'f, Petrov i Kheminguei..." in Ernst Zal'tsberg, ed., *Russkie evrei v Amerike: Kniga 10* (Toronto: Giperion, 2015), 41.

[12] Vladimir Germanovich Bogoraz-Tan, *USA: Liudi i nravy Ameriki* (Moscow: Federatsiia, 1932), 130.

[13] Kevin Maier, "Hunting," in Suzanne Del Gizzo and Debra Moddelmog, eds., *Ernest Hemingway in Context* (New York: Cambridge University Press, 2013), 274.

[14] Meredith L. Roman, *Opposing Jim Crow: African Americans and the Soviet Indictment of US Racism, 1928–1937* (Lincoln: University of Nebraska Press, 2012), 25–55.

as mutually and violently reinforcing in the way Hemingway suggested.[15] Ilf and Petrov were not prepared to grasp the dynamics of American racism embedded in the author's invitation to enjoy the manly pleasure of dominating a demeaned and racialized Other.

To the extent that Ilf and Petrov told the story of Black New York at all, they relied on a "romantic racialization" of African Americans as naturally spiritual and musical. Their approach owed much to the Russian reception of *Uncle Tom's Cabin*. Harriet Beecher Stowe's novel, with its indelible and heartfelt image of Black people as "more simple, docile, child-like and affectionate than other races," had the status of a "classic" in Russia. Between 1880 and 1917, Russian publishers brought out more than fifty editions, often in large print runs. In the 1920s and 1930s, the Soviet state published at least thirteen more editions. Ilf and Petrov clearly knew the novel, explicitly referencing it in the caption accompanying a photo of the Mississippi River.[16] The Soviet writers followed Stowe in ennobling – and sentimentalizing – African Americans by treating them as symbols rather than as human beings "with the normal range of virtues and vices."[17]

In the "Negroes" installment of their photo essay, Ilf and Petrov combined images and texts to depict an ostensibly positive, but also clearly racialized and decidedly primitive or childlike Harlem. Two pages of photographs documented what Ilf and Petrov identified as a "demonstration against war and fascism" that in October, as the *New York Times* reported, brought some 15,000 marchers from "lower Harlem to Central Park West and Sixty-Third Street, where they held a mass meeting."[18] Among the onlookers, Ilf captured a "respectable Negro mama" in a hat and pearl earrings alongside two children dressed in their Sunday best. A caption described an intent child looking directly into the camera as emblematic of "very inquisitive" African American children – a well-intentioned contrast to the lack of curiosity Ilf and Petrov deemed typical of (white) Americans.

---

[15] Mark Naison, *Communists in Harlem during the Depression* (Urbana: University of Illinois Press, 1983), 34–49; Kate Weigand, *Red Feminism: American Communism and the Making of Women's Liberation* (Baltimore: Johns Hopkins University Press, 2001), 24–37.

[16] I thank Debrorah Field for help developing this argument. George M. Fredrickson, *The Black Image in the White Mind: The Debate on Afro-American Character and Destiny, 1817–1914* (Middletown, CT: Wesleyan University Press, 1971), 110 (Stowe), 97–129; John MacKay, *True Songs of Freedom: "Uncle Tom's Cabin" in Russian Culture and Society* (Madison: University of Wisconsin Press, 2013), 61, 48; Il'ia Il'f and Evgenii Petrov, "Amerikanskie fotografii: X: Negry," *Ogonek*, no. 22 (10 August 1936): 15.

[17] Fredrickson, *Black Image*, 109.

[18] Il'f and Petrov, "Negry," 16–17; "15,000 March Here in Peace Parade," NYT, 27 October 1935.

Ignoring, perhaps missing, the substantial presence of communist and communist-affiliated organizations in the "Peace Parade," Ilf and Petrov focused on the 2,000 followers of Father Divine. A spiritual leader who preached celibacy and promoted himself as the "Negro god" of Harlem, Father Divine was, as communists themselves recognized, an unlikely ally.[19] Since mid-1934, when party leaders had persuaded Father Divine to participate in communist-sponsored demonstrations, they had been defending this odd extension of the Popular Front on the grounds of shared anti-war and antiracist values. Earl Browder, the leader of the American party, explained that for communists, the distinction between "good" and disreputable religious organizations was meaningless.[20] In the photo essay, only the slogan "against war and fascism," tucked away in a caption above the photo of the woman and children, hinted at a communist connection. Ilf and Petrov accompanied an image of demonstrators carrying signs proclaiming Father Divine "God" with the information that, following a jazz orchestra, the marchers danced and sang hymns. They ended with an image of "God" himself in a "nice Rolls Royce" that, in true American fashion, was adorned with advertisements urging onlookers to "love Father Divine." Identifying oppressed but noble African Americans with dance, singing, curiosity, and religion, the essay also gently satirized Divine as a self-aggrandizing Black swindler.

That there was something demeaning in understanding Blacks as "naturally" curious and religious with an innate gift for song and dance seems not to have occurred to Ilf and Petrov – or indeed to many white Americans. A performance of *Porgy and Bess*, which they saw in November at the invitation of the opera's director Rouben Mamoulian, reinforced their romantic racialist conceptions of African Americans. The opera was an adaptation of Mamoulian's first great directorial success, DuBose and Dorothy Heyward's 1927 play *Porgy* that was in turn based on DuBose Heyward's 1925 novel of life and death on Catfish Row. Set in a semi-fictionalized Black tenement in Charleston, South Carolina, the opera told the story of the disabled beggar Porgy's ill-fated love for the abused and drug-addicted Bess. Written, directed, and scored by white outsiders, and sung by a conservatory-trained Black cast, *Porgy and Bess* presented Catfish Row as an isolated world of music, magic, and violence teeming with drug dealers, gamblers, prostitutes,

---

[19] Benjamin Kahan, "The Other Harlem Renaissance: Father Divine, Celibate Economics, and the Making of Black Sexuality," *Arizona Quarterly* 65 (Winter 2009): 37–61.
[20] Earl Browder, "What Is Communism? 6. Communism and Religion," *New Masses* 15 (11 June 1935): 18; Naison, *Communists in Harlem*, 129–30; Jill Watts, *God, Harlem USA: The Father Divine Story* (Berkeley: University of California Press, 1992), 119–21.

and murderers. In a letter to his wife, Ilf deemed the "opera of Negro life" "marvelous." He reported that its representation of "Negro mysticism, terrors, kindness, and credulity" had given him "much joy."[21] Like many American "white audiences and critics," Ilf unselfconsciously interpreted "*Porgy and Bess*'s characters and situations through a prism of deeply entrenched racist stereotypes."[22]

After the show, when Ilf and Petrov went backstage to meet the cast, it became clear that the accomplished African American actors and singers had little in common with the people they portrayed. Ilf expressed amazement that "of course, the blackest Negress" suddenly started speaking Russian: "It turned out that before the Revolution, she had spent eight years performing in Russia." This was likely Georgette Harvey, Maria in the opera, whose *Playbill* biography described her as having spent "fifteen years in Europe, twelve of them in Russia." Soon they were joined by an American Indian woman, a "real squaw," who "also began to speak Russian." She may have been one of the "girls" in Harvey's quartet, who had a part in the opera.[23] The linguistic familiarity unsettled, but did not dislodge, the primitive and racialized image that had given Ilf such joy.

Ilf and Petrov's encounters with Black New York fit uneasily into Soviet categories. Neither the Ubangi Club, nor the Peace Parade, nor *Porgy and Bess* offered a clear means of condemning American racism or trumpeting Soviet racial enlightenment. Ultimately, the authors opted to exclude from *Low-Rise America* not only the flamboyantly genderfluid Gladys Bentley, but also the celibate Father Divine, and the Russian-speaking African American singer. To sustain their image of soulful and upright African Americans, they neglected to mention that they ran into the respectable communist Paul Robeson at a queer cabaret. To preserve Hemingway's status as a cultured American writer, they withheld his racist "joke." Instead, as we will see, the authors focused their discussion of American racism on the more manageable topic of what they called the "Southern Negro states," where they could display their racial enlightenment by denouncing the obvious and pernicious effects of Jim Crow.

Restoring Ilf and Petrov's suppressed adventures allows us to see the complex America that the writers encountered and tried to understand. Their strategy for making sense of America often involved shoehorning it

---

[21] PIA, Il'f, 4 November 1935, 443–44.
[22] Ellen Noonan, *The Strange Career of Porgy and Bess: Race, Culture, and America's Most Famous Opera* (Chapel Hill: University of North Carolina Press, 2012), 153.
[23] *Playbill*, Rouben Mamoulian Papers, Manuscript Division, Library of Congress, Box 116, Folder 1; Nugent, *Gay Rebel*, 214.

into available Soviet categories. Often, as in their adventure at the Ubangi Club, they seemed at a loss as to how to manage this. At other times, they hinted at their fascination with the America that failed to fit into neat boxes. This is especially clear in their encounters with Russian Jewish immigrant New York, where they cultivated deeper and more intimate connections than in Black New York.

10   Complex Hybrids

> We required an ideal being, a rose without thorns, an angel without wings. We needed some kind of complex hybrid: a guide-chauffeur-translator-altruist.
>
> Ilf and Petrov, *Low-Rise America*

Ilf and Petrov's dream of seeing and understanding America faced two daunting obstacles: Neither spoke much English and neither knew how to drive. In their early adventures outside of New York City, they relied on fellow Soviets and immigrants from the Russian empire to show them around. The Soviet consul Jean Arens drove them to the Danbury Fair. A Soviet citizen they met on board the *Normandie*, Grigory Alekseevich Kardysh, who was in the United States to study subtropical plants and was traveling with a translator, a driver, and the agronomist Mikhail Yakovlevich Natanson, gave them a lift to Washington, DC, in his new Ford.[1] They returned by train. Ilf's Uncle William picked them up in New York City and drove the three-and-a-half-hours to Hartford.[2] Again, the writers returned by train. Ilf and Petrov omitted these details from the published travelogue, declining to mention how they got from New York to Danbury, Hartford, and Washington, DC, and back. But identifying their guides reveals a central and incompletely suppressed paradox of their quest: their impressions of "real" America came filtered through the eyes and mouths of outsiders or immigrants.

These early experiences seem to have convinced Ilf and Petrov of both the need to travel by car and the need for a driver and translator. A motorcycle cop pulled Arens over on the way to Danbury for failing to yield to passing cars, but let him off with a warning once he learned he was the Soviet consul.[3] On the way to Washington, they witnessed their first car "*eksident*," a word that Ilf transliterated into Cyrillic in his notebook. He described it as serious, noting the red flares the police

---

[1] ZK, 13 October, 433; PIA, Il′f, 13 October, 431.
[2] ZK, 22 October, 439; PIA, 23 October, 436.   [3] ZK, 12 October, 430.

placed on the ground.[4] The train rides home were less eventful and somehow less American.[5] As Ilf and Petrov noted in *Low-Rise America,* "you cannot see America from a train window. It is not the writer's business to do anything of the kind."[6]

On Ilf and Petrov's first day in New York City, Arens had offered to take the pair on a nineteen-day road trip through Buffalo, Niagara Falls, Chicago, Detroit, and Pittsburgh.[7] The writers jumped at the chance. This was hardly the ocean-to-ocean trip that they claimed to have been plotting as they sailed to the United States, but it was exciting enough and, above all, doable. However, Arens quickly backtracked; he could not leave town for so long.[8] Thus began the hunt, an abridged version of which Ilf and Petrov recounted in *Low-Rise America,* to find a "complex hybrid," who could drive, translate, and guide the search for "real" America and who, critically, "didn't like to make money."[9] Strapped for funds, the writers needed an angel willing to work cheap.

Their first prospect was less an "angel" than an editor in need of his own cheap way out of a fix. Before Ilf and Petrov's arrival, the Russian-language newspaper *Russky golos* (Russian Voice) had published their novel *The Twelve Chairs* without their permission and, more to the point, without paying royalties. At the time, *Russky golos,* based in New York, was the largest circulation Russian-language newspaper in the United States, and one sympathetic to the Soviet Union.[10] Ilf and Petrov were less flattered that their work had been published than put out that they had not been paid. Another *Russky golos* writer, Emanuel Pollack, an émigré who had recently visited the Soviet Union and published his approving observations in *SSSR v obrazakh i litsakh* (The USSR in Images and Faces), planted the idea that Ilf and Petrov demand remuneration. The result, according to Ilf's notes, was a standoff: The editor absolutely agreed with the authors that they should receive royalties but maintained that there was no money with which to pay them. Ilf and Petrov "monotonously" repeated their wish to be compensated.[11] Ten days later, on 19 October, they reached a deal. In lieu of royalties, the

---

[4] ZK, 14 October, 433.   [5] ZK, 15 October, 434.   [6] LGA, 28–29; OA, 34.

[7] ZK, 8 October, 426; PIA, Il'f, 8 October, 428; Petrov, 8 October, 427.

[8] ZK, 11 October, 428; OA, 33.   [9] OA, 34.

[10] David Shub, "The Russian Press in the United States," *Russian Review* 3 (Autumn 1943): 124; Yaroslav J. Chyz and Joseph Slabey Roucek, "The Russians in the United States: I," *Slavonic and East European Review* 17 (April 1939): 654; "Russkii golos (N'iu Iork, 1917–)," Emigrantika: Periodika russkogo zarubezh'ia, www.emigrantica.ru/item/ russkii-golos-niu-iork-1917 (accessed 29 December 2020).

[11] ZK, 10 October, 11 October, 429, 430, 432–33; PIA, Il'f, 20 October, 435; Emanuel Pollack, *SSSR v obrazakh i litsakh* (New York: Russian-American Publishing House, 1935).

newspaper would loan them one of its editors, Alexander Brailovksy, for two-and-a-half months as a translator and driver.[12]

Brailovksy was a more complex hybrid than Ilf and Petrov imagined in their description of the ideal creature. In 1902, at age eighteen, Brailovksy, the son of a Jewish merchant, had left the Pale behind to join the Russian revolutionary movement. In 1905, already an "old Bolshevik," he fled the Russian empire, escaping a sentence of hard labor in Siberia. He settled in Paris for a decade, writing poetry and drifting toward more moderate politics, ultimately emigrating to New York in 1917. After the October Revolution, he reengaged with Bolshevism, working for the pro-Soviet *Russky golos* and *Novyi mir*. In September 1920, in connection with a Wall Street bombing that killed 33 and injured about 300, the New York police briefly detained the alleged "Trotsky–Lenin" agent, whom an anonymous tipster put at the scene of the blast.[13] Scratched but unscathed by the Red Scare, Brailovsky lived in New York and worked at *Russky golos* until the early 1930s, when, losing faith in the Soviet experiment, he moved to Los Angeles. There he became an American citizen and remade himself into an arts journalist and editor at *Experimental Cinema*. Brailovsky had returned to New York and his old post at *Russky golos* shortly before Ilf and Petrov's visit. Soon thereafter, he decisively broke his communist ties.[14] With one foot in radical Russian émigré circles and one in Hollywood, Brailovsky would have been, to say the least, an engaging tour guide. However, at the end of October, *Russky golos*, too, backtracked. Brailovsky never left New York with the Soviet funnymen.

By the time *Russky golos*'s offer fell through, Ilf and Petrov had another prospective angel, Solomon A. Trone, the prototype for the fictionalized Mr. Adams. Trone, like his literary counterpart, was a retired engineer who had worked for General Electric (GE) in the Soviet Union. In the published work, they described meeting their angel at the consul's reception, where he greeted them effusively and pledged to help. In late October, Trone and his wife Florence agreed to take the writers to

[12] ZK, 19 October, 437–38.
[13] "Held as Undesirable Alien," NYT, 19 September 1920; Beverly Gage, *The Day Wall Street Exploded: A Story of America in Its First Age of Terror* (New York: Oxford University Press, 2009), 185–86.
[14] Evgenii Demenok, "Il'f, Petrov i Burliuk," *Novyi mir*, no. 9 (2015): 137–39; Vladimir Khazan, "'Ia sovremennik, ia syn veka': Ob Aleksandre Brailovskom," *Lekhaim*, 18 October 2017, https://lechaim.ru/academy/ob-aleksandre-brailovskom/ (accessed 29 December 2020); Thomas Brandon, "'The Advance Guard of a New Motion Picture Art': Experimental Cinema, 1930–1933," *Journal of the University Film Association* 30 (Winter 1978): 27–31; Alexander Brailovsky, US, Naturalization Records, Ancestry.com.

Schenectady. This trip was not, as narrated in *Low-Rise America*, the first leg of their coast-to-coast trip with "mama and papa" Adams but an overnight excursion. Given Trone's career with GE, it made sense for him and Florence to take the pair to Schenectady, the company's head-quarters. In a letter, Ilf described the Trones as "elderly and nice Americans."[15] On 4 November, he related to his wife that he and Petrov would likely be traveling with Trone, "an American who knows America perfectly," and his wife, who is a "superb" driver.[16]

Low-Rise America recovered some of the complexity obscured by Ilf's description of the Trones as "elderly and nice Americans." At the time of Ilf and Petrov's visit, Solomon Trone was in his early sixties and retired – so by some definitions "elderly." The same could not be said of Florence, his second wife, who was about thirty years his junior. In 1930, she was working as a secretary at General Electric. The two had married in July 1933 in Manhattan. Two months later, while the couple was honey-mooning in Jamaica, Florence gave birth to a girl, Vera Alexandra. *Low-Rise America* acknowledged the age difference, describing Mrs. Adams as a "young lady," who wore the same thick glasses as her husband, and several chapters later characterizing Mr. Adams as a "good-hearted elderly gentleman."[17] It described the happy family as living on Central Park West – not too far from their actual address at 390 Riverside Drive.[18]

The Trones' two-year-old daughter figured prominently in *Low-Rise America*'s plot. In Ilf and Petrov's telling, the couple's qualms about leaving their child behind in New York constituted the primary impedi-ment to enlisting them as guides. The authors' own letters home, full of longing for their children, make clear that they understood the gravity of what they were asking. Amid their campaign to coax the Trones into joining them, Petrov sent a "big, big kiss to little Petenka" and asked for news of everything from his son's health to his toys. Ilf ended his letters with a kiss for his wife and "little golden Sasha," and wanted to know, "When will little Sasha's second tooth come in?"[19] None of these per-sonal concerns show up in *Low-Rise America*. On the contrary, when the Adamses raised the question of "the baby," the writers reported that they answered "flippantly": "You can put the baby in a public nursery."

[15] ZK, 17 October, 436; PIA, Il'f, 29 October 1935, 441.
[16] PIA, Il'f, 4 November 1935, 443.
[17] OA, 47, 57; ZK, 31 October, 442; Solomon Trone, New York Marriage Index and Consular Reports of Births, Ancestry.com.
[18] Alex Gumberg to L. E. Browne, 5 February 1936, Gumberg Papers, Box 12; Mark Popovskii, "Odnoetazhnaia Amerika polveka spustia," *Grani*, no. 131 (1984): 287.
[19] PIA, Petrov, 23 October, 435; Il'f, 17 October, 31 October, 434, 443.

The suggestion, so sensible to the Soviet citizen, was met, in the published work, with Mr. Adams reminding Ilf and Petrov that "there are no nurseries here. You are not in Moscow!" Ultimately, the couple found a "respectable" woman to care for the child while they were away, and the writers agreed to complete the 10,000-mile trip "in two months, not a day longer." That Ilf and Petrov felt like "scoundrels" as they watched the Trones take leave of their daughter seems quite plausible.[20]

If *Low-Rise America* got many of the domestic complications right, it effectively obscured the complexity of Florence and Solomon Trone's status as "Americans." Both were American citizens and may well have seemed like Americans to Ilf and Petrov. But they were of more recent and Jewish vintage than the pseudonym "Adams" suggested. Florence Trone (née Wagner) was born in the United States; the daughter of Russian Jewish immigrants, she spoke Russian fluently.[21] Solomon, variously described as the son or grandson of a rabbi, emigrated in 1916 from the Russian empire (Mitau, now Jelgava, Latvia). Becoming a naturalized American citizen in 1934, he continued to identify with the Soviet project.[22] As early as 1920, the Russian Jewish immigrant, who promoted the Bolshevik cause among his colleagues at General Electric, attracted J. Edgar Hoover's attention as a "suspected radical."[23] Trone spent his career at GE facilitating American–Soviet economic exchange and technology transfer. In the late 1920s and early 1930s, he traveled widely in the Soviet Union, where he oversaw General Electric's work on major industrialization projects.[24] Anonymous FBI informants, who knew Trone in the 1930s, characterized him as a "philosophical Marxist who sincerely predicted that the world of tomorrow" would be communist.[25] In a letter to Ilf and Petrov after they returned to Moscow, Trone expressed a desire to move to the Soviet Union and contribute to building socialism – a dream abandoned in the wake of the Stalinist purges.[26]

[20] OA, 69–74.

[21] Florence Wagner, US Census, 1930, Ancestry.com; Popovskii, "Odnoetazhnaia Amerika," 284.

[22] *The American Who Electrified Russia*, directed by Michael Chanan (2005), https://vimeo.com/141921892 (accessed 13 August 2023); Andrew Roth, "'Mr. Point Four,'" *Nation* (27 January 1951): 83–84.

[23] Report made by D. F. Broderick, 11 September [1920]; Department of State to Mr. Hoover, 19 August 1920, FBI 100-NY-96127 (Trone FBI). I thank David Evans for sharing documents from Trone's FBI files.

[24] Trone, "Application for Federal Employment," Trone FBI.

[25] Report made at New York, 20 June 1950: Report made 16 June 1951, Trone FBI.

[26] Letter from Trone to Il'f and Petrov, 17 August 1936, quoted in ZK, 497n213; Report made 31 October 1949; Report made 21 February 1950, Trone FBI.

The name "Adams" clearly evoked America's white Anglo-Saxon Protestant founders. For Ilf and Petrov, the name was also connected to Alexander Gumberg's wife Francis "Frankie" Adams. A former suffragist and director of the New York chapter of the National Women's Trade Union League, Frankie Adams really was a descendant of the presidents.[27] Ilf and Petrov met the Gumbergs when they stopped for breakfast at their "dacha" in Norwalk, Connecticut, on the way to the Danbury Fair.[28] About a week later, the writers were among a large number of guests invited to a dinner at the Gumbergs', the key features of which Ilf listed in his notebook as cocktails, appetizers, and "beef roasted right there on a wire rack." His description of Frankie Adams "boldly driving a car and singing 'Stenka Razin'" resembled both the real Florence Trone and the fictionalized Becky Adams, who were also excellent drivers, spoke Russian, and knew many Russian songs.

While the charismatic Frankie Adams lent her name to Becky Adams, Gumberg, who had shepherded John Reed and other Americans around revolutionary Petrograd, left a less vivid impression. Ilf and Petrov neglected to credit him as the source of their letters of introduction to "two La Follettes, one a governor, the other a senator," whom they might have met had their itinerary taken them to Wisconsin.[29] Ilf dryly noted in his journal only that the husband "recounted his biography." Gumberg may have mentioned his work translating Russia and the Soviet experience into terms Americans could understand. More recently, he had been doing the reverse, assisting Soviet visitors, including in 1931 Boris Pilnyak, who had described Gumberg as "an old American wolf and my friend."[30]

In transforming Gumberg into a generic "New York friend," Ilf and Petrov not only concealed the identity of the person who offered to arrange a free "banana boat" cruise to Cuba and Jamaica. They Americanized and sanitized the invitation, which Ilf had initially characterized in his notebook as "American *blat*." A notoriously difficult-to-translate term, blat, sometimes rendered as "pull," denoted the pervasive, although officially condemned, Soviet practice of using informal networks and illicit exchanges to circumvent shortages and bureaucracy.

---

[27] Lynn Cole, "Biographical Sketch of Emma Francis Adams," *Online Biographical Dictionary of Militant Woman Suffragists, 1913–1920,* https://documents.alexanderstreet .com/d/1010595680 (accessed 2 January 2021).

[28] ZK, 12 October, 431.

[29] OA, 46; Alex Gumberg to Mr. Ilf and Mr. Petrov, 4 November 1935; Gumberg to Phil [LaFollette], 4 November 1935, Gumberg Papers, Box 8, Folder 5.

[30] As cited in ZK, 492n147.

Blat was something that Soviet authors were licensed to satirize.[31] In this case, the comparison was not too far off the mark. Arranging junkets on United Fruit vessels for free or at low cost appears to have been something of a Gumberg specialty. His papers include a contemporary letter from Wisconsin Governor Philip La Follette on behalf of himself and his senator brother Robert, Jr., about "accommodations on the United Fruit boat leaving New York Saturday, October 12." "Of course," the governor added, "Bob and I want to pay our way. If we can get rates that would, of course, be welcome."[32] Ilf and Petrov were not prominent politicians, but the free cruise on a United Fruit company ship – on which they would be seated at the captain's table, no less – clearly relied on "connections" to facilitate a mutually beneficial, off-the-books exchange.

Yet instead of calling out American blat, Ilf and Petrov used the episode to satirize the Soviet practice. Gumberg's promise, made over elaborate cocktails, became an emblem not of unsavory "pull" but of American efficiency and reliability. In *Low-Rise America*, businesslike transactions with Americans stood as the implicit antithesis of Soviet blat and red tape. The writers recounted that they sent a telegram to Gumberg on their way back to New York inquiring about the cruise. They characterized his reply as "a little bit offended: Your tropical journey arranged long ago."[33] An American, they concluded, kept his word with no fuss and no reminders – even when it was given over cocktails. The actual telegram, as preserved in Gumberg's papers, addressed Solomon Trone in more neutral language: "Tell Ilf Petrov tropical journey arranged. Happy New Year."[34] A letter that met Ilf and Petrov when they checked back into the Shelton Hotel in January 1936 more clearly expressed Gumberg's eagerness to help the authors see as much as possible. He regretted that the cruises including Cuba were sold out, but assured them that in addition to Jamaica, they would have the opportunity to visit the Panama Canal and, in Colombia, to "see how bananas grow and how they are shipped."[35] Even more telling of Gumberg's desire to promote friendly Russian–American relations is his

---

[31] ZK, 20 October, 438, 495n198; Fitzpatrick, *Everyday Stalinism*, 62–65; Alena Ledeneva, *Russia's Economy of Favours: "Blat," Networking & Informal Exchange* (Cambridge: Cambridge University Press, 1998), 22–25.

[32] Philip F. La Follette to Alex Gumberg, 3 October 1935, Gumberg Papers, Box 8, Folder 5.

[33] OA, 50.

[34] Gumberg to S. A. Trone, 30 December 1935, Gumberg Papers, Box 8, Folder 5; Ilf and Petrov to A. Gumberg, 30 December 1935, Gumberg Papers, Box 8, Folder 5.

[35] Gumberg to Mr. Ilf and Mr. Petrov, 6 January 1936, Gumberg Papers, Box 8, Folder 6.

letter to A. A. Pollen of the United Fruit Company, to whom he sent a copy of *The Little Golden Calf*. Seeking to impress upon his correspondent Ilf and Petrov's cultural importance, he advised Pollen, whose literary taste he apparently doubted, to "read the comment of various American critics on the jacket before you read the book."[36]

By turning the Trones into Mr. and Mrs. Adams and Gumberg into a New York friend, Ilf and Petrov concealed their reliance on Jewish Russian Americans who had prospered in the United States. The Russian immigrants identified as such in *Low-Rise America* tended to be unhappy, often struggling economically, and regretful of their decision to emigrate. Trone and Gumberg hardly fit this mold. To identify them as immigrants would raise uncomfortable, not to say impermissible, questions. Why did a Russian engineer, whose expertise was needed in the Soviet Union, choose to remain in the United States?[37] How could one explain the largesse of Russian Jews so successful in the land of capitalism and racism that they were able not only to donate their services as guides and translators, but to host lavish dinners, provide letters of introduction to prominent politicians, and arrange free tropical cruises?

If passing off their immigrant benefactors as unproblematically American allowed Ilf and Petrov to sharpen the divide between "ourselves" and the Other, it also blurred it. The American Mr. Adams was clearly "one of us" ideologically, as he called attention to the failings – if also the technical achievements – of American capitalism. Ilf and Petrov's Mr. Adams had much in common with the Solomon Trone described by the FBI's informants. The characteristics that the Soviet writers viewed as positive signs of his political enlightenment – his wide travels in the Soviet Union, Japan, and Germany; his ability and desire to converse with all sorts of people; his familiarity with the work of Marx and Lenin – the FBI took as indicators of potential subversion. From both Soviet and American perspectives, Mr. Adams/Trone "did not at all," as Ilf and Petrov asserted, "resemble an American."[38]

Ilf and Petrov tempered Trone's ideological correctness with a dose of absentmindedness. Thirty miles outside Schenectady, Mr. Adams realized that he had gotten so caught up in expounding his views on the Italian invasion of Ethiopia that he had forgotten his hat. An accommodating hotel keeper sent the hat to General Delivery in Detroit, where the parcel failed to arrive on time. And so, the hat followed one step behind the travelers for two months – forgotten,

---

[36] Gumberg to A. A. Pollen, 31 December 1935, Gumberg Papers, Box 8, Folder 5.
[37] Etkind, *Tolkovanie puteshestvii*, 163.   [38] Fedorova, *Yankees*, 88; LGA, 105; OA, 139.

misdirected, or late – finally reuniting with its owner at the journey's end in New York City. Fifty years later, Florence explained to a Russian émigré journalist that the hat was pure fiction. Solomon Trone did not even wear one. She, too, overstated the case; Ilf recorded in his notebook that Trone forgot his hat not at the outset of their trip, but in King City, California.[39] In any case, Florence Trone adamantly maintained that her husband was neither comic nor absentminded. "He was concerned with big, serious problems: economic, political, historical, and literary."[40] She might have agreed with an FBI informant, who in 1950 remembered Trone in the late 1920s and early 1930s as "an 'elder statesman' type of man of wide knowledge and experience," whose "opinions were respected by his listeners." In Moscow, where "he frequently discussed industrial matters," Trone was "regarded as a profound global thinker."[41]

Ilf and Petrov did not take Mr. Adams quite this seriously. They compared their guide to Charles Dickens's lovably eccentric Mr. Pickwick, himself "a reinvention of the Quixote figure for the Victorian age." Mr. Adams, like Mr. Pickwick, is prone to befuddlement, pratfalls, and comic indignation. Like Pickwick, too, Mr. Adams reminds his fellow travelers to write down what they see in their notebooks. As for the story of the hat chasing Mr. Adams across America, Ilf and Petrov simply inverted the "ludicrous distress" Mr. Pickwick experienced "in pursuit of his own hat."[42]

Still, the authors appreciated that everything Mr. Adams said "was interesting and wise" – even if they also sometimes feigned sleep to avoid his constant patter. They particularly valued another trait that a federal investigator flagged in 1920: Trone took every opportunity to "learn everything possible about America." "Not content to learn this merely" by reading newspapers, Trone, the agent reported, "goes out himself and mingles with all classes."[43] Ilf and Petrov, too, wanted to meet and converse with people of all sorts. The gregarious Trone, who in 1920 a suspicious colleague at GE characterized in a confidential letter to the State Department as "a disputatious nature, but always exceedingly insinuating, sincere [?] and friendly in intercourse," proved an excellent

---

[39] ZK, 9 December, 462.   [40] Popovskii, "Odnoetazhnaia Amerika," 286–87.
[41] Report made 20 June 1950.
[42] Jonathan Greenberg, *The Cambridge Introduction to Satire* (New York: Cambridge University Press, 2019), 195–96; PIA, Il'f, 10 December 1935, 469; Galina Zhilicheva, "Narrativnye osobennosti travelogov I. Il'fa, Evg. Petrova (zapisnye knizhki, 'Odnoetazhnaia Amerika')," *Novyi filologicheskii vestnik* 45, no. 2 (2018): 27–38; Fedorova, *Yankees*, 88–89.
[43] LGA, 104; OA, 138; Report made 15 December 1917, Trone FBI.

mediator. Ilf and Petrov described Mr. Adams as "born to mingle with people ... He derived the same pleasure from conversations with a waiter, a druggist ... a six-year-old Negro boy, whom he called 'sir,' the mistress of a tourist home, or the director of a large bank."[44] The Soviet travelers longed to know this diverse America, which they compared to a "long, fascinating novel." This desire to learn was apparently mutual. Florence recalled that the Trones had agreed to accompany Ilf and Petrov because they wanted to know how Soviet people would respond to America.[45]

Looking back from the vantage of 1984, Florence offered a pessimistic assessment of Ilf and Petrov's efforts to understand America. She judged *Low-Rise America* "not wrong, but life as seen by people who grew up in the USSR, with the views they acquired in the USSR."[46] Florence doubted that Ilf and Petrov's adventures had led them to the "real" America they sought. Focused on their rootedness in Soviet culture and politics, she slighted their engagement with people like herself and her husband, who to some extent shared their cultural and political perspectives.

Recounting their adventures in the alien land of the capitalists, Ilf and Petrov, too, downplayed their interactions with hybrids like Solomon Trone and Alexander Gumberg. But such interactions were nonetheless critical to their mission. Recovering Ilf and Petrov's connections with people like the Trones and the Gumbergs allows us to see cultural exchange as a process. Unable or unwilling to divest themselves of views "acquired in the USSR," the authors nonetheless worked to find and understand alternative perspectives. What looked at first blush very much like blat could become in a different context a laudable commitment to keeping one's word in all business dealings. Trone in particular, with his ability to combine a desire to know America in all its complexity with faith in the communist world of the future, provided a model for Ilf and Petrov's own investigations. The complex hybrids demonstrated that in capitalist America, Soviet citizens could find kindred spirits. Even if never explicitly acknowledged, this lesson played a central role in Ilf and Petrov's adventures.

---

[44] LGA, 106; OA, 141; Charles L. Clark to Secretary of State, 13 August 1920, Trone FBI.
[45] OA, 112; Popovskii, "Odnoetazhnaia Amerika," 284.
[46] Popovskii, "Odnoetazhnaia Amerika," 286.

11   Squaring the Circle

> New York was asleep … Immigrants from Scotland, from Ireland, from
> Hamburg and Vienna, from Kovno and Białystok, from Naples and
> Madrid … were asleep. … Gazing at the shimmering lights, we wanted
> to find out as soon as possible how these people work, how they amuse
> themselves, what they dream of, what they hope for, what they eat.
>
> Ilf and Petrov, *Low-Rise America*

Ilf and Petrov related that on their very first evening wandering around
New York, "at that very moment, when it occurred to us how far we now
were from Moscow," they stumbled on a familiar sight: the Soviet
animated feature *The New Gulliver* playing at the Cameo Theater. Here
they took some artistic license. The film, in which a young communist
Gulliver liberated the Lilliputians, opened several weeks after their
arrival. Moving up the date, they emphasized their early realization that
they would discover fragments of the Soviet world within the capitalist
one.[1] The Cameo, the movie house devoted to showing Soviet films that
had seemed to a State Department special agent a potential spreader site
for the virus of revolution, appeared to Ilf and Petrov as a comforting
slice of home.

In immigrant America, Ilf and Petrov found themselves in a foreign
land, paradoxically surrounded by things and people that felt familiar.
On the day after their arrival, the writers had dinner at a small restaurant
where "suddenly, girls started speaking Russian."[2] The consul's reception on 16 October was, to a degree elided in *Low-Rise America*, an
opportunity to mingle with Russian Americans.[3] Ilf and Petrov met
Rouben Mamoulian, who had grown up in Tiflis (now Tbilisi,
Georgia), had studied at the Moscow Art Theatre, and had arrived in
the United States in 1923. In his notebook, Ilf described Mamoulian as a
"tall, pale, bespectacled man of the Moscow type." Whatever Ilf had in

---

[1] OA, 16; "The Screen Calendar: For Week Ending Oct. 31," NYT, 27 October 1935.
[2] ZK, 8 October, 427.   [3] ZK, 16 October, 435–36; PIA, Il'f, 17 October 1935, 432–33.

mind with the description "Moscow type," it clearly evoked something close to home.[4]

After the reception, Ilf and Petrov had a drink with the Futurist poet, painter, and impresario David Burliuk, whose work Ilf had admired since he was a sixteen-year-old in Odesa. Perhaps best known in the West as a co-author, along with Vladimir Mayakovsky and other poets, of the 1912 Futurist manifesto "A Slap in the Face of Public Taste," Burliuk emigrated to the United States in 1922. By 1935, he was an American citizen. Although he remained connected to fellow émigrés and met Ilf and Petrov again before they left for home in January 1936, Burliuk was "quick," as the art historian John Bowlt asserts, to embrace the "American values of family, home, and automobile." Still, he was "moved" when Ilf addressed him warmly as "David Davidovich."[5]

These slivers of home, like the complex hybrids, facilitated Ilf and Petrov's efforts to see, if not accept, American perspectives. The simple matter of being able to converse in Russian helped. So did the shared reference points. Talking to relatively recent émigrés like Mamoulian and Burliuk, Ilf and Petrov could imagine how people with whom they to some extent identified had become American. Both Ilf and Petrov also had family ties to America, and in these cases less imagination was required. The pair visited Ilf's uncles in Hartford and saw Petrov's brother's play, *Squaring the Circle*, on Broadway. They detailed neither of these adventures in the published travelogue. But again, as with the complex hybrids, the contacts shed light on the process of cultural exchange. Seeing Ilf's Jewish Russian American relatives in Hartford and an American production of Valentin Kataev's popular Soviet farce on Broadway allowed Ilf and Petrov to reflect on the possibility of bridging divides and to grapple with the most difficult kind of cultural understanding: getting one another's jokes.

In *Low-Rise America*, Ilf and Petrov connected Hartford with Mark Twain, a favorite American author in the Soviet Union with whom they were often compared. They recalled that at Twain's "wonderful, restful home" in Hartford, then and now a museum, they saw "the original illustrations for *The Prince and the Pauper*, which we had known since our childhood."[6] Given Twain's popularity before and after the Revolution – Soviet readers bought more than a million and a half copies of his work in

[4] ZK, 16 October, 436.
[5] Demenok, "Il'f, Petrov,"131–33; John E. Bowlt, "David Burliuk," in Maria Rubins, ed., *Twentieth-Century Russian Emigre Writers*, Dictionary of Literary Biography Vol. 317 (Detroit: Gale, 2005), Gale Literature Resource Center.
[6] LGA, 140; ZK, 22 October, 439.

the mid-1930s – many of Ilf and Petrov's readers would have shared their recognition.[7]

The writers left out of the published work a more personal connection to Twain. Ilf's uncle, Nathan Finesilver (Nacham Feinsilber on the ship's manifest), had emigrated to the United States in 1893, at age nineteen. When Ilf and Petrov visited him in Hartford, Uncle Nathan told them that he had met Mark Twain. Working as a peddler in 1896, the young immigrant with long hair caught the author's attention. When Twain learned that Nathan was from Russia, "the great humorist questioned him for a long time about Russia and asked uncle to stop by whenever he came through with his goods."[8] Twain's interest in the Russian Jewish immigrant seems plausible. At the time, the author was a fiery advocate of "free Russia." Responding to an 1890 talk by the journalist George Kennan (a distant cousin of the diplomat George Kennan) on the inhumanity of the tsarist autocracy, Twain allegedly declared, "If such a government cannot be overthrown otherwise than by dynamite, then thank God for dynamite!"[9] However, in 1891 financial difficulties forced Twain to embark on a worldwide lecture tour. It is possible that Nathan Finesilver met the author during a last visit in 1896; Twain never returned to the house after the death of his daughter in Hartford that year.[10]

The published work omitted not only the story of the Russian immigrant who charmed Mark Twain, but the entire Finesilver clan. Ilf had met Nathan's daughter, his cousin Blanche, in Paris a few years before. In 1935, Blanche, then living in New York, had learned about his visit from the newspaper. They met in the city on 17 October and arranged a visit to Hartford for the following week. Ilf's Uncle William, then fifty-six, who in his younger days had worked as a chauffeur, and his wife Pauline came down from Hartford in their Chrysler and drove Ilf, Petrov, and Blanche up to Connecticut, where most of Ilf's father's family had settled. The "shy," white-haired William's mannerisms and gait reminded Ilf of his father, Arnold Fainzilburg, who had died in 1933.[11]

[7] Albert Parry, "Mark Twain in Russia," *Books Abroad* 15, no. 2 (Spring 1941): 168–69; Ia. S. Lur′e, "Mikhail Bulgakov between Mark Twain and Lev Tolstoy," *Russian Review* 50 (April 1991): 203–204.

[8] PIA, Il′f, 23 October 1935, 437.

[9] As quoted in Louis J. Budd, "Twain, Howells, and the Boston Nihilists," *New England Quarterly* 32 (September 1959): 351; Jane E. Good, "America and the Russian Revolutionary Movement, 1888–1905," *Russian Review* 41 (July 1982): 273–76.

[10] "The Mark Twain House," The Mark Twain House and Museum, https://marktwainhouse.org/about/the-house/HartfordHome/ (accessed 12 January 2021).

[11] PIA, Il′f, 17 October 1935, 433; ZK, 22 October, 439; "Finley, Blanche," *Hartford Courant*, 19 December 1994.

Ilf knew his family in Hartford primarily from photographs. Nathan had been the first to emigrate, four years before Ilf's birth. In August 1897, two months before Ilf's birth, Nathan's younger brother William (Wilhelm Feinsilber), then seventeen, and their father (Ilf's grandfather) Benjamin (age fifty) joined Nathan in Hartford. In 1902, Anna Finesilver (Hene Feinsilber, then forty-seven), Benjamin's wife, followed with her two youngest children, Minnie (Mane, age sixteen) and David (fourteen).[12] By the time Ilf arrived in the United States, Nathan, in his early sixties, was, according to Ilf, "sad; his children have grown up and moved to New York; his wife died in 1930; money is, evidently, short."[13] William and his sister Minnie had married a sister and a brother, Pauline and Meyer Cohn. Meyer, William, and David worked at the Prospect Garage in West Hartford, not far from the Mark Twain House, that Meyer had opened in 1920.[14] Benjamin Finesilver had died in 1915, and Ilf did not meet his eighty-year-old grandmother. She died in 1937, a week after Ilf.[15]

The Finesilvers managed at once to retain old-world ways, nurture ties with a Soviet homeland they had never visited, and enjoy some success in the capitalist economy. William's home in the Blue Hills section of Hartford – a step up from the immigrant enclave of the East Side, but less affluent and more Jewish than the West End, where the garage and Meyer Cohn's home were located – seemed to Ilf a fragment of Russia unstuck in time and space.[16] At his uncle's, he had a meal of "Jewish sweetbread and pickled watermelon" the likes of which he had not eaten in "fifteen years or more." If the food brought Ilf back to his Odesa youth, the political discussion centered on the contemporary Soviet Union and labor activism in the United States. The authors met with the local chapter of the Friends of the Soviet Union and a "100% American" who had been involved in an aircraft workers' strike, presumably the 1934 strike at Pratt and Whitney, which local communists had

---

[12] Michele Kallin, "Pyatyhory Residents' Immigration Data," https://kehilalinks.jewishgen .org/pyatyhory/documents/Pyatyhory_Immigration_March_2015.pdf (accessed 13 January 2021).

[13] ZK, 22 October, 439. Fannie Schechtman Finesilver, JewishGen Online Worldwide Burial Registry, Ancestry.com.

[14] Aleksandra Il'f, "'Vskryvaem korni' Il'i Il'fa," Lekhaim, no. 165 (2006), https://lechaim .ru/ARHIV/165/ilf.htm (accessed 10 January 2021); Cohen [sic], Meyer_1974/7/25, Oral History, Jewish Historical Society of Greater Hartford, Oral History Collection (JHSGH). I thank Leah Early for calling the interview to my attention.

[15] "Mrs. Annie Finesilver," Hartford Courant, 20 April 1937; Aleksandra Il'f, "'Vskryvaem korni.'"

[16] Betty N. Hoffman, Jewish Hearts: A Study of Dynamic Ethnicity in the United States and Soviet Union (Albany: State University of New York Press, 2001), 42–50, 67–68.

helped to organize.[17] These official "receptions" provided a contrast to the family business, where the brothers sold Chryslers, Plymouths, and Hudsons; serviced cars of all makes; and pumped gas.[18] Ilf concluded the entry in his notebook with the observation: "Convenience is everything. They live well. But it looks strange. Communists and salesmen."[19]

Ilf and Petrov declined to share this uncanny family portrait with their Soviet readers. For an American audience, they emphasized not the strangeness of what they saw, but shared "democratic" values and practices. If the interview published in the *Hartford Courant* is an accurate indication, Ilf and Petrov performed their role as ambassadors carefully, if not reluctantly. They "shied away from answering political questions." Through a translator, Anne Gitlin, they explained that "because of the recent protest from the Government of the United States, both were compelled to swear not to conduct propaganda for the Soviet Union." Whether or not this oath was the primary source of their reticence is impossible to tell. Petrov, who did most of the talking, was willing to offer "that the Soviet Government is slowly increasing the amount of democratic machinery" like the secret ballot. To questions about the freedom of noncommunists, Petrov "said simply" that he was not a party member, "yet there has been no attempt to interfere with his freedom of action or thought." More in the vein of defending the Soviet Union than conducting propaganda on its behalf, "both denied ... that they were compelled to write on any assigned topic, except as journalists may be requested to 'cover' a given event." They certainly had experience with such "requests." In 1933, Ilf and Petrov, along with more than 100 prominent Soviet authors, "covered" the opening of the White Sea Canal, a flagship project of the First Five-Year Plan constructed by convict labor. In that case, they had managed to avoid contributing to the collective volume that praised the marginally unusable canal as a technical feat that "reforged" prisoners into model Soviet citizens.[20] In Hartford, they framed their lack of "freedom" in terms designed to highlight their kinship with the journalist assigned to interview the two Soviet visitors.

[17] Harry Gannes, "The War Planes Stop," *New Masses* 11 (24 April 1934): 14–15; Susan D. Pennybacker and Paul Kershaw, "Hartford Labor Militants Fight the Spanish Civil War," *Hog River Review* 2, no. 3 (2004): 21.

[18] Prospect Garage, Hartford, Connecticut, City Directory, 1935, 84, Ancestry.com. Gitlen, Herbert,1985/04/22, Oral History, JHSGH.

[19] ZK, 22 October, 439–40.

[20] "Two Authors from Russia Visitors Here," *Hartford Courant*, 24 October 1935; Milne, *How They Laughed*, 134–35; Cynthia Rudder, *Making History for Stalin: The Story of the Belomor Canal* (Gainesville: University Press of Florida, 1998), 20–38.

Petrov's immigrant "relation" in the United States – his brother's creative offspring on Broadway – offered a fuller opportunity to reflect on how ideology and the market constrained, respectively, Soviet and American writers. Written and set in the late 1920s, *Squaring the Circle* gently satirized both the contemporary housing shortage and the 1926 marriage code that made divorce as simple as sending a postcard. The "vaudeville," as Kataev called it, was an early Soviet hit. Premiering in 1928, the play enjoyed a run of more than 600 performances at the Moscow Art Theater and became a favorite of amateur companies. It tells the story of two young communist men sharing a small apartment who, unbeknown to one another, get married on the same day. Each brings his bride home without telling her that he has a roommate. By the end of Act I, the two couples have settled into the crowded space, dividing it first with a chalk line and then with a curtain. It immediately becomes clear that the pairs are mismatched. Abram, an intellectual forever fretting over whether his actions are "ethical," falls for Vasya's partner, the petty-bourgeois housewife Liudmilla, who feeds him cutlets and mends his trousers. At the same time, the architect Vasya, who feels smothered by Liudmilla's homemaking, is attracted to Abram's wife, the bookish and ascetic communist Tonya Kuznetsova. After many comic misunderstandings and a few tears, the lovers divorce and happily remarry via the intervention of the wise old communist Comrade Flavius. The house lights go up, and in a coda of rhyming couplets, the players ask, "Why not laugh at things that seem funny?"[21]

While Kataev's comedy played on the realities of life in the late 1920s in the Soviet Union, viewers did not need a deep acquaintance with the Soviet Union or Soviet ideology to get the joke. Explaining their choices of mate, Abram and Tonya repeatedly mention the features of a lasting communist marriage: mutual understanding, membership in the same class, a common political platform, and labor solidarity. "Love" they dismissed as rotten, petty-bourgeois nonsense. This too-earnest appeal to political categories is clearly an object of satire. But the satire is not all that sharp. In the end, the old Bolshevik Flavius simply advises the young people to stop their foolishness, switch partners, and "love one another." What drives the comedy is the repetition of dialogue between the various pairs trying to maintain appearances while longing for their roommate's spouse. The farce reaches a crescendo when the two men, each elated

---

[21] Robert Russell, *Russian Drama of the Revolutionary Period* (Totowa, NJ: Barnes and Noble Books, 1988), 92–95; Valentin Kataev, *Kvadratura kruga*, in *Sobranie sochinenii*, vol. 9, *P'esy* (Moscow: Khudozhestvenaia literatura, 1986), 83–138 (couplets), 111–13 (ethical),.

that his own wife has left, slowly realize, in a brilliant bit of vaudeville business, that the other's elation means the object of his own desire is also gone.

VASYA (STOPS, LOOKING AT ABRAM): Gone! Ha-ha! Gone...
ABRAM (STOPS, LOOKING AT VASYA): Gone! It's a fact!
VASYA (LAUGHING, WINKING): Gone...
ABRAM (LAUGHING, WINKING): Gone!
VASYA: Stop! Who's gone!
EMILIAN [A POET, THE OFFICIAL REGISTERED OCCUPANT OF THE APARTMENT]:
    Stop! Who's gone!
ABRAM: And who left?
EMILIAN: And who left?
VASYA: It's clear who: Liudmilla [Vasya's wife].
EMILIAN: It's clear who: Liudmilla.
ABRAM: What ... Liudmilla left! ... Have you gone out of your mind?
    Kuznetsova [Abram's wife] left!
EMILIAN: Have you gone out of your mind? Kuznetsova left!
VASYA: What? Have you gone out of your mind? Tonka [Kuznetsova] ... left?
    You're joking?
EMILIAN: You're joking?
ABRAM: Stop! (Dumbfounded)
VASYA: Stop! (Dumbfounded).[22]

The confrontation escalates to the absurd conclusion of Abram and Vasya running off to fight a duel.

Retaining the farcical plot, the Broadway version paradoxically Americanized the play by exaggerating its Sovietness. A comparison of the Russian and English scripts belies the claim made in the Lyceum Theater's playbill that the production included "revisions which do not in the least alter the point of view of the original play."[23] Eugene Lyons and Charles Malamuth's translation larded Kataev's frothy comedy with Soviet political rhetoric. In both scripts, Abram cites the political prerequisites for a lasting marriage under communism. But the American version more forcefully satirized the application of official directives to private life, specifying that Abram finds these guidelines in a fictional manual titled *Marriage under Communism*.[24] Malamuth and Lyons also added the doctrinaire bureaucrat Rabinovitch, the chairman of the housing committee, who gets a few cheap laughs calling for the "liquidation" of Liudmilla's petty-bourgeois canary. The American play's new ending

[22] Kataev, *Kvadratura kruga*, 90, 108, 111–12, 135, 131.
[23] Valentin Kataev, *Squaring the Circle*, trans. Charles Malamuth and Eugene Lyons (New York: Samuel French, 1936), 3.
[24] Kataev, *Squaring the Circle*, 22, 102–103.

further emphasized and seemingly criticized the Soviet elements of the story. For Kataev's comic couplets, the New York production substituted a dark and ambiguous final scene in which a child, the explicit embodiment of the socialist future, refuses to say whether it will help to build the new world.[25]

At the same time, the American play took Soviet ideology with a deep seriousness that verged on self-parody. In Kataev's play, as soon as Comrade Flavius understands the problem, he quickly and easily resolves it without bothering to make a "serious moral point."[26] On Broadway, the resolution came wrapped in a tedious explanation that seems designed to defend, if not promote, the Soviet approach to marriage. The translators turned Flavius, a name as incongruous in Russian as in English, into the grandfatherly and respectable Novikov, who attributes the rushed and ill-considered marriages to a "bourgeois mistake," and carefully outlines the "Communist logic" of the spouses unregistering and reregistering their unions.

It was precisely the Broadway production's surfeit of supposedly authentic Soviet detail that attracted the attention of both American reviewers and the Soviet visitors. Reactions to the play centered around the questions of how and whether an American audience could understand Soviet humor. The *New York Times*'s influential drama critic Brooks Atkinson complained that for those without a comprehensive knowledge of the "Soviet dialectic," the play was "gibberish," "crammed with abstractions that are funny only to people who are accustomed to taking them seriously." Unaware that the American translators, not Kataev, were responsible for the "abstractions," he deemed the New York production "the private joke of Communists."[27]

Likewise, Joseph Wood Krutch's more sympathetic review in the *Nation* unsuspectingly homed in on the translators' work more than the playwright's, praising the play's adroit reconciliation of "lively, knockabout farce" and "a subtly effective profession of fervent faith in the Communist enterprise." He saw this reconciliation most clearly in a "subtle scene, in many ways the best in the play" that he assumed was Kataev's: "the starved husband who has just been fed by his neighbor's wife discusses with her the existence of countries where wheat is burned up and fruits dumped into the sea." Then they "seize the flag" and begin to march to these lands. Krutch imagined that this deft shift "from jest to

---

[25] Kataev, *Squaring the Circle*, 7, 105.   [26] Russell, *Russian Drama*, 94.

[27] Brooks Atkinson, "'Squaring the Circle,' in Which the Soviet Sense of Humor Is Represented," NYT, 4 October 1935.

earnest" would bring a "Soviet audience ... cheering to its feet."[28] However, Kataev's script made no such shift. Instead, the gratefully fed Abram resolves to "develop" Liudmilla, beginning with the "simplest text," an account of the "electromagnetic theory of light." He gets through two comically incomprehensible sentences before she interjects, "Abramchik, take me to the Zoological garden!" After confirming that she has the money for the outing, he readily agrees.[29]

What Krutch called the play's "elusively ironic conclusion" became a particularly contentious issue among American critics and audiences. Taking it as a faithful translation of the Russian original, Krutch speculated that the ending "in all probability left some Soviet officials wondering whether or not the author had succeeded in putting something over on them." As he described the Lyceum Theater's production, Novikov, having settled the issue of the mixed-up marriages, "points to the grotesque, blubbering figure of a child" and asks, "will you go on marching and building or will you destroy it all?" In the dramatic pause that follows, "the child turns his silent, uncomprehending face, the lights dim, and the curtain goes down." Krutch reported that at this "the balcony broke out into concerted 'boos.'" Why, he wondered, "should the comrades boo a play which the homeland has taken to its heart?" Krutch judged the play a biting, albeit officially sanctioned satire and the American comrades humorless.

If the mainstream critics accepted the playbill's disclaimer at face value, better informed viewers took issue with it. In a letter to the editor published in the *Nation* about a month after Krutch's review, Herman Brownstein, who in 1934 had staged his own translation of *Squaring the Circle* in Los Angeles, blamed the boos on the New York show's "intellectually dishonest translators and producers." Offering to send the editors the Russian script to verify his claims, he charged that, "With the exception of the quotation, 'Why does everything turn out unethical when it feels so ethical?' every speech quoted by Mr. Krutch is something Kataev had nothing to do with, and has obviously been added with the malicious intent of casting reflections [sic] upon the great cultural and industrial progress in the Soviet Union."[30]

The poet Stanley Burnshaw, a regular contributor to the communist-aligned *New Masses* corroborated the boos and likewise found them

---

[28] Joseph Wood Krutch, "Drama: Soviet Farce," *Nation* (23 October 1935): 490; Kataev, *Squaring the Circle*, 66–67.

[29] Kataev, *Kvadratura kruga*, 113.

[30] Herman Brownstein, "Correspondence: 'Squaring the Circle,'" *Nation* (20 November 1935): 590.

entirely warranted. In an open letter to Kataev, Burnshaw attributed "hisses and boos" from the second-night audience to dissatisfaction with the "anti-Soviet" liberties taken with the play. Shifting the setting from the 1920s to the mid-1930s allowed the adaptation to include an otherwise anachronistic and, Burnshaw alleged, slanderous reference to the First Five-Year Plan: Vasya, guarding a precious match, observes, "Comes another Five-Year Plan and I'll have another match." But nothing surpassed the offensiveness of the ending, in which, as Burnshaw described it, "the symbol of the future (a stage midget in grotesque posture, his back to the audience) remains in portentous silence as the curtain falls."[31] For Burnshaw, the source of the problem was obvious: Lyons, a former United Press correspondent in Moscow, who was in the process of distancing himself from his earlier Stalinist sympathies, was "one of the foremost slanderers of the U.S.S.R."[32]

A revision of the play undertaken within the first three weeks of its run, apparently a reaction to the early negative reviews and boos, only partially assuaged concerns that it slandered the Soviet Union. In the wake of Mike Gold's scathing criticism in the *Daily Worker*, the director Dmitri Ostrov, a Russian immigrant, clarified that he was "entirely sympathetic" to the Soviet Union. His hasty revisions eliminated the play's most egregiously "anti-Soviet" elements. They also resulted in a show that got a lot of laughs and ran a respectable 108 performances, a fact that hints that the producers' motives may have been at least as commercial as they were political. Burnshaw expressed his pleasure that the "blubbering, grotesque dwarf of the finale has been replaced by a bright-faced youngster who makes a sturdy 'symbol of the future.'" He concluded that "the present (revised) production should delight friends of the U.S.S.R. and warm the hearts of 'neutrals,'" but worried that even in its improved form, the play still offered "a great deal for Red-baiters to cackle over and use with joy."[33]

From the perspective of American communists, who saw themselves as champions of the Soviet cause, the Broadway production of *Squaring the Circle* was no laughing matter. The primary issue for Burnshaw was that a Soviet artist, "who has an international responsibility which extends far beyond the borders of the U.S.S.R.," had entrusted his work to any

---

[31] Stanley Burnshaw, "A Letter to the Author of 'Squaring the Circle,'" *New Masses* 17 (29 October 1935): 27.

[32] Burnshaw, "Letter," 28; "Current Theater," *New Masses* 17 (12 November 1935): 27; S. J. Taylor, *Stalin's Apologist: Walter Duranty: The New York Times's Man in Moscow* (Oxford: Oxford University Press, 1990), 168–69, 235.

[33] Michael Gold, "Change the World!" *Daily Worker*, 6 October 1935; Burnshaw, "Letter," 28.

"Tom, Dick or Harry" rather than "a politically responsible group who can assure him deep and impassioned understanding." But Burnshaw did not ignore the commercial side of the equation. He predicted somewhat optimistically that a "politically responsible" production would attract a "limitless audience," not only proletarians, but the "swelling number of middle-class people who are demanding of the theater fresh, real and fearless themes."[34] Soviet drama, Burnshaw suggested, was too important to be handed over to Broadway producers, who adulterated and disparaged Soviet culture in a misguided effort to entertain American audiences.

The staging of *Squaring the Circle* that Ilf and Petrov saw on 17 October may have been the revised version. As Ilf described it in a letter home, it was strangely American but "not at all anti-Soviet." He asked his wife to let Kataev know that "the first person wearing a top hat that I saw in New York was buying a ticket to his play." He emphasized that the play itself employed every Russian cliché in the book. Before the curtain went up, "five Americans in purple blouses performed Russian folk songs on small guitars and huge balalaikas." Behind the set's window, the obligatory snow fell. A red flag stood in the corner of the room. Ilf reported that the public laughed and seemed to like the play. He judged the acting "not brilliant, but not bad." As to the changes to Kataev's script, Ilf noted the "insertion of several Broadway jokes that would make the author wince." Among the wince-inducing one-liners that Ilf may have had in mind: Emilian reacts to Abram's news that "Vasya and I got married," with a startled, "Vasya and you got married! That's not allowed."[35] (The misunderstanding would not be possible in Russian; Abram uses the verb *zhenitsia*, which denotes taking a wife.) Of course, Ilf also noticed that Lyons and Malamuth had given the play a "very serious and philosophical" ending – to the extent, he acidly added, that they were capable of philosophy. "We," evidently Ilf and Petrov, recommended to Malamuth that he delete the jokes and the philosophy. But overall, he concluded, "not bad."[36]

It is not surprising that Ilf and Petrov declined to include their family connections to America in *Low-Rise America*. They had come to the United States hoping to learn what "these people" dream, hope, and eat. But their encounters with people who often dreamed, hoped, and ate things familiar to the Soviet visitors destabilized the book's overarching structure. It turned out that both individuals and cultural products could at once remain recognizably "ours" and become distinctively American.

[34] Burnshaw, "Letter," 28.   [35] Kataev, *Squaring the Circle*, 49.
[36] PIA, Il'f, 17 October, 433.

The Hartford Finesilvers were ideological kin, communists, or at least sympathetic to the Soviet experiment. Yet they were also English-speaking salesmen, driving Chryslers and navigating the capitalist world. *Squaring the Circle* made a successful transition to Broadway in a version that highlighted its Soviet strangeness – or better, turned it into an American stereotype of Sovietness. The New York production spouted more stilted rhetoric than Kataev's original, in the process becoming both a more vicious satire of Soviet-speak and sympathetic evidence of the Soviet people's ability to laugh at their own excesses.[37] Of course, as Ilf and Petrov recognized, many of the play's "Soviet" jokes along with much of its "Soviet" philosophy, were cooked up by and for Americans.

Having emigrated to New York, *Squaring the Circle* was newly free to disparage or express fervent support of the Soviet Union. But it was also newly constrained by Broadway's commercial imperatives. Ilf character-ized the production's painful one-liners as "Broadway jokes," designed to appeal to a mass audience. The balalaikas and the snow served the same purpose. Ideological and market pressures were, of course, pro-foundly different, but they could produce similar dilemmas for artists and even artistic results with a family resemblance.

[37] Robert Benchley, "The Theater: (Laughter)," *New Yorker* (12 October 1935): 30.

12   The Apex of Middlebrow Culture

I firmly believe that while all entertainment is not art, all art
is entertainment.

Rouben Mamoulian, 1935

In the month they spent in New York, Ilf and Petrov became connoisseurs
of low culture. They appraised burlesque, nightclubs, penny arcades, an
auto race, a wrestling match, a boxing match, a rodeo, and self-serve
cafeterias. Indeed, they seemed to conclude that low culture *was*
American culture. Cheap, easily understandable, and crass, American
entertainments kept the masses distracted and docile. At the other end
of the spectrum, Ilf and Petrov endeavored to show that American high
culture consisted entirely of high-priced European imports. The rich and
"fashionable" sought status by taking "possession" of the "best musicians
in the world," but they appreciated their music only as a luxury commodity.[1] What Ilf and Petrov largely ignored, at least in the published travelogue, was middle culture – or the middlebrow. And it was in the middle
that Soviet and American cultural producers shared some of the same aims
and challenges – even as they operated under different constraints.

Comparing Ilf and Petrov's account of their experiences of American
high culture with reviews in the American press reveals their concern with
stressing its "bourgeois" and thus ultimately uncultured character.
Concerts at Carnegie Hall, where they heard the Russian émigré pianist
Sergei Rachmaninoff and saw the British-born Leopold Stokowski conducting the Philadelphia Orchestra, and in Chicago, where they heard the
Austrian violinist Fritz Kreisler, provided, they attested, "remarkable
music, remarkably played."[2] In this judgment, their account largely agrees
with contemporary reviews in the *New York Times* and the *Chicago Tribune*,
although the *Times*'s music critic Olin Downes thought that "in the early
part of his program, [Rachmaninoff] might not have been at this best."[3]

---

[1] OA, 148–49.   [2] LGA, 111; OA, 149.
[3] Olin Downes, "Audience Stirred by Rachmaninoff," NYT, 3 November 1935.

In some cases, the Soviet and American accounts depicted the same scene from slightly different angles. Both the critic and the funnymen commented on Rachmaninoff's ostentatiously aloof demeanor at his November Carnegie Hall appearance. Downes reported with perhaps exaggerated reverence: "The bell rings and a very tall, spare, grave gentleman, in afternoon garb of irreproachable correctness and sobriety, steps without smiling upon the stage. ... He does not smile once through the whole occasion."[4] Ilf and Petrov similarly described Rachmaninoff, wearing an "old-fashioned black tailcoat," as "tall, bent, and thin, with a long sad face." However, in their account, the pianist's habit of telling jokes in his dressing room before a concert (related to them by an unnamed composer) belied his studied performance of the "Russian exile's great sadness."[5]

At the same time, the American critics and the Soviet funnymen had entirely different perceptions – or at least descriptions – of American reactions to European high culture. Downes described the house at the Rachmaninoff concert, at which he played at least one of his own compositions, as "packed to overflowing" with both "celebrities of music" and students eager to "listen to an acknowledged master." All responded to the "musician-virtuoso" with "thunderous applause."[6] By contrast, Ilf and Petrov, expecting "an explosion" when Rachmaninoff finished, did not trust their ears when they heard only "normal applause" and a few scattered "enthusiastic exclamations" from the balcony.[7]

Ilf and Petrov asserted that the same pattern held at "all the concerts we attended in America." Their account of unmoved and uncomprehending American auditors in *Low-Rise America* hinged on the assumption that those who could afford the tickets were unlikely to appreciate the music.[8] They depicted the audience at a Philadelphia Orchestra concert at Carnegie Hall as a grotesque gallery of philistines – "meat and copper kings and chewing gum princes in tailcoats; railroad queens and dollar princesses in evening gowns and diamonds." The performance of the overture to *Die Meistersinger* was "faultless," but, they claimed, "stirred almost no emotions in the hall."[9] By contrast, in Downes's review, far from stirring no emotion, the first part of the concert, five of Stokowski's Bach transcriptions, reached "such a thrilling climax ... that the members of the audience cheered." He reported that the Wagner, too, was "furiously applauded."[10]

---

[4] Downes, "Audience Stirred."   [5] OA, 148.   [6] Downes, "Audience Stirred."
[7] LGA, 111–12; OA, 148–49; PIA, Il'f, 4 November 1935, 443.
[8] PIA, Il'f, 6 November 1935, 445; LGA, 112; OA, 149.   [9] OA, 149.
[10] Olin Downes, "Stokowski Offers Bach Work Here," NYT, 6 November 1935.

Ilf and Petrov's implicit comparison of American spectators and pur-portedly more cultured Soviet audiences apparently required them to suppress much cheering and thunderous applause. However, their pic-ture of musically unsophisticated American audiences was not wholly fictive. A brief item in the *Chicago Tribune* reviewing the Fritz Kreisler concert that Ilf and Petrov attended in November 1935 corroborates some of their critique.[11] In *Low-Rise America*, the authors described the concert as beginning and ending "in a half-empty hall." This detail does not square with the *Chicago Tribune*'s music critic's account. Edward Barry reported that "Twenty-five hundred persons crowded Orchestra hall [sic] to hear [Kreisler's] titanic fiddling." If we are willing to trust the *Tribune*, Ilf and Petrov appear intent on highlighting the "fact" that high ticket prices kept the masses out of American concert halls, whatever the actual size of the crowd. Still, the critic seemed to agree with the Soviet observers' larger point that the audience showed little musical discern-ment. Ilf and Petrov noted that in Chicago, as in New York, the "playing called forth no rapture from the public", although Kreisler played so "subtly, poetically, and wisely" that in Moscow he would have received a half-hour ovation. Feeling no "gratitude" in the Chicagoans' meager applause, Kreisler turned to pieces "which were increasingly banal – pretty little waltzes and other light pieces – the productions of low taste." These finally brought the audience to life. "It was," they concluded, "the great humiliation of a great artist who had begged for charity." The *Tribune*'s critic was only a bit more tactful: "The audience chose a very unspectacular little transcription of a Debussy piano piece as its especial favorite of the afternoon, and made him repeat it."[12]

The story of the virtuoso European musician pandering to a rich, uncultured audience is a central episode in Ilf and Petrov's account of their least favorite American city, "that horrible town, Chicago." On the shores of Lake Michigan, they found an emblem of the "triumph of absurdity" that was capitalism. While they discovered much to love and much to hate in New York, in Chicago they were "overcome with anger at people, who, in their pursuit of the almighty dollar, have reared on a fertile prairie … a huge, ugly poisonous fungus."[13] Here, a boorish bourgeoisie debased the "best musicians in the world."

Nothing, Ilf and Petrov emphasized, could be further from the situ-ation in the Soviet Union, where state-supported opera houses and

---

[11] ZK, 17 November, 448.
[12] LGA, 114; OA, 151–52; Edward Barry, "Fritz Kreisler's Titanic Fiddling Delights 2,500," *Chicago Tribune*, 18 November 1935.
[13] LGA, 109–10; OA, 146.

concert halls made high culture available to all. The American "bourgeoisie," Ilf and Petrov charged, "had stolen art from the people" and then
despoiled and neglected it.[14] As evidence of the crime, they related the
story of how "poor Italian immigrants" saved the New York Philharmonic.
When the "patrons of the arts" proved too busy with their businesses to
give a thought to the financial needs of the "clarinets, cellos, and bass
viols," the Philharmonic's star conductor, Arturo Toscanini turned to the
common folk who "did not have the money to buy tickets to a theater," but
avidly listened to radio concerts. After a broadcast, he offered anyone who
made a dollar donation an autographed photograph.[15] In fact, small
donations from the 1934 radio appeal, in which Toscanini promised a
personal response to all contributors, accounted for about $7,200 of the
Philharmonic's $500,000 fundraising goal.[16]

Condemning commodified American high culture, Ilf and Petrov had
little to say about American middle culture. Their story mocked the
unseemliness of a conductor begging for money, not the radio concert –
a format with which they would have been familiar. In the Soviet Union,
performances of the "classics," often accompanied by "explanations,"
constituted more than half of radio programming. Soviet radio also carried
literary works to the masses, everything from Pushkin to comedy skits by Ilf
and Petrov.[17] These sorts of self-consciously uplifting entertainments are
"middlebrow" in the sense proposed by the music critic John Rockwell:
They are "well-meaning, often naive efforts to elevate the masses through
high culture, and maybe to bend high culture in more populist directions."
Under this rubric, Rockwell includes Toscanini's radio concerts, George
Gershwin's *Porgy and Bess*, and Shostakovich's later works in which simpli-
city was perhaps "forced upon him."[18] As this catalog suggests, the middlebrow can be understood as crossing the socialist–capitalist divide.

In the United States, high-profile efforts to make high culture
accessible, even entertaining, generated an alarmist highbrow backlash.

---

[14] LGA, 112; OA, 149.   [15] LGA, 113; OA, 150.

[16] "Toscanini Appeals for Orchestra Aid," NYT, 7 February 1934; "Orchestra's Fund
Nearly Complete," NYT, 23 April 1934.

[17] Richard Stites, *Russian Popular Culture: Entertainment and Society since 1900* (New York:
Cambridge University Press, 1992), 82–83 (explanations at 82); Stephen Lovell, *Russia
in the Microphone Age: A History of Soviet Radio, 1919–1970* (New York: Oxford
University Press, 2015), 66–67, 81, 93, 101; Shawn Vancour, "Popularizing the
Classics: Radio's Role in the American Music Appreciation Movement, 1922–34,"
Media, Culture & Society 31 (2009): 294.

[18] John Rockwell, "1935, October 10: A Controversial Folk Opera Premiers on
Broadway," in Greil Marcus and Werner Sollors, eds., *A New Literary History of
America* (Cambridge, MA: Harvard University Press, 2009), Credo Reference; Pauline
Fairclough, "Was Soviet Music Middlebrow? Shostakovich's Fifth Symphony, Socialist
Realism, and the Mass Listener in the 1930s," *Journal of Musicology* 35 (2018): 336–67.

Art critic Clement Greenberg defined middlebrow "kitsch" as a "new commodity ... destined for those who, insensible to the values of genuine culture, are hungry nonetheless for the diversion that only culture of some sort can provide." While Rockwell's "friendly" definition of middlebrow culture credited its creators with an impulse to construct "work that speaks to real people with the most sophisticated means available," Greenberg imagined middlebrow cultural producers as looting, watering down, and repackaging the "fully matured" cultural tradition's "discoveries," and then selling them at a profit. Tellingly, and somewhat surprisingly given his emphasis on kitsch as demanding "nothing of its customers except their money," Greenberg's 1939 diatribe equated American kitsch and Soviet socialist realism. He rejected the notion that the "masses," whether in "backward Russia" or the "advanced West," preferred "kitsch simply because their governments condition them towards it." Instead, he imagined that a hypothetical Russian peasant would prefer the Russian realist painter Ilya Repin, whose work Greenberg deemed kitsch, to Pablo Picasso because the former required no "effort on the part of the spectator." Designed to "flatter the masses by bringing all culture down to their level," kitsch was, he argued, the same everywhere. Only its uses differed: it could make the capitalist money or provide an "inexpensive way" for "totalitarian regimes ... to ingratiate themselves with their subjects."[19]

Ilf and Petrov did not share Greenberg's contempt for art that moved the masses. At the same time, they were unwilling to describe, let alone judge, American efforts to make serious culture accessible. In New York, they consumed a good bit of what could be described as middlebrow in Rockwell's sense of elevated popular culture, or, less kindly, "high class kitsch."[20] On Broadway they saw not only *Squaring the Circle* but also *Porgy and Bess* and Lillian Hellman's *The Children's Hour*, which the *New York Times*'s reviewer called a "tragedy" set in the "precise key of hysteria."[21] They took in the blockbuster Van Gogh retrospective at the Museum of Modern Art that attracted more than 123,000 visitors in its two-month New York run.[22] And they were interviewed by reporters for a magazine Greenberg deemed a particular threat to the cause of true art, *The New Yorker.*[23] None of this showed up in their published work.

---

[19] Clement Greenberg, "Avant-Garde and Kitsch," *Partisan Review* 6, no. 5 (1939): 39, 40, 42, 43, 44, 47, 49; Joan Shelley Rubin, *The Making of Middlebrow Culture* (Chapel Hill: University of North Carolina Press, 1992), xiii–xiv; Denning, *Cultural Front*, 107–10.
[20] Greenberg, "Avant-Garde," 41.
[21] ZK, 23 October, 440; Brooks Atkinson, "Children's Hour," NYT, 2 December 1934.
[22] PIA, Il'f, 6 November 1935, 445; "Art Show Sets Record," NYT, 6 January 1936.
[23] Greenberg, "Avant-Garde," 41.

Rouben Mamoulian, who exemplified the aspiration to create entertaining art, likewise hardly figured in Ilf and Petrov's published work.
A photographic portrait of him in his signature round glasses and bow tie
appeared in the "Hollywood" installment of their photo essay. The
caption identified him as a "remarkably talented and unusually successful" film director, who in his eight years making motion pictures had
made only hits: *The Song of Songs* (1933, starring Marlene Dietrich), *Dr.
Jekyll and Mr. Hyde* (1931), *Queen Christina* (1933, starring Greta
Garbo), and *We Live Again* (based on the Lev Tolstoy novella
Resurrection, 1934).[24] Contrary to Ilf and Petrov's claim, the Tolstoy
adaption, *Queen Christina*, and *The Song of Songs* were box office duds.
But Mamoulian was a go-to director for the studio boss looking to make
a marketable "prestige picture."[25] In *Low-Rise America*, the writers do
not mention that they met the director in both New York and Los
Angeles. His name appears only on a list of the "best directors," whose
pictures delighted "cinematographic Moscow" alongside Lewis
Milestone, King Vidor, and John Ford.[26]

Ilf and Petrov's brief reference to Mamoulian established him as a
Hollywood director, who shared the socialist-realist commitment to
accessible art – although Mamoulian would likely not have put it that
way. He himself cultivated the image of a Hollywood heartthrob, who
made cosmopolitan style and taste available to the masses. A 1934 profile
of the director in *Modern Screen* that ran under the title "The Man Garbo
Loves" described Mamoulian as a "romantic Russian-Armenian from
the far-off Caucasus," who "speaks with a London accent" and relaxes in
a "poet's den" "lined with solid tomes in English, French and
Russian."[27] But he did not create art only for the cognoscenti. In 1935,
he directed both *Porgy and Bess* on Broadway and the pioneering technicolor feature *Becky Sharp*, an adaptation of William Makepeace
Thackery's 1848 novel *Vanity Fair*. Mamoulian promoted both as
innovative and entertaining artistic achievements. He maintained that
the new color process used in *Becky Sharp* gave the film the "aesthetic
quality of a painting," at the same time emphasizing that audiences

[24] Il'ia Il'f and Evgenii Petrov, "Amerikanskie fotografii: VII. Gollivud," *Ogonek*, no. 19–20
(20 July 1936): 20.
[25] David Luhrssen, *Mamoulian: Life on Stage and Screen* (Lexington: University Press of
Kentucky, 2013), 74 (prestige), 77; Douglas W. Churchill, "Taking a Look at the
Record," NYT, 25 November 1934.
[26] OA, 303.
[27] Cyril Vandour [Leon Surmelian], "The Man Garbo Loves," *Modern Screen*, June 1934,
Library of Congress Manuscript Division, Rouben Mamoulian Papers, Box 204,
Folder 1.

would instinctively understand the new medium.[28] In a 1934 *New York Times* interview, Mamoulian characterized himself as "devoted to the poetry of life" but denied that he was "arty or highbrow."[29] He "firmly" believed, as he told a radio audience in 1935, "that while all entertainment is not art, all art is entertainment." Some thirty-five years later, Mamoulian explained that "at the age of 18 I had a sort of artistic philosophy, art for art's sake. I outlived it by the time I was 19. Art is for life's sake!"[30]

Mamoulian's insistence that "all art is entertainment" bears an unexpected resemblance to the strictures of socialist realism. It calls to mind the pronouncements of Stalin's top enforcer of ideological purity, Andrei Zhdanov. His infamous 1948 directive to Soviet composers follows the same structure as Mamoulian's dictum: not everything that is "accessible" is a "work of genius," but all "works of genius" are accessible to the "broad masses."[31] This is not to suggest that Mamoulian was a Stalinist. Rather, the coincidence illuminates the transnational ramifications of the "deep-seated" Russian intelligentsia "tradition, existing long before 1917, of regarding the function of art as social transformation for the collective good."[32] It is striking that Mamoulian dated his abandonment of the philosophy of "art for art's sake" to his nineteenth year, when he was studying with Evgeny Vakhtangov at the Moscow Art Theater. Mamoulian never wrote about his years, about 1915 to 1918, at the Moscow Art Theater, but fragmentary evidence in his extensive archive suggests its importance.[33] Significantly, in these years Vakhtangov and other actors from the Moscow Art Theater "organized a troupe of about twenty workers who met twice a week to rehearse adaptations of stories by Chekhov, Turgenev, [Vladimir] Korolenko, and Gorky, as well as vaudevilles and light comic skits."[34] For all their differences, the dapper émigré and the Stalinist bureaucrat shared the middlebrow perspective that there was something wrong with elitist art.

---

[28] Typescript of interview, 9 July 1935, Mamoulian Papers, Box 54, Folder 2, pp. 2, 3; Luhrssen, *Mamoulian*, 77–80.

[29] "Rhythm on Screen," NYT, 11 February 1934.

[30] Radio talk and *Los Angeles Times*, 5 April 1970, as quoted in Joseph Horowitz, *"On My Way": The Untold Story of Rouben Mamoulian, George Gershwin, and Porgy and Bess* (New York: W. W. Norton, 2013), 15.

[31] Evgeny Dobrenko and Natalia Jonsson-Skradol, *State Laughter: Stalinism, Populism, and the Origins of Soviet Culture* (Oxford: Oxford University Press, 2022), 384.

[32] Fairclough, "Was Soviet Music Middlebrow?" 366; Michael David-Fox, *Crossing Borders: Modernity, Ideology, and Culture in Russia and the Soviet Union* (Pittsburgh: University of Pittsburgh Press, 2015), 48–71.

[33] Horowitz, *"On My Way,"* 10–11.

[34] E. Anthony Swift, *Popular Theater and Society in Tsarist Russia* (Berkeley: University of California Press, 2002), 200.

Mamoulian's invitation brought Ilf and Petrov to *Porgy and Bess* on 4 November 1935, shortly before high costs prompted the producers to trim the large eighty-two-member cast and forty-five-piece orchestra.[35] The opera impressed Ilf as both a mesmerizing representation of Black otherness and, somewhat paradoxically, a symbol of America. As we have seen, Ilf took pleasure in the "Negro mysticism" of Catfish Row. At the same time, he was fascinated by *Porgy and Bess*'s quintessentially American hybridity: "The Armenian Mamoulian staged it; the Jewish Girshfeld [sic] composed the music; [Sergei] Soudeikin, [best known for his work with Ballets Russes,] did the scenic design, and Negroes did the acting. Overall, a triumph of American art."[36] Ilf's assessment echoed almost verbatim an enthusiastic review in the American Jewish press that got the composer's name right: "That this cosmopolitan Jew [George Gershwin] should see a work by two 'Nordics' [playwrights DuBose and Dorothy Heyward], based upon the life of the humble Negro and produced by a polyglot Russian [Mamoulian], is a profoundly American symbol" and "a notable American achievement."[37] If Ilf's praise had a more ironic edge, he nonetheless shared a positive assessment of the cultural borrowing and mixing crucial to "American" art and identity.

Ilf's reactions were in line with Gershwin's own stated intentions for *Porgy and Bess*. The composer, too, framed his understandings of the story, the music, and the performers in the language of romantic racialism, while insisting on the opera's status as "American" art. Ten days after the show opened, Gershwin, in an article in the *New York Times*, tried to clarify *Porgy and Bess*'s often confusion-inducing subtitle, "an American folk opera." The story, he explained is a "folk tale" and "its people naturally would sing folk music." Wanting "the music to be all of one piece," he wrote his own spirituals and folksongs, thereby raising Black vernacular music into "a larger and more serious form."[38] Gershwin apparently saw no problem with writing his own "Black" folk music. African American critics, however, challenged what they viewed as his appropriation and distortion of the "Negro musical idiom." The composer Virgil Thomson called the opera "fake folk-lore." The *Amsterdam News*'s review charged that *Porgy and Bess* "smacks of minstrel days."[39] Indeed, Gershwin described himself as accepting the (from his perspective positive) stereotypes of the minstrel show. In composing his

---

[35] Horowitz, *"On My Way,"* 128; Noonan, *Strange Career*, 151–52.

[36] PIA, Il'f, 4 November 1935, 443.   [37] Noonan, *Strange Career*, 175 and 353n71.

[38] George Gershwin, "Rhapsody in Catfish Row," NYT, 20 October 1935.

[39] As quoted in Ray Allen, "An American Folk Opera: Triangulating Folkness, Blackness, and Americanness in Gershwin and Heyward's *Porgy and Bess*," *Journal of American Folklore* 117 (2004): 253.

opera of "Negro life," he explained, he utilized "the drama, the humor, the superstition, the religious fervor, the dancing and the irrepressible high spirits of the race." The music, he asserted, required of the performers only "what lies in their race." Yet even as he insisted on racialized difference, Gershwin clearly identified African American folk music and folklore as integral components of *American* identity. *Porgy and Bess*, he stressed, was "American, and I believe that American music should be based on American material." Gershwin's opera constructed a "pan-ethnic Americanism"[40] that anchored American identity in Black music as interpreted by the son of Russian Jewish immigrants.

In his brief note on the opera, Ilf did not concern himself with the question that preoccupied American critics: "What is it?"[41] For Ilf, *Porgy and Bess* was self-evidently "American art." By contrast, American reviewers found Mamoulian and Gershwin's production to be such a perplexing amalgam of serious art and crowd-pleasing entertainment that they struggled to categorize and judge it. Did *Porgy and Bess* succeed in transmuting a stew of jazz, spiritual, Tin Pan Alley, musical theater, recitative, and "synagogue chants"[42] into serious opera? On one hand, John Mason Brown's review in the *New York Post* praised Mamoulian's direction as "virtuoso," "filled with a visual music of its own, which is unfailingly rhythmic."[43] Downes, the *Times*'s music critic, urged the creators of grand opera to take note: "If the Metropolitan chorus could ever put one-half the action into the riot scene of the second act of 'Meistersinger' that the Negro cast put into the fight that followed the craps game, it would be not merely refreshing but miraculous."[44] By contrast, the *Times*'s theater critic Brooks Atkinson deemed Mamoulian less a virtuoso than an flashy entertainer: "He is not subtle, which is a virtue in showmanship. ... the rhythm is comfortably obvious."[45] Ready to praise the production, Downes sniffed that the music's style "is at one moment of opera and another of operetta or sheer Broadway entertainment. It goes without saying that many of the songs in the score of 'Porgy and Bess' will reap a quick popularity."[46] Gershwin may have taken this as a compliment. In his own piece in the *Times* he affirmed, "It was my idea that the opera should be entertaining."

[40] Denning, *Cultural Front*, 130.   [41] Horowitz, *"On My Way,"* 16, 98.
[42] Horowitz, *"On My Way,"* 162.   [43] As quoted in Horowitz, *"On My Way,"* 139.
[44] Olin Downes, "Exotic Richness of Negro Music and Color of Charleston, S. C., Admirably Conveyed in Score of Catfish Row Tragedy," NYT, 11 October 1935.
[45] Brooks Atkinson, "Dramatic Values of Community Legend Gloriously Transposed in New Form with Fine Regard for Its Verities," NYT, 11 October 1935.
[46] Downes, "Exotic Richness."

He aspired, he wrote, to create a "new form" "that would appeal to the many rather than the cultured few."[47]

Gershwin's strategy for creating a popular American art form had much in common with concurrent efforts in the Soviet Union to create accessible people's music. Like Gershwin, Soviet composers repurposed the methods of nineteenth-century romantic nationalism. They incorporated "indigenous folk melodies and harmonies into complex Western forms like opera" to create an "accessible, yet sophisticated, uniquely Soviet hybrid repertoire."[48] Like Gershwin, too, many of those who composed "national" music in the Soviet Union's constituent republics were outsiders to the folk traditions they ostensibly "enriched."[49] Although Soviet composers ultimately aimed to train natives to modernize their own folk traditions, these hybrid compositions reduced minority cultures to their "innate" or "immutable" national characteristics.[50] At once empowering and racializing, Sovietized folk music was "middlebrow" in the sense that that it aimed to "bend" classical music in more popular directions. But from the perspective of those who shared the impulse to create people's art, it was not middlebrow in the derisive sense of being vulgar or dumbed down.

Of course, American and Soviet producers of "people's art" worked within very different systems, one governed by the need for commercial success, the other by the state's ideological demands. While these differences were significant, they generated similar obstacles that could be negotiated in similar ways. Stalin, with his alleged fondness for hummable tunes, shaped the artistic agenda in the Soviet Union. In the United States, "artistically untrained movie, radio, and music executives did the same thing."[51] Gershwin, for one, was deeply insulted when MGM studio head Samuel Goldwyn asked him why he didn't write "hit songs you can whistle."[52] Frustrating or dangerous as they could be, neither the bean counters nor the apparatchiks exercised absolute control. A noncommercial theater like the Theater Guild, which

[47] Gershwin, "Rhapsody."

[48] Leah Goldman, "Nationally Informed: The Politics of National Minority Music during Late Stalinism," *Jahrbücher für Geschichte Osteuropas* 67 (2019): 377; Luhrssen, *Mamoulian*, 82.

[49] Goldman, "Nationally Informed," 379; Marina Frolova-Walker, "'National in Form, Socialist in Content': Musical Nation-Building in the Soviet Republics," *Journal of the American Musicological Society* 51 (Summer 1998): 335–36.

[50] Brigid O'Keeffe, "The Racialization of Soviet Gypsies: Roma, Nationality Politics, and Socialist Transformation in Stalin's Soviet Union," in David Rainbow, ed., *Ideologies of Race: Imperial Russia and the Soviet Union in Global Context* (Montreal: McGill-Queens University Press, 2019), 133.

[51] Stites, *Russian Popular Culture*, 95.   [52] Horowitz, *"On My Way,"* 171.

produced *Porgy and Bess* on Broadway, offered a way to stage an enormously expensive show that "closed in the red."[53] Even under Stalin there was some room to maneuver; state mandates and close party supervision relied on (unequal) "dialogue" between artists and ideologues.[54] Moreover, as the musicologist Pauline Fairclough notes in her discussion of whether Soviet music was middlebrow, the fact of state control did not rule out the possibility that Soviet composers (or other cultural producers) agreed with the notion that "'high art' had a clear duty to entertain, uplift, and inform," and that many found remarkable ways of expressing "their own taste" while performing their "civic duty."[55] Likewise, Gershwin, who died of a brain tumor in 1937 at age thirty-eight, might, like Mamoulian, have found a way to make money and art in Hollywood.

The decade of the 1930s was, in Rockwell's felicitous phrase, the "apex of middlebrow culture." New recording, broadcast, and film technologies allowed ambitious cultural productions to reach a "vast, democratized audience."[56] In the United States, pleasing this audience became big business. But even in America, middlebrow culture was about more than making money. It was part of what the American studies scholar Michael Denning calls the "laboring of American culture." Democratizing the production and consumption of art, middlebrow culture opened opportunities for immigrants, Jews, African Americans, women, children of working-class families, and other outsiders to create some of "the most powerful and lasting works of twentieth century American fiction, music, theater, and film."[57] In the Soviet Union, middlebrow culture "offered a way of legitimizing what had once been thought of as 'bourgeois' concerns." Rising numbers of newly literate urbanized peasants and educated workers eagerly engaged in "cultured consumption," which included consumption of literary and musical "classics."[58] And the Soviet middlebrow, too, could produce extraordinary works of art like Shostakovich's Fifth Symphony.[59]

[53] Horowitz, *"On My Way,"* 138; Luhrssen, *Mamoulian*, 89.
[54] Serhy Yekelchyk, "Diktat and Dialogue in Stalinist Culture: Staging Patriotic Historical Opera in Soviet Ukraine, 1936–1954," *Slavic Review* 59 (Autumn 2000): 624.
[55] Fairclough, "Was Soviet Music Middlebrow?" 366–67.
[56] Rockwell, "1935"; Joseph Horowitz, *Understanding Toscanini: A Social History of American Concert Life* (Berkeley: University of California Press, [1987] 1994), 7.
[57] Denning, *Cultural Front*, 117–18.
[58] Sheila Fitzpatrick, "Becoming Cultured: Socialist Realism and the Representation of Taste and Privilege," in *The Cultural Front: Power and Culture in Revolutionary Russia* (Ithaca, NY: Cornell University Press, 1992), 218.
[59] Fairclough, "Was Soviet Music Middlebrow?" 367; Laurel Fay, *Shostakovich: A Life* (New York: Oxford University Press, 1999), 104.

The desire for respectability and seriousness constituted a defining feature of middlebrow culture on both sides of the capitalist–socialist divide. In the Soviet Union, culturedness (*kulturnost*) was associated with "a sense of becoming, striving, and taking possession."[60] In 1936, *Ogonek* ran quizzes under the rubric, "Are You a Cultured Person?" that encouraged readers to gauge their own level of *kulturnost*: Can you recite a Pushkin poem by heart, summarize "the plots of Shakespeare's plays," and demonstrate "familiarity with mathematics, geography, and the classics of Marxism–Leninism"?[61] Socialist realism in the arts fed this hunger for culturedness as it demanded that artists produce paintings, novels, symphonies, or operas accessible to and thus capable of uplifting the masses.

In the United States, there was, of course, no state mandate for accessible, uplifting art. But Gershwin's desire for "the respect accorded classical composers" and his "dream of serious American musical theater"[62] point to an analogous interest in creating popular art that would raise the status of both its producers and consumers. For *Porgy and Bess*'s African American players, the production of respectability was particularly fraught. Barred from opera stages, the conservatory-trained singers had to balance the opportunity to perform against the show's perpetuation of racist stereotypes and the requirement that the cast "speak and sing in the dialect of the Negroes of 'Catfish Row.'" The African American press and the performers themselves took pains to highlight "the social, educational, and linguistic distance that separated them from the characters they portrayed onstage."[63] Fifty years after the Broadway premier, Anna Brown, the Julliard graduate who played Bess, remembered that her father, a doctor, "didn't like it at all. ... He said it perpetuated the image of blacks as lazy people, singing hymns and taking dope." But she herself believed "if it brought us forward in American music and in opera roles for black singers, then we should do it."[64] For critics, it was the "striving" aspect of middlebrow culture that gave it a bad name. Highbrows in the United States shared the fears expressed by Virginia Woolf that rather than raising up the masses, middlebrow culture succeeded only in "rather nastily" mixing art "with money, fame, power, or prestige."[65] But the concerns that cultural producers and consumers of middlebrow culture expressed about respectability,

[60] Fitzpatrick, "Becoming Cultured," 218.   [61] David-Fox, *Crossing Borders*, 64.
[62] Rockwell, "1935."   [63] Noonan, *Strange Career*, 166.
[64] As quoted in Noonan, *Strange Career*, 168.
[65] As quoted in Victoria Grieve, *The Federal Art Project and the Creation of Middlebrow Culture* (Urbana: University of Illinois Press, 2009), 4.

representation, and authenticity can also be read more generously as indicators of their faith in the transformative power of art.

To draw a sharp contrast between America and the Soviet Union, Ilf and Petrov largely ignored American middlebrow culture. They seem to have appreciated the ambition to produce a truly popular, pan-ethnic opera. But they disregarded or simply missed the possibility that Americans, no less than Soviet people, aspired to become cultured. Because Ilf and Petrov encountered middlebrow culture mainly in New York, they may have understood it, like skyscrapers, as existing outside the "real" America they sought. On the road, their main cultural fare was movies, which they dismissed as vulgar, violent, and formulaic trash. In low-rise America, Ilf and Petrov reported finding no middle culture, much less high culture; they did not recount hearing a classical concert west of Chicago. They told the story of their American road trip not as contrast between "high" and "low" but between technical marvels and cultural blight.

Part III

To the Pacific Ocean

With their sights set on what they called "Indian Country" and beyond that Hollywood, Ilf and Petrov traveled quickly, at least by 1935 standards, across the heart of low-rise America. Often covering more than 250 miles per day, they made the trip from Chicago to Santa Fe, New Mexico, in six days. Except for a stop in Mark Twain's hometown of Hannibal, Missouri, they did little sightseeing along the way. Maintaining a pace that required at least five hours of driving daily, they saw the Midwest primarily as a series of gas stations, diners, and small towns. On the road, they met "average" Americans by chance. Much to Ilf and Petrov's surprise, in Kansas City, Missouri, they encountered a Russian Jewish immigrant. Overhearing the travelers speaking Russian, the proprietor of a coffee shop, who had emigrated from Bessarabia thirty-five years earlier, asked where they lived, "told his full life story and showed photographs of his relatives."[1] More frequently, they – or to be precise, Solomon Trone – grilled the hitchhikers who joined them in their Ford.

The pace of Ilf and Petrov's travel slowed considerably when they reached the Southwest. The travelers spent nine days exploring Santa Fe, Taos, the Petrified Forest, the Grand Canyon, and Zion Canyon on their way to Boulder City, Nevada, where the Boulder Dam was in the final stages of construction. In the desert, Ilf and Petrov were less inter-ested in average Americans than in finding the mythical American West. Here, too, they attracted the unexpected attention of a Russian immigrant, who heard them speaking Russian in a gift shop in Taos, New Mexico.

Ilf and Petrov's route to Santa Fe followed US Route 66. Because the legendary highway, decommissioned in 1985, has inspired so many nostalgic guidebooks, it is possible to imagine the road as they would have seen it.[2] A historic Texaco station that looks much as it did in the

---

[1] PIA, Il'f, 19 November 1935, 453.
[2] Michael Dregli, ed., *Greetings from Route 66: The Ultimate Road Trip Back through Time along America's Main Street* (Minneapolis: Voyageur Press, 2010); Peter Dedek, *Hip to the Trip: A Cultural History of Route 66* (Albuquerque: University of New Mexico Press, 2007).

1940s serves as a visitor center in Dwight, Illinois, their first stop some seventy-five miles out of Chicago.[3] The visit to Hannibal, where visitors can still see the statue of Huck Finn and Tom Sawyer "starting out on a mischief bent" that charmed Ilf and Petrov, required a detour.[4] After a night in Nevada, Missouri, they picked up Route 66 again, overnighting in Oklahoma City and Amarillo, Texas, before reaching Santa Fe on 22 November. They stayed at the unassuming Montezuma Hotel (at Water and Galisteo Streets), a building, since replaced, that did not conform to the "old Santa Fe" architectural style that began to dominate the city in the early twentieth century.[5]

While much of old Route 66 no longer exists, the Native American villages and national parks that Ilf and Petrov visited in the Southwest appear today much as they would have seen them. Following their usually quite accurate notes, I followed their itinerary from Santa Fe to Boulder City, stopping at some of the same roadside attractions and hotels, and eating some of the same foods. In Santa Fe, the enchiladas are still as Ilf and Petrov described them: "appetizing blintzes stuffed with red pepper and finely chopped gunpowder, and sprinkled with nitroglycerine."[6] I investigated archival, library, and museum collections in Santa Fe, Taos, Albuquerque, and Boulder City, where I located letters, newspaper clippings, and paintings that shed light on the people and places with whom the Soviet visitors interacted.

Retracing Ilf and Petrov's footsteps, locating the spots where Ilf shot his photographs, I tried to see the country through their eyes. The process posed fundamental questions of how and whether we can understand people separated from us by identity, ideology, language – and time. This is in many ways the basic problem of historical research. Historians always operate as outsiders, separated from the object of their study by time and often much else besides. Investigating Ilf and Petrov's efforts to observe, understand, and empathize across political, cultural, and linguistic boundaries raised essential historical questions in particularly acute forms. How does outsider status shape, warp, or perhaps enhance our powers of observation? Where does interpretation end and judgment begin? Can we set aside, however briefly, our own presuppositions and glimpse the world and the Other anew? Appreciating the Other's perspective, can we laugh at ourselves?

---

[3] Joe Sonderman and Cheryl Eichar Jett, *Route 66 in Illinois* (Charleston, SC: Arcadia Publishing, 2014), 38–40.

[4] "Starting Out on a Mischief Bent," https://twain.lib.virginia.edu/tomsawye/nostalgia/26nemisshp.html (accessed 31 July 2021).

[5] Don D. Fowler, *A Laboratory of Anthropology: Science and Romanticism in the American Southwest, 1846–1930* (Albuquerque: University of New Mexico Press, 2000), 348–50.

[6] LGA, 138; OA, 186.

13   The Road

> When you close your eyes and try to resurrect the memory of the country in which you spent four months – you imagine not Washington with its gardens, columns, and full complement of monuments, nor New York with its skyscrapers and its poverty and wealth, nor San Francisco with its steep streets and suspension bridges, not mountains, factories, or canyons, but the intersection of two roads and a gas station against the background of wires and advertising billboards.
>
> Ilf and Petrov, *Low-Rise America*

Ilf and Petrov were masters of the literary road trip. In the Ostap Bender novels, they sent the smooth operator across the Soviet Union from the Black Sea to Siberia. As in a classical picaresque, the *pícaro*, the rogue or rascal at the center of the story, was an "amoral outsider but not an outright villain." The time–space of the road structured the chance meetings, incidents, and accidents that occasioned the pícaro's satirical "survey of the world in its vast social heterogeneity."[1] In the Soviet case, the road provided an especially effective satirical motif; Bender's travels evoked the governing metaphor of Soviet ideology, the "road to communism."[2] Set during the moderate New Economic Policy of the 1920s, *The Twelve Chairs* provided a panorama of Soviet society in transition and of the shady characters hoping to profit along the gradual path to socialism. By the time of Bender's journey in *The Little Golden Calf*,

---

[1] Jonathan Greenberg, *The Cambridge Introduction to Satire* (New York: Cambridge University Press, 2019): 186, 187; Karen L. Ryan, "Imagining America: Il'f and Petrov's 'Odnoetazhnaia Amerika' and Ideological Alterity," *Canadian Slavonic Papers* 44 (September–December 2002): 267; Milla Fedorova, *Yankees in Petrograd, Bolsheviks in New York: America and Americans in Russian Literary Perception* (DeKalb: Northern Illinois University Press, 2006), 90–92; Lesley Milne, *How They Laughed: Zoshchenko and the Ilf–Petrov Partnership* (Birmingham: Centre for Russian and East European Studies, 2003), 145.

[2] Lars Lih, "The Soviet Union and the Road to Communism," in Ronald Grigor Suny, ed., *The Cambridge History of Russia*, vol. 3, *The Twentieth Century* (New York: Cambridge University Press, 2006), 706.

gradualism had given way to breakneck industrialization, and alongside the satirized remnants of the former world, Bender also encountered the earnest builders of the road to communism, specifically the Turkestan–Siberian Railway.[3]

Low-Rise America, too, can be read as a picaresque. Narrating their own fictionalized autobiography in the first-person plural, Ilf and Petrov were not exactly rogues; although they admitted to feeling like scoundrels when convincing the Trones to leave their baby in New York. Casting Solomon Trone as Charles Dickens's "Pickwick," Ilf and Petrov became members of the Pickwick Club, who traveled around provincial England, avidly recording what they saw and the tall tales they heard on the road.[4] In conformity with the norms of the picaresque, and in violation of "official Soviet literary doctrine," *Low-Rise America*'s collective narrator appeared as a pawn of "Capricious Fortune," buffeted by the unexpected circumstances, strange coincidences, and characters met along the road.[5]

Low-Rise America deviated from the traditional picaresque in one important way: Ilf and Petrov turned their gaze on the ideological Other, not on their own society. With an ironic nod to Mark Twain, they posed as innocents abroad. Still, as they affirmed at the end of their travelogue, they constantly saw the Soviet "road to communism" reflected in the mirror of the beautifully paved American "road to nowhere."[6] Ilf and Petrov's American road trip never led them to doubt the superiority of the Soviet destination. However, it did "make them think about concrete flaws in Soviet life."[7] As they navigated America, they critiqued both the United States and their own society, however gently and implicitly.

The road, of course, was more than a metaphor. It was the central material reality of Ilf and Petrov's trip. For the reader acquainted with real Soviet roads, the unspoken contrast with American highways would have been obvious. For those of us without the required frame of reference, an American account of the inverse road trip – a 6,000-mile (approximately 10,000-kilometer) journey across the Soviet Union – offers a useful means of contextualizing Ilf and Petrov's observations. In 1929, George S. Counts, a progressive educator and professor at

[3] Cassio Ferreira de Oliveira, "Writing Rogues: The Soviet Picaresque, 1921–1938" (PhD diss., Yale University, 2014), 119–20.

[4] PIA, Il'f, 10 December 1935, 469.

[5] Deming Brown, "O. Henry in Russia," *Russian Review* 12 (October 1953): 258; Greenberg, *Cambridge Introduction*, 187.

[6] Jason Spangler, "We're on a Road to Nowhere: Steinbeck, Kerouac, and the Legacy of the Great Depression," *Studies in the Novel* 40 (Fall 2008): 308–27.

[7] Fedorova, *Yankees*, 93.

Columbia University's Teachers College, who was sympathetic to Soviet pedagogical experiments, spent the late summer and early fall exploring the country in a new two-door Ford he imported for the purpose. Traveling at the beginning of the First Five-Year Plan, Counts optimistically predicted "a better road ahead" and advised that "the foreign motorist, who desires to encounter the conditions which I have described ... should not postpone his journey to the distant future."[8] This advice turned out to be unfounded.

Counts's 1929 travelogue allows us to picture the Soviet roads that in 1935 Ilf and Petrov carried in their minds' eyes. The six years that separated Counts's journey from theirs hardly affected the Soviet highway system. In 1928, there were perhaps 20,000 motor vehicles in the Soviet Union, not all in working order. During the industrialization drive of the early 1930s, Soviet planners focused on increasing production of tractors and trucks, not passenger cars.[9] By 1937, there were a few more auto tourists on the road than in 1929, when on the 500-mile trip from Leningrad to Moscow, "one of the best roads between the two largest and most famous cities in Soviet Russia," Counts "saw but two automobiles beyond the limits of the cities."[10] But the traffic on Soviet highways remained sparse and slow; gas stations few and far between; and guidebooks nonexistent.[11] Ilf and Petrov were wholly unprepared for the unnerving experience of "tens of thousands" of cars "sweeping you along with them in their satanic flight."[12] Even on the eve of World War II, the "vast majority" of Soviet roads were not merely unpaved; they were ungraded, rutted dirt. Only in 1965, when the Soviet highway system included about 132,000 kilometers (82,000 miles) of paved asphalt or concrete highway, did it roughly match the US highway system of 1920.[13]

The Soviet context allows us to better appreciate Ilf and Petrov's tone, at once awestruck and tongue-in-cheek. They described the American gas station as a minor miracle. In their enraptured telling, a mechanic in a cap, striped overalls, and "a black leather bow tie ... inserted a rubber hose into the opening of the tank, and the pump began to automatically count the number of gallons our car swallowed up. Simultaneously, figures popped up on the pump's counter, indicating the cost of the petrol. With each new gallon, the apparatus emitted a melodious ring."

[8] George S. Counts, *A Ford Crosses Soviet Russia* (Boston: Stratford Co., 1930), 31, 43.
[9] Lewis H. Siegelbaum, *Cars for Comrades: The Life of the Soviet Automobile* (Ithaca, NY: Cornell University Press, 2011), 183, 21.
[10] Counts, *Ford Crosses Soviet Russia*, 77 (quotation), 28.
[11] Siegelbaum, *Cars for Comrades*, 206.   [12] LGA, 61; OA, 79.
[13] Siegelbaum, *Cars for Comrades*, 157, 169, 127, 205–206.

The ringing, like the leather bow tie, was mere "technical chic"; the process worked as well without it. Hardly had the melodious ringing subsided than the "great American *servis*" began. The attendant with the leather tie checked the oil and the tires, cleaned the windshield, adjusted a door, proffered an up-to-date map indicating stretches of road under construction and places to spend the night, and shared the weather forecast. This overwhelming service was, they reported, entirely free of charge, regardless of the amount of gas purchased or whether one was driving an old Chevy (*shevrolishka*) or a sparkling Deusenberg that cost thousands.[14]

Nothing could be further from Counts's description of the forty-five- or even ninety-minute ordeal of filling up in the Soviet Union. Seeking gas, he encountered not the "small, neat building" with "six, eight, or even ten red or yellow pumps" that greeted Ilf and Petrov everywhere in the United States, but a "primitive," out-of-the-way warehouse that kept odd and inconvenient hours. He found not an eager attendant, but a "complete absence of what might be called the spirit and tactics of salesmanship." Before obtaining any gasoline, you had to "convince those who dispense it that your cause is a worthy one." This might require a permit from the local police. Although Counts suggests no such thing, a less scrupulous traveler might have tried a bribe. Then the process could begin in earnest: "After you have signed an order for the amount of gasoline required you wait patiently while it is drained out of a cask and weighed. It is then brought to your car in a pail, often from a considerable distance, and poured into the tank through a funnel. In some cases, however, the funnel may be lacking, so you soon discover that you should carry one of your own." This was, Counts concluded, a "slow" and "wasteful" process, as "gasoline is spilled at both ends of the service." No wonder Ilf and Petrov made the ringing gas pump into a symbol of what Counts called "luxuriously standardized" American automobile travel.[15]

Both Counts and the Soviet travelers understood the road as an index of progress. When Counts reflected on "Russia today," he thought of "the grass-covered highways of the north with their hidden ruts that lay in wait for the wheels of the car." He took the reactions of dogs to his Ford as a clear indicator of a society "not adjusted to the automobile": "On seeing the car approach," village dogs "run in front of the automobile and then discover too late that it is more fleet than they." Anticipating

[14] OA, 79–81.   [15] Counts, *Ford Crosses Soviet Russia*, 102–103, 60.

change, Counts explained empty, unpaved, unmarked Soviet roads as relics "of a simple rural civilization."[16]

By contrast, Ilf and Petrov rhapsodized over pavement that was "ideally smooth"; the abundance and accuracy of road signs; and the reliable availability of gasoline, maps, and "service." They deemed the highway "one of the most remarkable phenomena of American life." "Wise American dogs" were already used to it: they "never race after cars with an optimistic bark. They know how that ends. They will be crushed – and that's it."[17] When they closed their eyes and conjured the country they had visited, they saw a gas station at an empty crossroads. In their photo essay, they captioned an image of just such an intersection "This is America!"[18] The statement can be read as both a satirical comment on the cultural barrenness of capitalist America and, given the miracle of the gas pump, an emblem of luxurious standardization.

On the road, as in American cities, Ilf and Petrov highlighted the paradox of poverty in a land of technical wonders. In two chapters of *Low-Rise America*, they presented the tales of woe that Solomon Trone extracted from the hitchhikers they picked up along the magnificent highway. When a "young marine" climbed into their Ford in Oklahoma, Trone immediately set to work "dissecting" him "before our eyes."[19] The twenty-one-year-old and his traveling companion, who hitched a ride in a black Buick, had taken a month's leave to make the trip from New York to their new post in San Francisco. He immediately revealed himself as uncultured if not downright immoral. The two marines, the hitchhiker confessed, were running behind schedule, having spent not three hours but nine days in Chicago, where, he explained, "We met some nice girls." The marine told them, too, about an "enormous scandal" he and six of his shipmates had caused when, on leave in Paris, they dodged a check, telling the restaurant manager to "Deduct the price of our dinner from the war debt France still owes to America."[20]

On more serious matters, the hitchhiker articulated clear understandings of political and personal problems but demonstrated little hope that his opinion mattered or that he had any control over his own fate. When asked what he thought about war, the young marine expressed the view that "we fought" the recent war in Nicaragua, "not in the interests of the United States but in the interests of United Fruit." (This was a largely

---

[16] Counts, *Ford Crosses Soviet Russia*, 139–40, 75–76, 41.   [17] OA, 78, 83–84.
[18] OA, 84; Il'ia Il'f and Evgenii Petrov, "Amerikanskie fotografii: Doroga," *Ogonek*, no. 11 (20 April 1936): 6.
[19] OA, 170.   [20] LGA, 128; OA, 171; ZK, 21 November, 450.

correct, if simplified analysis of US businesses' support for the jungle war waged between 1927 and 1933 against a "small army of peasants, workers, and foreign volunteers" led by Augusto Sandino.) The marine's scathing assessment notwithstanding, he suggested there was nothing he could do: "I am a soldier, so I must submit to discipline."[21] He also needed to keep his job. As an enlisted man, he earned about twenty-five dollars per month, out of which he sent ten dollars to his wife and child in New York.[22] The marine told the travelers that he regretted marrying so young, but fatalistically concluded, "what could you do about it?" Seeing the man off in Amarillo, the writers did not judge him too harshly. He had such a "winning smile" and was so "refreshingly young" that "his misbehavior did not seem offensive to us."[23]

Soon after they left Amarillo, the travelers picked up another hitchhiker, who, unlike most of the "ordinary" Americans Ilf and Petrov met, left a small mark in the historical record. As usual, Trone immediately began his questioning.[24] He quickly realized that he had read their passenger's story in an Oklahoma newspaper. The hitchhiker, identified as "Roberts" in *Low-Rise America*, Ilf's notebook, and the newspaper, but for some reason as "Rogers" in *Little Golden America*, was heading to Arizona. Explaining that his wife was in the hospital in Oklahoma City, he pulled out the clipping that Trone had seen and that I was able to track down. Ilf and Petrov slightly reworked the headline, translating "Months in Bed Fail to Dim Smile" into "She Smiles on Her Bed of Suffering." But their account of Roberts's story matches the article's, which emphasized his wife's good spirits in the face of an accident that had left her paralyzed. The short profile that ran on page twelve of the 20 November 1935 issue of the *Daily Oklahoman* included, just as Ilf and Petrov reported, a photograph of the cheerful, bedridden Mrs. Roberts. The hitchhiker told them that he was going to Phoenix, where a friend was earning eighteen dollars a week packing fruit; he planned to live on six or seven dollars and set aside the rest to pay for his wife's medical treatments[25] (Figure 13.1).

Ilf and Petrov described Roberts as typically American: straightforward, sociable, uncomplaining, and incurious. He obligingly answered

---

[21] LGA, 128; OA, 172; Robert Edgar Conrad, "Translator's Introduction," in Sergio Ramírez, ed., and Robert Edgar Conrad, ed. and trans., *Sandino: The Testimony of a Nicaraguan Patriot, 1921–1934* (Princeton, NJ: Princeton University Press, 1990), 14 (army), 3–19.

[22] OA, 172; "Enlisted Pay Chart 1922–1940," Navy CyberSpace, www.navycs.com/charts/1922-enlisted-pay-chart.html (accessed 13 October 2022).

[23] LGA, 128; OA, 172; ZK, 21 November, 450–51.   [24] OA, 175.

[25] ZK, 22 November, 451: LGA, 130–31; OA, 175.

Figure 13.1 Some of the Americans Ilf and Petrov met on their road trip. Clockwise, from top right: the hitchhiker Roberts; a Mexican from Santa Fe, New Mexico; the assistant to the director of Sing Sing prison; the former boxing champion Mr. Sharkey. From the "Americans" installment of "American Photographs," *Ogonek*, no. 13 (10 May 1936): 12. Courtesy Library of Congress.

"a hundred questions," but asked none. To Ilf and Petrov's surprise, the fact that the travelers talked among themselves in Russian, a language "he had never heard before," did not rouse Roberts's interest.[26] That the hitchhiker, intent on getting where he was going, had more serious things on his mind than asking questions of his Russian-speaking hosts seems not to have occurred to them.

Most fundamentally, Roberts personified what Ilf and Petrov deemed the distinctively American trait of blaming misfortune on "bad luck" rather than injustice. Over the course of several hours, he told them his life story "without appealing to pity or sympathy."[27] He graduated from high school but could not afford college. Instead, he became what they characterized as a "nomad," working as a foreman in a small cannery that followed the harvest. He married the owner's daughter, a teacher. Theirs was "a very happy marriage," centered on going to the movies, visiting friends, dancing, and building a comfortable life that included $2,000 in savings, "eighteen pedigreed cows," an automobile, and, according to Ilf's notebook, a truck.[28] Then suddenly, in February 1934, disaster struck. In the newspaper, Mrs. Roberts described the accident as a "silly way to get hurt"; she fell though the trapdoor of the hayloft of their Arkansas farm and suffered a "compound fracture of the first lumbar." The couple emptied their savings and sold the cows and the car to pay for operations, treatments, and specialists. According to Ilf and Petrov, Roberts told them that the local hospital had charged $25 a week; the hospital in Oklahoma City, identified in the article as McBride Reconstruction, charged twice that. A necessary "metal corset" cost $120. For Ilf and Petrov, "it looked more like a bandit raid than humane medical help." But "Roberts did not in the least complain." Like the marine, he concluded, "It can't be helped. Tough luck!"[29]

Generalizing from their encounters with a handful of passengers, Ilf and Petrov drew broad conclusions about the "American character." While their informants' stories illustrated limited opportunities, the writers' narrative stressed engrained traits. In Roberts's case, they speculated in language they likely did not perceive as racist that it was "perchance the admixture of Indian blood that made our fellow traveler so stoically calm!" Ilf and Petrov represented the hitchhikers they met along the wondrous American highway as congenitally incapable of grasping that it was capitalism – not a lack of luck, frugality, or grit – that sent them down a road to nowhere.

---

[26] LGA, 133; OA, 178–79.   [27] OA, 176.
[28] LGA, 131–32; OA, 176–77; ZK, 22 November, 452.
[29] LGA, 132–33; OA, 177–78; ZK, 22 November, 452.

Low-Rise America echoed only faintly the work of American writers and photographers such as John Steinbeck, Margaret Bouke-White, and Dorothea Lange, who made the barren highway a symbol of dispossession and disillusionment.[30] The grim picture Ilf and Petrov elaborated on the basis of their hitchhikers' misfortunes ran up against the reality that from a Soviet perspective, American poverty could look prosperous. The simple fact that hitchhiking was a reliable mode of travel demonstrated the ubiquity of the American car. The hitchhiker could count on being picked up if not by the first car he saw, then, they noted, "by the fifth, seventh, or tenth."[31] Such a plan was simply unthinkable in the nearly carless Soviet Union. Similarly, the "most important" indication of having passed from the "industrial East" to the "real West" was the appearance of scores of twenty-five-year-old Fords driven by farmers in overalls and cowboys in ten-gallon hats.[32] In his notebook, Ilf described the occupants of one such car heading from Kansas to California: a father looking for work, a mother, a "tow-haired, tear-stained boy, and a dog." The car itself was full of pillows and quilts.[33] These were likely Dust Bowl refugees. But Ilf and Petrov did not include them in their account of the American road.

What impressed Ilf and Petrov was not the migrants' distress, but their cars. *Low-Rise America* included only one brief description of a family on the road: a young Black husband and wife with a "grey-haired mother-in-law" and small children fascinated by the yellow New York license plate of the writers' Ford.[34] Ilf and Petrov did not emphasize the family's poverty – or the rarity of African American travelers.[35] Instead, they sang the praises of the durable, cheap, slightly comical "Old Henry," with a bucket and a step ladder strapped to the side, that carried them. The sight of one of these ancient Fords, with its canvas top in tatters and "nothing but a rusty rim of the spare wheel," elicited their "candid joy."[36] Who could imagine a Russian peasant with a private car, even an ancient one?

Innocents abroad on the American highway, Ilf and Petrov found much to love and much to criticize – about both the United States and the Soviet Union. *Low-Rise America*'s descriptions of astoundingly smooth roads and farmers and cowboys driving their own cars invited readers to draw sharp and unflattering comparisons with the Soviet

---

[30] Christine Bold, "The View from the Road," *American Studies* 29 (Fall 1988): 6–7.
[31] OA, 170.
[32] OA, 159, 174; Jack Reid, *Roadside Americans: The Rise and Fall of Hitchhiking in a Changing Nation* (Chapel Hill: University of North Carolina Press, 2020), 24.
[33] ZK, 22 November, 452.   [34] LGA, 119; OA, 159.
[35] Dedek, *Hip to the Trip*, 38–39.   [36] LGA, 119; OA, 160.

Union. Much of what Ilf and Petrov reported would have been pure fantasy at home. A reflective sign warning, "Dip 30 Feet Away" preceded every dip by precisely thirty feet but was "met with as rarely as the dip itself."[37] A dense network of service stations, restaurants, hotels, motor courts, and rooms for rent made it easy to have the oil changed every 1,000 miles, gather information about the road ahead, and find a meal and a comfortable bed in the most remote places. Here, the unspoken object of their satirical gaze was the Soviet road.

At the same time, Ilf and Petrov implicitly touted the superiority of the rutted but hopeful Soviet road to communism. The hitchhikers' sad stories served as clear reminders that the land of the capitalists was hell. Roberts's tale provided an object lesson in how the lack of affordable healthcare could turn a personal tragedy into a financial disaster. Lamenting the shortcomings of the "American character," Ilf and Petrov pitied Roberts. They reserved their scorn for the upbeat way in which the press reported his experience. The photograph of his smiling, paralyzed wife illustrated how the American fixation on individual responsibility obscured systemic and heartbreaking injustice. They condemned the American "poverty propaganda" that, as a more recent critic notes, turns the "inhumanity of capitalist culture" into a heartwarming human-interest story.[38]

Still, Ilf and Petrov did not dwell on the hard-luck cases. While they dutifully documented the failings of capitalism, they usually worked in a lighter vein, making fun of the extremes to which American capitalism took efficiency and standardization. Here, they relied less on American informants than their own sensations. As they ate their way across America, they granted that food was plentiful and usually cheap. But, they insisted, it was rarely tasty.

---

[37] LGA, 64; OA, 83.
[38] Kali Holloway, "'Feel Good' News Story or Poverty Propaganda?" *Nation* (1 October 2021): 7.

14 Frozen Meat, Salty Butter, and Other American Delicacies

> For a long time, we could not understand why American dishes, so lovely to look at, are so unappealing in taste. At first, we thought that they just didn't know how to cook there. But then we learned that this was not the whole story; the cause lay in the organization itself, in the very essence of the American economic system.
>
> Ilf and Petrov, *Low-Rise America*

In the United States, Ilf and Petrov ate lots of steaks but claimed they never enjoyed them. Why, one wonders, did they keep ordering a food that always disappointed? Perhaps it was their devotion to thorough investigation and a sense of responsibility to their readers. Or perhaps they overstated their aversion to frozen meat.

Praising American food presented greater challenges than praising American roads. No one pretended that the Soviet Union had a modern highway system. This was an aspiration for which the United States could provide a legitimate model. But by 1935, Soviet promises of plenty were everywhere. The food ministry had its own advertising branch that extolled the pleasures of foods and other consumer goods that allegedly filled – or would soon fill – store shelves.[1] This food fantasy – the historian Sheila Fitzpatrick calls it "consumer-goods pornography" – was part and parcel of socialist realism, the aesthetic conflation of what was and what would be.[2] In the United States, the abundance the Soviet state promised was widely, if not equitably, available. Ilf and Petrov could not deny this, but nor could they fully concede it. So, readers were treated to descriptions of T-bone steaks and exotic juices accompanied by disclaimers that these foods rarely tasted as good as they looked or sounded.

---

[1] Edward Geist, "Cooking Bolshevik: Anastas Mikoian and the Making of the *Book about Delicious and Healthy Food*," *Russian Review* 71 (April 2012): 303.

[2] Sheila Fitzpatrick, *Everyday Stalinism: Ordinary Life in Extraordinary Times: Soviet Russia in the 1930s* (New York: Oxford University Press, 1999), 90; Ronald D. LeBlanc, "The Mikoyan Mini-Hamburger, or How the Socialist Realist Novel about the Meat Industry Was Created," *Gastronomica* 16, no. 2 (2016): 39–40.

The most alluring description of American food in *Low-Rise America* comes in an early chapter that describes the wonders of a Manhattan cafeteria. Ilf and Petrov took Soviet readers, who in 1937 were struggling to find staples,[3] down the cafeteria line with them. The tour is overwhelming, even to someone acquainted with such buffets. As Ilf and Petrov pushed their trays along the "three rows of nickeled pipes," they surveyed the glass cases "filled with beautiful, appetizing dishes":

soups, chunks of roast, sausages of various lengths and thickness, legs of pork, roulades, mashed, fried, and boiled potatoes and potatoes shaped into some kind of balls, Brussels sprouts, spinach, carrots, and many more side dishes. ... Then came salads and vinaigrettes, various hors d'oeuvres, fish in cream sauce and jellied fish. Then came bread, sweet rolls, traditional round pies with apple, strawberry, and pineapple fillings.

Finally came coffee and milk followed by compote and ice cream, oranges, grapefruit halves (which tasted like "an orange with a dash of lemon"), and large and small glasses of various juices – orange, grapefruit, and tomato – all displayed on chipped ice. On each table the diner found bottles of oil, vinegar, ketchup, and other condiments along with "granulated sugar in a glass bottle set up like a pepper shaker with holes in the metal stopper."[4]

Ilf and Petrov were as amazed by the organization of the cafeteria as the plentiful, varied, and strange foods on offer. Before getting in line, customers took a ticket dispensed with a "melodic ring" from a metal slot. As they selected dishes, "neat but heavily rouged and permed girls in pink headdresses" punched their tickets with the cost of each item. Leaving the establishment required passing the cashier, presenting the ticket, and paying for the meal. At this final stage, patrons could buy cigarettes and help themselves to a free toothpick. "The process of eating," they concluded, "was just as superbly rationalized as the production of automobiles and typewriters."[5]

Only several pages, and further descriptions of splendidly organized, immaculately clean, well-provisioned, low-cost restaurants later did readers learn the problem with this capitalist cornucopia: "All this beautifully prepared food is quite tasteless." It filled the stomach, might even be healthy, but did not offer "any delights, any gustatory satisfaction." Ilf and Petrov warned their readers that eating the "attractive piece of roast" always made "you feel like a buyer of shoes which proved to be more handsome than substantial."[6] It is hard to believe that Soviet consumers, who rarely encountered shoes, let alone the dazzling array of foods

[3] Geist, "Cooking Bolshevik," 308; Fitzpatrick, *Everyday Stalinism*, 40–44.
[4] OA, 28–29.   [5] LGA, 24–25; OA, 28–29.   [6] LGA, 26–27; OA, 31.

available at a budget New York cafeteria, would take this "trouble" too seriously. An insubstantial piece of roast was surely better than no roast all. Nonetheless, Ilf and Petrov stuck to this objection to American food throughout their journey.

Ilf and Petrov emphasized that "rationalized" American food was not only tasteless; it was monotonous. On the road, they were in the habit of eating at drugstore lunch counters that they claimed everywhere offered identical but allegedly unsatisfying choices. Early in their trip they stopped at a small-town pharmacy north of New York City, where they encountered the reality that American druggists, whom big pharmaceutical companies had largely pushed out of the business of compounding medicines, sold more cigarettes, sundries, lunches, and ice-cream sodas than drugs.[7] However similar, few of these drugstores, especially in small towns, would have been part of national chains. In 1935, when there were more than 58,000 drugstores in the United States, the largest chain, Chicago-based Walgreen Company, had 500 corner locations, mostly in Midwestern cities.[8]

Still, in Ilf and Petrov's telling, drugstore menus across America had a sad sameness. The diner always faced a choice between Dinner #1, Dinner #2, Dinner #3, and Dinner #4. "Dinner #4," they reported "costs twice as much as Dinner #2, but that doesn't mean it is twice as good," simply that there is "twice as much of it": "If in Dinner #2 a course called '*kantri sosidzh*' [country sausage] consists of three chopped off sausages, then in Dinner #4 there will be six chopped off sausages, but the taste will be exactly the same." Clear across the country in Santa Fe, they found the same "numbered, standardized, and centralized food," featuring such culinary delights as "sweet and sour pickles"; "bacon fried to the consistency of plywood"; and "blindingly white" bread that tasted like cotton.[9] They neglected to mention that the bread came with butter.

Did Ilf and Petrov perhaps enjoy some of their lunches more than they let on? Drugstore meals, the fast food of the 1930s, certainly had their critics; the food writer Duncan Hines deemed the drugstore lunch counter the most "sinister" influence "in the modern social order." "How in God's name," he wondered, "can anyone who regularly eats drugstore snacks ever be expected to recognize a good meal when it's served?"[10]

---

[7] OA, 85; Oscar Lerner, "What Is Left of the Drug Business?" *Nation* (23 May 1934): 590–91; Louis Browdy, "Lo, the Poor Druggist," *Forum and Century* (September 1936): 129–33; Henrietta Ripperger, "The Business Man Orders Luncheon," NYT, 21 October 1934; Benjamin Y. Urick and Emily V. Meggs, "Toward a Greater Professional Standing: Evolution of Pharmacy Practice and Education, 1920–2020," *Pharmacy* 7, no. 98 (2019): 1–3.

[8] "500 Corner Drugstores," *Fortune* (September 1935): 71–80, 100.

[9] LGA, 66, 138; OA, 86, 185.

[10] As quoted in Louis Hatchett, *Duncan Hines: How a Traveling Salesman Became the Most Trusted Name in Food* (Lexington: University Press of Kentucky, 2014), 138.

By contrast, essayist Edward O'Brien made the "hot miniature dinners" that drugstores offered "for a fixed reasonable price" sound pretty tempting: "chilled fruit juice, a bowl of excellent soup, a salad, and such entrées as boiled beef tongue with raisin gravy, potato, and spinach, or chow mein with rice and noodles – even leg of lamb with potato, diced carrots and mint jelly. Desserts include everything from plain pie" to a hot fudge sundae over a brownie.[11]

Soviet readers may have paid more attention to the regular, hearty, and affordable servings of sausage and steak than to the culinary uniformity that Ilf and Petrov decried. Again, George Counts's description of the food he ate during his 1929 trip across the Soviet Union offers useful context. In the villages, he reported, "the traveler is fortunate if he finds borsch, black bread, tea, sugar, boiled eggs, and a little jam." Ready to grant that "this diet may seem quite sufficient to one who has never tried to subsist upon it," he emphasized that "it becomes excessively monotonous after the first day and a half." In some peasant households, he found the diet "even more restricted." Still, the only foods that he "really missed and which were absent in many restaurants, even in the larger cities, were white bread and butter." Counts found that the Soviet Union bested the United States only in the beverage department, thanks to Prohibition. While it was true that even in the cities, water had to be boiled, he enjoyed a "wide range of drinks which the American citizen, while at home, can secure only at the risk of arrest."[12] By the time of Ilf and Petrov's trip in 1935, rationing had ended in the Soviet Union and the state was advertising socialist abundance. But the provisioning of villages remained essentially as Counts had described it. The Soviet beverage advantage ended in December 1933 with the repeal of Prohibition.

Given persistent scarcity at home, it is perhaps unsurprising that Ilf and Petrov's explicit comparisons with the Soviet Union focused not on actual provisioning but on the principles of tastiness and variety. P. A. Bogdanov, the former head of Amtorg in New York City and an advocate of Amerikanizm, employed the same strategy. In his 1935 articles, he noted only one downside of American efficiency: the dull uniformity of American goods. He grumbled that there was "only one standard type of water-melon." He of course imagined that in their adoption of American tekhnika, the Soviets would do better, securing "variety in the objects of

---

[11] Edward O'Brien, "Drug Store Lunch," in Mark Kurlansky, ed., *The Food of a Younger Land: A Portrait of American Food from the Lost WPA Files* (New York: Riverhead Books, 2009), ebook; Megan Elias, "Lunch," in Andrew F. Smith, ed., *Savoring Gotham: A Food Lover's Companion to New York City* (New York: Oxford University Press, 2015), 357.

[12] Counts, *Ford Crosses Soviet Russia*, 123, 122, 124.

home consumption ... in order to avoid the leveling effect ... which in the end has a bad effect and simplifies the psychology of individuals."[13]

The criticism of "standardized" American food may seem strange at a time when food in the Soviet Union was "still scarce and of poor quality."[14] But Bogdanov's and Ilf and Petrov's complaints make sense in the context of the Soviet media's celebration of the forthcoming fruits of socialism. In the mid-1930s, newspapers routinely offered readers mouthwatering images of plenty. Bogdanov's gripe about the single type of watermelon available under capitalism stood in stark contrast to a contemporary newspaper's description of a recently opened grocery store in Moscow that featured "38 types of sausage."[15] Ilf and Petrov grounded their comparison in the propaganda produced by the Soviet food ministry. Regularly eating allegedly bad steaks, the writers claimed that the slogan "food in a socialist country must be delicious" sounded like poetry.[16]

By contrast, the ostensible author of the slogan, People's Commissar of Food Industries Anastas Mikoyan, the "father of Soviet cuisine," seemed to take the tastiness of industrially produced food for granted. In 1936, Mikoyan, an Armenian communist, who had the rare good fortune of serving under Lenin and surviving Stalin to retire peacefully in the 1970s, made his own two-month journey across the United States.[17] Deputized by Stalin to study American tekhnika that might turn promises of Soviet abundance into reality, the commissar envisioned his trip as a grand fact-finding and procurement mission. Thirty-five years later, he fondly cataloged visits to "almost 100 different enterprises." No aspect of the food industry seems to have escaped his gaze. Mikoyan and his entourage investigated the production of canned food, ice cream, crackers, biscuits, bread, shaved ice, candy, mayonnaise, powdered milk, coffee, beer, wine, and champagne. They toured refrigerated storage facilities, poultry farms, the Chicago slaughterhouses, "and so on and so forth."[18]

Like Ilf and Petrov, Mikoyan surveyed not only American production methods but also American "service." Macy's style of "cultured trade" made a particularly powerful impression.[19] Occasionally, the Soviet travelers' itineraries overlapped. Mikoyan may have visited the same cafeteria on

---

[13] P. A. Bogdanov, "Notes on American Business Efficiency," *Pravda*, 19 May 1935 as translated in Bullitt to Secretary of State, 22 June 1935, NACP, RG 59, 711.61/527.

[14] Fitzpatrick, *Everyday Stalinism*, 93.

[15] As quoted in Fitzpatrick, *Everyday Stalinism*, 94.   [16] OA, 32.

[17] Geist, "Cooking Bolshevik," 297.

[18] A. I. Mikoian, "Dva mesiatsa v SShA," *SShA – ekonomika, politika, ideologiia*, no. 11 (1971): 73.

[19] Philippa Hetherington, "Dressing the Shop Window of Socialism: Gender and Consumption in the Soviet Union in the Era of 'Cultured Trade,' 1935–53," *Gender and History* 27 (August 2015): 425; Jukka Gronow, *Caviar with Champagne: Common Luxury and the Ideals of the Good Life in Stalin's Russia* (Oxford: Berg, 2003), 56.

Forty-Second Street in New York City that mesmerized Ilf and Petrov.[20] Making the standard Soviet pilgrimages to Ford Motor Company and General Electric, Mikoyan, again like the writers, saw the model employee cafeteria at GE and noted with surprise the lack of any dining facilities at the Ford plant, where workers ate their lunches on the factory floor.[21]

While Mikoyan understood that all he saw issued from the "bowels of capitalism,"[22] his interest was less in unmasking the unpalatable reality of American abundance than in learning its secrets. Since the early 1930s, the commissar had been involved in (ultimately failed) efforts to raise Soviet per capita meat consumption to something approaching American levels by constructing huge industrial meat-processing plants. Even before he made his own trip to the United States, he had become enamored of American hot dogs and mass-produced ice cream as potential markers of socialist abundance.[23] Mikoyan emphasized in his 1971 account of the trip that he had no interest in "wasting time looking for the vices of American capitalism." Whenever his traveling companions started to complain, he reminded them that they had come "to study and borrow all the best technical achievements so that we can introduce them at home."[24] He returned dreaming of bringing hamburgers, frozen foods, and fruit juices to Soviet consumers.[25]

For Mikoyan, the "hot cutlet" was the industrial food par excellence. He ordered 25 of the machines capable of turning out 5,000 hamburger patties per hour. In a report upon his return from the United States, he explained that the "hamburger" was served inside a sliced bun with tomato, pickle, and mustard. "For the busy person," Mikoyan concluded, "it is very convenient."[26] He did not bother to specify whether it was also delicious. But far from sharing Ilf and Petrov's distaste for frozen meat, Mikoyan promoted the wonders of the so-called Birdseye process of flash freezing.[27] While Ilf and Petrov downplayed, however unconvincingly, the appeal of large "*ti-boun-steiki*," which they described as "steaks of frozen meat with a T-shaped bone," Mikoyan championed the hamburger, rebranded as a "hot cutlet," "Moscow cutlet," or

---

[20] Mikoian, "Dva mesiatsa," 74.

[21] Mikoian, "Dva mesiatsa," 79; LeBlanc, "Mikoyan," 32; OA, 122–23.

[22] Mikoian, Dva mesiatsa," 79.   [23] Geist, "Cooking Bolshevik," 289–99.

[24] Mikoian, "Dva mesiatsa," 74; "Report of People's Commissar of the Food Industry of the USSR Comrade A. I. Mikoyan on his trip to America," 14 November 1936, National Security Archive, https://nsarchive.gwu.edu/sites/default/files/documents/7338777/National-Security-Archive-Doc-01-Anastas-Mikoyan.pdf, 2 (accessed 2 September 2021).

[25] Mikoian, "Dva mesiatsa," 77; LeBlanc, "Mikoyan," 32.

[26] Mikoian, "Dva mesiatsa," 77.

[27] Mikloian, "Dva mesiatsa," 75; Donald J. Cleland, "The History of Food Freezing," *ASHRAE Transactions* 126, part 1 (2020): 619.

"Mikoyan cutlet," as a means of fulfilling the Soviet goal of providing meat for the masses.[28]

Mikoyan likewise saw a model for the Soviet food industry in the impressive American production of nonalcoholic beverages. Given the scarcity of apples in the Soviet Union, he focused on tomatoes, and "dreamed of producing such a quantity of tomato juice that it would become a truly popular product of consumption."[29] While he did not envision introducing Coca-Cola to the Soviet Union, he proposed applying the process of producing a beverage of uniform quality and taste from concentrates to the production of lemonade and kvass, a traditional drink made from fermented rye.[30]

On tomato juice at least, Ilf and Petrov grudgingly agreed. They admitted that over the course of their travels, they eventually succumbed to the "persistent advertising" that, in the service of profit, "taught Americans to drink juices before breakfast and lunch." Skeptical that the vitamins in the juices benefited consumers as much as the sales benefitted fruit merchants, they nonetheless took a shine to peppered tomato juice. It was both tasty and refreshing, and agreed with their "Southern Russian stomachs." Coca-Cola, on the other hand, they dismissed as a capitalist con. Finally giving in to the onslaught of advertising, they attested with scathing irony that Coke refreshes "the throat, stimulates the nerves, soothes health disturbances, softens the torments of the soul, and makes a man a genius like Leo Tolstoy."[31]

While Ilf and Petrov exposed how advertising ginned up profits, Mikoyan focused on how advertising could be adapted to Soviet needs. *The Book about Delicious and Healthy Food*, a lavishly illustrated cookbook first published in 1939, transformed capitalist advertising into socialist realism. Scarcely reflecting the realities of Soviet food supply, it codified a "*vision* of the idealized food future."[32] Teaching housewives how to use products like ketchup and canned corn that existed mainly in the tome's photographs and the commissariat's colorful posters, the book exaggerated both the wonders and the availability of newfangled foods.[33]

---

[28] OA, 82; LGA, 63; LeBlanc, "Mikoyan," 31.   [29] Mikoian, "Dva mesiatsa," 77.

[30] Mikoian, "Dva mesiatsa," 75; Amanda Ciafone, *Counter-Cola: A Multinational History of the Global Corporation* (Berkeley: University of California Press, 2019), 19–22.

[31] LGA, 25, 87; OA, 28–29, 113–14.

[32] Geist, "Cooking Bolshevik," 298; LeBlanc, "Mikoyan," 39.

[33] Geist, "Cooking Bolshevik," 295–96; Jean-Louis Cohen, *Building a New New World: Amerikanizm in Russian Architecture* (New Haven, CT: Yale University Press, 2021), 345–48; Helena Goscilo, "Luxuriating in Lack: Plentitude and Consuming Happiness in Soviet Paintings and Posters, 1930s–1953," in Marina Balina and Evgeny Dobrenko, eds., *Petrified Utopia: Happiness Soviet Style* (London: Anthem Press, 2009), 56–73; Anton Masterovoy, "Engineering Tastes: Food and the Senses," in Matthew P.

Low-Rise America, by contrast, exposed capitalist plenty as a mirage produced by flavorless and monotonous food. And yet, just as the Soviet cookbook occasionally acknowledged the "gaping gulf between the aspirations of the Soviet food industry and its actual achievements,"[34] the travelogue provided tantalizing descriptions of American bounty that sounded genuinely alluring. Ilf and Petrov's dutiful assertions of tastelessness notwithstanding, lists of exotic foods such as freshly squeezed orange juice, pancakes and maple syrup, and "America's national dish, bacon or ham and eggs"[35] may have fueled food fantasies.

Moreover, as Ilf and Petrov acknowledged, there was more to American cuisine than the cafeteria and the lunch counter. Their description of Atlantic & Pacific grocery stores, the largest retail chain in the United States, emphasized wearisome standardization, but also standardized luxury.[36] A&P stores, they reported, "are built according to one model, and no matter in what corner of the land a customer may find himself, he always knows that in an Atlantic and Pacific store pepper stands on a certain shelf, vanilla on such and such a shelf, and coconut on such and such a shelf."[37] This expensive and rarified shopping list hardly squared with the image of Americans filling up on food as unceremoniously as they filled up their cars with gas.

Ilf and Petrov also documented regional and ethnic cuisines that could provide pleasure and sometimes pain. As they entered what they deemed the "real West" beyond Chicago, they noted that ubiquitous advertisements for hot dogs disappeared, replaced by "advertising of a purely Western edible: '*bar-bi-k'iu*' sandwiches of grilled pork." They left the taste of these barbeque sandwiches to the reader's imagination. Whenever they got sick of numbered drugstore dinners, they availed themselves of "other kinds of edibles – Italian, Chinese, Jewish."[38] In New York, they reported, it was possible to "secure any dish" from "Russian caviar and vodka to Chilean soup and Italian macaroni." Beyond New York, too, they found restaurants run by immigrants. At a diner outside Santa Rosa, New Mexico, run by a Mexican who "did not know a word of English," the "sensible calm American service disappeared." The food, however, remained blandly "American": cheese and "canned ham" sandwiches for which the proprietor charged twice the usual price.[39] But in Santa Fe, they found a self-proclaimed "original"

Romaniello and Trica Starks, eds., *Russian History through the Senses: From 1700 to the Present* (London: Bloomsbury, 2016), 173–76.
[34] Geist, "Cooking Bolshevik," 307.   [35] LGA, 78; OA, 102.
[36] Tracey Deutsch, "A & P," in Smith, ed., *Savoring Gotham*, 1–3.
[37] LGA, 118; OA, 158.   [38] LGA, 138; OA, 185.
[39] LGA, 118, 138, 26, 133; OA, 159, 185, 30, 179.

Mexican restaurant staffed by waiters in "orange silk blouses and satin neckties." Alas, the enchiladas, which, Ilf noted, had to be served with a fire extinguisher, defeated the travelers, who ran, "hungry, angry, dying of thirst," from the restaurant to a nearby drugstore where they resigned themselves to eating numbered food.[40]

In Ilf and Petrov's telling, authentic American food was plentiful, efficiently produced and distributed, often attractive to the eye, but incapable of satisfying the stomach. Unsurprisingly, they explained this paradoxical situation as rooted in capitalism. Granting that even in the most remote towns they found abundance, they emphasized that the "American business of feeding people" concerned itself only with profit. Because it "did not pay to raise cattle and to have truck gardens in New York," people ate "frozen meat" from Chicago's slaughterhouses, "salty butter, and unripe tomatoes" shipped green from California.[41] Such geographic specialization was indeed an important feature of the American food industry, as, for example, Chicago came to dominate meat and grain processing. However, what the writers, who visited in the late fall and early winter, failed to realize was that New Yorkers enjoyed local New Jersey tomatoes – when they were in season. The California or Florida tomato was the "year-round" tomato.[42]

At the same time, Ilf and Petrov suggested that capitalism was not the full story. They outlined a distinctively *American* problem: Capitalists benefitted from, perhaps exacerbated, a fundamental American trait, the lack of a "natural human desire to get some satisfaction out of food."[43] Thus, they suggested, American technique could be put to more humane use in the Soviet Union. Representing the Chinese, Italian, Mexican, and Jewish foods they encountered, and the less-than-stellar service that might accompany these cuisines, as not really "American," they blamed the shortcomings of American foods on the American character. They implicitly accepted a racialized vision of America as divided between "cold" Americans, well-suited to capitalism, who prized convenience above all else, and colorful Others, who, if not actively resisting capitalism were not easily assimilated into the American mainstream.

---

[40] ZK, 22 November, 452; LGA, 138; OA, 186.   [41] LGA, 27; OA, 52.
[42] John Hoenig, "A Tomato for All Seasons: Innovation in American Agricultural Production, 1900–1945," *Business History Review* 88 (Autumn 2014): 524–44.
[43] LGA, 27; OA, 31.

15   The Nationalities Question

> To a Soviet person, used to the nationality policy of the USSR, all the mistakes of the American government's Indian policy are evident from the first glance. The mistakes are, of course, intentional.
>
> Ilf and Petrov, "American Photographs: VI: Indians"

In the desert Southwest, surrounded by rock formations that looked like "recumbent elephants and antediluvian lizards," Ilf and Petrov felt like "interplanetary travelers."[1] The indigenous people seemed to them the natural products of this "desolate and wild" landscape.[2] The "unique" "redness of Indian skin" matched "the color of their porous cliffs." The desert hills appeared to have provided the "models" for Native American "wigwams."[3] Armed with an understanding of American Indians gleaned from *The Last of the Mohicans*, Ilf and Petrov applied the Algonquin word for tents made of animal skins or birch bark to traditional Navajo (Diné) hogans made of earth or sod.[4] Even when they encountered American Indians living in a modern way, like the pair they saw in Santa Fe getting out of an automobile and going into the cinema, Ilf and Petrov underlined picturesque otherness: "On the Indian man's forehead was a broad bright-red sash. On the Indian women's legs could be seen thick white puttees."[5]

Yet paradoxically, Ilf and Petrov found in the desert a familiar problem, known in the Soviet Union as the "nationalities question": How could formerly colonized peoples be liberated, modernized, and integrated as equals into a multinational state? They represented American Indians as exotic but also akin to the varied national minorities – from Azerbaijanis to Yakuts – who had been subject to Russian imperial

---

[1] OA, 213, 238.   [2] LGA, 157; OA, 211.   [3] OA, 192, 229.

[4] Where possible, I use specific tribal designations to identify indigenous peoples; on the case for using "American Indian," see Robert Warrior, "Indian," in Bruce Burgett and Glenn Hendler, eds., *Keywords for American Cultural Studies*, 2nd ed. (New York: NYU Press, 2014), 130–31; Peter Nabokov and Robert Easton, *Native American Architecture* (New York: Oxford University Press, 1990), 56–62, 322–36.

[5] OA, 186; Fedorova, *Yankees*, 167.

power. The difference, they claimed, was that whereas the Soviet state had given its minorities the benefit of a presumptively "correct" nationalities policy, American Indians remained marginalized, oppressed, and on the verge of extinction.

We can see in Ilf and Petrov's insistence that the American government made "intentional" mistakes in its treatment of Native American peoples yet another example of their tendency to apply Soviet categories to American realities. Doing so, they provided oversimplified depictions of both American Indian policy and Soviet nationalities policy. The shortcomings of their analyses notwithstanding, reconstructing Ilf and Petrov's encounters and observations in the desert Southwest opens a revealing perspective on the role of racialized difference in Soviet and American understandings of ethnic minorities. As historian Brigid O'Keeffe has argued in reference to Soviet Gypsies (Roma), one of the "core tensions" of Soviet nationalities policy was its simultaneous commitment to the notion of "human malleability" and its insistence on the immutability of "so-called 'national character.'"[6] Ilf and Petrov's adventures throw this fundamental tension into sharp relief and expose the ways in which it crossed the capitalist–socialist divide. Like the white American connoisseurs of Native American culture with whom they interacted, Ilf and Petrov took for granted that indigenous peoples could and should be uplifted and "modernized," while also romanticizing and racializing American Indians as the timeless, natural, and unspoiled denizens of mythical domains. Behind this shared sensibility lay a long history of Russian–American anthropological exchanges that was coming to an end as Ilf and Petrov crossed the United States.

The closest Soviet analogue to American Indian policy was policy toward the numerically small indigenous peoples of Siberia, whom Russian anthropologists conceptualized as "Russia's own Indians."[7] An influential Soviet expert in this area, Vladimir Bogoraz, had important ties with American anthropologists, especially Franz Boas, and with the United States. In the 1890s, Bogoroz and his colleague Lev Shternberg had become distinguished ethnographers largely by accident. Sentenced to long terms of political exile in Siberia for their radical political activities, they took up the study of local indigenous populations as a socially useful extension of their revolutionary commitments. In

---

[6] Brigid O'Keeffe, "The Racialization of Soviet Gypsies: Roma, Nationality Politics, and Socialist Transformation in Stalin's Soviet Union," in David Rainbow, ed., *Ideologies of Race: Imperial Russia and the Soviet in Global Context* (Montreal: McGill-Queen's University Press, 2019), 133.

[7] Yuri Slezkine, *Arctic Mirrors: Russia and the Small Peoples of the North* (Ithaca, NY: Cornell University Press, 1994), 124.

1899, Boas, who that year became a professor at Columbia University, invited Bogoraz, as well as another exile-turned-anthropologist, Vladimir Jochelson, to participate in the Jesup North Pacific Expedition to investigate indigenous cultures on both sides of the Bering Strait. Bogoraz and Boas's intellectual exchanges and friendship solidified when the former, once again in political hot water at home, spent several years in the United States, where he wrote up his findings on the Chukchi (Luoravetlan) and the Siberian Eskimos (Yupik) for publication. Bogoraz also collected material for works about the United States, including autobiographical sketches, short stories, and a novel.[8] His "American stories," published under the pseudonym N. A. Tan, constituted an important prerevolutionary source of Russian understandings of the United States.[9] In preparation for their trip, Ilf and Petrov perhaps read his *USA: American People and Mores*, published in 1932.[10]

The central assumption of Soviet nationalities policy was evolutionism. This theory, as developed by Karl Marx and Friedrich Engels from the work of American ethnologist Lewis Henry Morgan, held that all human groups moved through a series of hierarchical, evolutionary stages from primitive communism through slaveholding, feudalism, capitalism, and socialism, ultimately to communism. By means of a process that historian Francine Hirsch terms "state-sponsored evolutionism," Soviet policymakers sought to usher "primitive" peoples through these stages. State-sponsored evolutionism was a "civilizing mission." But in contrast to the French or British civilizing missions that served to rationalize and whitewash colonial exploitation, the Soviet program promised to redress the wrongs of tsarist imperialism and bring the benefits of socialist modernity to all.[11]

---

[8] Franz Boas, "Waldemar Bogoras," *American Anthropologist* 39 (April–June 1937): 314–15; Bruce Grant, "Missing Links: Indigenous Life and Evolutionary Thought in the History of Russian Ethnography," *Berichte zur Wissenschaftsgeschichte* 43 (2020): 119–29; Sergei Kan, "'My Old Friend in a Dead-End of Empiricism and Skepticism': Bogoras, Boas, and the Politics of Soviet Anthropology of the Late 1920s–Early 1930s," *Histories of Anthropology Annual* 2 (2006): 34–35; Sergei Kan, "Evolutionism and Historical Particularism at the St. Petersburg Museum of Anthropology and Ethnography," *Museum Anthropology* 31 (2008): 30–32; Vladimir Germanovich Bororaz, *Publications of the Jesup North Pacific Expedition*, vol. 7, *The Chukchee* (New York: Johnson Reprint, [1904–1909] 1966); Vladimir Germanovich Bogoraz, *Publications of the Jesup North Pacific Expedition*, vol. 8, pt. 3, *The Eskimo of Siberia* (New York: AMS Press, [1913] 1975).

[9] Fedorova, *Yankees*, 25–26, 116–28, 150–55.

[10] Vladimir Germanovich Tan-Bogoraz, *USA: Liudi i nravy Ameriki* (Moscow: Federatsiia, 1932).

[11] Francine Hirsch, *Empire of Nations: Ethnographic Knowledge and the Making of the Soviet Union* (Ithaca, NY: Cornell University Press, 2005), 7–8, 21–30, 103.

Initially, Soviet nationality policy permitted relatively open debate among experts. In the 1920s, Bogoraz and other Russian ethnographers drew on evolutionist concepts to argue that the indigenous peoples of Siberia were naïve "primitive communists," whose unique culture should be preserved.[12] Bogoraz advocated the view, unorthodox and eventually "scandalous" in the Soviet context, that the protection of indigenous cultures required the establishment of native reservations along American lines. A "merger" with the neighboring Russian population, he warned, "is a virtual end to the natives – they are crushed into smithereens like an earthenware pot tossed with iron kettles."[13]

Likening native culture to a fragile earthenware pot in need of conservation, Bogoraz expressed a "romantic sensibility" that crossed political and theoretical divides. This sensibility essentialized the supposedly harmonious and authentic cultures that anthropologists yearned to study and preserve.[14] It brought together Bogoraz, the ostensible evolutionist wary of progress that threatened to smash beautiful, primordial cultures, and Boas, the brash anti-evolutionist and cultural relativist, who likewise romanticized "primitive" cultures even as he forcefully rejected the hierarchical ranking of cultures from primitive to civilized.[15] This romantic sensibility animated their shared understanding of ethnographic fieldwork as an urgent salvage operation, a race to safeguard, describe, and interpret genuine indigenous languages, rituals, and artifacts before they succumbed to historical change. It shaped the museum displays that Boas and Shternberg installed in the early twentieth century at the American Museum of Natural History in New York and the Museum of Anthropology and Ethnography in St. Petersburg. Both employed artifacts, mannequins, and painted panoramas to construct ahistorical

---

[12] Slezkine, *Arctic Mirrors*, 147–48.

[13] Soviet historian Mikhail Sergeev ("scandalous") and Bogoraz, both as cited in Bruce Grant, *In the Soviet House of Culture: A Century of Perestroikas* (Princeton, NJ: Princeton University Press, 1995), 70; Slezkine, *Arctic Mirrors*, 148–49; Dmitry V. Arzyutov, "'American Dreams' of Early Soviet Ethnography," *Ab Imperio*, no. 1 (2020): 79–81.

[14] George W. Stocking, Jr., "Romantic Motives and the History of Anthropology," in George W. Stocking, Jr., ed., *Romantic Motives: Essays on Anthropological Sensibility* (Madison: University of Wisconsin Press, 1989), 5, 6; George W. Stocking, Jr., "Ideas and Institutions in American Anthropology: Thoughts Toward a History of the Interwar Years," in *The Ethnographer's Magic* (Madison: University of Wisconsin Press, 1992), 160–65; Regna Darnell, *Invisible Genealogies: A History of Americanist Anthropology* (Lincoln: University of Nebraska Press, 2001), 187–88, 287, 311.

[15] Darnell, *Invisible Genealogies*, 34–51; Stocking, "Ideas and Institutions," 119–27; Franz Boas, "The Aims of Anthropological Research," *Science* 76 (30 December 1932): 605–13.

tableaus of "timeless subjects" and vanishing cultures.[16] Boas's North Coast Hall remained largely intact until 2017, when the museum announced a multiyear project to update the exhibits with the collaboration of representatives from the First Nations of the Pacific Northwest.[17] As we will see, Shternberg's vision of "timeless" peoples had a far shorter lifespan, falling victim to the Stalinist modernization drive of the early 1930s.

In the early 1920s, Boas and Bogoraz took advantage of the warming of Soviet relations with the West inaugurated by the New Economic Policy to renew their scholarly exchanges. Boas, concerned about the intellectual and physical well-being of his Russian colleagues, sent them books, journals, and food parcels. Up to and long after Shternberg's death in 1927, Boas worked to put together an English edition of his work on the Gilyaks (Nivkh) of Sakhalin Island.[18] Bogoraz managed to get back to New York City in 1928 for the International Congress of Americanists. By then, he was promoting a more conventionally evolutionist approach, publicly arguing against efforts to "artificially" preserve traditional ways of life.[19] Nonetheless, he and Boas, the most prominent of American anti-evolutionists, came up with the idea of organizing a graduate student exchange that would facilitate cooperation between Western and Soviet anthropologists doing fieldwork in the Arctic.

Boas arranged the funding, and in 1929 was able to invite the first (and, it turned out, last) Soviet student, Yuliia Averkieva, who, at twenty-two, had already done extensive fieldwork in her native Karelia. She spent a year at Barnard, and, posing as "Papa Franz's" granddaughter in order to enter Canada without a visa, conducted six months of fieldwork among the Kwakiutl tribe on Vancouver Island.[20] After returning to

---

[16] Tony Bennett, "Liberal Government and the Practical History of Anthropology," *History and Anthropology* 25 (2014): 155–61 (quotation at 155); Steven Conn, *History's Shadow: Native Americans and Historical Consciousness in the Nineteenth Century* (Chicago: University of Chicago Press, 2004), 195–96; Grant, *In the Soviet House of Culture*, 8–11, 70–71; Slezkine, *Arctic Mirrors*, 125–29, 387–90; Wendy Leeds-Hurwitz, "The Committee on Research in Native American Languages," *Proceedings of the American Philosophical Society* 129 (June 1985): 129–37; Kan, "Evolutionism and Historical Particularism," 33–37.

[17] "Northwest Coast Hall," American Museum of Natural History, www.amnh.org/exhibitions/permanent/northwest-coast (accessed 2 September 2021).

[18] Arzyutov, "'American Dreams,'" 79–81; Bruce Grant, "Foreword," in Lev Shternberg, *The Social Organization of the Gilyak*, ed. Bruce Grant (New York: American Museum of Natural History, 1999), xliv–liv.

[19] Kan, "My Old Friend," 51.

[20] Kan, "My Old Friend," 52–53; Grant, "Foreword," xlvi–xlix; Boas to Bogoraz, 24 November 1928, Franz Boas Papers, American Philosophical Society; E. L. Nitoburg, "Iu. P. Petrova-Averkieva (1907–1980): Sud'ba I vremia," *Novaia i*

Leningrad in 1931, Averkieva, who devoted the rest of her career to the study of American Indians, adhered to a dogmatic evolutionist line in print even as she continued to address Boas as "Papa Franz" in her letters.[21] The only American participant in the exchange, Archie Phinney, a member of the Idaho Nez Percé (Niimíipu) tribe and the first American Indian to graduate from the University of Kansas, left for the Soviet Union in 1932. He spent five years there, mostly at the Academy of Sciences in Leningrad. Upon his return to the United States in 1937, he took a job at the Bureau of Indian Affairs (BIA), where he worked until his death in 1949.[22]

While Averkieva was in North America, the Stalinist cultural revolution put intense pressure on social scientists such as Bogoraz to commit to modernizing, rather than preserving, indigenous cultures. The effort to turn Soviet ethnography into a tool of socialist construction occasioned often vicious attacks on the older generation of so-called bourgeois specialists – even those like Bogoraz with a history of political opposition and exile under tsarism. Bogoraz's personal anguish comes through in a 1930 letter to Boas. Offering his condolences to the American anthropologist, whose wife had recently died, Bogoraz reminded his friend that "You have at least your sons and grandsons, the whole clan Boas. I have none and nobody, only my students who want to take from me everything and give me nothing."[23]

In the early 1930s, Soviet nationalities policy became more uncompromising as advocates of state-sponsored evolutionism demanded a war on "backwardness." Policy toward the small peoples of the North now targeted "survivals of tribalism" such as polygamy and the timeless "savage," personified by the shaman.[24] An intensification of the persistent, if not always acknowledged, association of "civilization" with

noveishaia istoriia, no. 1 (2004): 209–10; Julia Averkieva and Mark A. Sherman, *Kwakiutl String Figures* (Vancouver: UBC Press, 1992), xvii–xxii.

[21] Averkieva to Boas, 4 May 1932; Boas to Averkieva, 19 May 1932, Boas Papers; Iu. Averkieva, "Sovremenaia amerikanskaia etnografiia," *Sovetskaia etnografiia*, no. 2 (1932): 101, 102. Arzyutov, "'American Dreams,'" 83–85; Kan, "My Old Friend," 58, 54, 63n37.

[22] Boas to Phinney, 11 July 1935; Phinney to Boas, 9 September 1935; Boas to Collier, 13 May 1935; Collier to Boas, 17 June 1935, Boas papers; Willard William, "American Anthropologists on the Neva: 1930–1940," *History of Anthropology Newsletter* 27 (2000): 3–9; Benjamin Balthaser, "From Lapwai to Leningrad: Archie Phinney, Marxism, and the Making of Indigenous Modernity," *Ab Imperio*, no. 1 (2020): 43.

[23] Bogoraz to Boas, 13 January 1930, Boas Papers; Kan, "My Old Friend," 55–57; Slezkine, *Arctic Mirrors*, 188–93, 253–55.

[24] Slezkine, *Arctic Mirrors*, 226, 124–28; Grant, *In the Soviet House of Culture*, 53–58, 93–96; Hirsch, *Empire of Nations*, 217–20, 246–58; Kan, "My Old Friend," 34–35; Kan, "Evolutionism and Historical Particularism," 28–46.

Russian culture and language delegitimated earlier efforts to preserve ethnic particularities and indigenous languages. By 1934, Soviet education authorities, touting the benefits of Russian-language instruction for indigenous children, began scaling back native language schools, and some indigenous parents were inclined to agree that literacy in Russian opened more opportunities than literacy in, say, Evenk. In 1938, an official decree made the study of Russian compulsory in all Soviet schools.[25]

In the 1930s, American Indian policy, too, was in flux. The Indian Reorganization Act of 1934, the so-called Indian New Deal, aimed to revive and modernize American Indian institutions and cultures. It reinstated communal ownership of tribal lands, encouraged tribal self-government, and accelerated the replacement of English-only boarding schools, where Native American people "were made to feel inferior and insecure," with bilingual community day schools that taught them "the value of their origins" and "belief in themselves." In an article published in the *New York Times* early in his tenure, the Commissioner of Indian Affairs John Collier described the new approach as rejecting schemes for "whitening" Indians that produced only "shame of race." Instead, he proposed restoring the Indians' "sense of belonging" to their own civilization in order to "prepare [them] to enter into our civilization."[26] As Collier's presumption that American Indians should ultimately enter into "our" civilization suggests, the new policies could in practice be both coercive and culturally insensitive.[27] But officials insisted that the "objective of the Indian Reorganization Act is humane – rehabilitation of broken, pauperized, and demoralized, Indian groups."[28]

Ilf and Petrov overlooked, misunderstood, or underestimated recent changes in both Soviet and American policy. Their blind spots are particularly clear in the case of language, where they identified English-only instruction as the American government's chief "intentional" mistake. Mocking the excuse that the multiplicity of Native American

[25] Lenore A. Grenoble, *Language Policy in the Soviet Union* (New York: Kluwer Academic Publishing, 2003), 60–61; Slezkine, *Arctic Mirrors*, 243.

[26] Scudder Mekeel, "An Appraisal of the Indian Reorganization Act," *American Anthropologist* 46 (1944): 209; John Collier, "A Lift for the Forgotten Red Man, Too," NYT, 6 May 1934.

[27] John J. Laukaitis, "Indians at Work and John Collier's Campaign for Progressive Educational Reform, 1933–1945," *American Educational History Journal* 33 (2006): 99–104; Joseph Watras, "Progressive Education and Native American Schools, 1929–1950," *Educational Foundations* 18 (Summer–Fall 2004): 81–105; Thomas James, "Rhetoric and Resistance: Social Science and Community Schools for Navajos in the 1930s," *History of Education Quarterly* 28 (Winter 1988): 599–626.

[28] Mekeel, "An Appraisal," 217.

languages necessitated the use of English, they claimed that "the many American specialists who have fallen in love with Indian culture" could "in a short time" produce "Indian written languages." Failure to do so was "imperialism," plain and simple.[29] What Ilf and Petrov did not mention – perhaps did not know – was that Soviet experts, too, had struggled to create written forms of indigenous languages and proposed instruction in Russian as a necessary stopgap. Only in 1924, with the establishment of the Committee of the North (more properly, the Committee for the Assistance to Peoples of the Northern Borderlands), did linguists begin working systematically to develop nine "base" languages for the twenty-six linguistic-ethnic groups they identified in Siberia. In the meantime, the Committee, one of whose founding members was Bogoraz, established Russian-language schools at their "culture bases" in Siberia. In the early 1930s, as Soviet policy increasingly focused on modernization, authorities created boarding schools in which children from different tribes and linguistic groups studied together in Russian. This may have been practical, but it also reflected the new assimilationist approach. As in the notorious boarding schools for American Indian children, students could be punished for speaking their native languages.[30]

While Ilf and Petrov understood that changes were afoot in American policy, they expressed skepticism that reforms recently undertaken by the "liberal gentleman" who ran the Office of Indian Affairs would amount to much. A "few beautifully equipped schools," "museums of Indian culture," and efforts to promote the sale of American Indian crafts would not, they argued, overcome the Native Americans' deep and fully justified hatred of white society. "This hatred," Ilf and Petrov observed, "drips from an Indian's every glance." They imagined that, whatever the proven benefits of modern hygiene and childcare practices, the Native American "will tie a newborn child to a flat board and place him right on the dirty earth floor of a wigwam" rather than "take any culture from a white man."[31] Ilf and Petrov here endorsed what Archie Phinney, the Nez Percé who studied for five years in the Soviet Union,

---

[29] ART, 65; Il'ia Il'f and Evgenii Petrov, "Amerikanskie fotografii: VI. Indeitsy," *Ogonek*, no. 16 (10 June 1936), 9; LGA, 168; OA, 226–27.

[30] Grant, *In the Soviet House of Culture*, 41, 72, 85; Grenoble, *Language Policy*, 161–73; Slezkine, *Arctic Mirrors*, 242–45; Ruth Spack, *America's Second Tongue: American Indian Education and the Ownership of the English Language* (Lincoln: University of Nebraska Press, 2002), 59; Margaret D. Jacobs, "A Battle for the Children: American Indian Child Removal in Arizona in the Era of Assimilation," *Journal of Arizona History* 45 (Spring 2004): 41.

[31] ART, 64–65; OA, 226.

cited as the foundation of Soviet nationalities policy: The only way to overcome the "antagonisms of the tribespeople" was to demonstratively and systematically "abolish all privileges once enjoyed by any national group."[32]

At the same time, Ilf and Petrov were ambivalent about the modernization that they faulted the American government for failing to undertake. Recoiling at the thought of babies strapped to boards and placed on dirt floors, they nonetheless saw in the Native Americans' "stubborn resistance" evidence of their "pride and their spiritual purity."[33] In other words, they were caught in the fundamental tension that structured Soviet nationalities policy as a whole: a commitment to remaking "backward" peoples pulled against a belief in real and immutable (and in this case, romanticized) "national character." As Ilf and Petrov learned in the Southwest, this friction between a desire to bring American Indians into "our" civilization and a belief in the impossibility, even undesirability, of doing so shaped American policy, too. In *Low-Rise America*, in addition to criticizing English-only instruction, they quoted with seeming approval the white director of an English-language Pueblo school who told them that to remain "real Indians," Native American peoples consciously rejected "electricity, automobiles, and other nonsense."[34]

A comparison of Ilf and Petrov's account of "meeting the Indians" with Phinney's analysis of the plight of the Niimíipu people and the small peoples of the North highlights the similar ways in which the Indian New Deal and Soviet nationalities policy perpetuated the racialized stereotypes or "shame of race" that they claimed modernization would erase. Phinney's five years in the Soviet Union hardly made him a fan of Soviet nationalities policy. In the margins of his notes from a class on Marxism at the Leningrad Academy of Sciences, he commented that the Soviets had succeeded only in moving "the native ... from the plane of the pitiful to [the] plane of the tragic."[35] Nevertheless, two articles he wrote while in the Soviet Union, including one conceived as part of his application for a job at the Bureau of Indian Affairs, took the Soviet commitment to modernization, shorn of its tendency toward romantic racialization, as a critical component of any effort to improve the lives of indigenous peoples.

---

[32] Archie Phinney, "Racial Minorities in the Soviet Union," *Pacific Affairs* 8 (September 1935): 322.

[33] ART, 65.   [34] LGA, 148; OA, 199.

[35] As cited in Benjamin Balthasar, "'A New Indian Intelligentsia': Archie Phinney and the Search for a Radical Native American Modernity," in Ned Blackhawk and Isaiah Lorado Wilner, eds., *Indigenous Visions: Rediscovering the World of Franz Boas* (New Haven, CT: Yale University Press, 2018), 263.

Phinney's 1935 article "Racial Minorities in the Soviet Union" focused on Soviet developments but substituted the American term "racial minorities" for the Soviet term "national minorities." This shift may have been an effort to make the material accessible to a North American audience more familiar with the concept of "race," which Phinney did not bother to define, than the Soviet concept of "nation." The translation of Soviet policy into the language of race also suggests that Phinney understood "race" and "nation" as functional equivalents. While imperialists used the ascription of "national character" no less than the cataloging of "racial" characteristics to justify the exploitation of supposedly natural inferiors, neither race nor nation was, from Phinney's perspective, immutable.

In his discussion of Soviet "racial" policy, Phinney focused on human malleability, the possibility of overcoming the "utter backwardness" that defined the peoples of Northern Siberia. He praised the markers of the "new life" already visible among these peoples: medical stations, motor-boats, fish canneries, radios, "air lines for mail and passenger service," native councils, and institutes for training "technicians, teachers, health workers, social and political organizers, and creators of native art and literature." Unlike the salvage ethnographers, Phinney evinced no nostalgia for the "abject and primitive" indigenous life "annihilated" by rapid modernization. He cheered the historically necessary destruction of "primitive social relations" as a means of "reanimating the traditional elements and forms of culture and bringing them into a new synthesis."[36] As the scholar Steven Lee has noted in another context, Soviet nationalities policy offered, in theory if not in practice, a means of embracing "descent-based particularism in a way that advanced universal equality."[37] To borrow Bogoraz's resonant metaphor, Phinney wished neither to preserve nor smash the earthenware pot of "backward" native culture. Instead, he favored remodeling the brittle clay artifact into a sturdy modern vessel that remained somehow authentically American Indian.

While in the Soviet Union, Phinney also wrote an essay directly addressing American Indian problems, which he included in his BIA application. In this essay, probably written in 1936 or 1937, he did not mention Soviet policy as an inspiration or model.[38] Perhaps unsurprisingly in an essay designed to win him a job, Phinney expressed general

---

[36] Phinney, "Racial Minorities," 321–22, 324–25, 327; Balthasar, "A New Indian Intelligentsia," 258–60.

[37] Steven S. Lee, *The Ethnic Avant-Garde: Minority Cultures and World Revolution* (New York: Columbia University Press, 2015), 30.

[38] Archie Phinney, "Numipu among the White Settlers," *Wicazo Sa Review* 17 (Autumn 2002): 21–42.

agreement with Collier's basic assumption that the "social and economic regeneration of Indian populations" required both bringing "modern conveniences and scientific apparatus within the reach of every Indian" and cherishing American Indian "heritage" – art, songs, dances, rituals, and cooperative institutions. This "ideological formulation," as Phinney called it, begged the question of how the government could at once modernize and preserve American Indian culture.[39]

Phinney emphatically rejected the solution of modernization plus colorful displays of native crafts, dances, or food that passed among policymakers in both the United States and the Soviet Union as a commitment to antiracism or anti-imperialism. Instead, he envisioned modern Native Americans who had nothing in common with "befeathered museum specimens" living in modern communities distinct from the "the general white population."[40] For him, "wild west" displays were symptoms of a "disrupted ... tribal order." Pandering to white society's romanticization of the "glorious savage," American Indians reworked traditional tribal performances into "theatrical" spectacles featuring "flashy regalia." This did not, he argued, signify a renewal of Native American culture. On the contrary, the younger generation, unable to speak the Native American language fluently, did "not know tribal mythology, songs, and dances," and "turned to white American social practices."[41] Phinney also knew firsthand how such displays could demean Native American culture and knowledge. In 1935, his Soviet colleagues had quite literally turned him into a specimen, prevailing upon him to wear a feathered headdress borrowed from the museum in order to play an "authentic Indian" in the documentary film *The Language of North American Indian Gestures.*[42]

Writing at the same moment as Phinney, Ilf and Petrov shared with him the optimistic belief in the possibility of remaking "abject and primitive" cultures, a category into which they placed the Native American cultures they encountered in New Mexico and Arizona. That such modernization was not happening in the United States they blamed on centuries of imperialism and intentionally mistaken policy. They also shared Phinney's view that to turn the American Indian into a "befeathered museum specimen" – or in their telling, an "old lion" in a cage – was to dehumanize him, to reduce him to a passive and pathetic cliché. They sympathized with the Native Americans' plight. And yet they romanticized the "museum specimen" in a way that Phinney, who knew what it

[39] Phinney, "Numipu," 37, 39.　　[40] Phinney, "Numipu," 41.
[41] Phinney, "Numipu," 33–34.
[42] Igor Kuznetsov, "Archie Phinney, A Soviet Ethnographer," *Ab Imperio*, no. 1 (2020): 69–70.

meant to be regarded as a voiceless stereotype, could not. Ilf and Petrov stood in awe of the timeless, indestructible, mythical American Indian "almost completely unassimilated into white culture."[43] Indeed, they had come to the Southwest in part to see such "glorious savages."[44] Unlike Phinney, the Nez Percé anthropologist who wanted to escape the white man's museum, they identified with the white anthropologists and antiquarians who wanted to help American Indians but also to preserve them as pristine relics of the ancient past. In the vast, beautiful, and alien desert, their commitment to modern nationalities, not to mention modern hygiene, medicine, and "service," ran aground on the desire for the spiritual, the natural, the timeless, and the exotic.

[43] ART, 64–65; OA, 226.   [44] Fedorova, *Yankees*, 162, 165–69; OA, 194–95.

16   A Laboratory of Anthropology

> Among the austere red hills beyond [Santa Fe] stands the fine building
> of the Rockefeller Institute of Anthropology. The institute is supported
> by one of Rockefeller's sons. But what would happen if Rockefeller's
> son had not been interested in anthropology? That, we dare say, could
> not be answered even by the assistant director, Mr. Chapman himself,
> who was acquainting us with the work of the institute.
>
> Ilf and Petrov, *Low-Rise America*

Ilf and Petrov's efforts to learn about American Indians relied more on
interactions with white lovers of Indian culture than with Native
American people themselves. They seem to have been particularly
impressed by their visit to the Laboratory of Anthropology, which they
misidentified as the Rockefeller Institute of Anthropology. In the
"Indians" installment of their photo essay, a photograph of its assistant
director, Kenneth Chapman, immediately follows their reference to
"American specialists who have fallen in love with Indian culture."[1]
In his journal, Ilf noted no details of the visit, but sketched a two-
sentence portrait of Chapman: He had come to the Southwest thirty-
five years earlier to treat a lung ailment, and had stayed. He was gaunt,
with an "Anglo-British" face. That Ilf condensed the encounter into a
medical condition that mirrored his own suggests – the "Anglo-British"
face notwithstanding – a certain kinship. In *Low-Rise America*, only a
shadow of this kinship remains, as Chapman became "a man with an
excellent, energetic, and gaunt American face"[2] (Figure 16.1).

It is impossible to say how much more of his own story Chapman told
the visiting Soviet writers. It may not have been much. Chapman, it
seems, preferred talking about his work to talking about himself.[3] But
showing Ilf and Petrov around the Laboratory, he undoubtedly communicated his enthusiasm, more as artist than as anthropologist, for its

---

[1] Il'f and Petrov, "Indeitsy," 10.   [2] ZK, 23 November, 452; OA, 188.
[3] Janet Chapman and Karen Barrie, *Kenneth Milton Chapman: A Life Dedicated to Indian
Arts and Artists* (Albuquerque: University of New Mexico Press, 2008), xii, 204–205.

Figure 16.1 Archaeologist Kenneth Chapman sketching designs on Pueblo pottery, New Mexico, c. 1915. Courtesy Palace of the Governors Photo Archives (NMHM/DCA), Negative No. 013312.

collection of Native American pottery, much of which he himself had acquired. In *Low-Rise America*, they recounted that Chapman led them through "excellently organized storage areas, where on thin metallic shelves the rich collections of decorated Indian pots were neatly displayed; temperature-controlled storerooms, where Indian rugs and textiles were preserved; laboratories in which young scientists sat thoughtfully over apparently ordinary rocks." Having demonstrated the institute's careful and scientific efforts to preserve and understand American Indian material culture, Chapman, they reported, informed them that "The Indians are doomed to disappear. We study them well, but we do little to preserve them as a people."[4]

Chapman's gloomy conclusion regarding the failure to "preserve them as a people" can be read as a broad condemnation of US Indian policy or more narrowly as a criticism of the Laboratory's failure to live up to its mission. In either case, the failure struck at the heart of his own

---

[4] LGA, 139; OA, 187–88.

identification with the project of revitalizing and promoting Native American art. Chapman was twenty-three when he arrived in the territory of New Mexico in 1899 from the Midwest, where he had studied at the Art Institute of Chicago and worked as a commercial illustrator. As he recalled in an unpublished memoir written in the 1950s, he quickly learned the "accepted formula" for producing the romanticized depictions of the "land of enchantment" demanded by tourists traveling via the Atchison, Topeka, and Santa Fe Railway. He did a "thriving business" selling watercolors featuring "an old adobe house on a hillside, with an outdoor oven, a string of chile peppers hanging beside the door, and for good measure, a native and a burro loaded with wood."[5] His paintings gained him local attention and a job teaching art at the New Mexico Normal School (now New Mexico Highlands University) in Las Vegas, New Mexico. Accompanying the school's president, the self-taught archeologist Edgar Lee Hewett, on archeological expeditions, notably to remote Chaco Canyon, Chapman became fascinated with prehistoric potsherds and met American Indian artists. He began bringing Native American pots into his art classes; in a 1965 interview he reflected, "I am probably the first one to use Indian art in school instruction in the United States."[6]

With his move to Santa Fe in 1909, Chapman became interested not only in teaching white people about American Indian pottery but in reacquainting Native American craftspeople with their ancient traditions. Working as the head of the illustration department at the Museum of New Mexico, the politically well-connected Hewett's new institutional home, Chapman participated in the excavation of local archeological sites. On the Pajarito Plateau, twenty miles west of Santa Fe, he worked with some of the future luminaries of Southwestern anthropology, including Alfred V. Kidder. He also interacted with the local Tewa men employed, Kidder wrote, as "shovelmen," who helped the archeologists "identify many specimens which would otherwise have been puzzling." Particularly important was Chapman's acquaintance with Julián Martínez of the nearby pueblo of San Ildefonso. He and his wife María, who made the pots that Julián painted, pioneered the black-on-black pottery for which the pueblo is still known.[7] The Museum's

---

[5] As quoted in Chapman and Barrie, *Chapman*, 38.
[6] As quoted in Chapman and Barrie, *Chapman*, 49–52 (quotation).
[7] A. V. Kidder, "Introduction," in Carl E. Guthe, *Pueblo Pottery Making: A Study at the Village of San Ildefonso* (New Haven, CT: Yale University Press, 1925), 13; Chapman and Barrie, *Chapman*, 63, 69, 72, 78; Jennifer McLerran, *A New Deal for Native Art: Indian Arts and Federal Policy, 1933–1943* (Tucson: University of Arizona Press, 2009), 51–54.

collection of ancient pots provided them with inspiration for shaping and decorating their innovative and highly marketable "new old" designs.[8]

Increasingly interested in connecting Native Americans to their own "lost" cultural production, Chapman in 1924 was among the founders of the Pueblo Pottery Fund (later the Indian Arts Fund) devoted to making sure that the best examples of Native American arts remained in the Southwest, where contemporary Native American craftspeople could learn from them. White artists, activists, and anthropologists organized the Fund without any input from the Pueblo people. They sought to counter the trend toward what they viewed as shoddy souvenirs by establishing clear standards for Native American crafts. The Fund collected exemplary pots with the paradoxical, perhaps incompatible, aims of both ensuring the timeless authenticity of Native American art and of allowing American Indian artists to respond creatively to – and profit from – the Anglo (a synonym in the Southwest for "white") art market. The Fund's organizers encouraged dealers to demand better quality, which would allow American Indians to sell higher-priced goods and tourists to take home more tasteful souvenirs. The project at once treated Native Americans as in need of white paternalism and as capable of entering the modern marketplace and becoming self-sufficient. In 1936, these same goals led Commissioner of Indian Affairs John Collier to establish the Indian Arts and Crafts Board on which Chapman worked to certify Native American art as "authentic" in design and technique.[9]

In 1929, the Indian Arts Fund found a home for its collection in a new institution, the Laboratory of Anthropology. The Laboratory, as its name suggests, took a rather more scientific approach to anthropology than Chapman and other local collectors. It emerged out of a convoluted institutional battle that pitted local cultural entrepreneur Hewett and the Archeological Institute of America against the Indian Arts Fund and a consortium of university-based, mostly East Coast anthropologists.[10] The anthropologists sought a graduate field school. Chapman's goals were more "parochial," the study and preservation of Native

---

[8] Margaret D. Jacobs, "Shaping a New Way: White Women and the Movement to Promote Pueblo Indian Arts and Crafts, 1900–1935," *Journal of the Southwest* 40 (Summer 1998): 207.

[9] Chapman and Barrie, *Chapman*, 170, 175–76; Kidder, "Introduction," 11–15; Mclerran, *A New Deal*, 2–4; Jacobs, "Shaping a New Way," 188–95.

[10] Chapman and Barrie, *Chapman*, 228–50; George W. Stocking, Jr., "The Santa Fe Style in American Anthropology: Regional Interest, Academic Initiative, and Philanthropic Policy in the First Two Decades of the Laboratory of Anthropology, Inc.," *Journal of the History of Behavioral Sciences* 18 (1982): 3–9; Fowler, *Laboratory*, 366–71.

American pottery.[11] But it was precisely these provincial aims that attracted the interest of John D. Rockefeller, Jr., who on a 1926 visit to Santa Fe had been captivated by the Indian Art Fund's collection of pottery, then languishing in the basement of Hewett's museum. The Laboratory brought these national and local visions together in an ambitious, ultimately unsustainable, mission to promote "the collection and preservation of outstanding examples of Indian Art, anthropological research, public education, field training for graduate students in anthropology, and improvement of the condition of the Indian tribes of the Southwest."[12]

Conceived between 1927 and 1929, "when the country was in the full tide of prosperity," the Laboratory was a hybrid institution with sweeping goals and no endowment. Rockefeller pledged $200,000 for a purpose-built structure, the first of a proposed Laboratory campus in the Santa Fe style on the outskirts of the city, and another $135,000 in outright and matching grants to cover a diminishing percentage of the annual operating budget ($40,000) for five years. However, as Kidder, the chair of the Laboratory's board of trustees, noted at the board's November 1935 meeting, by the time the Laboratory's new building was ready in 1931, the "financial collapse late in 1929 and the ensuing period of depression" made raising the funds necessary to carrying out its goals extraordinarily difficult. After the five-year term of Rockefeller's initial grant came to an end in 1934, the Lab's director, Jesse Nusbaum, made "heroic" efforts to "engender collateral support," but managed to raise less than $5,000.[13]

Contrary to what Ilf and Petrov imagined, Chapman had a pretty good idea of the consequences of the Laboratory's reliance on Rockefeller funding. Soon after they left, he learned exactly what would happen if Rockefeller lost interest in anthropology. In early November, unbeknown to Chapman, Nusbaum, facing the prospect of limited additional funding from Rockefeller, resigned from his post as director to become supervisor of Mesa Verde National Park. The resignation came just ten days before the board's annual meeting at the Museum of Natural History in New York. Proposing an extensive self-study to determine the way forward, the board named Chapman acting director.[14] Kidder's letter informing Chapman of his appointment was dated 22 November, so when Ilf and

[11] Chapman and Barrie, *Chapman*, 229.
[12] "Minutes of the Ninth Annual Meeting of the Board of Trustees of the Laboratory of Anthropology," 152–53, November 1935, Laboratory of Anthropology Institutional Archives (LOA), Archives of the Laboratory of Anthropology/Museum of Indian Arts and Culture, Santa Fe, 89LA0.0001.1.
[13] "Minutes of the Ninth Annual," 153–54.
[14] "Minutes of the Ninth Annual," 154–55.

Petrov visited on the twenty-third, Chapman was still introducing himself as the assistant director. He learned the full extent of the financial
crisis in early 1936.[15] When he did, he quickly realized that the persistent
and inaccurate public impression – shared by Ilf and Petrov – that the
Laboratory was "the half-million dollar Santa Fe institution backed by
Rockefeller" hampered efforts to raise money from other sources.[16]
By the summer of 1936, Chapman's pitch to potential local donors began
by emphasizing that the Laboratory was "one of Santa Fe's institutions,
not Mr. Rockefeller's."[17]

Through the remainder of the Depression and World War II, the Lab's
leadership struggled to find funding and to redefine its mission. Finally,
in 1947, when Hewett's death ended his long grudge against the
Laboratory, it merged with the publicly funded Museum of New
Mexico. Today, the Laboratory's building stands alongside the much
larger Museum of Indian Arts and Culture, opened in 1987, which has
nearly 300 pottery vessels from the Laboratory's collection on long-
term display.[18]

Ilf and Petrov's visit to the Laboratory of Anthropology did not generate new knowledge. Rather, it affirmed their assumptions about both
capitalism and American Indians. Even without understanding the Lab's
current financial crisis, they highlighted its precariousness as a scientific
institution funded not by the state, but by a Rockefeller. This arrange-
ment corroborated their ideas about the irrationality of capitalism.
To some extent, their criticism of American private philanthropy echoed
that of American anthropologists. In his own letter of resignation from
the Laboratory's board in December 1935, Kidder warned of the "evil
effects of prostituting one's aims to please private donors and of shaping
research programs with an eye to the wishes of foundations."[19] For Ilf
and Petrov, the absurdity of the American situation stood in implicit
contrast to that in the Soviet Union, where ethnographers worked closely
with the Soviet government to solve the nationalities question.[20]

If the Laboratory's reliance on Rockefeller supported Ilf and Petrov's
assessment of the evils of capitalism, its exhibits, and perhaps Chapman's

[15] Chapman and Barrie, *Chapman*, 266–69, 399n46.
[16] Editorial as quoted in A. V. Kidder to Arthur Packard, 25 November 1935, LOA,
89LA3.074; ZK, 452.
[17] As quoted in Chapman and Barrie, *Chapman*, 271.
[18] Stocking, "Santa Fe Style," 9–17; The Buchsbaum Gallery of Southwestern Pottery,
Museum of Indian Arts and Culture/Laboratory of Anthropology, http://
indianartsandculture.org/current?&eventID=39 (accessed 7 June 2020).
[19] A. V. Kidder to Board of Trustees, 31 December 1935, LOA, 89LA3.016; Chapman
and Barrie, *Chapman*, 226.
[20] Grant, *In the Soviet House of Culture*, 76.

explanation of them, offered confirmation of their view of American Indians as romantic relics. The Laboratory's 1934–1935 annual report provides a sense of what the two writers would have seen: seven cases devoted to Navajo and Pueblo baskets; three to Navajo and Pueblo silver; four to post-Spanish Pueblo pottery; and one each to Hopi Kachinas, Mexican archeology, prehistoric textiles, and dendro-chronology, a new tree-ring dating technique.[21] The side-by-side study and exhibition of relatively recent and prehistoric cultural products suggested that contemporary American Indians differed but little from the makers of the artifacts on display. The comment Ilf and Petrov attributed to Chapman – that the Indians were "doomed to disappear" – validated their view of American Indians as stubbornly and perhaps heroically unwilling to become modern (capitalist) Americans.

[21] Annual report of the Director, 31 October 1935, LOA, 89LA0.0005.2.

17 New Mexico Moderns

"Where does the Russian lady live? The village of Rio Chiquito, New Mexico, United States."

Ilya Ilf, letter home, 26 November 1935

For Ilf and Petrov, finding "real" America proved challenging in part because, as the letter quoted in the epigraph suggests, they kept meeting Russians in places such as New Mexico that they imagined as a world away from Russia. In the case of the "Russian lady" living in Rio Chiquito, the meeting was unplanned and unexpected. Overhearing the writers and the Trones speaking Russian, a "little lady in a black suit" eagerly sought an introduction.[1]

Ilf and Petrov identify the lady in black as Alexandra Feshina, the former wife of the painter Nicolai Fechin, who had studied with the great Russian realist Ilya Repin. In the United States, Alexandra went by a French-inflected version of her last name, "Fechin," dropping the feminine ending and transliterating the Russian "ш" as "ch." When she met the Russian travelers, she may have reverted to the feminine form. Or perhaps Ilf and Petrov corrected what to them sounded like a mistake. Here, I identify her in a hybrid way as Alexandra Fechina, retaining the Russian ending, but using what has become the standard English spelling.

Like most of the people whom Ilf and Petrov identified as Russian immigrants in *Low-Rise America*, Fechina stood for the bankruptcy of the American dream. The writers reported that she could not afford to heat the house that her then-husband Fechin had built in Taos. Instead, she was renting a place for three dollars a month in a village that lacked both electricity and English speakers. The Depression, she complained, prevented her from selling the residence in Taos. Expanded at the cost of some $20,000, it would not bring more than $5,000 under the current circumstances.[2]

---

[1] PIA, Il'f, 26 November 1935, 457–58.
[2] ZK, 24 November, 455; Alexandra [Fechin] to Spud [Johnson], 8 November 1935, The University of Texas at Austin, Harry Ransom Center, Walter Willard "Spud" Johnson Papers, (Johnson Papers), Box 7, Folder 5.

When they asked why, given her apparent dissatisfaction with life in the United States, she didn't return to the Soviet Union, the "lady" explained, "They are all new people there. I don't know anybody."[3]

Unlike other Russian immigrants described by Ilf and Petrov, Fechina had emigrated from the Soviet Union, not the Russian empire, and revolutionary dreams held little allure for her. She told the writers that in 1923, she had left Kazan, a city on the Volga about 715 kilometers (450 miles) east of Moscow. Given the fact that Ilf described her in his journal as "unable to stop talking," she may well have shared her harrowing experiences of the civil war and famine in the village of Vasilevo.[4] She had struggled to survive and care for her young daughter in the village, while Fechin continued teaching in nearby Kazan. His fame as an artist – before the Revolution he had shown his work in the United States and Europe – ultimately opened the way for the Fechins to leave for the United States with the assistance of the American Relief Administration. The family settled in New York, where Fechin immediately received lucrative commissions as a portrait painter.[5] Fechin's poor health, and perhaps also an aversion to urban life, led him to look for alternatives to the city. At the suggestion of the English artist John Young Hunter, who insisted that Fechin see the "real America," the family spent the summer of 1926 in Taos.[6]

In Taos, Fechin joined a vibrant arts community presided over by Mabel Dodge Luhan. In 1918, as Mabel Dodge Sterne, she had brought her Greenwich Village salon to Taos. She soon separated from her third husband, the artist Maurice Sterne, and in 1923, violating both Anglo and Pueblo notions of propriety, married a Tiwa man, Tony Lujan. She imagined that her marriage would serve as a "bridge between cultures," an embodiment of her commitment to modernist "primitivism." Like other writers, scholars, artists, and intellectuals who came to the Southwest, Luhan was what the anthropologist Oliver LaFarge called a "yearner." She embraced the exotic and the primitive not as a rejection of modernism, but as its source, as a means of throwing off constraining social and aesthetic traditions. In articles in popular magazines and literary journals, Luhan promoted Taos, which had been a destination

[3] LGA, 147; OA, 198.   [4] ZK, 24 November, 454.
[5] Bertrande M. Patenaude, *The Big Show in Bololand: The American Relief Expedition to Soviet Russia in the Famine of 1921* (Stanford, CA: Stanford University Press, 2002), 310; Douglas Smith, *The Russian Job: The Forgotten Story of How America Saved the Soviet Union from Ruin* (New York: Farrar, Straus and Giroux, 2019), 74–75, 201–202; Frank Waters, "Nicolai Fechin," *Arizona Highways* (February 1952): 14–26; John Jellico, "Nicolai Fechin," *American Artist* 23 (1 March 1959): 22–27, 63–64.
[6] Eya Fechin, "Fechin's House in Taos," *Southwestern Art* 7 (1978): 5.

for artists since the turn of the century, as a place where Anglos could learn from the Native Americans to value community and the natural environment above the accumulation of wealth.[7]

Hoping to make the city a beacon and catalyst of a new American civilization, Luhan set about luring artists and activists to Taos. Most famously, she attracted Georgia O'Keeffe, D. H. Lawrence, Ansel Adams, and John Collier.[8] The Fechins were not the only Russians drawn to the Taos colony. Leon Gaspard, born in 1882 in Vitebsk (now in Belarus and more famous as Marc Chagall's hometown), had arrived in Taos in 1919. A notorious teller of tall tales, he spent the years before the war in Paris, painting Jewish shtetls and Russian villages and, he claimed, hobnobbing with Monet, Picasso, Matisse, Chagall, and Modigliani. Shot down flying for the French Aviation Corps, he came to New Mexico to recover, and began painting Western landscapes and American Indians, although he never stopped painting Russia.[9]

Their first summer in Taos, the Fechins stayed in a house on Luhan's property. But soon after they returned in 1927, Fechina and Luhan apparently had a falling out.[10] Fechin purchased seven acres nearby and set about reconstructing and expanding the small adobe house on the property with the help of local Hispanic (Nuevomexicano) and Tiwa laborers from the Taos Pueblo. In 1933, before he had completed the renovation, the couple divorced. Fechin left with their daughter, settling ultimately in southern California, and returning only occasionally to his beloved Taos.[11]

In the early 1930s, the Fechins became American citizens.[12] But the question of their self-identification is difficult to answer. At the time of his death in 1955, Fechin asked that his remains be buried in Russia;

[7] Lois Palken Rudnick, *Mabel Dodge Luhan: New Woman, New Worlds* (Albuquerque: University of New Mexico Press, 1984), xi; Fowler, *Laboratory*, 357–65; Marianna Torgovnick, *Gone Primitive: Savage Intellects, Modern Lives* (Chicago: University of Chicago Press, 1990), 119–40; Sieglinde Lemke, *Primitivist Modernism: Black Culture and the Origins of Transatlantic Modernism* (New York: Oxford University Press, 1998), 144–51; Flannery Burke, *From Greenwich Village to Taos: Primitivism and Place at Mabel Dodge Luhan's* (Lawrence: University Press of Kansas, 2008).

[8] Rudnick, *Mable Dodge Luhan*, 172–75, 191–224, 234–38; Mabel Dodge Luhan, *Taos and Its Artists* (New York: Duell, Sloane and Pearce, 1947).

[9] John Jellico, "Leon Gaspard: Veteran Painter of Taos," *American Artist* 25 (May 1961): 46–50, 68; Frank Waters, *On Time and Change: A Memoir* (Denver: MacMurray & Beck, 1998), 101–30.

[10] Fechin, "Fechin's House," 5.

[11] Fechin "Fechin's House," 5–12; Taos Art Museum at Fechin House, www .taosartmuseum.org/nicolai-fechin.html (accessed 7 June 2020).

[12] Alexandra Fechin and Nicolai Fechin, New Mexico, Federal Naturalization Records, Ancestry.com.

twenty years later, his daughter Eya traveled to the Soviet Union to inter his ashes in Kazan.[13] On the other hand, in 1950 he categorized himself as a Southwestern painter. Working with the novelist Frank Waters to get a book of his paintings published, he wrote that, "It would be very nice if the University of New Mexico Press prints some of my work. To tell the truth my art belongs to this country more than to any other."[14] The artist's American biographers characterize him as an American painter with a Russian soul. Waters, who spent time in Taos in the 1930s and after World War II, deemed Fechin a "perennial peasant" and emphasized that the landscapes and native people of Taos reminded the painter of his roots in "the dark Slavic forests and native villages" of the Volga.[15] The house Fechin built was likewise a hybrid. It included niches for Spanish *santos* and Russian icons as well as the most modern bathrooms in Taos – plumbing so modern that no one in town knew how to install it. (Renovated in the 2000s, the house is now the Taos Art Museum at Fechin House.)[16] More recently, Russian collectors have claimed Fechin as a Russian painter unjustly neglected in the West.[17]

Although Fechina knew English better than her husband, it is possible that she saw herself, as Ilf and Petrov did, as a "Russian lady." In 1939, she sent Waters an icon of the "Prophet Ilya." The gift was part of a campaign to enlist Waters's help in her efforts to persuade Myron Brinig, a closeted gay Jewish novelist, to marry her. The gambit – which failed – relied on the appeal of a Russian exoticism similar to the "primitivism" that attracted so many of the white artists in Taos. The icon, she wrote Waters, reminded her of childhood: At the sound of thunder her nurse would cross herself and light candles before the icon of the prophet, who was "passing in His blazing chariot across the sky."[18]

Such reminiscences of old Russia suggest why Fechina did not wish to begin a new life among the "new" people of Soviet Russia. Yet, as Ilf and Petrov also reported, she could imagine herself as successful in modern America. They recorded that she planned to earn the money she needed by writing "for the cinema," undaunted by the fact that "so far she has not earned anything." That this Russian lady living in a remote village in

[13] Forrest Fenn, *The Genius of Nicolai Fechin* as cited at http://mysteriouswritings.com/a-personal-reflection-on-nicolai-fechin-by-forrest-fenn/ (accessed 7 June 2020).
[14] Waters, *On Time and Change*, 190.   [15] Waters, "Nicolai Fechin," 24.
[16] I thank Christy Schoedinger Coleman for an informative tour.
[17] Melanie Gurlis, "Soviet Realist for London," *Art Newspaper* 23 (October 2013): 6; Alexander Rozhin, "All Is New, and All Is Exciting!" *Tretyakov Gallery Magazine* 35 (2012): 36–47.
[18] Alexandra Fechin to Frank Waters, 11 December 1939, Frank Waters Papers (MSS-332-BC), Box 23, Folder 6, Center for Southwest Research, University Libraries, University of New Mexico.

New Mexico dreamed of making a living, if not a fortune, by writing for the movies appears comically impractical, even a bit tragic. Ilf and Petrov present Fechina as yet another immigrant deluded by the mass media and unable to perceive the deficiencies of capitalism.

Fechina's contemporary letters corroborate her plan to support herself by writing – a book or stories, not screenplays.[19] What may have allowed her to believe that her scheme was more practical or at least less delusional than Ilf and Petrov implied was that, like them, she was linked to a network of artists, writers, and patrons who might open doors in Hollywood or New York. Among the people in Taos who could have provided useful connections was Luhan's secretary Willard "Spud" Johnson, who had worked briefly for the *New Yorker* and returned frequently to the city.[20] Myron Brinig had connections in both New York and Hollywood. His 1937 novel *The Sisters* was made into a film starring Bette Davis and Errol Flynn and directed by Anatole Litvak, who had left the Soviet Union in 1925. I have found no evidence that Fechina ever sold a screenplay. However, in 1937 she published a small collection of stories based on her experiences during the civil war, which received a generally favorable review in the *New York Times*.[21]

The problem for Fechina was not that she lacked connections but that her relations with the people in her network were often strained, even antagonistic. As Waters noted in his 1998 memoir, she "periodically ... developed crushes on younger men, many of them homosexuals." Her aggressive pursuit of men who had no interest "reduced her invitations to homes whose hostesses feared ... upsetting scenes."[22] The earliest of her "crushes" was on Johnson, an infatuation which contributed to her decision to file for divorce in 1933. When she met Ilf and Petrov in November 1935, she was still relentlessly pursuing Johnson, repeatedly declaring her love in long, histrionic letters to which he responded with anger and irritation. He vented his rage at her unwanted attentions in a 1935 journal entry: Why, he wrote, did "no one but unattractive bitches like the Fechin woman fall for me."[23] By late 1939, Fechina had shifted her attentions to the closeted Brinig. The letters in which she pursued

[19] Alexandra to Spud, 8 November 1935, 27[?] November 1935, 17 November 1936, Johnson Papers, Box 7, Folder 5.
[20] Flannery Burke, "Spud Johnson and a Gay Man's Place in the Taos Creative Arts Community," *Pacific Historical Review* 79 (February 2010): 94.
[21] Alexandra Fechin, *March of the Past* (Santa Fe, NM: Writers' Editions, 1937); John Cournos, "Tales of Russia," NYT, 16 January 1938.
[22] Waters, *On Time and Change*, 171–72.
[23] Fechina's letters and his replies in Johnson Papers, Box 7, Folder 5; Box 4, Folder 2; Burke, "Spud Johnson," 97–104 (quotation).

him reveal her need for and tendency to damage personal networks. In a January 1941 letter to Brinig, then in New York, she pledged to follow him anywhere and pleaded, "just send me a rail-road ticket and a little money, because at the present moment I have none of my own, and having quarreled with all my friends could not go and ask for loans. I rather ask *you* [underlined twice] and you won't refuse me, will you? ... I love you."[24] She actively sought Waters's assistance with money and her relationship with Brinig, while also reprimanding him for "keeping such a close friendship with Mabel Luhan." She asked, apparently rhetorically, "don't you know what an accursed and disgusting part Mabel *has* and still *is* trying to play in my affairs?"[25]

Whether they knew it or not, Ilf and Petrov's American network overlapped with Fechina's in the Santa Fe home of the poet Witter "Hal" Bynner. The communities of artists in Taos and Santa Fe (some seventy miles apart) were closely linked to one another by personal ties and by their members' efforts to preserve and celebrate what they understood to be the purity and power of American Indian culture. But they were also riven by disagreements, jealousies, and personal rivalries. Among the most public were Bynner's confrontations with Fechina's nemesis, Mabel Luhan.

Bynner, who had come to Santa Fe in 1922, shared Luhan's affinity for "primitivism." While teaching at Berkeley, he translated Chinese poetry and adopted "the philosophy of Taoism as the means by which to live a sane and simple existence in a confusing and overly complex modern world." When he came to the Southwest, he found "striking parallels" between Taoist values and behaviors and those of the Pueblo people. He spent part of his first summer in New Mexico as Luhan's guest in Taos. (She was then Mabel Dodge Sterne.) In a letter to his mother, Bynner described the spirt of her house as one of "ease and calm," conducive to writing poetry.[26]

The harmony was short-lived. Within a year, admiration turned into mutual recrimination. Bynner was angered by Luhan's hiring of Johnson, his business partner and lover, as her secretary. Luhan resented his 1923 trip to Mexico with D. H. Lawrence and his friendship with Lawrence's wife Frieda. In 1929, Bynner cruelly, if wittily, satirized Luhan in the absurdist play *Cake: An Indulgence* as "a woman jaded by

[24] Fechin to Myron Brinig, 7 January 1941, Waters Papers, Box 23, Folder 6.

[25] Fechin to Frank Waters, 24 November 1941, Waters Papers, Box 23, Folder 6; Alexandra Fechin to E. Dana Johnson, 10 July 1937, E. Dana Johnson Papers (AC 116), Folder 9, Fray Angélico Chávez Library, Santa Fe, NM.

[26] Rudnick, *Mabel Dodge Luhan*, 243–44.

life who seeks relief from her boredom in travel, drink, sex, religion, death, and finally cake." To Bynner's annoyance, Johnson worked as Luhan's secretary and publicist for most of his life. Bynner and Luhan remained bitter rivals for the next thirty years.[27]

A letter from John Dos Passos to Bynner gave Ilf and Petrov entrée into this community of New Mexico moderns, but they learned little about it. Dos Passos introduced them as "the authors of 'The Little Golden Calf,' who are touring around the US." He suggested that Bynner "tell them some funny stories about N.M." Ilf and Petrov mention the letter (from a "famous New York writer") in *Low-Rise America*, focusing in particular on what they deemed its "strange" description of them as admiring Mark Twain "more than anybody."[28] They attributed Dos Passos's exaggeration to their strained efforts to describe Mark Twain's home in Hartford in "far from remarkable English." The animated gestures that accompanied their story apparently gave the New York writer the "impression that we were fanatical devotees of Mark Twain." Dos Passos's letter passed this impression on to Bynner, who "dragged" Ilf and Petrov up a stairway to admire a photograph of Twain inscribed, unusually for the author, with verses. This in turn gave Ilf and Petrov the impression that Bynner himself was a fanatical Twain devotee.[29]

Ilf and Petrov spent an evening with Bynner, learning over whiskey and water "precisely where we should go to see Indians." But they gained little sense of Bynner as anything more than a generically "famous American poet" with a penchant for Mark Twain.[30] This was among the great lost opportunities of the trip. Bynner was a literary trickster of the sort that the two Soviet funnymen would have appreciated. In 1916, he and fellow poet Arthur Davison Ficke perpetrated what Bynner's biographer calls the "greatest hoax in American letters."[31] As Emanuel Morgan (Bynner) and Anne Knish (Ficke), they cooked up their own "school" of poetry, Spectrism, to parody the pretensions of Imagism, Futurism, and other modernist isms. They published *Spectra: A Book of Poetic Experiments* complete with a manifesto. Much to the poets' surprise and joy, their mock modernism was taken for the real thing. For a year and half serious critics analyzed and serious journals published Spectric poems. Bynner even agreed to write a review of the collection. Only in 1918, with Ficke a major in the US Army in France, did Bynner come

---

[27] James Kraft, *Who Is Witter Bynner? A Biography* (Albuquerque: University of New Mexico Press, 1995), 55–57 (quotation at 55); Rudnick, *Mable Dodge Luhan*, 244–48; Burke, "Spud Johnson," 94.

[28] OA, 189; John Dos Passos to Hal Bynner, Houghton Library, Harvard College Library, Witter Bynner Papers, MS Am 1891-1891.7, bMS Am 1891, (222).

[29] LGA, 140–41.   [30] OA, 189–90; ZK, 23 November, 453.   [31] Kraft, *Who Is*, 2.

clean.[32] Taking Bynner's advice about where to look for American Indians, Ilf and Petrov did not seem to realize that they were dealing with a joker, a man able to undertake a review of his own literary hoax with a straight face.

Bynner certainly looked the part of an expert on American Indians. His house at the corner of East Buena Vista Street and Old Santa Fe Trail was a monument to his interest in American Indian culture. Ilf and Petrov describe it as a veritable museum, "filled from its foundation to its roof with Indian rugs, Indian ware, and silver ornaments." Bynner also displayed scrolls and jade purchased on his trips to China. The sprawling, eccentric adobe incorporated Chinese, American Indian, and Nuevomexicano architectural details.[33] (Restored in the 1990s, it is now a bed and breakfast, the Inn of the Turquoise Bear, and listed on the National Register of Historic Places.) Bynner promoted the "regional myth" of the Southwest as a place where "ancient civilizations" – Spanish, Nuevomexicano, and Native American – combined to create an alternative to contemporary America. Without considering the impact of Anglo artists on these "civilizations," Bynner also introduced Ilf and Petrov to the problem of gentrification. He explained that pioneering artists inevitably attracted millionaires eager to despoil the landscape with their villas. Finally, Bynner advised the writers to visit Taos Pueblo and the Native American village of San Ildefonso. It was following his directions on how to meet American Indians that they met the incongruous "Russian lady."[34] They quickly classified her as another unhappy immigrant. That she might have moved in the same American modernist circles as "the famous American poet" Witter Bynner does not seem to have crossed their minds.

---

[32] Paul Thompson, "Soulful Spectrism Nothing But a Hoax," NYT, 2 June 1918; Kraft, *Who Is*, 40; Jason Guriel, "The Spectric Poets," *Poetry* 201 (February 2013): 568–70.
[33] OA, 190; Kraft, *Who Is*, 2.   [34] Fowler, *Laboratory*, 343–56; OA, 190.

18   Can You Kid a Kidder?

> The amazing thing is that in the center of the United States, ...
> surrounded on all sides by power plants, oil wells, railroads, millions
> of automobiles, thousands of banks, stock markets, and churches,
> deafened by the din of jazz bands, movies, and gangsters' machine
> guns, Indians have preserved their way of life completely untouched.
>
> Ilf and Petrov, "American Photographs: VI: Indians"

Ilf and Petrov presented their visit to "Indian Country" as an encounter
with a timeless world completely cut off from the American mainstream.
Petrov was probably correct when he wrote that they were stopping in
places where no Soviet person had ever previously set foot.[1] But plenty of
tourists had. The sites the poet Witter Bynner recommended that they
visit – the village of San Ildefonso and Taos Pueblo – had long been
popular destinations for white American yearners.

While the Pueblo peoples of the Southwest remained on their ancestral
lands and maintained traditional ways to an extent unknown among the
tribes of the Eastern United States, they were hardly unaffected by centuries of colonialism or unfamiliar with the modern world.[2] However, it
was precisely the myth of the "untouched" Native American that drew the
tourists. In 1926, the Fred Harvey Company, whose hotels and restaurants had been serving travelers on the Atchison, Topeka and Santa
Fe Railway since the 1870s, developed "Indian Detours," multiday side
trips by motor coach for train passengers who wanted to travel "off the
beaten path" in luxury. The company's 1936 brochure described San
Ildefonso as a place to see the "characteristic features of pueblo life – the
quaint church, the plaza, the 'dobe houses ... the mud ovens shaped like
gigantic beehives." It promised visitors to Taos Pueblo the "changeless,
picturesque life" that "made Taos a mecca for artists of national

---

[1] PIA, Petrov, 26 November 1935, 459.
[2] Alfonso Ortiz, "The Dynamics of Pueblo Cultural Survival," in Raymond J. DeMallie
and Alfonso Ortiz, eds., *North American Indian Anthropology: Essays on Society and Culture*
(Norman: University of Oklahoma Press, 1994), 296–306.

reputation."[3] New Mexico writers such as Bynner actively participated in inventing this mythology. In a contribution to the Harvey Company's 1928 booklet *They Know New Mexico*, he tempted readers with the possibility that at one of the "strict villages" along the Indian Detour they might see dances performed with "a devout beauty which explains to us moderns what the ancients meant when they danced before the Lord."[4]

It was this myth of "pride and spiritual purity" that Ilf and Petrov perpetuated in their account of meeting Pueblo people – despite meeting few Native Americans who personified such sublime notions.[5] The "Indians" episode of their photo essay includes a conversation with only one Pueblo man, Agapito Pino of San Ildefonso. In both the book and photo essay, Ilf and Petrov reported with straight faces that Pino "didn't know about the existence of Europe or oceans" and had only a dim understanding "that there was such a thing as the city of New York." They also identified him as "the local jokester." Bynner, Ilf noted in his journal, had called Pino a "clown."[6] It is not clear whether the Soviet funnymen knew that the Pueblo clown was having a little fun with them by playing up the stereotype of the naïve primitive ignorant of the modern world. Was the joke on them or on their readers? (Figure 18.1).

The question of whether Ilf and Petrov got the joke goes to the core of their efforts to understand America. If, as pioneering anthropologist Bronislaw Malinowski claimed, anthropology is the "science of the sense of humor," Ilf and Petrov were well-qualified practitioners. For Malinowski, cross-cultural understanding required the ability "to see ourselves as others see us," which in turn required the ability to see the comical, ironic, absurd, or "savage" sides of ourselves and our own society. Writing in 1937, Malinowski depicted this "savage" side of "civilization" in explicitly political terms, asking rhetorically, "Where can we find cruder magic than in the political propaganda of today?"[7] Ilf and Petrov's satire targeted precisely the crude magic of political incantations: Ostap Bender even devised his own spell book, the "Complete Celebrator's Kit," a compendium of ideologically correct charms that could be strung together to construct a news story, sketch, novel, play, or poem for any occasion.[8]

[3] [Atchison, Topeka and Santa Fe Railway Company], *Indian Detours: Off the Beaten Path in the Great Southwest* (Chicago: Rand McNally and Co., 1936), 14, 23.

[4] As quoted in Elizabeth Lloyd Oliphant, "Marketing the Southwest: Modernism, the Fred Harvey Company, and the Indian Detour," *American Literature* 89 (March 2017): 107.

[5] Il'f and Petrov, "Indeitsy," 9.   [6] ART, 66; ZK, 24 November, 454.

[7] Bronislaw Malinowski, "Anthropology Is the Science of the Sense of Humour: An Introduction to Julius Lips' *The Savage Hits Back, or the White Man through Native Eyes*," *Hau: The Journal of Ethnographic Theory* 5 (2015): 301.

[8] Il'ia Il'f and Evgenii Petrov, *The Little Golden Calf*, trans. Anne O. Fischer (Montpelier, VT: Russian Life Books, 2009), 344–48.

Figure 18.1 Agapito Pino was not as naïve about the world beyond the pueblo as he tried to make Ilf and Petrov believe. Agapito Pino photographs his mother washing clothes, c. 1920. Courtesy of the Palace of the Governors Photo Archives (NMHM/DCA), Twitchell Collection, Negative No. 003740.

In *Low-Rise America*, Ilf and Petrov turned their satirical gaze on the Other, an easier and safer target. Thus, the writers mocked a young Baptist hitchhiker, who conceded that in the Soviet Union "everybody is well fed and happy" but nonetheless maintained that, as atheists, Soviet people would inevitably suffer the "the tortures of hell."[9] But they retained the essential ability to see the comical side of themselves. Nowhere was this more necessary than in Indian Country, where they confronted a unique challenge: Native Americans who saw (and mocked) them not as Soviet people but as "Whitemen."[10] Released from the need to defend Soviet values, Ilf and Petrov were somewhat freer to recognize and laugh at their own desire to find unspoiled American Indians who had only the vaguest notion of the existence of jazz, moving pictures, and a place called New York City.

It is highly unlikely that in 1935 any resident of San Ildefonso was in fact ignorant of the existence of New York City. María and Julián Martínez, who became the pueblo's most well-known potter and painter, spent their honeymoon at the 1904 World's Fair in St. Louis, where they and other inhabitants of San Ildefonso inhabited a faux "Cliff Dwelling,"

---

[9] LGA, 177–78; OA, 239.
[10] Lidia Dina Sciama, "Introduction," in Lidia Dina Sciama, ed., *Humour, Comedy and Laughter: Obscenities, Paradoxes, Insights and the Renewal of Life* (New York: Berghahn, 2016), 8–9.

danced, and demonstrated American Indian crafts. In 1915, they traveled to San Diego to live in the "Painted Desert" exhibit at the Panama–California Exposition. Designed by Kenneth Chapman and built by Jesse Nusbaum and a crew of workers from San Ildefonso, the display featured replicas of Taos Pueblo and a San Ildefonso kiva. Representatives from a number of Southwest tribes demonstrated Native American crafts. María Martínez was one of the potters.[11]

The pueblo of San Ildefonso itself had been a tourist attraction since at least the 1920s. In 1921, San Ildefonso's Comanche Dance attracted spectators from Santa Fe.[12] As the village emerged as an important center of Pueblo pottery making, the tourist traffic increased. In 1925, María Martínez opened a shop in her house, and, having taught her neighbors how to make the blackware so popular among the white tourists, encouraged them to do the same.[13] By the early 1930s, the village was enmeshed in the international art market.[14] Pueblo art was displayed in Denver, San Francisco, Chicago, Madrid, and Prague, not to mention a major show in 1931 in New York City billed as "the first exhibition of American Indian art selected entirely with consideration of esthetic value."[15]

Allowing themselves to become tourist attractions, the Pueblo people rendered outsiders "symbolically" harmless by playfully imitating them and laughing at their ignorance.[16] In 1904, with a clear sense of the fairgoers' desire for an "authentic" spectacle, the San Ildefonso villagers in St. Louis spoke Tewa and pretended to know little or no English. That ruse, María Martínez told her biographer in 1948, gave them "something to laugh about when the white people had gone home."[17] Late into the twentieth century, "tourists from back East," a term used to designate visitors who expected the Pueblo people to match the "Hollywood image of the Plains Indian warrior," constituted favorite targets.[18]

Burlesquing tourists was the particular purview of the Pueblo clown (*kossa* or *koshare*). In Pueblo society, the "sacred clowns" constituted a

---

[11] Fowler, *Laboratory*, 274.

[12] "Comanche Dance at San Ildefonso, January 23, 1921," *El Palacio* 10 (29 January 1921): 5–7.

[13] *Tewa Basin Study, 1935*, vol. 1: *The Indian Pueblos* (Albuquerque: Soil Conservation Service, Region Eight, Division of Economic Surveys, 1939), 54–78; Chapman and Barrie, *Chapman*, 190–91.

[14] Fowler, *Laboratory*, 351.

[15] Janet Catherine Berlo, "The Art of Indigenous Americans and American Art History: A Century of Exhibitions," *Perspective* 2 (2015): 2.

[16] Jill D. Sweet, "Burlesquing 'the Other' in Pueblo Performance," *Annals of Tourism Research* 16 (January 1989): 66; Ortiz, "The Dynamics," 303.

[17] As quoted in Fowler, *Laboratory*, 217.   [18] Sweet, "Burlesquing," 70.

special group with "punitive and policing" functions. As the anthropologist Elsie Clews Parsons observed in 1934, the clowns used the "weapon" of "ridicule" to enforce social norms among their neighbors. Central to "clown comedy" were "take-offs on other tribes or races – Navaho, Mexicans, Americans." Parsons understood such comedy as a vital "emotional release."[19] Making fun of outsiders also offered a way of simultaneously expressing "what is Pueblo and what is not Pueblo."[20] The clowns inspired laughter and also fear, as they might mock and bully anyone in the audience at a ceremonial dance. They parodied the archeologist enthralled with a homely pot dug out of the ground, the white woman squealing over a bargain piece of pottery, the tourist taking photographs of the exotic spectacle.[21]

In 1935, the head of the clown society in San Ildefonso, the *Kossa Sendo*, was none other than Ilf and Petrov's informant Agapito Pino. Born in about 1878, Pino was well-known to locals such as Bynner and to the anthropologists who studied the Pueblo people.[22] Parsons's 1929 *The Social Organization of the Tewa of New Mexico* includes a photograph of Pino dressed for a ceremonial dance. He may have been the San Ildefonso informant she identified with some frustration as a "man whose social position is of the best, but whose veracity is of the worst according to both white and Indian standards," but who nonetheless "has probably been hitherto one of our sources of authority on the Tewa."[23] William Whitman, III, a student of Franz Boas's, who did fieldwork in San Ildefonso around the time of Ilf and Petrov's visit, likewise encountered Agapito Pino. The Kossa Sendo is one of the most vivid characters in Whitman's study *The Pueblo Indians of San Ildefonso*. Whitman described Pino as "the only man in the pueblo whom we ever heard make a sexual joke. Large, fat, and coarse, he enjoyed burlesque and trickery. He was blustering in manner and thoroughly unreliable as an informant." In his discussion of the village's "religious officers," Whitman depicted Pino as the quintessential Kossa Sendo: "obscene, brutal, domineering. He loved to dance and to drink, and he took great pleasure in lying. ...

---

[19] Elsie Clews Parsons and Ralph L. Beals, "The Sacred Clowns of the Pueblo and Mayo-Yaqui Indians," *American Anthropologist*, New Series, 36 (October–December 1934): 499–500, Table 1.

[20] Sweet, "Burlesquing," 73.

[21] William Whitman, III, *The Pueblo Indians of San Ildefonso: A Changing Culture* (New York: AMS, [1947] 1969), 136–37; Eric Knight, "The Funny Men," in George Fitzpatrick, ed., *This Is New Mexico* (Albuquerque: Horn & Wallace, 1962), 232–36.

[22] Agapito Pino, US, Indian Census Rolls, and US Federal Census, 1880, 1910, 1930, Ancestry.com.

[23] Elsie Clews Parsons, *The Social Organization of the Tewa of New Mexico* (New York: Kraus Reprint Corporation, [1929] 1964), plate 26, 8 (quotation), 56n9, 114.

In any other capacity he would not have been accepted by the pueblo, and, even so, there were villagers who resented and distrusted him despite his privileged role."[24]

Ilf and Petrov's description of Pino was rather less harsh. In the published account they claimed that they had run into the clown by accident. They initially mistook Agapito Pino for a woman; he wore two long braids that fell onto a "fat chest" and had "holes from earrings in his meaty ears." Ushering them into his home, he sang and danced for his visitors and told them about the village. They represent themselves as taking him at his word. And perhaps they were fooled, like the anthropologists who had relied on the native of San Ildefonso who lied "from secretiveness, from his sense of burlesque, and from sheer laziness."[25] Petrov wrote his wife about "Indians" who said they knew almost nothing of the world beyond the reservation, without any indication that he thought they might be pulling his leg. While in the published texts Ilf and Petrov identified Pino as a "jokester," they connected this designation more with his interest in singing, dancing, and having his picture taken than with the possibility that he was a teller of tall tales.[26]

So perhaps the Pueblo clown did kid the kidders. Still, one wonders whether the writers had some inkling that they were being conned. After all, Pino's modus operandum resembled that of Ilf and Petrov's most famous creation, Ostap Bender, who worked by quickly reducing his intended victim "to a formula" and then "identifying the appropriate set of clichés for manipulating him."[27] Differences between the published versions of the story and Ilf's brief notes about the encounter with Agapito Pino suggest that the authors might have been on to him.

In *Low-Rise America*, Ilf and Petrov made the clown's claim of ignorance about the outside world more plausible by playing up his remoteness from the modern world of commerce. They expressed their relief that Pino did not pressure them to buy one of the photographs of American Indians performing a "war dance" that were lying about his house. (The San Ildefonso "war dance" was actually a send-up of a Comanche war dance.)[28] Despite Pino's stock of souvenir photographs, the writers happily reported that "our redskin brothers" remained outside American capitalism, regarding tourists without the "commercial passion" of the "pale-faces."[29]

---

[24] Whitman, *Pueblo Indians*, 16, 26–27.   [25] Parsons, *Social Organization*, 8.
[26] PIA, Petrov, 26 November 1935, 459; ART, 66; Il'f and Petrov, "Indeitsy," 11.
[27] Alexander Zholkovsky, "Dreaming Right and Reading Right: Five Keys to One of Il'f and Petrov's Ridiculous Men," *Slavic Review* 48 (Spring 1989): 37.
[28] Parsons, *Social Organization*, 215.   [29] OA, 192; LGA, 142.

The "Indians" installment of Ilf and Petrov's photo essay does not include the story of Pino's apparent lack of "passion" for selling tourist souvenirs. But it features a photograph that matches the general description ("war dance") of the ones Ilf and Petrov claimed not to have bought. Given that their visit did not coincide with the dates of ceremonial dances observed by contemporary anthropologists – and that Ilf and Petrov never asserted that they saw such a dance – Pino seems to be the likely source of the photograph.[30] Ilf's journal supports the impression that they bought a photograph from the clown. In that version of the story, in addition to singing, Pino "offered a photograph, took a dollar, and calmed down."[31] Pino's engagement in the souvenir trade calls into question his pose of naiveté and Ilf and Petrov's representation of pre-capitalist Pueblo purity.

Portraying Pino as an innocent, Ilf and Petrov may not have been dupes but straight men, who helped Pino to spring his joke on their readers. At the same time, their exaggerated portrait took the venom out of the clown's burlesque of the gullible tourist, turning it into a validation of the stereotype of the pure and majestic American Indian that it was designed to mock. Ilf and Petrov may have omitted complicating details and embroidered the story not in order to allow Pino to have the last laugh but to confirm their own and perhaps their readers' bias.

Ilf and Petrov shared with many Russian readers a picture of the American West and American Indians shaped by the nineteenth-century adventure stories of Gustave Aimard, "the French Fennimore Cooper," and Mayne Reid, a Scots Irish American author better known in Russian translation than in English. Reid in particular remained popular throughout the Soviet period; even Stalin read him.[32] While still in New York, Ilf, at least, had already expressed this desire to see the mythical realms inhabited by American Indians. He described Schenectady, the home of General Electric, as the former domain of the Mohicans.[33] In the alien desert landscape of the Southwest, the dream of finding American Indians who matched the literary clichés finally seemed realizable. The desire for the Western romance and the familiar Other may explain why Ilf

---

[30] ART, 62; Whitman, *Pueblo Indians*, 130–40; Parsons, *Social Organization*, 179–236.

[31] ZK, 24 November, 454.

[32] Virgil L. Jones, "Gustave Aimard," *Southwest Review* 15 (Summer 1930): 452–68; Yulia Pushkarevskaya Naughton and Gerald David Naughton, "'Westward Went I in Search of Romance': The Transnational Reception of Thomas Mayne Reid's Western Novels," *CEA Critic* 75 (July 2013): 142–57; "Mayne Reid in Russian Translation," *Soviet Literature* 4 (1968): 177–78; Fedorova, *Yankees*, 162–67.

[33] PIA, Il'f, 29 October 1935, 441.

and Petrov let their readers (and themselves) imagine that in Pino they had found if not a "noble" savage, then at least a naïve and unspoiled one.

Similarly, Ilf and Petrov reported that at the nearly 1,000-year-old Taos Pueblo, they found a fragment of the past they "knew" from adventure stories. They exalted when they met the governor of the pueblo, who embodied their childhood image of a "bloodthirsty and honorable Indian": Reid and Aimard had not "deceived" them after all! The governor, appropriately enough, was dying (Figure 18.2). But they seemed to take some heart from the young Tiwa men, who "behaved like young lions"; although the only outlet for their fearlessness was

Figure 18.2 Ilf and Petrov described the governor of the Taos Pueblo, an unnamed Santana Sandoval, as a real-life version of the "bloodthirsty and noble" Indians they had read about in Western novels. Arthur Rothstein photographed the governor in 1936. Farm Security Administration – Office of War Information photograph collection, Prints and Photographs Division, Library of Congress, LC-USF346-002956-E.

demanding five cents from the visitors, and then turning contemptuously when they were refused.[34]

Emphasizing the "centuries" that separated Taos Pueblo from the Anglo town that grew up alongside it, Ilf and Petrov read the sign requiring that visitors secure the governor's permission before entering as indicating the Pueblo's isolation, not a need to regulate the flow of tourists. (Today Taos Pueblo is a World Heritage Site, where visitors are greeted by a sign prohibiting "all electronic devices.") In his journal, Ilf noted that one of the residents of Taos Pueblo told them that he knew a Russian painter – the same Gaspard that Fechina had mentioned.[35] But in their published accounts, Ilf and Petrov declined to mention the connections between Taos Pueblo and the Taos art colony, where many Tiwa worked as artists' models, domestics, and laborers.[36]

The degree to which Ilf and Petrov's picture of Pueblo villages reflected less a communist perspective than their own romantic preconceptions of American Indians comes into sharp relief when compared with a nearly contemporary description by Mike Gold. A self-identified proletarian writer, founding editor of the communist-aligned *New Masses*, and native New Yorker, Gold visited New Mexico in 1936. He appreciated that the Southwestern desert "stuns the city visitor." But he had no patience for "postcard picturesqueness" or "shallow Bohemian mysticism." Invoking the doyen of the Taos art colony, Gold dubbed the Native American pueblos "Mabel Luhan's slums." At all the pueblos he visited, including Taos, "the wealthiest and most famous," Gold found "familiar" poverty: "It was nothing but the East Side slum I had known in boyhood ... Flies, excreta, dirt, and disease sores everywhere." Where Ilf and Petrov saw "stately redskins, as proud as ancient Romans," Gold saw a "backward nation" enslaved by imperialists. Ilf and Petrov seemed ready to agree with white "lovers" of Pueblo culture that the "real Indians" were those "without electricity, automobiles, and other nonsense." From Gold's perspective, such backwardness was the real "Indian problem." For a solution, he looked to Mexico and the "Soviet East," where the American Indians' "blood brothers" had joined the "the mainstream of modern life." Far from an exotic landscape out of time, Gold saw in the Southwest a familiar struggle.[37]

---

[34] OA, 195.   [35] ZK, 25 November, 455.

[36] Burke, "Spud Johnson," 89–90; Sylvia Rodríguez, "Art, Tourism, and Race Relations in Taos: Toward a Sociology of the Art Colony," *Journal of Anthropological Research* 45 (Spring 1989): 80–90.

[37] Michael Gold, "Mabel Luhan's Slums," *New Masses* 20 (1 September 1936): 11–13; LGA, 148: OA, 199–200.

Paradoxically, for Ilf and Petrov the Southwest's exotic Native Americans and Native American spaces were "ours," the ones Russians grew up with in the pages of translated Western novels. Like the American Indians they knew from Aimard and Reid, the Pueblo people they met in San Ildefonso and Taos Pueblo seemed anti-American, or at least anti-American capitalism. Thus, although they did not picture American Indians as potential revolutionaries, they depicted them as instinctive, pure, and majestic allies of Soviet anti-capitalism. Understanding that Pino was a kidder, Ilf and Petrov may have succeeded in catching a fleeting glimpse of themselves as the Pueblo clown saw them – credulous romantics in search of an imagined American Indian. Still, they did not entirely get the joke. Turning Pino's burlesque into evidence of his unspoiled, anti-capitalist Indian nature, Ilf and Petrov remained blind to their own tendency to racialize and romanticize the Other. They failed to fully register that Native American contempt for white people might extend to them.[38]

[38] LGA, 148; OA, 199.

19   The Man in the Red Shirt

So, here in the desert, where for two hundred miles around there is not a single settled habitation, we found: excellent beds, electric lights, steam heat, hot and cold water ... In the dining room we were served tomato juice in little glasses and *"steik"* with a bone in the shape of the letter T ... and for all this they charged us almost the same price as in Gallup, Chicago, or New York, although, if they wanted to take advantage of the travelers' desperate situation, they could have charged as much as they liked.

Ilf and Petrov, *Low-Rise America*

One of the first things Ilf and Petrov did upon their return to Moscow was write a letter to Stalin. The spot they chose to describe to the Soviet leader was a motel in the desert between the Grand Canyon and Zion Canyon. The roadhouse shows up in *Low-Rise America*, too. In both the ten-page, typewritten letter and the book, it stands as an emblem of the high American standard of living.[1] But there are telling differences. In the case of the desert lodge, they spun their "great literary material" into two distinctive literary products: a "weapon" in the "struggle for socialism"[2] that they presented to Stalin and a sympathetic portrait of an American missionary, "the man in the red shirt." To reverse engineer these transformations, I followed the clues in the travelogue and Ilf's notebooks to the source of their impressions. Armed with maps and local histories, I was able not only to find the lodge but also to put a name to the man who joked, pointing to his red shirt, "I'm a Bolshevik!"

In the missive directed to Stalin, Ilf and Petrov focused on the importance of introducing American-style comfort and service at home. Assuring the dictator that they wrote as people eager to see their homeland "the strongest, richest, and most cultured in the world," the writers described their American road trip as an exploration of the Soviet Union:

---

[1] Milne, *How They Laughed*, 228; OA, 229.
[2] Letter as published in Iu. Murin, "Daesh Gollivud!" *Iskusstvo kino*, no. 11 (November 1992): 85.

"We drove all day on American roads, but thought about Soviet roads; we stayed in American hotels, but thought of Soviet hotels; we toured Ford plants but saw the Gorky automobile works." "Quite naturally," they concluded, "we tried to apply all we saw to our Soviet life." It was in the spirit of seeing the Soviet future in the astonishing American present that Ilf and Petrov narrated the story of the day they drove through the Arizona desert.[3]

The writers told Stalin nearly the same story that they recounted in a jauntier register in *Low-Rise America*. In the letter, as in the book, Ilf and Petrov emphasized the remoteness and barrenness of the locale. "This was," they wrote Stalin, "desert in the full sense of the word." They "went two-hundred miles without meeting a single living soul, if you don't count a few highway workers repairing the road." The road crew, an "excellent bridge," and finally the well-equipped hostelry attested to the reach of modern infrastructure into the most isolated corners of the United States.[4] In *Low-Rise America*, the lodge appeared more dramatically as a providential oasis: The writers caught sight of the little house's lights just as they ran out of gas and Mr. Adams, always ready with a worst-case scenario, opined that the hungry and cold travelers would have to spend the night in the Ford.[5] For Stalin's benefit, Ilf and Petrov itemized a few amenities left out of the published work. To the excellent beds, electricity, steam heat, hot and cold water, and radio mentioned in the travelogue they added "perfectly white sheets and towels" and a bathroom. For both Stalin and their broader readership, they emphasized that deep in the American desert "was absolutely everything that could be found in New York, Washington or San Francisco." Omitting the droll "Gallup" from the list of comparable cities they presented to Stalin, Ilf and Petrov stressed that they cited "this example not as an exception, but as the rule. 16,000 kilometers on the road gives us the right to assert that anywhere in the United States, a person can find absolutely every comfort."[6]

However, only in the letter to Stalin did Ilf and Petrov provide an explicit and unflattering Soviet parallel of the sort we have been relying on George Counts to supply. They attributed the comparison to a contingent of workers who had been in the United States to study the automobile industry. Ilf and Petrov befriended them on the ocean voyage home, and met them again at the Soviet border, where the returning autoworkers rapturously drank Russian tea and ate black bread. But by that evening, when Ilf and Petrov ran into the group in the train's

---

[3] Murin, "Daesh Gollivud," 85, 87.   [4] Murin, "Daesh Gollivud," 87.   [5] OA, 229.
[6] Murin, "Daesh Gollivud," 87–88.

restaurant car, joy had given way to anger. The workers responded to the writers' "what's the matter, comrades?" with a catalog of unhygienic and inefficient service: a dirty tablecloth and napkins, a chattering waitress without a headscarf, an obsequious but inept waiter with a wine stain on his jacket, and the overpowering stench from the kitchen. Hearing this litany, Ilf and Petrov asked for an honest answer to one question: before their trip to the United States, "what would you have said about a tablecloth like this?" The irate workers admitted that they would have deemed it "entirely satisfactory." But now they found it unconscionable, and eagerly turned to discussing how they would implement a new regime of "perfect cleanliness" in their own workplace.[7]

Ilf and Petrov reported this conversation to Stalin with "stenographic exactness" as proof that the staggering American standard of living had to be seen to be believed – and imitated. The returning workers "suffered," Ilf and Petrov promised Stalin, "as only a person who loves his country deeply can suffer." This was mobilizing suffering, as the fuming autoworkers immediately set their minds to raising their own standards. Thus, the writers proposed that not only technicians, but secretaries of local party committees be sent to America to learn what was possible in the Soviet Union. To quickly improve the Soviet standard of living, local officials had to "see with their own eyes and understand the meaning of mass consumer service." They needed to see hundreds of "exceptionally important things," including a gas station; a cafeteria; clean tablecloths, lavatories, and showers; a concrete road; a long-distance bus; a dime store; "the ideally simple and businesslike office environment"; and "cheap and primitive but exceptionally comfortable tourist cabins." Seeing all of this, party secretaries, like the autoworkers, would return, Ilf and Petrov were certain, not despondent that "we are far behind," but "itching" to work "smarter, better, and more product-ively to achieve the American level, and then overtake it." "Well-organ-ized trips to America for party workers," they concluded, "could bring great benefits" to the Soviet Union.[8]

Much of *Low-Rise America* operates on the assumption that "to develop the taste"[9] for service and standardized comfort, Soviet people had to experience it for themselves. As literary scholar Leslie Milne notes, Ilf and Petrov's perhaps "hopelessly naïve" letter to Stalin reveals a key purpose of their travelogue: "If they could not organize tour-groups to the USA, they could bring the American experience to readers in a

[7] Murin, "Daesh Gollivud," 88.
[8] Murin, "Daesh Gollivud," 88–89; Milne, *How They Laughed*, 230–31.
[9] Murin, "Daesh Gollivud," 89.

book."[10] Omitting the explicit, if diluted, critique of Soviet conditions that they included in the letter, Ilf and Petrov relied on their readers to supply the contrasts.

Soviet readers would have recognized that the remote American road-house offered more amenities than many big-city Soviet hotels. Again, we can turn to Counts to fill in the missing comparison. He reported that in the better Soviet establishments, a fortunate traveler might find "bath-tubs or showers, but no warm water" and a cot "with inadequate springs and mattress." The small town "house of peasants," where the public spaces smelled of the manure caked on the guests' boots, offered a bed that "probably" lacked springs, a blanket, and an unwashed sheet. For Counts, "Without doubt the most repulsive feature about travel in Russia is the quality and condition of toilet arrangements"; the rare working toilets were "terribly abused by those who patronize them."[11] This was a topic that Ilf and Petrov broached only indirectly in the letter, including a clean lavatory on their list of must-see American attractions. Toilets figured not at all in *Low-Rise America*. But the attentive reader might have guessed that a lodge fitted with steam heat, excellent beds, and running hot and cold water had working toilets, although they might not have imagined them as clean.

Like their readers, Ilf and Petrov made comparisons not only, or even primarily, with New York, Chicago, and Gallup. Their implicit reference points were Moscow, Leningrad, and provincial Russian towns such as Yaroslavl, which they had written about in 1929.[12] They thus missed or overlooked the shortcomings of the desert lodge that vexed guests from American cities. A visitor from London, the artist Nora Cundell, who spent the fall and winter of 1935 in northern Arizona, found tourists from Southern California to be "the worst" complainers: "They came from a land of plenty and just couldn't understand that many of the commod-ities that they were in the habit of taking for granted," such as fresh milk, "were extremely hard to come by in the remote and arid deserts of Arizona." They likewise failed to appreciate that because coal had to be trucked in from more than 300 miles away, "running 'hot and cold'" was not always available. While American tourists grumbled about roughing it, Ilf and Petrov exulted in "complete comfort."[13]

[10] Milne, *How They Laughed*, 232.
[11] Counts, *Ford Crosses Soviet Russia*, 134, 126–27, 132–33.
[12] Il'ia Il'f and Evgenii Petrov, "Iaroslavl' pered shturmom," *Chudak*, no. 7 (September 1929): 8–9. Thanks to Kira Stevens for the citation.
[13] Nora Cundell, *Unsentimental Journey* (London: Methuen & Co., 1940), 215–16; OA, 230.

What is perhaps most notable about the desert roadhouse as Ilf and Petrov described it in both their letter to Stalin and the travelogue is that it seemed to operate outside the normal capitalist drive for profit. Understanding that their pressing need for gasoline and lodging coupled with a total lack of alternatives opened them to higher charges if not price gouging, they were pleasantly surprised when the innkeeper billed little more than the same accommodation would have cost in New York, Chicago, or Gallup. Ironically, American tourists were more prone to gripe about the elevated prices in the desert. Cundell marveled that Californians expected gasoline, bread, or bootlaces "hauled by road all the way from Flagstaff," to be "sold for the same sum" as in Los Angeles.[14]

Ilf and Petrov offered no explanation of the innkeeper's remarkable failure to "rip off" the helpless travelers.[15] In the letter to Stalin, they implicitly adopted Mikoyan's strategy of declining to waste the leader's time analyzing the workings of capitalism. In the published work, they tempered their wide-eyed eagerness to share the "spectacle of the American *standard of life*," a phrase they rendered in English, with the caveat that the cozy little house existed alongside the "Indians' pauper hovels."[16] But such contrasts hardly influenced their narrative. Focused on the people they met at the lodge more than the system in which it was embedded, Ilf and Petrov managed to suggest the possibility of big-hearted capitalists. Soviet reviewers generally well-disposed to the book criticized Ilf and Petrov's "fetishization" of "service with a smile." The pair's beloved *servis*, critics reminded their readers, was merely a "species of commerce," which the authors mistook for real "respect for humankind."[17]

Ilf and Petrov's description of their route through the Arizona desert is accurate enough to guide a curious historian to the lodge at the heart of their story. The travelers left the south rim of the Grand Canyon on Thanksgiving morning, heading east along the canyon's rim on a "new road," Desert View Drive completed in 1931 and designated a "scenic road," a term they provided in English and Russian.[18] As they noted, this road brings travelers into Navajo land and to the trading post at

[14] Cundell, *Unsentimental Journey*, 116.   [15] Murin, "Daesh Gollivud," 88.

[16] OA, 229–30; LGA, 170.

[17] A. Mingulina, "Ocherki puteshestviia po Amerike," *Kniga i proletarskaia revoluiutsiia*, no. 5 (1937): 115 (fetishization); Lev Nikulin, "'Odnoetazhnaia Amerika' I. Il'fa i E. Petrova," *Kniga i proletarskaia revoluitsiia*, no. 2 (1937): 122 (smile, species); Milne, *How They Laughed*, 123 (respect).

[18] "Along Desert View Drive," www.nps.gov/grca/planyourvisit/desert-view-drive.htm (accessed 13 September 2021); OA, 225.

Cameron, Arizona.[19] From Cameron, the travelers followed a "splendid road" through "Navajo territory."[20] The "Indians" installment of their photo essay includes a photograph of the suspension bridge (built in 1911) spanning the Little Colorado River that they would have crossed as they headed north out of town.[21] (A new deck truss bridge replaced it in 1959.) The road, US Highway 89, was almost entirely paved and oil surfaced when Ilf and Petrov traveled it.[22] "The Desert" installment of the photo essay features a photograph of the highway and one of the "dark-grey" rock formations between the trading post and Marble Canyon[23] (Figures 19.1 and 19.2).

In *Low-Rise America*, Ilf and Petrov placed the suspension bridge at the end of their five-hour drive through the desert, confusing it with the Navajo Bridge that spanned the Colorado River at the Marble Gorge of the Grand Canyon. While the Navajo Bridge was not a suspension bridge, they correctly identified its eastern landing as marking the boundary of the Navajo reservation. Ilf and Petrov's description of the "little house" and nearby gas station that they found on the far side of the bridge closely matches contemporary photographs of what was then called Vermilion Cliffs Lodge. Now part of Marble Canyon Lodge, the building looks much as it did in the 1930s, down to the "chunks of petrified wood" flanking the porch[24] (Figures 19.3 and 19.4).

Trone immediately set to work extracting the story of the man who owned the place. According to Ilf and Petrov, the proprietor, a cowboy from Texas, had become an innkeeper by chance. Having built a small homestead in the remote desert, he decided to take advantage of the wave of tourists traveling the newly widened highway by converting his home into a hotel and building a gas station. Despite this entrepreneurial turn, Ilf and Petrov portray the cowboy as out of step with American capitalism. He showed the visitors two Indian rugs that he refused to sell, "although he had been offered two-hundred and fifty dollars apiece" for them. These

---

[19] OA, 226–27; Russ Tall Chief (Osage), "On the Beaten Path: Cameron Trading Post," *Native Peoples* 25 (May–June 2012): 56.
[20] OA, 228.   [21] ART, 68–70; Il'f and Petrov, "Indeitsy," 12.
[22] P. T. Reilly, *Lee's Ferry: From Mormon Crossing to National Park* (Logan: Utah State University Press, 1999), 401; "Arizona Leads West in Oiled Roads," *Arizona Highways* 9 (October 1933): 12; Norman G. Wallace, "Scenic 89 (Continued)," *Arizona Highways* 11 (April 1935): 22.
[23] OA, 229; ART, 56–57; Il'ia Il'f and Evgenii Petrov, "Pustynia," *Ogonek*, no. 15 (30 May 1936): 16.
[24] PIA, Il'f, 28 November, 459–60; LGA, 170; OA, 230; Carolyn O'Bagy Davis, *Arizona's Historic Trading Posts* (Charleston, SC: Arcadia Publishing, 2014), 22; W. L. Rusho, *Lee's Ferry: Desert River Crossing* (Page, AZ: Glen Canyon Natural History Association, 2016), 139–59; Reilly, *Lee's Ferry*, 383, 504n52.

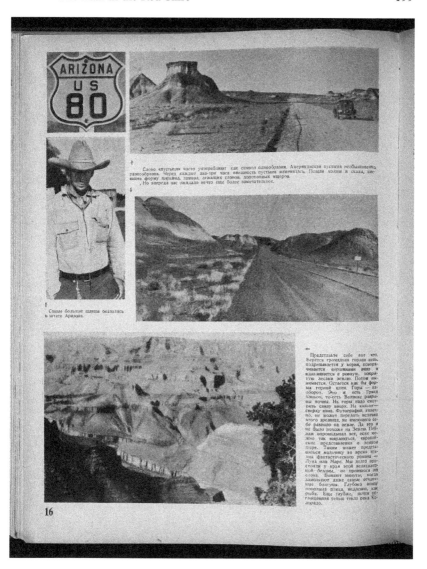

Figure 19.1 Photographs from "The Desert" installment of "American Photographs": Two views of US Highway 89 between Cameron, Arizona, and Marble Canyon; a photograph illustrating the claim that "the biggest hats were found in the state of Arizona"; a view of the Grand Canyon from the rim. *Ogonek*, no. 15 (30 May 1936): 16. Courtesy Library of Congress.

Figure 19.2 US Highway 89 today: the road is wider, but the rocks are the same. Photo by author, 2019.

were, their host explained, "religious rugs" that he had acquired many years before and that he kept because the Navajo used them in their healing rituals.[25] Ilf and Petrov depicted him as more friend of the Navajo than businessman. Their sketch bears a surprising resemblance to a laudatory 1942 obituary of one of the best-known traders to the Hopi and Navajo, Lorenzo Hubbell, Jr., that declared, "he wasn't a trader with an adding machine. He was a trader with a big and kind heart."[26]

The proprietor of Vermilion Cliffs Lodge, David Crockett "Buck" Lowery, did look and sound very much like a cowboy. A local historian describes him as a "'John Wayne' type, tough man of the West."[27] In the summer of 1935, he and his son were involved in one of the most dramatic events ever to shake the quiet of Marble Canyon. Learning that the man who had murdered a gas station attendant at the lodge a month earlier had escaped from jail in Flagstaff, father and son blocked the road

[25] OA, 230–31; LGA, 170–71. Malamuth misstates the price.
[26] "Lorenzo Hubbell: Trader to the Hopi and the Navajo," *Arizona Highways* 13 (April 1942): 2.
[27] Rusho, *Lee's Ferry*, 142.

Figure 19.3 D. C. Lowrey and his Marble Canyon Lodge, c. 1935.
NAU.PH.97.46.120.46, P. T. Reilly Collection, Special Collections
and Archives, Cline Library, Northern Arizona University.

at the bridge and shot and killed the fugitive as he attempted to run them
down. The coroners' jury not only exonerated the Lowerys, but also
praised them for their service to the county.[28]

For all his Western toughness, Buck Lowery was not a cowboy, and Ilf
and Petrov underplayed or perhaps failed to understand the calculation
behind the establishment of the lodge. Born in 1889 in Tennessee and
married in 1907 to Florence Wilmeth, Buck Lowery came to Arizona via
Texas in about 1918 to trade with the Navajo, not to raise cattle.[29] When
he filed a homestead entry in the mid-1920s, he already knew that the site
was adjacent to the proposed bridge across the Colorado and thus "an
ideal place for a lodge and store."[30] Buck and Florence also applied to
open a post office; she was appointed postmaster of Marble Canyon,
Arizona, in 1927.[31] As the bridge went up, Buck Lowrey simultaneously
established a trading post on the Navajo side of the river and built a lodge
on the other side that opened its doors the day the span was dedicated,
14 June 1929. The "Indian rugs and trinkets" for sale that Ilf and Petrov

[28] Kel M. Fox, "Murder at Marble Canyon," *Journal of Arizona History* 24 (Winter
1983): 331–38.
[29] David Crockett "Buck" Lowrey, Jr., Find a Grave, www.findagrave.com/memorial/
120832802/david-crockett-lowrey (accessed 22 August 2022); David C. Lowrey, US
Federal Census, 1920, Ancestry.com.
[30] Rusho, *Lee's Ferry*, 142.
[31] Florence L. Lowrey, Appointments of US Postmasters, Ancestry.com.

Figure 19.4 The lodge today looks much as it did in the 1930s, down to the "chunks of petrified wood" flanking the porch. Photo by author, 2019.

represented as evidence of an embryonic "future large hotel," were Buck's stock in trade.[32]

Although Lowery was not quite the accidental capitalist Ilf and Petrov described, he seems to have been a rather "poor businessman."[33] In 1929, he had borrowed $10,000 from Hubbell at 8 percent interest for three years – a fairly typical arrangement before the advent of the New Deal and fixed-rate, long-term mortgages. But in 1933, when Lowrey was granted the patent to his homestead, the entire debt remained; he had paid neither interest nor principal. He also owed $1,000 plus interest to a lumber company in Flagstaff. A local historian calculated that the lodge "grossed about $15,000 each year" in the early 1930s, but judged that Lowrey was "weak in accounting and budgeting." He may also have been affected by a drop in tourist traffic during the Depression.[34]

[32] Rusho, *Lee's Ferry*, 145; Reilly, *Lee's Ferry*, 322–28; OA, 231; LGA, 171.

[33] Reilly, *Lee's Ferry*, 391.

[34] Dan Cooper and Brian Grinder, "Financing the American Dream: A History of the Fully-Amortized 30-Year Mortgage," *Financial History*, no. 113 (Spring 2015): 10–11; Reilly, *Lee's Ferry*, 366; David C. Lowrey, US, General Land Office Records, Ancestry. com.

In 1936, the lumber company got a judgment against the Lowreys for the entire debt, interest, and attorney fees. Unable to come up with the money, and certainly unable to pay his outstanding obligation to Hubbell, Buck tried to sell. In 1937, he and Florence signed the property over to Hubbell, with Buck staying on as manager for another year. By 1940, the family had relocated to Flagstaff, where Buck was working as a state investigator.[35]

Buck Lowrey's work as a trader on the Navajo reservation and the couple's financial woes add poignancy to a story of Buck's related by Ilf and Petrov. In their retelling, the innkeeper began by describing the Navajo as "irreproachably honest" people, whom he both respected and pitied. Navajo children, he told the travelers, were "dying at a great rate," but the Navajos did not want and would not accept "help from the whites." Lowrey illustrated the incompatibility of Navajo and white cultures with the tale of "a certain Indian of the Navajo tribe who suddenly decided to take up trade." With $200 in capital from selling cattle or finding "a little oil on his property," the man "bought two hundred dollars' worth of various merchandise" to sell on the reservation. This, Lowrey emphasized was a first, "an Indian engaged in commerce!" But the Navajo trader's methods were "peculiar." "You see," the host explained to his visitors from the world of socialism, "he was selling his merchandise for exactly the same price he had paid for it himself." Lowrey tried to make him see that a trader had to add a markup. But the idea of making a profit seemed to the Navajo nothing but "fraud" and deception.[36]

Lowrey evidently viewed the story as a humorous illustration of why "the only commercial enterprise with Indian capital in the Navajo tribe had to close up." But Ilf and Petrov took it as further evidence of the contrast between pure, instinctively anti-capitalist Native Americans and greedy white Americans – among whom they did not necessarily include the innkeeper, a sympathetic character unwilling to sell his "religious rugs."[37]

The cowboy who unwittingly unmasked the "fraud" of American capitalism was not the most memorable personality Ilf and Petrov met at Vermilion Cliffs Lodge. That distinction went to the tall man with greying red hair sporting horn-rimmed glasses, boots, a red shirt cinched with a cartridge belt, and a "dazzling smile," whom they encountered in the lodge's dining room. According to their "cowboy host," the man in the red shirt was "the only white man, whom the Indians have accepted

---

[35] Reilly, *Lee's Ferry*, 391, 399, 404; David Lowry [sic], US Federal Census, 1940, Ancestry.com.
[36] LGA, 171–72; OA, 231–33.   [37] LGA, 173; OA, 233.

Figure 19.5 Shine Smith, Buck Lowrey, river guide Clyde Eddy, 1927. NAU.PH.97.46.120.28, P. T. Reilly Collection, Special Collections and Archives, Cline Library, Northern Arizona University.

as one of their own." Like Solomon Trone, the unnamed man had "an insatiable and insane desire to talk." The two hit it off immediately. With an "extraordinary" biography that constituted an indictment of the hypocrisy of American religion, the man in the red shirt turned out to be "one of the most interesting people we met in the United States."[38]

The man who charmed the travelers was likely Hugh Dickson "Shine" Smith (Figures 19.5 and 19.6). Smith was something of a local legend. Born in Georgia in 1882, he had been ordained as a Presbyterian minister in 1911. He had preached to cowboys in west Texas until 1917, when the church sent him to northern Arizona as a missionary to the Navajo. How he acquired the nickname Shine was, as his friend Gladwell Richardson noted in a 1946 profile, "the subject of many stories." Richardson gave most credence to the version that dated the moniker to the hard winter of 1921, when Smith brought food and medicine to isolated Native American settlements where children were dying of

[38] OA, 233–35.

Figure 19.6 The "man in the red shirt" in "The Indians" installment of "American Photographs." At the top is Vermillion Cliffs Lodge. Ilf and Petrov misidentified the suspension bridge across the Colorado River at Cameron, Arizona as the bridge across the Little Colorado at Marble Canyon. *Ogonek*, no. 16 (10 June 1936): 12. Courtesy Library of Congress.

influenza and malnutrition. The grateful Navajos, so the tale goes, began to say, "He brings hope and life like the sun shining upon the earth." Smith quickly became known as "Sunshine" and then simply "Shine."[39]

Like Ilf and Petrov's man in the red shirt, Smith came to Arizona as a representative of a Christian church, worked diligently to learn fluent Navajo, and then, in the early 1920s, become a "freelance missionary." Covering the 25,000-square-mile reservation on horseback and, by 1935, in a "beat-up old Model-T Ford," Smith "preached sanitation and child welfare as often as he told them about the Bible and the white man's God."[40] This sounds very much like the man in the red shirt, who told Ilf and Petrov that he was interested not in converting the Native Americans but in helping them by calling doctors and explaining "how they must care for their children."[41]

As with the case of his nickname, stories abounded about why Smith left – or was kicked out of – the church. In his 1946 profile, Richardson attributed "Shine's decision to withdraw from organized missionary service" to a desire for more "freedom of movement and action." Emphasizing that the split was discouraged by church officials, Richards sought to dispel rumors that Smith was unfrocked for "misconduct." Still, he granted that Smith's sympathy for Native American ways, which led him to assist at "pagan Navajo tribal ceremonies," infuriated church officials.[42] These activities square with Ilf and Petrov's account of the man in the red shirt, who told them that he wanted to be "accepted by the Indians as one of them." In their telling, Smith became a freelancer because the church administration "fired him" when he "refused" to "act like all missionaries." Rather than making Christians of the Indians, he told the travelers "they made an Indian out of me."[43]

Where Ilf and Petrov's portrait differs most clearly from Smith's biography is their assertion that he was married and that they met his wife. Overhearing the travelers speaking "in some foreign tongue," the man in the red shirt said to the woman accompanying him to dinner, "Well, wife, these must be Frenchmen. Now you'll have a chance to speak French." To her insistence that she did not know French, he allegedly replied, "We have been married for fifteen years and all this time every

---

[39] Gladwell Richardson, "Shine Smith: Friend of the Navajo," *Arizona Highways* 22 (August 1946): 27; Marshall Trimble, "Shine Smith," *True West Magazine*, 31 March 2018, https://truewestmagazine.com/shine-smith/ (accessed 16 September 2021); Dan L. Thrap, "Smith, Hugh Dickson (Shine)," in *Encyclopedia of Frontier Biography: In Three Volumes*, vol. 3 (Lincoln: University of Nebraska Press, 1988), 1328.

[40] Trimble, "Shine Smith" (freelance); Barry Goldwater, "Shine Smith: Navajo Friend," *McCall's* (December 1967): 168 (Ford); Richardson, "Shine Smith," 28 (preached).

[41] OA, 235.   [42] Richardson, "Shine Smith," 28–29.   [43] LGA, 174–75; OA, 235–36.

day you told me you were born two hours' ride from Paris." And so she was, she responded, in London, which is "actually two hours' ride from Paris if you go by airplane." The man's laughter suggested that this was a "family joke," "repeated every time the couple met foreigners."[44]

The woman could not have been Smith's wife, as he never married.[45] However, in the fall of 1935, he may well have been dining and joking with a visitor from London, who also spent a good bit of time at Vermilion Cliffs Lodge, the artist Nora Cundell. She had been coming to Arizona and staying with the Lowreys since 1934, and she was there in 1938 when they finally turned the place over to Hubbell. In her own account of her visits to northern Arizona, *Unsentimental Journey*, Cundell fondly remembered Smith at a Navajo gathering, in "his enormous hat and horn-rimmed spectacles," towering above the 700 Native Americans, all of whom he seemed to know by name, and making "execrable puns in two languages." He even joined in during some of the dances, "weaving in and out among the performers with obvious enjoyment."[46]

Given Cundell and Smith's joking familiarity, the travelers may have mistaken them for husband and wife. However, Ilf's notebook identifies the woman not as the missionary's wife, but as his "neighbor," and more importantly, quotes her as affirming that she *lived* in London – not that she was born there.[47] Ilf's contemporary notes suggest that the authors chose to turn the pair into husband and wife. This choice simplified the story and heightened its pathos. In *Low-Rise America*, they emphasized that this "odd fellow stuck to his dangerous ideas, with his wife and without a penny to his name." The man's reflection that the Indians "taught me to love the sun, the moon, the desert, to understand nature," brought a tear to Mr. Adams's eye. The happy, if fictive, marriage along with the man's jocular farewell, which Ilf and Petrov rendered as "*Ai em Bolshevik!*" only added to his aura of goodness.[48]

In both *Low-Rise America* and their letter to Stalin, Ilf and Petrov used the little house in the desert to illustrate the high American standard of living. But while the letter ended with a sincere plea to send Soviet functionaries to the United States to learn how to construct American comfort at home, the tale in the book took a more wistful turn. As they departed, Ilf and Petrov found the missionary pumping gas because the

[44] LGA, 173; OA, 233–34.
[45] Rev. Hugh Dickson "Shine" Smith, Find a Grave, www.findagrave.com/memorial/116472525/hugh-dickson-smith (accessed 16 September 2021).
[46] Cundell, *Unsentimental Journey*, 143; Carolyn O'Bagy Davis, "Nora L. M. Cundell, Artist," www.noracundell.com/the-artist/ (accessed 16 September 2021); Rusho, *Lee's Ferry*, 151–53.
[47] ZK, 29 November, 459.   [48] OA, 235–37.

cowboy was "busy with his homestead."[49] Their farewell left readers with indelible images of a real cowboy who had the tourist trade thrust upon him and a "Bolshevik" missionary helping a friend. Reflecting on how the Navajo had managed to resist the modern capitalist world of gangsters, jazz clubs, and banks that surrounded them, the writers seemed almost ready to emulate the white man who had abandoned American comforts for the sun, moon, and desert. As they drove away from the lodge, Ilf and Petrov watched the little house, the gas station, and the man in red slowly fade into the glorious landscape. American service itself became a kind of natural wonder.

[49] OA, 237.

20   Natural Wonders and Technical Marvels

> It's probably impossible to find anything on earth more majestic and
> beautiful than the American desert. We raced along it for a whole week
> and never stopped marveling.
> Ilf and Petrov, "The Desert," *American Photographs*

As they traveled through the Southwest, Ilf and Petrov stood amazed
before one natural wonder after another: the Painted Desert, the
Petrified Forest, the Grand Canyon, the Sonoran Desert. They made
the desire to communicate this amazement to their readers the starting
point of "The Desert" installment of "American Photographs." In at
least one case, that of the photographer Alexander Rodchenko, they
failed spectacularly. Looking at Ilf's photos of the desert, Rodchenko
experienced not amazement, but exasperation.

In a review published in August 1936, three months after the "The
Desert" appeared in *Ogonek*, the renowned avant-garde photographer
characterized Ilf's photographs as "passive and mild" and lacking "the
gunpowder of satire." Rodchenko imagined that "Ilf gets out of the car,
stands to the side, and simply photographs." Unlike a "professional
photographer," he did not capture "some prominent car detail" or use
filters "to play up the clouds or the shadows." Instead, Ilf shot landscapes
"honestly: half sky, half ground. The bending line of the road and the
back of automobile are in the photo." He photographed "markers, sig-
nals, and inscriptions ... as simply as if he were jotting this down in his
notebook." These photographs were "documentary records" that
Rodchenko derided as "bookkeeping."[1]

As in the case of his assessment of Ilf's New York photographs,
Rodchenko unaccountably ignored the captions in "American
Photographs" and then advised Ilf and Petrov to write "sharp and
funny!" captions. When taken together with their captions, the desert
photographs, like those of New York City, are quite sharp and funny.

---

[1] Alexander Rodchenko, "Ilya Ilf's American Photographs," in ART, 149, 151–52.

Nonetheless, Rodchenko does have a point. On their own, Ilf's desert panoramas are unimpressive. They do appear shot in a hurry. Ilf seems more interested in "striving to document a phenomenon simply" than in expressing his "special point of view." For Rodchenko, Ilf's photographs suggested "bookkeeping" or indifference. A more generous and useful label might be "deadpan."[2] When we pay attention to the captions and to the photo essay's juxtapositions of texts and images, we can perceive a "special point of view," although not the charged perspective that Rodchenko desired. In their exchanges with the captions, the photographs play it straight, getting a laugh by failing to react to the contradictions and absurdities that swirl around them. More seriously, they allowed the writers and their readers to observe the United States before judging it.

Ilf and Petrov found the unifying thread of the ever-changing desert landscape in the "scenic road." As they explained in an early installment of the photo essay, the American scenic road made it possible for travelers to "get the entire required quantity of emotions" without leaving their car and having to "scramble around on the cliffs in search of a convenient observation point."[3] Nowhere did they find scenic highways more magnificent, convenient, or necessary than in the desert. Because their guides insisted that the trip last no more than two months, the writers moved quickly. On their way to and from California, they spent seventeen days covering more than 2,500 miles through Oklahoma, Texas, New Mexico, Arizona, Utah, and Nevada. Their hurried timetable limited Ilf to taking snapshots during brief stops along the road. Four of the five panoramic views of the desert landscape in "The Desert" include wide swaths of the smooth highway. The writers' beloved Ford makes a cameo appearance in three of them. The automobile, with three travelers still seated inside, also appears in Ilf's portrait of a saguaro cactus raising its "prickly arms up to the heavens in despair."[4]

Even when it appears that the travelers ventured further afield, retracing their route makes it clear that Ilf shot from the most accessible roadside vantages. His photograph of the Grand Canyon positions the viewer at the rim looking down at the canyon's "mountains in reverse" (see Figure 19.1). It provides no context. But, as the writers explain in Low-Rise America, and as my visit to the area confirms, they viewed the

---

[2] Aron Vinegar, "Ed Ruscha, Heidegger, and Deadpan Photography," *Art History* 32 (December 2009): 852–73.
[3] ART, 5; Il'ia Il'f and Evgenii Petrov, "Amerikanskie fotografii," *Ogonek*, no. 11 (20 April 1936): 3.
[4] ART, 60; Il'f and Petrov, "Pustynia," 17.

canyon from the lookout directly across from Bright Angel Lodge, the complex of cozy cabins where they spent the night, and from the over-looks along Desert View Drive. Likewise, Ilf's images of petroglyphs created by ancestral Puebloan people may suggest a remote location. But they are from Newspaper Rock, a stop on the twenty-eight-mile tourist road through Petrified Forest National Park. Ilf photographed the petrified logs themselves through the windows of the visitor center's museum.[5]

Ilf and Petrov's rushed tour of natural wonders produced a fundamental insight: The scenic highway was a mundane marvel. It conquered space and time with nothing more spectacular than regular road maintenance, cheap motels, plentiful gas stations, and accurate signage. In contrast to Soviet technical marvels, always represented as heroic prospects or the fruits of epic battles with nature, the American scenic road, whatever feats of engineering underpinned it, seemed to be part of the landscape. It was extraordinary mainly because it was so pervasive and predictable.[6]

Structuring the "The Desert" around the marvelous and banal scenic road allowed the writers to question, even erase, the "distinction between pristine landscape and modern development."[7] The photo essay's first lines emphasize the purity of the American desert. The writers observe that as they traveled West, the sun shone brighter, the sky became bluer, and the "annoying advertising billboards almost disappeared." "Soon," they informed their readers, "the first cowboy appeared." And sure enough, the first photograph in "The Desert" is of a cowboy on the range. In the caption, as in their descriptions of Agapito Pino, Ilf and Petrov verified their and their readers' romantic preconceptions. The cowboy, allegedly the first one they spotted, "wore, as expected, a wide hat and a checkered flannel shirt. He carried a pistol on his belt. Spurs glittered on boots with high curved heels. The toes of the boots were tucked into stirrups with thick leather shields." None of these details,

---

[5] ART, 57; Il'f and Petrov, "Pustynia," 15, 16.

[6] Katerina Clark, *The Soviet Novel: History as Ritual* (Chicago: University of Chicago Press, 1985), 100–106; Aglaya Glebova, "Elements of Photography: Avant-Garde Aesthetics and the Reforging of Nature," *Representations*, no. 142 (Spring 2018): 57–61; Nicholas Kupensky, "The Soviet Industrial Sublime: The Awe and Fear of Dneprostroi, 1927–1932 (PhD diss., Yale University, 2017), 216–17; PIA, Il'f, 7 December 1935, 464–65.

[7] Cécile Whiting, "The Sublime and the Banal in Postwar Photography of the American West," *American Art* 27, no. 2 (2013): 61; Kelly Dennis, "Landscape and the West: Irony and Critique in New Topographic Photography," Unpublished paper presented at the Forum UNESCO University and Heritage 10th International Seminar "Cultural Landscapes in the 21st Century" (2005), 1; Fedorova, *Yankees*, 95–96.

save the silhouette of the wide hat, are visible in the photograph. Nonetheless, the image of a cowboy on horseback following perhaps a dozen or so head of cattle under a wide-open sky matched the caption's sense of the "expected" features of the American West. The other cowboy in the photo essay, a young man looking directly into the camera, lacked the pistol and the checkered shirt. He stood as evidence of the fact, reported in the laconic caption, that "the biggest hats were found in the state of Arizona." If we discount the barely visible travelers waiting in the car while Ilf took pictures, the cowboys are the only people who appear in "The Desert."[8]

But no sooner had Ilf and Petrov established the reality of the mythic West than they called it into question. Alongside the cowboy and his "cows," "The Desert" set an image of an art deco monolith emblazoned with the word "Texas" that stood on a pedestal marked with a five-pointed star. In the caption, Ilf and Petrov explained that this "strange" monument, which looked to them like a "small grain elevator," marked the Oklahoma–Texas border, and served no purpose beyond indulging Texans' "love of decorating the borders of their state." They informed their readers that the monument's star was the "emblem of Texas, the biggest and most romantic state in America." The straightforward photograph and the caption's neutral tone leave unresolved the question of whether the writers were simply reporting a fact – Texas was the biggest and most romantic state – or mocking the Texans' passion for garish markers that marred the landscape and spoiled the romance (Figure 20.1).

Ilf and Petrov applied the same noncommittal approach to the least appealing images in "The Desert," four photographs of gas stations. The first, showing a couple of nondescript single-story buildings facing a barren patch of earth adjacent to the road, appears on the essay's first page. For the twenty-first-century reader, Ilf's gas stations call to mind Edward Ruscha's deadpan *Twentysix Gasoline Stations*, a 1963 compendium also shot from a car along Route 66 between Los Angeles and Oklahoma (Figure 20.2). Ilf and Petrov provided more elaborate captions for their gas stations, but they, like Ruscha, seem willing to accept them as signifying at once "progress and degradation."[9] In this case, Ilf and Petrov's ironic caption naturalized the unlovely spot as a "small oasis, typical for the American desert." In a single page of the photo

[8] ART, 51; Il'f and Petrov, "Pustynia," 13, 16.
[9] Britt Salvesen as quoted in Juha Tolonen, "Contemporary Photographic Practice in Landscape," in Rod Giblett and Juha Tolonen, *Photography and Landscape* (Chicago: Intellect Books, 2012), 163.

Figure 20.1 The first page of "The Desert" installment of "American Photographs": the "expected" cowboy; a monument marking the Oklahoma-Texas; and the treeless desert "oasis" with an "abundance of life-giving rivulets of oil." *Ogonek*, no. 15 (30 May 1936): 13. Courtesy Library of Congress.

Figure 20.2 Twenty-seven years after Ilf, Ed Ruscha captured gas stations along the same stretch of Route 66. Ed Ruscha, *Standard, Amarillo, Texas*, 1962, Gelatin silver print, 11.8 × 12.1 cm (4 5/8 × 4 3/4 in.), J. Paul Getty Museum. © Ed Ruscha.

essay, they moved from the desert's bright sun and pure air to a treeless "oasis" with an "abundance of life-giving rivulets of oil."[10]

Only at the bottom of the second page of the five-page spread, following photographs of a cattle guard, a second gas station, and a sign proclaiming, "Leave Texas Enter New Mexico," did Ilf and Petrov provide a view of the "majestic and beautiful" landscape promised in the photo essay's opening lines. This was perhaps one of the photographs that irritated Rodchenko. We see the bending line of the road and, almost

[10] ART, 51; Il'f and Petrov, "Pustynia," 13.

in the center of the frame, the Ford, its back toward the photographer. But the text that accompanies Ilf's photograph directs our gaze elsewhere. Ignoring both the highway and the vehicle, the caption tries to get us to see the overwhelming beauty of the "painted desert," a term rendered in English: "The desert has been brightly, wonderfully painted by nature. The colors are dark blue, pink, deep red, pale yellow. The hues are blindingly pure."[11]

We can understand Ilf and Petrov's recourse to listing the "pure" colors of the Painted Desert as an admission of the limits of photography in the face of natural wonders. In a letter to his wife, Ilf described his encounter with saguaro cactuses, which he anthropomorphized as "praying," "hugging," and standing in "proud tranquility." He wrote that he had sent her postcards with photographs of cactuses and had taken many pictures of his own. But he doubted any photo would give her a true impression: "you have to see this with your own eyes."[12] The caption accompanying a rather unremarkable view of the Grand Canyon similarly asserts that "a photograph, of course, can't convey the grandeur of this sight." Ilf and Petrov thus supplemented the image with a series of ingenious and evocative metaphors, likening the canyon to the impression made by an enormous upside-down mountain range pressed into the earth; to the surface of the Moon or Mars; to a vast bowl in which a bird slowly floated like a fish. They ended by recounting their own awe in the face of the otherworldly landscape: They "stood at the edge of this magnificent abyss for a long time, not saying a word. There are times," they concluded, "when even the most incorrigible chatterboxes can keep quiet."[13] Here, Ilf and Petrov explicitly used their caption to compensate for the photographs' inability (any photograph's, not just Ilf's) to capture the ineffable canyon.

This reading of the photo essay – the captions supply what the camera cannot – makes sense but misses the degree to which the elaborate captions play off the indifferent images.[14] Like the scenic road itself, the photo essay is full of contrasts and contradictions: the "blindingly pure" colors of the desert, smooth highways, unsightly "oases," vulgar monuments. To draw out these contrasts, Ilf and Petrov relied on the ironic back and forth between text and images. The photograph of the Painted Desert is only recognizable as such because the caption fills in the colors. But the text does more than make up for the inadequate black and white reproduction. It attempts to recast the photograph entirely. Looking past the road and the Ford, the caption encourages readers to

---

[11] ART, 56; Il'f and Petrov, "Pustynia," 14.   [12] PIA, Il'f, 27 December, 460.
[13] Nesbet, "Skyscrapers," 388; ART, 57.   [14] Reischl, *Photographic Literacy*, 175.

see not a prosaic scene – a bend in the highway, the back of the car, some indistinct desert – but a fantastic, almost surreal landscape.

Other images and captions on the page work in the opposite direction, guiding the viewer's gaze from the sublime desert to the ordinary technologies of the road. At the top of the page with the car in the Painted Desert, the viewer encounters a shot of textured pavement and a bit of metal fence. Here, the landscape that surrounds the Ford is reduced to a sliver, as the highway itself takes center stage. A long and involved caption explains that the photograph shows a structure that Ilf and Petrov thought unique to Texas. Having no Russian equivalent, they transliterated it as *kattl garden*. The unpretentious photograph inspired them to give a short lesson on the economics of cattle ranching, to joke about trigger-happy cowboys, and to sing the praises of a low-tech example of American ingenuity, the humble cattle guard. Ranchers, they explained, separated their "enormous parcels of land" with barbed wire. This kept cattle from straying onto a neighbor's property, thus avoiding lawsuits and preventing "the picturesque cowboys from having to engage their Colts." But where the highway intersected the fence line, there was nothing to detain cows interested in crossing the road. To solve this problem, "some unknown inventor came up with the bright idea" to extend the fence with a "metallic grate covering a pit." The grate, they affirmed, "doesn't bother automobiles at all, but the cows are afraid that their hooves will fall though the bars, and so they refrain from undesirable excursions into foreign territory." The cattle guard, they concluded, typified the "American way: simple and effective!"[15]

Ilf's straightforward photographs of two additional "simple and effective" features of the American highway – the gas pump and the highway marker – similarly allowed readers to observe the scenic road as both technical marvel and natural wonder. At a New Mexico gas station, Ilf captured the Ford and a gas pump against a background of open desert and a dark rock formation. As their description of gas pumps in *Low-Rise America* makes clear, Ilf and Petrov viewed them not as aberrant growths on "unspoiled" nature, but as a magnificent example of American "service." Here, the landscape seems to coexist with, even overshadow, the human-altered environment. The adjacent caption positioned alongside the image of a highway marker transports the seemingly mundane to the realm of the divine: The sign's "slightly ceremonial" announcement, "Leave Texas Enter New Mexico," "sounds as if you were leaving the earth and entering heaven."[16]

---

[15] ART, 52–53; Il'f and Petrov, "Pustynia," 14.   [16] ART, 53.

What immediately brings the writers back down to Earth is not the modern amenities' deformation of the "pure" desert landscape, but American capitalism's deformation of modernization. In the caption, the pictured station turns out to be less benign than it looks: "they took two cents more per gallon from us than in Texas." Ilf and Petrov warned readers used to centralized planning that, "the price of gasoline fluctuates in the most capricious way in America. Every state has its own price."[17] It went without saying that the distribution of gasoline in the Soviet Union (if there were gas pumps!) would be pleasingly rationalized.

Like a good sidekick, Ilf's photos fed the writers observations that occasioned all manner of ironic, critical, and whimsical rejoinders. Because Ilf shot everything – from the Grand Canyon to a highway marker – head-on, with none of the professional photographer's flourishes, filters, or foreshortening, the photos seemed to give everything equal weight. It was precisely this refusal to take a stand that bothered Rodchenko. He disdained as "bookkeeping" photographs that asked viewers merely to "recognize" rather than "see" that at which they looked.[18] In "pursuit of some distanced and more 'knowing' condition," Rodchenko ascribed no value to mere observation. But for Ilf and Petrov, documentary "recognition" facilitated "comic acknowledgment" of the unknown.[19]

The spread on the Petrified Forest illustrates how Ilf's seemingly inexpressive photographs allowed the writers to highlight, without necessarily judging, modern capitalist America's (comic) contradictions. Two photos set side by side on the top half of the photo essay's third page provide views of Petrified Forest National Park. One, apparently shot in front of the visitor center, foregrounds a patch of empty ground, likely the parking lot. In the center of the photo, petrified logs surround a flagpole at the top of which the American flag twists in the wind. In the other photograph, as noted earlier, the viewer peers through the museum's window to glimpse petrified logs lining a gently sloping path. The travelers, as Ilf informed his wife and as the photographs of the petroglyphs attest, drove the park road, which provides plenty of opportunities to photograph a "whole forest" of petrified trees.[20] Nonetheless, Ilf and Petrov chose photographs that pictured not the Petrified Forest, but the National Park, where the facilities – a parking lot, a visitor center – made it easy and comfortable to see "nature." Ironically, the image that gives the most satisfying sense of the petrified logs' grandeur is of a "gas station hemmed in with a fence made of pieces of petrified wood." In this final photograph, taking up the entire bottom half of the page, Ilf

[17] RT, 53, 56.   [18] Glebova, "Elements of Photography," 90n38.
[19] Vinegar, "Ed Ruscha," 870, 868.   [20] PIA, Il'f, 27 November 1935, 459.

foregrounded the impressive wall of petrified logs above which hovered a small "Texaco" sign (Figure 20.3).

The text accompanying the Petrified Forest images contrasts the careful preservation of national park lands and the unregulated capitalist

Figure 20.3 Page from the "The Desert" installment of "American Photographs" showing the Rainbow Forest Museum and a gas station outside the park. *Ogonek*, no. 15 (30 May 1936): 15. Courtesy Library of Congress.

exploitation of nature. The caption that ran alongside the two views of the visitor center explain that the "process of replacing particles of wood with particles of salt, lime, and iron took place over millions of years." The resulting petrified tree rings sparkled with "red, dark blue, and yellow veins." The rangers carefully guarded these treasures, prohibiting travelers from taking even a "single grain of sand" out of the park. However, as soon as they left the preserve, the writers encountered the pictured gas station, where the proprietor was doing a brisk business selling tacky souvenirs fashioned from polished pieces of petrified wood. Taking the petrified tree's perspective, Ilf and Petrov wondered, "Was it worth it to lie around for so many millions of years just to be turned into an unattractive brooch?"[21] Whatever the tree might think, the writers, as they reveal in *Low-Rise America*, found the souvenirs irresistible, and bought "several pieces of wood." As they packed them into the Ford, they imagined "how in due time they would travel inside our valises across the ocean."[22]

The image of bits of petrified wood stuffed into the writers' suitcases offers an effective coda to "The Desert." Ultimately, the photographs and the captions displayed not a "special point of view," but a panorama of the banal marks technology and consumerism left on nature. In *Low-Rise America*, which did not include photographs, the writers riffed more extensively on the incongruity of a modern visitor center in a barren landscape. As in "The Desert," they reported that they learned at the museum that "these trees were a hundred and fifty-million years old." They added the observation that "the museum itself was probably no more than a year old." (The building, which still houses the Rainbow Forest Museum, was completed in 1931.)[23] It was, they emphasized, a "small but quite modern building" with metal-frame windows and running hot and cold water. "Emerging from such a building," they concluded, one would expect to find a subway and a department store. Instead, just outside the door they found, as Ilf tried to document in his photograph, "a desert extending for hundreds of miles."[24] When I visited in 2019, the museum still looked like a chunk of the modern world unexpectedly stranded in the desert (Figure 20.4).

This focus on the startling presence of standardized modernity woven into a vast wilderness helps to explain why Ilf and Petrov treated readers to photographs of the Petrified Forest museum, multiple gas stations, highway markers, and a cattle guard, but omitted the most impressive

---

[21] ART, 57.   [22] LGA, 159; OA, 214.

[23] "Rainbow Forest Museum," National Park Service, www.nps.gov/pefo/learn/historyculture/rainbow-forest-museum.htm (accessed 5 June 2022).

[24] LGA, 159; OA, 214.

Figure 20.4 The Rainbow Forest Museum today still looks like a chunk of the modern world unexpectedly stranded in the desert. Photo by author, 2019.

technical marvel they encountered in the desert: Boulder Dam. When they arrived in late December 1935, the dam was already a busy tourist attraction.[25] In his notebook, Ilf recorded that he shot more than one roll of film there,[26] so the problem does not appear to have been a ban on photography. A "Topics of the Times" column that ran in the *New York Times* shortly after Boulder Dam's 30 September 1935 dedication suggests that the issue may have been on the Soviet side. The unsigned article pointedly asked why, after all the commotion around the construction of the Dneprostroi Dam in Ukraine, the more impressive Boulder Dam, with two and a half times the sustained generating capacity of the Dnepr Hydroelectric Station, had attracted so little attention in the Soviet Union. It concluded that the Soviets ignored Boulder Dam because it served only to "remind people that the capitalist system, too, can build hydroelectric plants." Why, Ilf and Petrov may have asked

[25] Hoover Dam – Tourists and Tourism (1920s–1950s), Boulder Dam Museum and Archive (BDMA), Boulder City, Nevada, Subject Files.
[26] ZK, 476.

themselves, publish a photo of an American dam that dwarfs the "star feature of the First Five-Year Plan"?[27]

The writers may well have been disinclined to present an image of an American dam that surpassed Soviet achievements. Still, they managed to finesse this problem in *Low-Rise America*, which devoted an entire chapter to Boulder Dam. I would argue that they left it out of the photo essay not because they hesitated to remind people that capitalists could build dams, but because there was no way to integrate the massive project into a story of the ordinariness of American technical marvels. The Soviet Union already had a heroic dam that conquered recalcitrant nature, brought the peasantry into the modern world, and promised to light the socialist future.[28] What it needed, Ilf and Petrov suggested, was the "simple and effective" everyday technologies that made even the remote American desert modern and convenient.

---

[27] "Topics of the Times," NYT, 2 October 1935.
[28] Kupensky, "Soviet Industrial Sublime," 21.

21   The American Dneprostroi

> Standing at the summit of one of the most glorious constructions of our century, about which is known only that no one knows who built it, we spoke of fame in the United States.
>
> Ilf and Petrov, *Low-Rise America*

Boulder Dam, the "biggest job in the world today," as the *Las Vegas Review-Journal* boasted in 1931, invited comparisons between socialist and capitalist construction.[1] In late November 1935, two months after its official dedication, Ilf and Petrov recognized the colossus that tamed the Colorado River as akin to the monumental projects that propelled and came to symbolize Soviet industrialization. When Bruce Bliven, the editor of the *New Republic*, made his own cross-country trip (by train) in December 1935, he too stopped at Boulder Dam; the item on his visit ran under the headline "The American Dnieperstroy." Bliven mentioned the Dnepr Hydroelectric Station only once in the body of the article, noting that Boulder Dam would have a "maximum electric capacity four times that of Niagara, three times that of Muscle Shoals, two and one-half times that of the great Russian [sic] dam." However, his description of the project's workforce suggested a less favorable comparison with the Soviet system. He noted that "a large proportion of the workers had been college men who, because of the vagaries of our economic system, had been unable to get jobs more appropriate to their training." He also observed that "the work is exceedingly hard, often dangerous, and not particularly well paid."[2]

By contrast, Ilf and Petrov took surprisingly little notice of the workers or their working conditions. What troubled them was the fact that no one in America knew the names of those who constructed the "biggest dam in the world." This failure to accord the builders their due provided Ilf and Petrov with a means of at once praising American technology and

---

[1] As quoted in Anthony F. Arrigo, *Imagining Hoover Dam: The Making of a Cultural Icon* (Reno: University of Nevada Press, 2014), 91.
[2] Bruce Bliven, "The American Dnieperstroy," *New Republic* 85 (11 December 1935): 125.

criticizing American capitalism. Gazing at "one of the most glorious constructions of our century," they contrasted it to an imagined Soviet Boulder Dam that would generate both electricity and heroes of socialist labor. Their tour guide at the dam, GE engineer Charles John Thomson, was well positioned to help them make such comparisons. In charge of installing the generating turbines at Boulder Dam, he had received the Order of the Red Banner of Labor for doing the same job at Dneprostroi.[3]

Despite his status as one of the few foreigners to win a Soviet order, Thomson has left relatively little mark in the historical record. His last name often appears as "Thompson" and sources sometimes identify him as "James" or by incorrect initials. Ilf and Petrov introduced their guide as "Mr. Tomson" a forty-year-old native of Scotland with a ruddy complexion and lively eyes. They observed that his "profession had almost deprived him of his homeland": He was "a Brit, working for an American company, who travels the world" installing machinery.[4]

Immigration documents and a short contemporary article in a Las Vegas newspaper corroborate Ilf and Petrov's portrait of the peripatetic engineer. Between a stint in the 1920s at Muscle Shoals dam in Alabama and his employment at Boulder Dam, Thomson worked in the Soviet Union, South America, and South Africa. I was unable to verify Ilf and Petrov's claim that he served during World War I as a British aviator. But there is no reason to doubt their assertion that he had the "shadow of sadness" characteristic of "those who had given several years of their life to war."[5] In 1927 and again in 1934, Thomson filed declarations of intention to become an American citizen, but he never followed through. His wife Eleanor (née Dichmont), whom he married in 1927 in New York City, was born in England and grew up in South Africa. On travel documents, they listed residences in both Schenectady, New York (GE's headquarters) and Cape Town, South Africa.[6]

In line with GE policy, Thomson rarely discussed his experiences at Dneprostroi. To protect its interests and its reputation, General Electric "instructed its engineers not to discuss conditions in the U.S.S.R. with

---

[3] OA, 246–47, 251; "Inzhenery GE pomogli osushchestvit' samyi znakovyi proekt SSSR v 1930kh – stroitesl'stvo Gidroelektrostantsii DneproGES," GE v Rossii, 4 September 2014, www.ge.com/news/reports/инженеры-ге-помогли-осуществить-самый-з (accessed 6 June 2022); "Soviet Dedicates Dnieprostroy Dam," NYT, 11 October 1932.

[4] OA, 248.   [5] LGA, 183; OA, 248.

[6] "Electrical Generating Units Weighing Hundreds of Tons Being Installed at Dam Now," clipping, [c. 30 September 1935], Las Vegas (Nevada) Evening Review-Journal, BDMA, Thompson, CJ BF 6631; ZK, 30 November, 460; Charles Thomson, New York, Arriving Passenger and Crew Lists; Alabama Naturalization Records; New York Naturalization Records; New York Marriage License Indexes, Ancestry.com.

the State Department," and apparently "destroyed" corporate records covering its work there. When the historian Harold H. Fisher contacted "a number" of engineers about their experiences on Soviet projects, only two replied. In a 1934 letter, "C. Thomson, G. E. chief erector," confirmed that he had worked on the Stalingrad and Dneprostroi hydroelectric stations. However, he refused to elaborate, noting that the fact that he might have to return "plus the danger of involving my Company in an unpleasant situation bars me from making any statements."[7] Thomson and other GE personnel thus declined to publicize the complaints about lax work habits, disregard for proper procedures, and poor hygiene that filled their contemporary correspondence with the local Soviet authorities at Dneprostroi.[8]

Thomson was nonetheless willing to share stories about his time at Dneprostroi with the Soviet funnymen. The presence of Solomon Trone, a retired GE engineer, who had overseen work at Dneprostroi, Magnitogorsk, Stalingrad, and other Soviet industrial sites, likely put Thomson at ease. In March 1933, before the normalization of Soviet–American relations, Trone himself had violated company policy and discussed conditions in the Soviet Union with an official at the American consulate in Riga. He apparently saw no harm – and maybe some benefit – in outlining the potential of the Soviet market for American technology and implicitly pressing for formal recognition of the Soviet government. Trone conveyed his sense that at the close of the Five-Year Plan, Soviet people were "disappointed and underfed, but not hopeless." Overall, he expressed so much "enthusiasm for the industrialization project as a whole, and especially for Russian accomplishments in the electrical field" that the American vice consul found it "difficult to interview him with regard to actual accomplishments."[9]

With the writers and their guide, Thomson reminisced about his time in the Soviet Union and disclosed some sense of the frustrations of working there. He recounted the dramatic moment when the Soviet engineer A. V. Vinter switched on the power at the Dnepr Hydroelectric Station for the first time. "The soup is ready," Thomson

[7] Antony C. Sutton, *Western Technology and Soviet Economic Development, 1930 to 1945*, vol. 2 (Stanford, CA: Hoover Institution Press, 1971), 164n44, 270n45.

[8] Kupensky, "Soviet Industrial Sublime," 164–65n8; O. M. Ihnatusha, "Amerykans'ke predstavnytstvo na Dniprobudi: dokumenty z fondiv Derzhavnoho arkhivu Zaporiz'koï oblasti," *Pivdenna Ukraina XX stolittia: zapysky naukovo-doslidnoi labaratorii istorii Pivdennoi Ukrainy ZDU* 1, no. 4 (2008): 45–75. I thank Nick Kupensky for sharing this article.

[9] "Memorandum of Conversation with Solomon Trone," 15 March 1933, NACP, RG 59, 861.5017-Living conditions/616, pp. 5, 6.

recalled telling Vinter, who had tears in his eyes. He confided that, because "my wife and I have no children," he regarded the machines he installed as his offspring; some of his "most beloved" were in the Soviet Union. In his notebook, Ilf recorded that Thomson judged Soviet engineers and workers 30 percent less productive than some unspecified reference group, presumably their foreign or American counterparts. (A "Mr. Tompson," identified as an American engineer, had told a Soviet reporter virtually the same thing in 1930.[10]) In the published travelogue, however, the closest Thomson came to voicing doubts was noting that even some Soviet engineers had been skeptical "that your untrained workers and young engineers could ever master the complex and complicated production process." Echoing, consciously or not, Soviet propaganda, he ended by exclaiming: "You did it! Now it's a fact which no one can deny!"[11]

In Ilf and Petrov's telling, Thomson guided them around Boulder Dam with an eye to producing maximum amazement. He started by showing them the dam from below. They marveled at the canyon's three towering walls: two natural "dark-red cliffs" and a human-made "wall of reinforced concrete" that looked like "a petrified waterfall." On the crest of the dam, Thomson walked them first along the downstream side, where "from a tremendous height we saw the dried-out bottom of the canyon littered with remainders of the great construction."[12] About a month later, Bliven described the same view. But at the bottom of the canyon, alongside the "the usual appalling litter that goes with construction," he discerned workers "moving about amid their rubbish heaps." They appeared to him "incredibly small and weak; the mind refuses to grasp the fact that these tiny dolls and others like them ... built that vast cliff of concrete."[13] Ilf and Petrov toured the dam on a Sunday, so there may have been few people working. Still, like Bliven, they noticed "a railway car suspended from a steel cable slowly descending to the bottom of the abyss" (Figure 21.1); the activity suggests the presence of at least a skeleton crew at the bottom. Finally, in a "well-prepared effect," Thomson directed the travelers to the upstream side, where they saw a "large, clear, cool lake." The dam, Ilf and Petrov (like Bliven) explained, "gives the desert not only electricity, but also water."[14]

Eager to see the dam and hear Thomson's stories of working on Dneprostroi, Ilf and Petrov overlooked the workers and do not seem to

[10] N. Anov, "Dneprostroi," *Nashi dostizheniia*, no. 4 (April 1930): 12.

[11] LGA, 184; OA, 248, 249; ZK, 30 December, 460; Kupensky, "Soviet Industrial Sublime," 225.

[12] LGA, 184–85; OA, 249.   [13] Bliven, "American Dnieperstroy," 126.   [14] OA, 249.

Figure 21.1 What Bliven called a "large cage" and Ilf and Petrov a "railway car" transported workers to the bottom of the dam. The photograph shows "workmen going on shift in skip operated over Six Companies Inc., Cableway No. 9," 26 March 1933. National Archives at Denver (NAD), 293826.

have asked any questions about their living and working conditions. They missed the significance of the fact that all visitors to Boulder City had to pass through a government checkpoint; they likened it to the innocuous booth "you find at the entrance to every American national park." The town itself, built to house the dam's workforce, enchanted them with its "many lawns, flowerbeds, basketball and tennis courts." It offered a welcome contrast to Las Vegas, just thirty miles away, which despite its evocative name, turned out to be a twin of Gallup, all gas pumps, drugstores, and "streets clogged with automobiles."[15] Bliven more frankly reported that "So far as anyone can discern from casual observation, the only occupations of Las Vegas, Nevada are drinking, gambling, and prostitution." He, too, preferred Boulder City. However, he fathomed, as Ilf and Petrov did not, that the town was a strictly regulated government installation. Owned and run by the federal government, not "private industry," it was a "pleasant community of curving boulevards along the hillsides, bastard-Mediterranean architecture, green lawns, palms and bright flowerbeds."[16] The government-appointed manager barred the entry of unemployed men seeking work and "labor agitators"; "banished" undesirables; and prohibited gambling, prostitution, and the sale of "high-powered liquor"[17] (Figure 21.2).

Ilf and Petrov seemed to take the cozy town as evidence that American workers (when they worked) lived well – better, a reader might infer, than many Soviet workers. They apparently had no inkling of the brutal conditions that had prevailed on the site in the summer of 1931, when, in a hurry to employ legions of jobless men, the Hoover administration started the project six months ahead of schedule. While Boulder City remained a "barren desert" and daytime temperatures hovered 12 degrees above normal, around 120 degrees Fahrenheit (48 degrees Celsius), hundreds of workers labored without adequate housing or clean water. As the government prioritized "speed over safety," the Boulder Dam project in its initial stages bore an uncanny resemblance to the chaotic and dangerous jobsites characteristic of Soviet industrial construction. The difference was that in the United States, union organizers documented and publicized the deadly consequences of men "handling dynamite in a rocky gorge" under unforgiving conditions.[18] A strike in

---

[15] OA, 247, 245.   [16] Bliven, "American Dnieperstroy," 127, 125.

[17] Guy Louis Rocha, "The IWW and the Boulder Canyon Project: The Final Death Throes of American Syndicalism," *Nevada Historical Society Quarterly* 21 (Spring 1978): 11 (agitators, radicals); "Boulder City Shrinks in Size But Will Not Join Ghost List When Big Dam Is Complete," *Christian Science Monitor*, 29 January 1935, Hoover Dam – Construction (1935–36), Subject Files, BDMA.

[18] Judson King, "Open Shop at Boulder Dam," *New Republic* 67 (24 June 1931): 148.

Figure 21.2 Ben D. Glaha, Street scene in residential section, Boulder City, Nevada, 1934. In album Boulder Dam: a portfolio of photographs prepared for Hon. Harold L. Ickes, Secretary of the Interior, Prints and Photographs Division, Library of Congress, LOT 7365, photo 06.

August 1931 precipitated by a wage cut ended without a pay increase, but the unrest helped to speed the installation of cooling systems, the construction of housing and a mess hall, and the delivery of fresh water. By the time Ilf and Petrov arrived, it was easy to assume that the orderly government-run "reservation" of dormitories and "family cottages" with "all the basic conveniences" had existed from the start.[19]

Nor did Ilf and Petrov seem to know that only a few months before their visit, a labor dispute had shut down construction for two weeks. In July 1935, the largely un-unionized workforce had gone on strike to demand higher wages, a six-day work week, and a lunch break on company time. A day after the walkout began, a "special agent" for the contractor, Six Companies, "had his men dynamite the old road from

[19] Rocha, "IWW," 2–24 (quotations at 19); "Nevada and U.S. to Study Strike at Dam," *Chicago Daily Tribune*, 12 August 1931.

Las Vegas." This made it possible to force "all traffic to enter the government reservation by the new road, which can be controlled by a gate, and forestall the entrance of radicals who might incite further trouble."[20] By fall 1935, arbitration and government intervention resulted in the workers winning all their demands.[21] But the gate remained.

The tour of the dam prompted Ilf and Petrov to raise questions not about the mass of workers but about the identity of the "author of the Boulder Dam project." They were appalled that Thomson did not know; he could tell them only the name of the contractor, Six Companies, Inc. The engineer informed them that if they were to ask a worker to tell them who was installing the turbines, "he would not be able to give you my name. He would simply tell you that General Electric is doing the installation." This was how things worked in America: "engineers don't enjoy fame. Only the firms are known."[22]

Ilf and Petrov regarded as a "great injustice" the fact that the company, not the engineer, got the glory. They made the contrast with the Soviet Union explicit: "In the USSR, engineers and workers enjoy great popularity. Newspapers write about them; magazines print their portraits." Just like the builders of St. Peter's in Rome, they argued, the "authors of Boulder Dam … deserve fame." They understood the failure to celebrate individual heroes as of a piece with the American press's "strange" lack of attention to the Boulder Dam project. They claimed that only when President Roosevelt "participated in its solemn opening, did the newsreels devote a few flashes to it."[23]

To sharpen the contrast between the fame enjoyed by workers and engineers in the Soviet Union and their total obscurity in the United States, Ilf and Petrov misrepresented (or perhaps misunderstood) the president's speech. The writers arrived in New York on 7 October, a full week after Boulder Dam's dedication. By then, the opening of the dam would have been stale news, pushed off the front pages by Italian fascist victories in Ethiopia. Nonetheless, Ilf and Petrov claimed that they "had seen the newsreel and we remembered the president's speech." As they summarized it, Roosevelt "spoke about the significance of this government enterprise, praised some governors and senators, but did not say one word about the men who designed the project and who built the

---

[20] "Strike Halts All Work on Boulder Dam as Truck Drivers Join Walkout over Hours," NYT, 14 July 1935.

[21] "Dam Strike Ends, Men Are Back at Work," *Las Vegas Age*, 26 July 1935; Bill Vincent, "Organized Labor and Hoover Dam," *The Nevadan*, Sunday supplement (3 November 1968): 27; clippings in Hoover Dam – Labor and Labor Issues, BDHA, Subject Files; "Boulder Dam Strike Up to Ickes," NYT, 26 July 1935.

[22] LGA, 185; OA, 250.   [23] LGA, 185, 183; OA, 246, 250.

dam – the great monument to man's triumph over nature."[24] In fact, Roosevelt represented the dam precisely as a triumph over nature: Where ten years earlier there had been only an "unpeopled, forbidding" and "cactus-covered waste" there now stood a "twentieth century marvel." He also offered a "tribute" to the "genius" of the dam's designers and the "energy, resourcefulness, and zeal" of its builders; although the only people he thanked by name were the senator and congressperson who had introduced the legislation authorizing the project.[25] Perhaps these clips did not make the newsreel. Or perhaps they were forgotten because they did not fit the writers' preferred critique of the American dam.

Even as they expressed indignation about the American failure to lionize the people who built the dam, Ilf and Petrov not only noted that Mr. Thomson disagreed with them; they carefully recorded his objections. He could not name the single author of the dam, he explained, because "contemporary tekhnika" relied on the routine work of hundreds of professionals diligently producing incremental advancements. Personally, he was satisfied with recognition from specialists in his field. The Soviet Union, Thomson remarked, was "carried away by construction." He predicted that when modern marvels became ordinary and expected, the Soviets, too, would "stop proclaiming the fame of engineers and workers."[26]

Ilf and Petrov's paean to the scenic road suggested that they got Thomson's point. They did not refute his argument that in the United States "progress" was so widely and readily available that people were no longer "carried away" by it. Nonetheless, they gave themselves the last word and insisted on the correctness of the Soviet convention of representing technical marvels as the work of exemplary individuals. That Americans failed to fete heroes of labor they attributed to the distorting effect of money on American values. In the United States, boxers, football players, movie stars, even gangsters enjoyed fame (or glory, *slava*), they observed, because their fame made money for someone – themselves, promoters, producers, newspapers. But no one, they reasoned, stood to profit by making the people who built "cars, power plants, bridges, and irrigation systems" famous. On the contrary, their bosses stood to lose because "they would have to pay a famous person a higher salary."[27] Thus, GE was famous, and Mr. Thomson was not. In America, the capitalists appropriated the fame that under socialism belonged to the workers.

On the summit of the glorious dam created by unglorified laborers and engineers, Ilf and Petrov saw both the promise and the failure of

[24] LGA, 183; OA, 247.   [25] "President's Talk at Boulder Dam," NYT, 1 October 1935.
[26] LGA, 185; OA, 250–51; ZK, 30 November, 460.   [27] OA, 251.

capitalism. In the Soviet Union, they emphasized, the workers would have enjoyed the fame that rewarded real accomplishment. In America, fame turned out to be a commodity that "like any commodity profited not those who produced it, but those who sold it."[28] Maybe, they mused, Thomson was right to reject *American* fame and focus on the good opinion of his professional peers. Was it worth being famous in America? The question was not purely theoretical. Driving into the desert sunset, reflecting on celebrity culture, Ilf and Petrov were headed for Hollywood. They hoped to sell a screenplay.

---

[28] OA, 252.

Part IV

The Golden State

The drive from Santa Fe to Gallup, New Mexico, was the worst of Ilf and Petrov's entire road trip. It gave Ilf nightmares. In *Low-Rise America*, the writers dubbed the journey the "day of misfortunes." When the Ford spun out on the slushy highway, the travelers had to "get out of our warm car and, wearing only thin city shoes, plunge our feet into icy water." It took an hour to put chains on the tires. Having survived the ice at the cost of a broken chain and a damaged fender, they then encountered an eleven-mile detour through what appeared to be the worst stretch of road in the United States. Each time the car got stuck "in immense puddles of thin mud," the pair got out and pushed. Their "shoes, trousers, the edges of our overcoats, our shoulders and even our faces" ended up "covered in pink clay." The travelers arrived in Gallup hungry, tired, and dirty, but not yet through with mishaps. As they drove along the main street, a small truck struck their car, denting the side but causing no serious damage. Mr. Adams prevailed upon Ilf and Petrov to go no further on this "day of bad luck." Instead, he went to the local Ford dealership to find out about repairing the car. Caught up in conversation, he walked through a plate glass window. Fortunately, he emerged unscathed; only his glasses were broken.[1]

In *Low-Rise America*, Ilf and Petrov embellished the day of misfortunes for comic effect and omitted its most dramatic element. Trone really did walk unharmed through a plate glass window. However, the accident occurred a year earlier at a Chrysler dealership.[2] The day ended not with Trone's pratfall, but with a blowup between the writers. In reminiscences of Ilf written two years after his death, Petrov recalled that in Gallup they had, for the first and only time in their partnership, quarreled about something other than a "figure of speech or an epithet." The "shouting, swearing, and terrible accusations" went on for about two hours. Looking back, Petrov suggested that perhaps the exhausting journey triggered the argument. Certainly Ilf, whose health was deteriorating, would have felt

---

[1] ZK, 26 November, 456; OA, 204–206.   [2] ZK, 29 November, 459.

acutely the misery of standing for an hour in ankle-deep slush installing chains.[3]

Petrov recalled that the confrontation ended with the two men reaffirming their friendship. Suddenly, both started to laugh. At the same moment, they realized it was "pointless" to argue: "A writer who had lived for ten years and composed a half dozen books cannot disappear just because his component parts quarreled like two housewives in a communal kitchen." The argument gave way to a "heartfelt conversation" in which they disclosed their "most secret thoughts and feelings" and confessed their fear of facing a blank sheet of paper alone.[4]

However, the stress of the trip did not abate. Less than a week later, the sixteen-hour drive from somewhere in the California high desert to Fresno rivaled the miseries of the day of mishaps. As Ilf and Petrov tell the story, they reluctantly agreed to Mr. Adams's suggestion that they make a "five-minute" stop at Sequoia National Park in the southern Sierra Nevada mountains. On the map, the park appeared tantalizingly close to the main highway. The short side trip turned into a harrowing five- or six-hour adventure on icy mountain roads. The Ford almost skidded off a cliff. Ilf and Petrov set about putting on their one set of undamaged tire chains, maintaining, as they recounted in *Low-Rise America*, their habit of enduring difficulties in "proud silence." They gave the chapter on this segment of the road trip the cheerful title "Mrs. Adams Sets a Record": she had driven 375 miles. In his notebook, Ilf logged a succinct, but decidedly grimmer summation of the day: "Snow, ice, terror, moon, cold."[5]

By the time Ilf and Petrov arrived in San Francisco they had been in a car, as Petrov noted in a letter, for twenty-five days.[6] They had been away from home for seventy-two days – since 19 September. They were tired and most of all homesick. In *Low-Rise America*, the writers projected their longing onto the Adamses. It was their guides who insisted on limiting the trip to two months, unwilling to "torment our baby more than sixty days."[7] But Ilf and Petrov's letters make clear that they missed their children at least as much as their guides missed theirs. Writing from San Francisco on 3 December, Ilf confided to his wife that during the two weeks in the desert when he had had no news from her, he "so yearned for home" that it was sometimes terrifying. He was overjoyed to find two letters and a telegram waiting for him at the consulate in San Francisco and vowed to "never leave you again." On 10 December,

[3] Evgenii Petrov, "Iz vospominanii ob Il'fe," in V. D. Ostrogordskaia, ed., *Sbornik vospaminanii ob I. Il'fe i E. Petrove* (Moscow: Sovetskii pisatel', 1963), 8; Lesley Milne, *How They Laughed: Zoshchenko and the Ilf–Petrov Partnership* (Birmingham: Centre for Russian and East European Studies, 2003), 226–27.

[4] Petrov, "Iz vospominanii," 9.   [5] OA, 260–65; ZK, 1 December, 461.

[6] PIA, Petrov, 3 December, 461.   [7] LGA, 261, 214; OA, 359, 291.

Petrov wrote from Hollywood, "I want to go home to Moscow"; he missed the snow, the cold, his wife, and his son. Both writers asked anxiously about their children and about whether their wives had enough money, bought gifts, and sent kisses. By the time they left California on 26 December, they were ready to race back to the Atlantic.[8]

However, because they had work to do, Ilf and Petrov remained in California for nearly a month despite their longing for home. They engaged in endless meetings with Soviet diplomats, American leftists, and film actors and directors. Many of these encounters, notably with the journalists Lincoln Steffens and Albert Rhys Williams, show up in *Low-Rise America*. But in the published work they ignored the task that emerges in their letters as the most pressing, making effective and lucrative connections in Hollywood.

Following Ilf and Petrov's footsteps and searching for traces of their visit to the Golden State, I wanted to understand how each side responded when it encountered the Other. The California adventures offer a particularly fruitful place to consider this question. There the writers became active participants in American life as both Soviet cultural emissaries and minor Hollywood players. This more direct engagement with Americans potentially tested everyone's presuppositions. Did the encounters between the Soviet writers and American communists and fellow travelers allow either side to see the other anew? To what extent did Ilf and Petrov and the Russian (Jewish) directors with whom they met understand and identify with one another? Did these encounters manage to bridge cultural or political divides?

Because many of Ilf and Petrov's contacts preserved their personal papers, I was often able to find evidence of their visit. In some cases, the archives revealed people quite different from those Ilf and Petrov described. The trickiest problem was reconstructing the perspectives of the "ordinary" Russian immigrants who appear in *Low-Rise America*. Here, I was aided by a remarkable project overseen by the anthropologist Paul Radin that in 1935 employed hundreds of amateur interviewers to collect the life stories of foreign-born San Franciscans, including Russians and Jews from the Russian empire. Although Radin's team and Ilf and Petrov likely interviewed different immigrants, they asked similar questions.

Walking to the San Francisco Public Library, which holds the unpublished records of Radin's survey, I felt more acutely than at any moment in my research that I was returning to the place Ilf and Petrov had visited.[9] The Main Library is still located in the San Francisco Civic Center, just around the corner from the building it occupied in 1935,

---

[8] PIA, Il'f, 3 December 1935, 460; Petrov, 10 December, 26 December, 467, 479.
[9] Susan Goldstein, "The Daniel E. Koshland San Francisco History Center, San Francisco Public Library," *California History* 96 (2019): 50–51.

Figure IV.1 Dorothea Lange, "Unemployed men sitting on the sunny side of the San Francisco Public Library, California," 1937. Farm Security Administration – Office of War Information Photograph Collection, Prints and Photographs Division, Library of Congress, LC-USF34-016147-C.

which now houses the Asian Art Museum. In the mid-1930s, Dorothea Lange photographed the "ragged senate of unemployed philosophers" that, according to the Works Progress Administration (WPA) guide to the City by the Bay, regularly gathered "along the 'wailing wall'" adjacent to the building's south entrance (Figure IV.1) . During the Depression, Marshall Square, the site of the new library, hosted "great mass meetings" of the unemployed.[10] Across from the park stood the offices of the *Western Worker*, the West Coast organ of the Communist Party. In July 1934, during the San Francisco General Strike, vigilantes had vandalized the building[11] (Figure IV.2). "American Photographs" does

[10] Federal Writers' Project of the Works Progress Administration, *San Francisco in the 1930s: The WPA Guide to the City by the Bay* (Berkeley: University of California Press, [1940] 2011), 169, 171.
[11] Robert W. Cherny, "Prelude to the Popular Front: The Communist Party in California, 1931–35," *American Communist History* 1 (2002): 36.

Figure IV.2 Ilf and Petrov did not mention the San Francisco General Strike, but included a photograph of the vandalized offices of the *Western Worker*. AAF-0601, San Francisco History Center, San Francisco Public Library.

not mention the strike, but includes a photo of the damage caused by "future stormtroopers."[12] When I visited, the two-story structure at 37 Grove Street was still there, now serving as a resource center offering social and medical services for at-risk and homeless families.

Ilf and Petrov found in San Francisco, as they did everywhere in America, "limitless wealth and limitless poverty standing side by side." But in the City by the Bay, they thought the "poverty was at least picturesque." Through their "foreign" eyes the city looked "more like a European than an American city," and they were able to fall in love with it. Today, the contrasts are if anything even sharper than they were in 1935, as homeless encampments rise in the shadow of luxury condominiums and tech giants' sleek headquarters. In September 2018, the city established a "proactive unit" to remove human waste from the sidewalks of one of "America's beacons of urban beauty." Perhaps even today, Ilf and Petrov, like so many visitors, would experience San Francisco as "one of those cities one begins to like from the very first moment and continues to like more and more everyday thereafter."[13] Or would they be unable to overlook the staggering inequality bred of capitalism?

---

[12] Miriam Allen De Ford, "San Francisco: An Autopsy of the General Strike," *Nation* 139 (1 August 1934): 121–22; ART, 80; Il'ia Il'f and Evgenii Petrov, "Amerikanskie fotografii: VII: Kaliforniia," *Ogonek*, no. 17 (20 June 1936): 13.

[13] Thomas Fuller, "The Vile Side: Life on the Dirtiest Block in San Francisco," NYT, 9 October 2018; LGA, 199–200; OA, 271–72.

22 Irrational Presuppositions

> [C]ontact with these minorities tended to break down the irrational presuppositions with which most Americans operated and opened their eyes to the fact that the cry against the foreigners was largely a slogan used by individuals and groups for economic exploitation.
>
> Paul Radin, "The Survey of San Francisco's Minorities: Its Purpose and Results," 1935

On San Francisco's Potrero Hill, Ilf and Petrov found an immigrant neighborhood that transported them back to provincial Russia. The people who lived there, Molokans, Christian sectarians who had faced religious persecution in tsarist Russia, defied the writers' stereotype of Russian Americans as uprooted and demoralized. The Molokans spoke Russian untainted by English, and they expressed no disillusionment with the United States. In *Low-Rise America*, the writers usually disguised or excised such confounding immigrants – as in the cases of their guides and Ilf's family. But in recounting their San Francisco adventure, Ilf and Petrov opted instead to investigate the complexity of Russian American identities and experiences.

In 1935, Ilf and Petrov were not the only people investigating San Francisco's Russian immigrants. They came on the heels of a nine-month project supervised by the anthropologist Paul Radin to study the city's ethnic minorities. Radin's survey, conducted under the auspices of the State Emergency Relief Administration and the WPA's Federal Writers' Project, was far broader than Ilf and Petrov's. Designed to employ "so-called 'white-collar' people who were temporarily on relief," the project engaged at least 200 largely untrained interviewers. Radin aimed to "study the steps in the adjustment and assimilation of minority groups … from the time of their first arrival to the present time." Tasking his researchers with surveying more than thirty ethnic groups, Radin planned sixteen monographs, including one on "The Russians" and one on "The Jews."[1] As it

---

[1] Paul Radin, "The Survey of San Francisco's Minorities: Its Purpose and Results," Abstract from the SERA Project 2-F2–98 (3-F2–145), September 1935, pp. 1, 4, 9–10,

turned out, the sprawling project resulted in only one published study, *The Italians of San Francisco: Their Adjustment and Acculturation*, which appeared in 1935 in two mimeographed volumes.[2]

Like the Soviet writers, Radin came to his study of immigrants as an outsider. By his own "practical" definition, Radin was not an "American": Although he was raised in New York, neither he nor his parents were born in the United States.[3] In 1884, Johanna and Adolph Radin (Radyn), a Reform rabbi, had emigrated with their infant son Paul and three other children from Łodz, then in the Russian empire (now Poland).[4] A student of Franz Boas, Radin, best known for his work on Winnebago (Ho-Chunk) trickster tales, has been described as an "anthropological trickster." Restless and peripatetic, with a penchant for "scathing" critiques of other members of the "Boasian family," Radin was an innovative but marginal figure in the discipline.[5]

Central to Radin's project – and also, if less explicitly, to Ilf and Petrov's journey – was the premise that when cultures came into meaningful contact, people on both sides "acculturated." In the 1930s, anthropologists understood acculturation as "internal processes of reaction to foreign cultural influences."[6] Radin was rather unusual in applying the concept to immigrant groups in the United States rather than to colonial encounters.[7] His survey anticipated transnational histories of

Box 4, Folder 20, Paul Radin Papers (SFH 23), San Francisco History Center, San Francisco Public Library.

[2] Paul Radin, *The Italians of San Francisco: Their Adjustment and Acculturation*, vol. 1, *Introduction and Part I* ([San Francisco]: SERA Project, July 1935); Paul Radin, *The Italians of San Francisco: Their Adjustment and Acculturation*, vol. 2, *Part II* ([San Francisco]: SERA Project, August 1935); Jon Lee, *Chinese Tales Told in California* (San Francisco: Sutro Branch, California State Library, 1940).

[3] Radin, *The Italians*, 1: 2–3.

[4] Stanley Diamond, "Paul Radin," in Sydel Silverman, ed., *Totems and Teachers: Key Figures in the History of Anthropology*, 2nd ed. (Walnut Creek, CA: AltaMira Press, 2004), 53.

[5] Paul Radin with Karl Kerény and C. G. Jung, *The Trickster: A Study in American Indian Mythology* (New York: Greenwood Press, [1956] 1969); Christer Lindberg, "Paul Radin: The Anthropological Trickster," *European Review of Native American Studies* 14 (2000): 1–9; George W. Stocking, Jr., "Ideas and Institutions in American Anthropology: Thoughts toward a History of the Interwar Years," in *The Ethnographer's Magic and Other Essays in the History of Anthropology* (Madison: University of Wisconsin Press, 1992), 127 (Boasian family), 144 (scathing).

[6] João Leal, "'The Past Is a Foreign Country'? Acculturation Theory and the Anthropology of Globalization," *Etnográfica: Revista do Centro em Rede de Investigação em Antropologia* 15 (2011): 316.

[7] Stocking, "Ideas and Institutions," 136–37, 142–45; Robert Redfield, Ralph Linton, and Melville J. Herskovits, "Memorandum for the Study of Acculturation," in George W. Stocking, Jr., ed., *American Anthropology, 1921–1945: Papers from the "American Anthropologist"* (Lincoln: University of Nebraska Press, 1976), 257–62; Melville J. Herskovits, "Some Comments on the Study of Cultural Contact," in Stocking, ed.,

immigration that assess the diverse ways and degrees to which immigrants both "Americanized" and maintained identities, cultures, and institutions that linked them to their countries of origin.[8] Importantly, Radin saw acculturation as a two-way street. As his description of the project made clear, he assumed that immigrants "assimilated" into American culture. But he also insisted that "intimate," face-to-face contacts between immigrants and his mostly American investigators, who had previously known ethnic minorities only from hearsay, "chance contacts," and "highly colored newspaper accounts," would break down the latter's "irrational presuppositions" about the inferiority of other ethnic groups.[9] He asserted as fact, not hope, that cross-cultural communication necessarily resulted in a new awareness of human universals.[10]

Given this framework, Ilf and Petrov's entire trip can be understood as a laboratory of acculturation. A comparison of their travelogue with the life stories in Radin's project files offers a means of assessing and contextualizing their more limited fieldwork. Like trained anthropologists, Ilf and Petrov traveled to "acquire and collate" experiences of otherness. Less systematic than the professionals, and clearly constrained by their "prejudices" about America, the writers were not "imprisoned" by them.[11] As they avidly collected the stories of immigrants working to adapt to new American contexts (and Americans working to adapt to the Depression), they grappled with their own "presuppositions" (irrational or otherwise) and their complex reactions to a country that at once repelled and attracted them.

To study immigrants' inner experiences of acculturation, the anthropologist-trickster and the Soviet funnymen adopted essentially the same method: gathering, retelling, and interpreting life histories. Early in his career, Radin unsettled accepted anthropological practice by publishing an informant's autobiography, the reminiscences of Jasper Blowsnake.[12] Life stories remained central to his work, which emphasized the relationship of "real and specific men and women" to their

American Anthropology, 448–58; Melford E. Spiro, "The Acculturation of American Ethnic Groups," *American Anthropologist* 57 (December 1955): 1240–41.

[8] Daniel Soyer, "Transnationalism and Americanization in East European Jewish Immigrant Public Life," in Jack Wertheimer, ed., *Imagining the American Jewish Community* (Waltham, MA: Brandeis University Press, 2007), 47–66.

[9] Radin, "Survey," 5–6; Radin, *The Italians*, 1: 7–26.

[10] Lindberg, "Paul Radin," 8; Regna Darnell, *Invisible Genealogies: A History of Americanist Anthropology* (Lincoln: University of Nebraska Press, 2001), 187.

[11] Justin Stagl and Christopher Pinney, "Introduction: From Travel Writing to Ethnography," *History and Anthropology* 9 (1996): 121–22.

[12] Paul Radin, "Personal Reminiscences of a Winnebago Indian," *Journal of American Folklore* 26 (October–December 1913): 293–318; Paul Radin, ed., *Crashing Thunder: The Autobiography of an American Indian* (Ann Arbor: University of Michigan Press, [1926] 1999).

cultures.[13] It is thus not surprising that in the San Francisco survey Radin rejected "that gift of the gods, a formal and detailed question-naire" as unduly narrowing the investigation of "complex processes."[14] He opted instead to have interviewers ask each informant to "tell the story of his life as he thought best." A "hidden questionnaire" encour-aged investigators to elicit the "nature of adjustment to American life" and the "survival of old native customs." This indirect method, Radin argued, had the advantage of keeping "the salient events of the narrator's life in their proper sequence and their correct perspective."[15]

From Radin's perspective, relying on untrained interviewers to collect the "primary facts" turned out to be an unexpected advantage. In his September 1935 report on the project, Radin confessed that at the outset it had seemed to him "somewhat optimistic to anticipate any illuminating information from individuals approached at random by non-trained interrogators selected at random." However, the "first week's data" dispelled his doubts; "it became perfectly clear that most individuals are more than willing to speak about themselves and that almost an equally large number are adept in asking them to do so."[16]

Radin's survey was hardly a comprehensive portrait of San Francisco's 7,000 foreign-born Russians.[17] Rather, the 100 or so life stories served to illustrate the uneven and highly individual process of acculturation. In *The Italians*, as in his earlier work on the Winnebago tribe, Radin included lengthy excerpts from the texts produced on the basis of inter-views, allowing the study's subjects to tell their own stories.[18] The final section of the first volume, "Human Types as Indicated by Illustrative Autobiographies," featured twenty-one "life sketches" meant to afford a "concrete and vivid" picture of the city's Italian population.[19] Defending this approach, Radin wrote, "Far more important and devastating infer-ences have been, and still are, drawn, from infinitely more inadequate and inferior material."[20]

Ilf and Petrov's interviews with immigrants likewise constituted not a comprehensive portrait but a "concrete and vivid" picture of Russian (Jewish) American lives. As we have seen, they emphasized that

---

[13] Radin as quoted in Darnell, *Invisible Genealogies*, 151; Diamond, "Paul Radin," 51; James L. Peacock and Dorothy C. Holland, "The Narrated Self: Life Stories in Process," *Ethos* 21 (December 1993): 367–68.

[14] Radin, "Survey," 1.   [15] Radin, *The Italians*, 1: 4–5.   [16] Radin, "Survey," 2.

[17] Bureau of the Census, *Sixteenth Census of the United States: 1940: Population*, vol. 2, *Characteristics of the Population*, part 1, *United States Summary and Alabama – District of Columbia* (Washington, DC: Government Printing Office, 1943), 565.

[18] Lindberg, "Paul Radin," 3–4.   [19] Radin, *The Italians*, 1: 71–111 (quotations at 71).

[20] Radin, *The Italians*, 1: 11.

everywhere from New York to Kansas City to Taos they encountered immigrants whose American dreams had not panned out. Their conversations with a deckhand they chanced to meet as they traveled by ferry from Oakland to San Francisco began in the typical way. Overhearing the travelers chatting in Russian, and eager to talk about himself, the sailor explained that he was a native of Blagoveshchensk, in Siberia, and had emigrated in 1919 to escape the civil war. He clearly regretted his decision to "run away." His three brothers, "navigating on the Amur," were all captains, "each in command of a steamer." But in the United States, he was only a "common sailor!" "On a ferryboat!" Still, he exclaimed as he hurried away when the ferry approached the shore, he had "comforts," pronouncing "the word English fashion." Ilf and Petrov could not make out "whether he was speaking seriously or with bitter irony about his ferryboat 'comforts.'"[21] Although lacking the social distinction of his brother-captains, their acquaintance, they allowed, perhaps enjoyed a higher standard of living.

As it happens, the San Francisco investigators also interviewed Russian ferryboat deckhands, and their reports suggest that Ilf and Petrov's man may have been speaking earnestly. A short, handwritten account, produced by a researcher with a Russian surname, gives concrete form to the sailor's "comforts." The unnamed informant had arrived in San Francisco in 1923. Working as a laborer, he never earned more than $100 per month. Then, in 1926, he got his current "steady job" on the Southern Pacific ferryboats, where he earned $139.40 per month. In 1934, eight months before the interview, he moved into a two-room apartment, which he rented for $25 per month. The narrative does not include information about the interviewee's background or where he emigrated from.[22] But it suggests that, amid the Depression, the deckhand experienced some upward mobility. We can imagine Ilf and Petrov hearing in their deckhand's story pride in similar success.

In addition to chance encounters with individual, often isolated, immigrants like the deckhand, Ilf and Petrov described a meeting with a distinctive immigrant community, the Molokans. Members of a pacifist sect that the tsarist state had barely tolerated, many Molokans had left the Russian empire in the early twentieth century.[23] A small group had arrived in San Francisco in 1906, shortly after the earthquake.

---

[21] LGA, 197–98; OA, 269–70.
[22] John Gruzdeff, untitled, n.d., Radin Papers, Box 2, Folder 26.
[23] Nicholas B. Breyfogle, *Heretics and Colonizers: Forging Russia's Empire in the South Caucasus* (Ithaca, NY: Cornell University Press, 2005), 299–304; Christel O. Lane, "Socio-political Accommodation and Religious Decline: The Case of the Molokan Sect in Soviet Society," *Comparative Studies in Society and History* 17 (April 1975): 221–37.

By 1911, some 1,000 Molokans lived in San Francisco; a larger group of about 5,000 settled in Los Angeles. In both places, Molokans worked to preserve their religion and their Russian traditions.[24] In 1940, the WPA guide to San Francisco described the "little colony" on Potrero Hill as the place in the city where Russian "folkways" were most "apparent." By contrast, the aristocratic postrevolutionary émigrés who settled in the Western Addition honored the "customs of their forbears [sic]" by annually squandering "the savings of a twelvemonth on a grand ball in honor of their Petrograd days."[25]

In Ilf and Petrov's account, it was the Molokans' ability to maintain both their aloofness from American life and their ties with the Soviet "homeland" that, paradoxically, spared them from disillusionment. The writers emphasized that the San Francisco Molokans had constructed an uncanny and quaint slice of old Russia in a modern city. The men gathered to meet Ilf and Petrov resembled "prerevolutionary Russian workers." The women were "Russian peasant women, white-faced and rosy-cheeked, in good holiday blouses with puff sleeves and full skirts" (Figure 22.1). The Molokans served their guests familiar Russian foods – pirozhki, pickles, sweet bread, glasses of tea – and sang the classic Russian ballad, "It's not the wind that bends the bough." So Russian was Potrero Hill, Ilf and Petrov related, that it had acquired the nickname "Russian Hill." They seemed to have missed the irony of affixing the name of one of the city's poshest neighborhoods to an immigrant enclave overlooking the shipyards.[26]

In Ilf and Petrov's telling, it was primarily as proletarians that the Molokans maintained, even strengthened, their ties to their new "old country," the Soviet Union, and distanced themselves from the land of the capitalists. After the Bolshevik victory, according to the writers, the immigrants "For the first time in their lives felt that they had a motherland" rather than a "stepmother" – a formulation that suggests they had never identified themselves as in any way "American." The portraits of Stalin, Kliment Voroshilov, and Mikhail Kalinin hanging in the meeting room where the community had tea with the visiting writers offered a

---

[24] John K. Berokoff, *Molokans in America* (Los Angeles: Self-published, 1969), unpaginated [15]; Willard B. Moore, "Communal Experiments as Resolution of Sectarian Identity Crises," *International Review of Modern Sociology* 6 (Spring 1976): 89–90; Susan W. Hardwick, "Religion and Migration: The Molokan Experience," *Yearbook of the Association of Pacific Coast Geographers* 55 (1993): 129–39; Pauline V. Young, "The Russian Molokan Community in Los Angeles," *American Journal of Sociology* 35 (November 1929): 393–402.

[25] Federal Writers' Project, *San Francisco*, 285.

[26] OA, 287–89; LGA, 211–13; Federal Writers' Project, *San Francisco*, 253–54.

Figure 22.1 Russian Molokan congregation, Potrero Hill, San Francisco, 1938. Ilf and Petrov described the people they met on Potrero Hill as resembling prerevolutionary workers and peasants. Photograph by Syndey Robertson Cowell, W. P. A. California Folk Music Project collection (AFC 1940/001), American Folklife Center, Library of Congress.

prominent indicator of the Molokans' Soviet sympathies. Under the watchful eyes of the Soviet leaders, the sectarians asked their guests about "collective farms, factories, and Moscow." They told Ilf and Petrov that, at the time of the collectivization of agriculture, one of the "respected Molokan elders" in San Francisco had received a letter from his nephews in the Soviet Union asking whether they should join the kolkhoz. The nephews wrote that a church elder in the USSR had discouraged them from joining. But, according to Ilf and Petrov, the uncle in San Francisco, as much an old Molokan preacher as an old longshoreman, advised them to join. He "proudly told us that he now often receives grateful letters from his nephews."[27]

---

[27] OA, 287–89.

Ilf and Petrov concluded the story of their visit to Russian Hill with an elegiac reflection on the Molokans' "yearning" (*toska*) for home. In the dazzling City by the Bay, alongside the surging vitality of its cosmopolitan population and the technological wonders of its bridges under construction, the Molokans, they asserted, lived in a "kind of voluntary prison" with their "Russian songs and Russian tea." Having lost their homeland, "they remembered it every minute, and in remembrance of it had hung a portrait of Stalin."[28] The writers' final assessment of these immigrants who ignored America in favor of nurturing their transnational ties was decidedly ambivalent. Only the Molokans' commitment to living in their own Russian/Soviet "prison" – presided over by Stalin – inoculated them against the disappointment that plagued the other Russian immigrants who appeared in *Low-Rise America*.

What Ilf and Petrov did not mention (and perhaps did not know, although the history of the Molokans provided by their host was pretty thorough) was that in the mid-1920s a group of Molokans from Potrero Hill had re-emigrated to the Soviet Union, only to return to the United States at the end of the decade. At the outset of the New Economic Policy in 1921, the Soviet state had tried to lure prerevolutionary emigrants from the Russian empire, who constituted a source of hard currency and technical know-how.[29] For the Bolshevik leadership, "left sectarians" constituted a particularly attractive subset of Russians abroad. Familiar with the research of Vladimir Bonch-Bruevich – himself a Bolshevik – on religious dissenters, they viewed groups like the Molokans, with their history of oppression under tsarism and their social solidarity, strong work ethic, and sobriety, as a good fit for the Soviet project.[30] For their part, many Molokans "hailed the new social order as an expression of Molokan values of equality, brotherhood and intellectual progress."[31] The San Francisco branch of the Society for Technical Aid to Soviet Russia encouraged their interest. In 1921, the Potrero Hill community worked with the organization to send famine relief to

[28] OA, 290–91.
[29] Phillip Gillette, "Armand Hammer, Lenin, and the First American Concession in Soviet Russia," *Slavic Review* 40 (Autumn 1981): 362; Antony C. Sutton, *Western Technology and Soviet Economic Development, 1917 to 1930* (Stanford, CA: Hoover Institution on War, Revolution and Peace, 1968), 126–32.
[30] Benjamin Warren Sawyer, "American 'Know-How' on the Soviet Frontier: Soviet Institutions and American Immigration to the Soviet Union in the Era of the New Economic Policy" (PhD diss., Michigan State University, 2013), 8; Elena Danilova, "'Vyrazhaem polnuiu gotovnost' pomogat' Sovetskoi vlasti...': Nedolgii opyt integratsii dukhovnykh khristian v sovetskuiu ekonomiku 1920kh-gg," *Gosudarstvo, religiia, tserkov' v Rossii i za rubezhom* 36, no. 3 (2018): 64–65.
[31] Lane, "Socio-political Accommodation," 226.

Ukraine and South Russia; they deputized Ivan M. Seliznoff (or Seleznev) as their agent to ensure that the aid they collected was properly distributed and to "scout out the living conditions under the new regime."[32]

In the early 1920s, satisfied with their scout's report, a group of thirty Molokan families in San Francisco began to plan and save for their re-emigration. The Soviet state required immigrants to bring enough supplies to support themselves for at least a year. Each family pledged $300 for the purchase of farm machinery, seeds, and other basic household goods such as stoves and tents. The first group, including the venture's organizer, Vasily Fetisoff, left San Francisco in May 1923; a second group left in 1925. In all, twelve families from San Francisco emigrated. They settled in the North Caucasus alongside villages inhabited by other sectarians (Molokans, Dukhobors, and New Israelites) returning from Uruguay and the Kars region of Turkey, which had been part of the Russian empire. The Molokans from San Francisco founded a village variously identified in oral histories as "California" or "New California."[33]

The Molokan agricultural settlements seem to have become – as Soviet officials had hoped – prosperous models of modern agriculture. Initially facing some of the same difficulties with inadequate land and malaria as their secular neighbors, the Molokans benefited from their advanced American threshing machine, their ability to speak Russian, and their proximity to communes founded by their co-religionists and the closely related Dukhobors (some of whom came from Canada). By 1924, a Molokan dairy farm and cheese factory were producing impressive yields.[34]

Four years later, the experiment came to an unhappy end. By then it was clear that, overall, the program had failed to realize its economic promise. The Commissariat of Foreign Affairs, which had long warned that returnees posed a security risk, stepped up its attacks on re-emigration as a potentially dangerous conduit of counterrevolutionary forces.[35] At the same time, Soviet policy grew increasingly intolerant of religious sectarians, who were not assimilating into Soviet life and whose numbers were growing. In 1927, the state simultaneously ended

---

[32] Quotation from Berokoff, *Molokans in America*, [32]; Sawyer, "American 'Know-How,'" 226.

[33] Several communes were named "California" or "New California." Sawyer, "American 'Know-How,'" 100, 182, 225–26; Moore, "Communal Experiments," 96–97 (California); Ethel Dunn and Stephen P. Dunn, "The Molokans in America," *Dialectical Anthropology* 3 (November 1978): 353–54 (New California).

[34] Danilova, "'Vyrazhaem,'" 71; Moore, "Communal Experiments," 97; Sawyer, "American 'Know-How,'" 184.

[35] Sawyer, "American 'Know-How,'" 219.

the re-emigration program and rescinded the pacifist sectarians' exemption from military service. The collectivization of agriculture the following year further undermined the largely autonomous sectarian communes.[36] In 1928, the Soviet authorities allowed Molokan and Dukhobor re-emigrants to return to North America.[37] Given this history, one wonders if Ilf and Petrov's report that the immigrants "asked us if it would be possible to arrange the Molokans' return to their native land" was less factual reporting than an attempt to deflect questions about why peasant proletarians sympathetic to the Soviet Union remained in San Francisco.[38] The writers did not record their response.

Omitting the failure of the sectarians' return to Russia, Ilf and Petrov's travelogue registered no Molokan doubts about the Soviet Union, but only a deep, even anguished emotional connection, an overwhelming sense of *toska*. If their account is an accurate reflection of the Molokans' attitude, this yearning can be explained at least in part as a result of fortunate timing. Leaving in 1928, the San Francisco re-emigrants escaped the most violent and coercive phase of the collectivization drive in the Don region, when prosperous sectarians, now denied the right to emigrate, were arrested, exiled, or shot.[39] Their paradoxical ability to yearn for a "homeland" that betrayed their hopes may also have had a religious basis; the *pokhod*, the flight to spiritual refuge, constituted a key component of the Molokan faith.[40] But secular re-immigrants, too, often refused to condemn the Soviet Union. They returned to the United States disappointed that the Soviet state had failed to make good on the terms offered upon their departure, but still committed to the Soviet project overall.[41]

Because, as Ilf and Petrov reported, many of the Molokans worked as longshoremen, the experience of the eighty-three-day waterfront strike

---

[36] Danilova, "'Vyrazhaem,'" 75; Moore, "Communal Experiments," 97–98; Dunn and Dunn, "Molokans in America," 353.

[37] Moore, "Communal Experiments," 98; Vadim Kukushkin, "A Roundtrip to the Homeland: Doukhobor Remigration to Soviet Russia in the 1920s," Doukhobor Heritage, https://doukhobor.org/a-roundtrip-to-the-homeland-doukhobor-remigration-to-soviet-russia-in-the-1920s/ (accessed 18 August 2023); Alexis Fetisoff, New York, Passenger and Crew Lists; Alex Fetesoff, US Federal Census, 1940, Ancestry.com.

[38] LGA, 213; OA, 290.

[39] E. N. Danilova, "Immigratsionnaia politika i sozdanie trudovykh kommun iz immigrantov i reimigrantov v SSSR v 1920-e gody," *Vestnik Moskovskogo Universiteta*, ser. 8, *Istoriia*, no. 1 (2002): 26–29.

[40] Moore, "Communal Experiments," 93; Berokoff, "Molokans in America," [34]; Dunn and Dunn, "Molokans in America," 352–54.

[41] Sawyer, "American 'Know-How,'" 3–4, 10–11, 18–19, 230; Seth Bernstein and Robert Cherny, "Searching for the Soviet Dream: Prosperity and Disillusionment on the Soviet Seattle Agricultural Commune, 1922–1927," *Agricultural History* 88 (Winter 2014): 22–44.

that shook the West Coast in the spring and summer of 1934 may have (re)invigorated their ties to the Soviet Union.[42] Somewhat surprisingly, Ilf and Petrov, focused on the Molokans' preservation of prerevolutionary habits and their reactions to the Revolution, ignored radical activities closer to home, where the dockworkers' union was closely, although rarely publicly, affiliated with the Communist Party. I have found no direct testimony from the Molokan side that might shed light on whether the longshoremen told the Soviet visitors about the dramatic events of 1934.

But those who participated in the Big Strike could scarcely have forgotten what came to be known as "Bloody Thursday." On 5 July 1934, as police armed with tear gas, clubs, and pistols attempted to force open the port of San Francisco, violent confrontations with thousands of picketers erupted along the Embarcadero. Near the longshoremen's union headquarters, the police shot three strikers, killing two. On 9 July, tens of thousands of marchers participated in a silent funeral procession that bore the dead the entire length of Market Street. The violence catalyzed more than 100,000 organized and unorganized workers in San Francisco, Oakland, and Alameda County to join a four-day General Strike in support of the maritime unions. Shortly after the inconclusive end of the General Strike, the longshoremen's union voted to return to work. In October 1934, the stevedores won their chief demands through arbitration. Just four months before Ilf and Petrov's visit, on 5 July 1935, San Francisco longshore workers had marked the first anniversary of Bloody Thursday by shutting down the port. Today the date, a turning point in the union's history, is enshrined as an official holiday in the International Longshore and Warehouse Union's collective bargaining agreement.[43] However, in Ilf and Petrov's telling, these unique Russian immigrants made their way in America not by fighting or even criticizing capitalism, but by retreating to "Russian Hill," where time stood still.

Ilf and Petrov's nostalgic and ambivalent vision of "Russian Hill" finds little corroboration in Radin's survey. The only interview I found with a

---

[42] Hardwick, "Religion and Migration," 134.

[43] Fred B. Glass, *From Mission to Microchip: A History of the California Labor Movement* (Berkeley: University of California Press, 2016), 239–46; Victoria Johnson, *How Many Machine Guns Does It Take to Cook One Meal? The Seattle and San Francisco General Strikes* (Seattle: University of Washington Press, 2008), 71–104; Michael Johns, "Winning for Losing: A New Look at Harry Bridges and the 'Big Strike' of 1934," *American Communist History* 13 (2014): 1–24; Cherny, "Prelude," 5–42; Bruce Nelson, *Workers on the Waterfront: Seamen, Longshoremen, and Unionism in the 1930s* (Urbana: University of Illinois Press, 1990), 127–55; "2023 ILWU/PMA Paid Holidays," https://apps.pmanet.org/pubs/Payroll/Holiday_Calendar_2023.pdf (accessed 11 April 2023).

clearly identified resident of Potrero Hill, albeit not one labeled a Molokan, was a story of domestic violence and alcoholism. The unnamed subject of the interview, a fifty-five-year-old Russian stevedore, had arrived in the United States in about 1905, and worked on the waterfront in New York before moving to San Francisco in about 1915. Married to "a fellow Russian," he had "two big boys, about twenty years old." According to the report, the man's "great vice, shared by his wife and sons, is drink." Here, the investigator provided a measure of how much the man drank based on cultural stereotypes: "He does not drink as the Italian does, moderately and as a freshening to his food, nor as an American, quickly and for a pick up, but vastly, unendingly, and for days at a time ... In fact he is well known to the Potrero police, for it is his playful habit in times of drink, to beat up his wife and sons, wreck the furniture, and amble out in the street like a great mad bear seeking a fight." The "sodden hulk" was also cheating on his wife, sharing his paycheck with the seventeen-year-old daughter of a "family of Slavs" who lived next door on Potrero Hill. The wife, apparently in a separate interview, said that she solved that problem by bringing her case to what the interviewer took to be "some sort of fixer among the Russians," perhaps a church elder. Evincing more condescension and aversion than empathy, the investigator conjectured that "the old man gets his revenge, because his lawful wedded spouse was a battered old lady the last time I saw her."[44]

Much of the difference in these accounts owed to the fact that while Ilf and Petrov described a carefully staged community reception, the interviewer focused, as the writers did on other occasions, on capturing a single life story. But the difference hinged, too, on the observers' different cultural "presuppositions." Where Ilf and Petrov felt some kinship with the immigrants' folkways, the project interviewer's mocking, incongruously jocular tone communicated an overriding sense of his informants' otherness.[45]

The Radin survey offers clearer collaboration of the "yearning" for home so central to Ilf and Petrov's account of the Molokans. In one of the longest (at twenty pages) and most elaborate stories in the files, the informant, Matthew, expressed a profound, if still ambivalent, desire to return. In 1913, pushed by a quarrel with his father and economic hardship, he had left Volhynia province (now Zhytomyr oblast, Ukraine) for America. By 1917, Matthew was able to send his wife

---

[44] Undated interview, typescript and manuscript, Radin Papers, Box 2, Folder 26.
[45] On the interviewer Dominick Twomey, see Ocean Howell, *Making the Mission: Planning and Ethnicity in San Francisco* (Chicago: University of Chicago Press, 2015), 344n34.

$1,000 for the passage to join him. But the chaos of war and revolution and, his father cryptically suggested in a dictated letter, Matthew's wife's questionable faithfulness, left him without any word from her. Still, he hoped. Until in 1926, he learned that she had taken advantage of the new Soviet marriage code to divorce him in absentia.[46]

In the nine years between this news and the interview, "he became reconciled to the fact that he had no wife." But his "personal problems had kept him aloof and far from assimilating the main fundamentals of living in this new country," despite his apparent ability to speak and read English. Paraphrasing Matthew's words or drawing his or her own conclusions, the interviewer wrote that twenty-one years after leaving Russia, Matthew "remained a Russian in heart and mind. There was nothing in the new country, save comfort and general conditions of earning a livelihood, which could replace the old love and the old country ties." Matthew seemed to find little solace in "comfort," perhaps less than Ilf and Petrov's deckhand. Yearning for what he still considered home, he tried to learn about the "new Russia," but found only conflicting information: Those who praised the Soviet Union "did not remain over there, but came back here." So, Matthew decided to "go there personally and decide for himself."[47]

The planned return faced numerous obstacles, first on the American and then on the Soviet side. In 1931, the problem was that the building and loan to which Matthew had entrusted his $500 in savings "suspended all payments." Then he lost his job. By the time he had saved enough to make the trip, the political situation had changed. With normalized relations between the United States and the Soviet Union came a Soviet consul in San Francisco. Expecting "the new democratic Russia to employ lesser and simpler formalities than its Czarist predecessor," he met with "far more despotic demands and regulations." Months after making his application in 1934, he "was asked to write a life story about himself and his stay in this country and his doings." At the time of the interview, apparently in 1935, he was still "waiting for the decision." In the final section of the report titled "Russian Americans," the interviewer reflected, "Perhaps soon he will be on his way to the old country, the old country of his memories and dreams. Will he come back again to America? Or will he not? He admits both possibilities."[48]

---

[46] E. A. Martineau, "An Old Love," n.d., Radin papers, Box 3, Folder 1, pp. 8, 15, 16; Wendy Z. Goldman, *Women, the State, and Revolution: Soviet Family Policy and Social Life, 1917–1936* (New York: Cambridge University Press, 1993), 214–53.
[47] Martineau, "An Old Love," 16, 17.   [48] Martineau, "An Old Love," 18, 20.

Like the Molokans in Ilf and Petrov's account, Matthew remained homesick after more than twenty years in the United States. While the Molokans ostensibly understood and supported the "new Russia," he remained unsure about it. It was precisely stories like theirs that gave him pause: they "praised" the "new order," but "came back here." Never having become a US citizen, Matthew was careful to make sure that he would be able to return if the Soviet Union failed to live up to his expectations. Even as he continued "longing for home," he recognized that not only Russia but he himself had changed. No longer a peasant, he had become a "skilled worker in many specialities," of the sort he imagined would be quickly welcomed back.[49] Instead he encountered a "despotic" regime – an adjective that may have been the interviewer's, not his – that seems to have deepened his ambivalence, even if it did not quell his longing.

Reading the survey interviews against Ilf and Petrov's raises the question of whether, as Radin hopefully predicted, "intimate" contacts across ethnic (or in the writers' case, also ideological) divides fostered cross-cultural understanding. Did face-to-face encounters work to break down "irrational presuppositions" about Americans and American capitalism? In the cases described here, I would argue that Ilf and Petrov acquitted themselves creditably as amateur ethnographers, pushing against their own presuppositions in their efforts to consider their informants' perspectives. They granted, however tentatively, that the ferryboat deckhand may really have prized his "comfort." They expressed ambivalence about the Molokans' yearning for "home" that seemed at once to imprison them and spare them from disillusionment. The process of collecting life stories did not prompt Ilf and Petrov to disavow as irrational their presuppositions about capitalism. But nor did they allow their preconceptions to obscure their informants' humanity. While often highlighting immigrants' consciousness that life was better in the Soviet Union, they also produced portraits of Russian Americans as complex individuals, who were simultaneously homesick and at home in the United States. They proved less willing to explore the complexities of American radicals who longed for the Soviet Union.

[49] Martineau, "An Old Love," 18, 20.

23   The Soviet Colony in Carmel

> Our radical intelligentsia are good, honest people. Yes, yes, my good
> sirs, it would be foolish to think that America is only standardized, that
> it only chases after dollars, that it only plays bridge or poker.
>
> Mr. Adams in Ilf and Petrov, *Low-Rise America*

Carmel-by-the-Sea, where Ilf and Petrov stopped in early December
1935 on their way to Los Angeles, provided the rather incongruous setting
for *Low-Rise America*'s only sustained discussion of the radical intelligentsia. Often compared with Taos, New Mexico, Carmel, too, was an art
colony that promoted itself as "a hotbed of modernist activity and exclu-
sive site of leisure, pleasure and cultural enrichment." Its reputation as an
"upscale bohemia" dated to the early twentieth century, when the Carmel
Development Company enticed accomplished and aspiring, often wealthy,
artists and writers from the Bay Area to settle there. Among the early art
colonists were Upton Sinclair and Jack London.[1]

Unlike Taos, Carmel in the 1930s was not only a haven for artists, but
also an important center of communist-affiliated activism. At the time of
Ilf and Petrov's visit, the town's most famous radical was the muckraking
journalist and "intellectual Communist" Lincoln Steffens. He and his
wife Ella Winter, who moved to Carmel in 1927, drew a constant stream
of progressive visitors to The Getaway, their house overlooking the
ocean. Steffens and Winter supported numerous left-wing causes. They
raised funds for striking farmworkers and hosted an evening of proletarian poetry in support of the San Francisco dockworkers at which
Langston Hughes read his translations of Mayakovsky.[2] Mentioning

---

[1] Geneva M. Gano, *The Little Art Colony and US Modernism: Carmel, Provincetown, Taos*
(Edinburgh: Edinburgh University Press, 2020), 31–58 (hotbed), 85–86; Peter
Hartshorn, *I Have Seen the Future: A Life of Lincoln Steffens* (Berkeley, CA:
Counterpoint, 2011), 385 (upscale).

[2] Justin Kaplan, *Lincoln Steffens: A Biography* (New York: Simon & Schuster, 2013), 311
(intellectual); Hartshorn, *I Have Seen*, 415–29; Steven S. Lee, *The Ethnic Avant-Garde:
Minority Cultures and World Revolution* (New York: Columbia University Press,
2015), 74–80.

none of these specifics, Mr. Adams proposed that Ilf and Petrov visit the seaside town to meet Americans who "know how to be carried away by ideas." Adams called Steffens, then in the last months of his life, "one of the best people in America."[3]

Defining American radicals as "good and honest," Mr. Adams suggested that they had no clear political ideas or revolutionary commitments. Certainly, they stood in contrast to "standard" Americans addicted to making money and mindless entertainment. But they did not appear especially interested in challenging American capitalism. Advancing Lincoln Steffens as "one of the best" exemplars of American radicalism, Mr. Adams did not dredge up the journalist's famous (or notorious) 1919 pro-Soviet quip, "I have seen the future, and it works."[4] Mr. Adams – and by extension Ilf and Petrov – valued a radical intelligentsia sympathetic to Soviet values, but not necessarily committed to revolutionizing America in the Soviet image. Their expectations were a long way from the revolutionary prediction with which Boris Pilnyak began and ended his 1933 "American novel": "Betsy Ross passes the first American flag to the first president of the United States, and her granddaughter passes the red flag to the Detroit branch of the Communist Party."[5]

The high tide of antifascist international solidarity – still in the future when Ilf and Petrov visited the United States – underpinned their portrait of the "good and honest," but not necessarily revolutionary, American radical intelligentsia. Articulated at the Seventh Comintern Congress in the summer of 1935, the "united front against fascism" prioritized broad leftist coalitions against "the bitterest enemy of all the toilers." The strategy postponed into the perhaps distant future efforts to "overthrow" capitalism and achieve "the victory of the proletarian revolution."[6] In *Low-Rise America*, Mr. Adams is deeply committed to the Popular Front cause of the moment, opposition to the 1935 Italian invasion of Ethiopia. By the time the book appeared in 1937, antifascism had become a powerful mobilizing strategy in the United States and globally, associated above all with the Spanish Republic's struggle against rebels backed by Nazi Germany and Fascist Italy.

---

[3] OA, 295–96.

[4] Hartshorn, *I Have Seen*, 315; Ella Winter, "Lincoln Steffens," *New Masses* 20 (8 September 1936): 13–14; Trone to Il'f and Petrov, 17 August 1936, as cited in ZK, 501n314.

[5] Boris Pil'niak, *O'kei: An American Novel*, trans. Ronald D. LeBlanc, Faculty Publications, 926, University of New Hampshire, 2020, 1, 198.

[6] "Resolution on Fascism, Working-Class Unity, and the Tasks of the Comintern," in Kevin McDermott and Jeremy Agnew, *The Comintern: A History of International Communism from Lenin to Stalin* (Basingstoke: Palgrave Macmillan, 1996), 243.

Mr. Adams's real-life counterpart Solomon Trone was himself connected to radical intelligentsia circles. He was friendly with both Steffens and his neighbor Albert Rhys Williams, whom Alexander Gumberg had guided around revolutionary Petrograd. In September 1935, shortly before Ilf and Petrov arrived in New York, Williams had turned to Trone for "any connections or ideas or materials" that might be of use in the journalist's encyclopedic work in progress, "The Soviets."[7] While shepherding Ilf and Petrov around San Francisco, if not before, Trone met others who had ties to Williams and the Carmel colony. Dr. Ralph A. Reynolds, the president of the San Francisco branch of the American-Russian Institute, hosted what Ilf described as a rather unpleasant cocktail party in the writers' honor. Alexander Kaun, an associate professor of Slavic languages at Berkeley, invited them to a lecture and a get-together with students. Ella Winter, Williams, and Kaun had all spoken at events organized by Reynolds's Institute.[8]

Carmel was a hub and haven for these radical intellectuals. In a letter to Boris Skvirsky, an official at the Soviet embassy in Washington, DC, Williams called the village "the Soviet colony in Carmel." The Soviet consul in San Francisco, Mosei Galkovich, who saw the travelers off from the city, often visited the seaside town and, according to Williams, was considering renting a cottage there.[9] Although Ilf and Petrov suggest that they went to Carmel on Mr. Adams's recommendation, the village was a standard stop on the West Coast itineraries of visiting Soviet luminaries. Winter, in a poem celebrating the publication of *The Soviets*, wrote that Williams had "sucked his visitors dry for ideas"; her list of informants who made the pilgrimage to Carmel included "Ilf and Petroff, the Soviet satirists" and unnamed "engineers and aviators / Journalists and economists, professors and artists, / Army men and poets from the Soviet Union."[10]

To emphasize Carmel's place in American radical networks, Ilf and Petrov in *Low-Rise America* rearranged the timeline of their trip. In the published travelogue, the prospect of visiting Carmel prompts Mr. Adams's observation regarding the goodness and honesty of the American radical intelligentsia. To substantiate his point, he asks the

---

[7] Gumberg to Williams, 19 April 1934, Rare Book and Manuscript Library, Columbia University Library, Albert Rhys Williams Papers (Williams Papers), Box 15, Williams to Trone, 24 September 1935, Williams Papers, Box 8. At the time of my research, the papers were unprocessed and did not include numbered folders.

[8] PIA, Il'f, 6 December 1935, 463; Norman Saul, *Friends or Foes? The United States and Soviet Russia, 1921–1941* (Lawrence: University Press of Kansas, 2006), 161–62, 368.

[9] Williams to [Boris] Skvirsky, 12 July 1935, Williams Papers, Box 8.

[10] Ella Winter "The Soviets," Williams Papers, Box 4; Williams to Elena [Arens], 15 April 1936, Williams Papers, Box 9.

writers to "remember the young gentleman with whom we recently spent an evening." Ilf and Petrov then proceed to describe the meeting in a "large industrial city" with an "old friend of Adams's," a young man who "renounced" his "aristocratic" family's wealth to join the Communist Party and fight against the "injustice of the capitalist system."[11] This incident largely matches Ilf's summary of a meeting with a communist organizer. In a journal entry dated New Year's Day 1936 – more than three weeks after their visit to Carmel – he noted that the travelers stopped by the apartment of a "friend of Trone's," a twenty-four-year-old "organizer," who "told us about the port strike in Houston" as well as his own efforts to organize farmworkers.[12] Here, Ilf and Petrov turned a future encounter into a memory.

In the published work, Ilf and Petrov filtered this actual meeting through cliched, although not necessarily incorrect, images of Russian radicalism. As they tell the story in *Low-Rise America*, a half hour after they arrived at the organizer's apartment, a "worker communist," looking like "any Moscow member of the Young Communist League," dropped by. Because there were no more chairs, the visitor simply sat on the floor. Identified as a dockworker "leading a strike of stevedores at the port," the guest does not appear in Ilf's notebook, and he may have been a literary invention. In *Low-Rise America*, he dramatically describes the violence that erupted in Houston "last night" as police tried to bring in strikebreakers. In fact, by the time Ilf and Petrov reached the Gulf Coast, the three-month longshore strike that involved 7,500 workers in ports from Pensacola, Florida, to Corpus Christi, Texas, had ended. However, the violence that the dockworker – or perhaps their host – described resembled widespread confrontations in October and November between strikers, strikebreakers, and police.[13] Making the story more immediate, Ilf and Petrov told a noble tale of committed "party workers living on two dollars a week." They mentioned in passing that Mrs. Adams's and the organizer's wife, a German communist, made sandwiches while the men finished their conversation. This relegation of women to the kitchen did not, from the writers' perspective, compromise their hosts' radical credentials. Ilf and Petrov emphasized that the scene in the poorly furnished apartment "was a spectacle of the kind we know only from museum pictures which portray the life of Russian revolutionists on the eve" of the 1905 Revolution.[14]

---

[11] OA, 293–94.   [12] ZK, 1 January 1936, 468–69.

[13] "Trend of Strikes and Lock-Outs," *Monthly Labor Review* 42 (February 1936): 392–95; Gilbert Mers, *Working the Waterfront: The Ups and Downs of a Rebel Longshoreman* (Austin: University of Texas Press, 1988), 88–114.

[14] OA, 294–95.

Although Ilf and Petrov noted the presence of a German communist, they scrubbed American radicals of all complicating ethnic, national, or racial markers and elided their connections to the Soviet Union. While the writers identified the exploited farmworkers as Mexican and Filipino, they emphasized that the young organizer's "ancestors had disembarked from the *Mayflower.*" The dockworker organizing the strike is presumptively a white American; although the Gulf Coast strike, as Ilf and Petrov may not have known, was notable for the solidarity of white, Black, and Hispanic stevedores.[15] Reynolds, the doctor who headed the local branch of the American-Russian Institute, an organization affiliated with the Soviet agency in charge of cultural relations with the West, did not get a mention in *Low-Rise America*, even though he apparently arranged their tour of the Oakland–San Francisco Bay Bridge then under construction.[16] Devoting a largely admiring passage to Kaun, the Berkeley professor, Ilf and Petrov neglected to mention that he was an immigrant.

Ilf associated Reynolds with the writers' most tedious obligations as cultural ambassadors. In a letter, he disparagingly described the doctor as hosting a reception for about "thirty Americans" at which they were fed unappetizing "microscopic appetizers on huge plates."[17] In this instance, Ilf and Petrov appear as incurious as the hitchhikers they derided. The gathering at the doctor's home in the St. Francis Wood neighborhood of San Francisco included some interesting guests, notably the young writer William Saroyan and the consul general of the Irish Free State, Matthew Murphy.[18] Ilf and Petrov seem to have learned little about any of the people who came to honor them or about Reynolds. The doctor had made numerous trips to the Soviet Union and, in 1929 and 1930, had published reports on Soviet medicine and public health that "shocked most of the American medical profession profoundly."[19] By the time *Low-Rise America* was published, Reynolds's enthusiasm for the progressive Soviet approach to divorce, contraception, and abortion was, to say the least, inconvenient. In 1936, the Stalinist state rolled back earlier policies by recriminalizing abortion, limiting access to birth control, and restricting divorce. Less problematic was the doctor's praise of socialized medicine. But Reynolds did not impress the writers. Even if he had

[15] Mers, *Working the Waterfront*, 90–112.   [16] ZK, 10 December, 463, 503n332.
[17] PIA, Il'f, 6 December 1935, 463.
[18] "Guests from Russia Are Given Honor," *San Francisco Chronicle*, 6 December 1935.
[19] "Dr. Ralph Reynolds: A Tribute," Bancroft Library, University of California, Berkeley, Ralph Reynolds Family Memoirs, circa 1956, BANC MSS 99/100 c, Box 1, Folder 1; Ralph A. Reynolds, "Social Hygiene in Soviet Russia," *American Journal of Social Hygiene* 16 (November 1930): 465–82; Ralph A. Reynolds, "The Doctor in the Soviet Union," *Nation* (24 September 1930): 316–19.

helped to arrange it, there was no reason to mention him in connection with their visit to the unfinished suspension span of the Bay Bridge. Ilf and Petrov turned that adventure into a comic set piece. Unpersuaded that the safety net below them ensured their safety, both the writers and the Adamses clung desperately to the steel cable, while obsessively intoning its excellence.[20]

Of course, Ilf and Petrov could not possibly describe everyone they met. But they clearly preferred the elegant and witty Professor Kaun as a representative of the American radical intelligentsia. Kaun was yet another of the Jewish immigrants whose roots in the Russian Empire Ilf and Petrov ignored. Born near Odesa, Kaun (aka Samuel Cohen) had emigrated in 1909 at age twenty; he became a US citizen in 1915.[21] *Low-Rise America* omits the detail, included in the English translation, that Kaun had published a biography of Maxim Gorky. He and his wife, the sculptor Valeria (née Tracewell), had spent time at Gorky's villa in Sorrento, Italy, where the author lived from 1924 to 1933, before he returned to the Soviet Union.[22] In both editions, Ilf and Petrov illustrated Kaun's expertise with a brief, appreciative summary of a lecture in which he displayed a volume of Tolstoy's stories translated into Tatar as evidence of the benefits of Soviet nationalities policy. He held his students rapt as he told them of a "distant land with a new and amazing way of life."[23]

Kaun's published work makes clear that the appreciation was mutual and confirms Ilf and Petrov's sense of him as enthusiastic about the "amazing way of life" under construction in the Soviet Union. In 1936, Kaun reviewed new editions of *The Twelve Chairs* and *The Little Golden Calf.* He predicted that the novels would become classics. Ilf and Petrov, he gushed, "are endowed with the divine gift of laughter, which mankind has never been capable of resisting." To the "fearful query of old maids," "Is there propaganda?" the professor responded, "To be sure!" He granted that the novels had a clear "message": the inevitable "loneliness of a money-seeker ... in the midst of a people drunk with the adventure of building a new life." Still, he found the message

[20] OA, 275–76.

[21] G. R. Noyes, "Alexander Kaun," *Books Abroad* 18 (Autumn 1944): 319–20; "Professor Alexander Samuel Kaun," Federal Bureau of Investigation, 100-SF-17879-889-p.103–104; Alexander Kaun [Samuel Cohen], US, Naturalization Record Indexes; Alexander S Kann, US, World War II Draft Registration Cards, 1942, Ancestry.com.

[22] Alexander Kaun, *Maxim Gorky and His Russia* (New York: J. Cape & H. Smith, 1931); Tovah Yedlin, *Maxim Gorky: A Political Biography* (Westport, CT: Praeger, 1999), 163, 243; LGA, 214; OA, 292.

[23] PIA, Il'f, 6 December 1935, 463–64; LGA, 201–202; OA, 274–76; Noyes, "Alexander Kaun," 322.

"unobtrusive," and perhaps agreeable. In any case he assured would-be readers that in Ilf and Petrov's novels "Hearty laughter over human foibles drowns all other voices."[24]

Enjoying the writers' company and apparently eager to introduce them to his students, Kaun invited Ilf and Petrov to join him and a group of about fifteen young people at his cottage on Point Richmond, just north of Berkeley. Completed in 1935, his modest modernist bungalow stood amid eucalyptus trees on a large beachfront lot. Ilf and Petrov did not describe the house. But their account of the evening suggests they were taken in by the beauty of the spot. They recalled that one of the young women briefly left the gathering to go for a swim, returning with "hair wet and flowing, like a mermaid's."[25]

Whether or not Ilf and Petrov knew it, Kaun's beach house, designed by the Austrian-born, Los Angeles-based architect Rudolph Schindler, connected the professor to the intelligentsia network that ran through Carmel. Schindler and Kaun had met in Chicago sometime between 1914, when Schindler emigrated to the city, and 1918, when Kaun left for Berkeley and Schindler left for Frank Lloyd Wright's studios in Taliesin, Wisconsin. Schindler and his wife Pauline moved to Los Angeles in 1920, where he soon began planning a house at 835 Kings Road in West Hollywood. A modernist masterpiece designed by Schindler to accommodate two families, the house gave architectural form to Pauline's desire to undertake an "experiment in communal living."[26] After the couple split in 1927, Pauline spent time in Carmel before returning in the late 1930s to live in the house with her former husband. Kings Road, which served as a residence and Schindler's studio, became a vibrant gathering place for artists, intellectuals, bohemians, and radicals from Los Angeles and beyond – Kaun among them.[27] (Today it is a unit of the Austrian Museum of Applied Arts, Vienna, the MAK Center for Art and Architecture at the Schindler House.) In 1934, Schindler, who worked primarily in Southern

[24] Alexander Kaun, Review of *Dvenadtset stulyev* and *Zolotoy telenok*, *Books Abroad* 10 (Summer 1936): 362.

[25] OA, 292.

[26] Robert Sweeney, "Shindler House, 1922," MAK Center for Art and Architecture, www .makcenter.org/schindler-house (accessed 4 July 2022).

[27] Robert Sweeney, "Life at Kings Road: As It Was, 1920–1940," in Elizabeth A. T. Smith and Michael Darling, eds., *The Architecture of R. M. Schindler* (Los Angeles: Museum of Contemporary Art, 2001), 86–115; John Crosse, "Pauline Gibling Schindler: Vagabond Agent for Modernism, 1927–1936," Southern California Architectural History, https:// socalarchhistory.blogspot.com/2010/07/pauline-gibling-schindler-vagabond.html (accessed 5 July 2022).

Figure 23.1 The modernist beach house in Richmond, California, where Professor Alexander Kaun and his students spent an evening with Ilf and Petrov. R. M. Schindler papers, Architecture and Design Collection. Art, Design & Architecture Museum; University of California, Santa Barbara.

California, agreed to undertake the beach house project in the Bay Area both because Kaun was an old friend and because he was drawn to the challenge of using innovative materials to construct an affordable ($1,500) modernist house[28] (Figure 23.1).

In the enchanting eucalyptus grove on the bay, Ilf and Petrov found the admirable representative of the American intelligentsia surrounded by the idiocy of American life. While they presented Kaun as effectively communicating the wonder of the new Soviet life, the "best" students invited to his home appear incorrigibly empty-headed. Sitting in a circle on the sand, they sang ("tunefully but rather weakly") several Cal fight songs that praised "Our Sturdy Golden Bear" and mocked "lowly Stanfurd." Anticipating that this would make no sense to their readers, the writers perhaps further befuddled them with the explanation that "the

[28] Steve Wallet, "RM Schindler's Kaun Beach House 1934–35," Steve Wallet, Architect, https://stevewallet.com/2011/04/30/rm-schindlers-kaun-beach-house-1934-35-part-1-of-3/; John Crosse, "Alexander 'Sasha' Kaun Beach Cottage, Richmond, CA, R. M. Schindler, Architect, 1935," Southern California Architectural History, 6 April 2017, https://socalarchhistory.blogspot.com/2017/04/ (accessed 23 June 2022).

students of the University of California call themselves 'Bears,'" and that Stanford students are their "sworn enemies" on the football field.[29]

Likely accurate as far as it went, Ilf and Petrov's depiction highlights the distance between American academic culture and the haughty seriousness of the Soviet intelligentsia. Kaun's Berkeley colleague George Noyes remembered similar details to very different effect. That Noyes was memorializing Kaun, who had died suddenly in 1944, clearly shaped his recollection. Nonetheless, it is telling that Noyes began with the essential fact, ignored by Ilf and Petrov, that the students singing Cal songs were also trying to learn about the wider world. They were members of "our little Slavic Society, to which all the students of any Slavic language might belong." That the writers, whose English was avowedly unremarkable, should disdain American college students learning Russian seems especially churlish. By contrast, Noyes fondly recalled the Society's gatherings at Kaun's "'private Riviera,' a rather chilly little beach adjoining his cottage at Richmond. The boys and girls toasted wienies, bathed in the turbid water, played ball, were happy." "Sasha" and Valeria, as Ilf and Petrov must have observed, "mingled with them without affectation or condescension."[30]

Kaun's 1938 review of *Low-Rise America* offers an oblique view of his perspective. He had ended his 1936 assessment of Ilf and Petrov's novels by noting that the pair "have recently motored across this continent, and have come in close contact with a variety of people, from cropsharers [sic] and hoboes thumbing for a lift to college students and factory directors." Neither here nor in his review of *Low-Rise America* did Kaun reveal that he and his Berkeley students had been among Ilf and Petrov's varied contacts. Marveling that "the gamut of their experiences is strikingly broad," Kaun did not seem persuaded by their "humorous but not altogether uncharitable impression" of the United States. "Most of their observations," he concluded, "are as nearly correct as might be expected from first visitors."[31] His strained politeness suggests that Ilf and Petrov's patronizing account of the "little Slavic Society" may have rubbed him the wrong way.

Ilf and Petrov's depiction of the Carmel intelligentsia was likewise "not altogether uncharitable." After two months in America, they found Williams's cottage a wonder to behold. It looked nothing like all the

---

[29] LGA, 215; OA, 292; Cal Songs, http://calband.berkeley.edu/media/cal-songs/ (accessed 22 June 2022).
[30] Noyes, "Alexander Kaun," 322.
[31] Alexander Kaun, "Review of *Odnoetazhnaya Amerika*," *Books Abroad* 12 (Spring 1938): 249.

other American houses they had seen. There were books and pamphlets everywhere: "In this house people actually read."[32] In *Low-Rise America*, the bedridden Steffens decries American capitalism, sobs and repents his own past inability to understand his fame as a bourgeois "bribe," and expresses his wish to "go to Moscow, so as to see before his death the land of socialism and die there."[33] In undated notes, Williams offers a slightly different perspective on the conversation. He describes Steffens as crying not over the support he unwittingly gave to "iniquitous" capitalism, but rather "over the inhumanity of man." In Williams's version, the dying Steffens expressed a desire "to go to Moscow and be buried there."[34] Where Ilf and Petrov emphasized the great man's desire to see the socialist promised land, Williams suggested that he was thinking about his legacy, perhaps imaging himself buried alongside John Reed at the Kremlin wall.

Unable to bear Americans' "idiotic optimistic laughter," Steffens clearly emerges in *Low-Rise America* as "one of us." Earlier in the travelogue, the American habit of meeting misfortune with a smile, which Steffens could not abide, provoked Ilf and Petrov to cutting sarcasm. A billboard on a garage in Bakersfield, California, "Here you will always be met with a friendly laugh," elicited a lengthy disquisition on why "American laughter, generally good, loud, and cheerful laughter, occasionally does irritate."[35] The problem, they concluded, was that "America is a land that loves primitive clarity in all its affairs and ideas": "It is better to laugh than to cry," so "an American must laugh."[36] Racializing this annoying trait, they imagined a laughing (white) "American" reasoning, "Let the Mexicans, Slavs, Jews, and Negroes whine and grieve."[37] Yet they represented Steffens as capable of transcending this unwarranted, debilitating, essentially American optimism. In *Low-Rise America*, they provide a simple explanation – or perhaps consequence – of this ability: "A year ago, Lincoln Steffens joined the Communist Party."[38] The line does not appear in Charles Malamuth's translation. In 1935, Steffens was more sympathetic to communism and the Soviet Union than at any time in his life. But he never became a card-carrying communist.[39]

Even as they embraced Steffens as one of their own, Ilf and Petrov registered something odd, if not slightly ridiculous, about a community of radicals living in a cozy town whose cypress-lined streets descended to the ocean. They deflated the pathos of Steffen's heartfelt confession with

[32] LGA, 218; OA, 296.   [33] LGA, 219; OA, 298; PIA, Il'f, 9 December 1935, 465–66.
[34] "Lincoln Steffens," typed by lw (Lucita Williams), September 1962, Williams Papers, Box 15.
[35] LGA, 219, 189; OA, 297, 258.   [36] OA, 259.   [37] LGA, 190; OA, 259.
[38] OA, 298.   [39] Hartshorn, *I Have Seen*, 423.

a recap of the visitors' long discussion at his bedside about how best to transport the dying man to the Soviet Union: "Could he go by boat from California by way of the Panama Canal to New York, and from there through the Mediterranean to the Black Sea coast?"[40] Their portrait of Lucita Squier, who had married Williams in 1923, when both were living in the Soviet Union, comes close to parody. The former writer of scenarios for silent films appears in *Low-Rise America* theatrically attired in a "homespun linen Mordovian dress with cross-stich embroidery," worn, she told the writers "in remembrance of Russia." Ostentatiously "pining" for the Soviet Union, Squier responded to their admiration for the Pacific Coast with, "the Black Sea is better."[41] Perhaps Ilf and Petrov rolled their eyes; they describe Williams rushing to explain that "obsession" impaired his wife's judgment. Since visiting the Soviet Union, "she has come to hate everything American ... She is even capable of saying the Black Sea is bigger than the Pacific Ocean, just because the Black Sea is Soviet."[42]

In Carmel, Ilf and Petrov found the intellectual Williams, no less than the intellectual Kaun, surrounded by standard American vacuousness. His wealthy neighbors, like all the wealthy art lovers in the travelogue, lacked taste and discernment. At one gathering, an architect offered "cooling drinks" to the "local intelligentsia." When the host's daughter played several pieces "loudly" on the piano, the guests listened with "utmost attention." Ilf and Petrov mocked their deferential politeness, likening it to the silent tableau at the end of Nikolai Gogol's satirical *The Inspector General*. They did not need to summarize the play's mute ending, which would have been familiar to their readers: When the "town's corrupt officials" learn that the real inspector general is arriving, they freeze, holding "horrified expressions" for a full ninety seconds.[43] In Carmel, when the music started, the partygoers signaled their "delicacy" by halting mid-gesture, with glasses to their lips or bent in conversation.[44] In a letter, Ilf described the company in less literary terms as "strange": "some strikingly ugly American old women, some daughters of impoverished millionaires engaged in making ladies' handbags in a nauseatingly intelligentsia style, timid and beautiful young people, and a former boxer, Mr. Sharkey."[45]

Mr. Sharkey, the only guest lacking the refinement to freeze when the music started, emerges as the most remarkable character in Ilf and

---

[40] LGA, 219; OA, 298.   [41] LGA, 218; OA, 296; ZK, 9 December 1935, 461 (pining).
[42] OA, 297.
[43] Judith Robey, "Modelling the Reading Act: Gogol's Mute Scene and its Intertexts," *Slavic Review* 56 (Summer 1997): 233–50 (quotations at 233).
[44] OA, 299.   [45] PIA, Il'f, 6 December 1935, 466.

Petrov's Carmel adventure (see Figure 13.1). Introducing himself as a rich former world champion boxer, he invited all the guests to feel his muscles and then proposed that they go to his oceanfront house for a drink. Ilf and Petrov described him as a prodigious liar, who claimed to have captained a schooner at the South Pole; a hard drinker, who had been a bootlegger and mixed "hellish" cocktails; a sentimental father, who showed them his sleeping daughters; and a flamboyant radical, who proclaimed that "in America, revolution must be made as soon as possible." Mr. Adams, who loved to try everything, could not resist the former champion's challenge to a "friendly bout." The evening ended with the two "fat men" in boxing gloves jumping around and laughing hysterically – and then one final drink.[46]

As they learned six months later, Ilf and Petrov had become extras in a comical truth-is-stranger-than-fiction plot to connect the Carmel intelligentsia to the Communist Party. In *Low-Rise America*, they explain that back in Moscow, they received a packet of clippings from Mr. Adams that revealed Mr. Sharkey's real identity. The published story is clearly based on a June 1936 letter and newspaper articles from Trone. The "world champion," Ilf and Petrov reported, turned out to be a "police agent connected with the fascist American Legion."[47] Their summary and the list of aliases under which Mr. Sharkey had operated – Captain Bakcsy, Berger, and Foster – mostly squares with the *Western Worker*'s May 1936 exposé of the "notorious labor spy and racketeer."[48] The writers used the most colorful of Sharkey's aliases, Captain X, as the title of their chapter on Carmel.

Giving top billing to the "spy and racketeer" rather than the intellectuals, Ilf and Petrov suggested that the villain was more fascinating – and perhaps more typically "American" – than the radical intelligentsia. Eager to turn Sharkey into a gangster, they asserted that he had used the name Captain X when he was a "Chicago racketeer," not, as the *Western Worker* reported, when, during World War I, he worked in military intelligence. They also left out – perhaps did not pick up on – a detail noted in US coverage. Bakcsy, as he was known in San Francisco, had a "thick Hungarian accent."[49] He was one of the many immigrant informers who leveraged their "alienism" to fight "radicalism."

---

[46] OA, 300.
[47] OA, 301; Trone to Il'f and Petrov, 9 June 1936, as cited in ZK, 502n320.
[48] "Notorious Labor Spy and Racketeer Hired by Waterfront Employers for Plot against Unions and Communists," *Western Worker*, 21 May 1936.
[49] Estlov E. Ward, *Harry Bridges on Trial: How Labor Won Its Biggest Case* (New York: Modern Age Books, 1940), 186; "Notorious Labor Spy."

Although Ilf and Petrov highlighted Captain X's affiliation with the "fascist" American Legion, they omitted a key piece of the story, which Trone had emphasized in the letter: its aggressive anticommunism. The elaborate scheme to incriminate Carmel's radical elite by plying them with alcohol at parties in a house "wired with dictaphones," aimed to "prove" that "Moscow Gold" financed the radical waterfront unions. Bakcsy was not in the employ of the American Legion, which had turned down his proposal, but rather the shipping interests, who had long sought to discredit (and perhaps deport) labor organizers as "Reds."[50] They wanted evidence to support the claim, made by the San Francisco Chamber of Commerce among others, that the 1934 waterfront strike was "not a conflict between employer and employee" but rather a conflict "between American values and un-American radicalism."[51] What interested Ilf and Petrov, by contrast, was not the red baiting but the "racket." As the *Western Worker* reported, Bakcsy was "netting ... plenty of dough in exchange for a few dummied dictaphone reports." What could be more American than that?

Yet Ilf and Petrov still expressed hope in the possibility of an authentic American radicalism. They gave the last word of the "Captain X" episode to Steffens. Reporting that the old muckraker died at his typewriter, Ilf and Petrov ended the chapter on Carmel with a quotation from Steffens's unfinished August 1936 article on the recent "Spanish events": "We Americans must remember that we shall have to wage a similar battle against the Fascists." This is a politically corrected translation of the statement Steffens wrote, at the request of the *New Masses*, a month after the war in Spain began: "Spain's is the first opening battle of man for man ... we realize as they fight that we have to finish what they are starting." Ella Winter forwarded the article to the journal with the note that it was "in Lincoln Steffens's typewriter when he died." Ilf and Petrov's version made Steffens's message more closely match the explicitly antifascist statements among which it was published. However, they did not go so far as to attribute to Steffens anything like Theodore Dreiser's prediction that "In the victory of communism in Spain will be every possibility for a new life for the people, and a new hope for the ignorant and oppressed."[52] Even the few American communists who appeared in *Low-Rise America* did not look forward to the "victory of communism."

---

[50] Trone to Il'f and Petrov, 9 June 1936; "Notorious Labor Spy"; Hartshorn, *I Have Seen*, 429–30; "Solomon A. Trone: Internal Security – R," 19 October 1945, Trone FBI.

[51] As quoted in Nelson, *Workers on the Waterfront*, 144; Ella Winter, "Stevedores on Strike," *New Republic* 79 (13 June 1934): 121.

[52] LGA, 221; OA, 301; "¡Viva España Libre!" *New Masses* 20 (18 August 1936): 11; Ella Winter, *And Not to Yield: An Autobiography* (New York: Harcourt, Brace & World, 1963), 219.

Communism Is Twentieth Century Americanism.
American Communist Party slogan, 1935

In late December 1935, two weeks after their visit to the Soviet colony in Carmel, Ilf and Petrov met an actual prerevolutionary Russian radical. Not mentioned in *Low-Rise America*, the encounter with the president of the American-Russian Institute of Southern California, Dr. Nahum Kavinoky, provides a fitting epilogue to Ilf and Petrov's at once dismissive and admiring portrait of the American radical intelligentsia. In many ways, the episode echoed the disagreeable reception at the American-Russian Institute in San Francisco. In a letter to his wife, Ilf wrote that they "had to have lunch with a certain doctor, a friend of the Soviet Union." The unwanted obligation sent them to Pasadena, where they were served a "cold, but tasty," Russian-style meal.[1]

But Ilf and Petrov offered conflicting descriptions of Nahum Kavinoky as, on the one hand, engaged in the pursuit of the almighty dollar and, on the other, as connected to the Soviet intelligentsia. In Petrov's telling, the doctor was a canny adept of the capitalist system. Kavinoky, he informed his wife, was an "old man, who had become famous mainly because he was insured against illness, had fallen ill with chronic heart disease, and now receives 600 dollars per month from the insurance company." By contrast, Ilf highlighted an unexpected link with Soviet culture. The doctor's daughter, he wrote to his wife, "lives in Moscow and is married to [Vasily] Katanyan, a literary critic, who it seems you know."[2] Katanyan was an expert on Mayakovsky; in the 1920s he had been active in the avant-garde journals *Lef* (Left Front of the Arts) and *Novyi lef* (New Lef), which Mayakovsky edited. In 1937, he left his wife Galina for Lili Brik, an author famous for having been Mayakovsky's muse. Katanyan lived with Brik until her suicide in 1978. How the doctor's daughter ended up in

---

[1] PIA, Il'f, 22 December 1935, 476.
[2] PIA, Petrov, 23 December 1935; Il'f, 22 December 1935, 478, 476.

Moscow attached to the most rarefied Soviet cultural circles Ilf did not say.[3]

The writers' brief accounts of the Sunday brunch do not mention whether the doctor's wife, Dr. Nadina Kavinoky was also at the table. It seems likely that she, too, would have been interested in meeting the Soviet writers. Their failure to notice her suggests that they may have missed their hosts' connection to the Soviet colony in Carmel; Boris Reinstein, Nadina Kavinoky's father, was a Jewish return immigrant to the Soviet Union, who had guided Albert Rhys Williams and John Reed around revolutionary Russia and then employed them in the Soviet foreign ministry's "bureau of propaganda."[4]

While I found no evidence of the writers' visit or the insurance scheme in the family archive, it does shed light on a complex history that includes both revolutionary radicalism and immigrant striving. In an undated auto-biography that seems to have been drafted around the time of Ilf and Petrov's visit – it mentions in passing the "horror which grips [Berlin] today" – Nahum Kavinoky described the dramatic circumstances that led him in 1905 to abandon his wife and daughter in Russia and emigrate to the United States. Born in 1875 in Grodno (in today's Belarus), Kavinoky was one of eleven children raised in a "pious Jewish" family. As he told the story, at an early age he had chosen science over religion, and "emanci-pated" himself "from nearly all of the orthodox rites." Graduating "high school with sufficient honors" to earn one of the small number of places open to Jews, he enrolled at Kiev (Kyiv) University. There he became "a member of the international socialist movement," as a means of alleviating "the suffering I saw all around me." Kavinoky, like many radicals in the Russian empire, ultimately chose medicine as a practical way to serve the people. He studied in Vienna, worked for the local government (*zemstvo*) clinic in a small village about thirty miles from Minsk, and then undertook additional medical training in Berlin.[5]

In 1905, Kavinoky was drafted for service during the war with Japan and also stuck in an "unsuccessful and unhappy married life." As he remembered it, "the majority of us" – it is not clear who the "us" encompassed – were "wishing for defeat of the Russian Armies, because we expected that defeat would bring more liberalism in Russia." He was

---

[3] Bengt Jangfeldt, *Mayakovsky: A Biography* (Chicago: University of Chicago Press, 2014), 578–79.

[4] Albert Rhys Williams, *Journey into the Revolution: Petrograd, 1917–1918* (Chicago: Quadrangle Books, 1969), 168–69.

[5] Nahum Kavinoky, "I Think Back," n.d., typescript, 10, 4, 2, 6, University of California, Santa Barbara, UC Santa Barbara Library, Department of Special Research Collections, Schott Family papers, SBHC Mss 112, Box 1, Folder 8.

actively working to achieve this desired result, distributing revolutionary pamphlets, until his superior tipped him off that he was about to be arrested. He "escaped prison" and "at the same time ended my unsuccessful marriage," by emigrating. He left behind a six-month-old daughter and a wife, who remarried about a year later. Only much later, at age nineteen or twenty, did Galina learn the truth. When she expressed "anti-Jewish feelings in the presence of a friend of her mother's, who himself was a Jew," the friend "lost control and answered her that if she knew who her father was she wouldn't speak that way about the Jews." At that point, Galina "began to dig around" and learned that her father was in the United States. In 1925, he received his "first letter from her and we have been in constant correspondence since."[6] According to Ilf, the writers "talked and talked" over lunch. But how much of this story Kavinoky related is unclear.

Nadina Kavinoky's parents' story closely paralleled her husband's. Anna Reinstein (née Mogliva), a decade older than Nahum Kavinoky, had, like him, been attracted to a medical career in order to "treat the peasants" afflicted with "epidemic diseases." In the 1880s, she joined the large number of Russian women who since the 1860s had been studying medicine and organizing radical youth groups at the University of Zurich.[7] In a "Circle of the Young People's Will Party Adherents," a group committed to terrorism rather than Marxism, she met fellow student Boris Reinstein. Brought up in a secular Jewish family in Rostov-on-Don, Reinstein arrived in Zurich with a knowledge of English and a love of American folk songs, the fruit of his wealthy father's effort to instill some discipline by dispatching him to North Dakota for a year. As Nadina told the story, the two radicals, "fell in love and married." Nadina was born in 1888 in Switzerland. A year later, Boris attended the founding congress of the Second International in Paris, where, as he remembered in 1936, he began "to find the path towards a more consistent Marxist position and tactic."[8] In 1891, Anna completed her medical degree, the couple narrowly avoided deportation from France, and they emigrated to Buffalo, New York.[9]

---

[6] Kavinoky, "I Think Back," 11, 13.

[7] Richard Stites, *The Women's Liberation Movement in Russia: Feminism, Nihilism, and Bolshevism, 1860–1930* (Princeton, NJ: Princeton University Press, 1978), 131–32; Faith Hillis, *Utopia's Discontents: Russian Émigrés and the Quest for Freedom, 1830s–1930s* (New York: Oxford University Press, 2021), 28–32.

[8] Boris Reinstein, "Clara Zetkin at the Cradle of the Second International," *The Communist* 15 (June 1936): 563.

[9] Nadina Kavinoky, "My Five Identities," typescript of manuscript written 2 August 1969, [2, 3], Schott Family Papers, Box 1 Folder 11.

In many ways the Reinsteins were typical immigrants working to make a comfortable life. Anna Reinstein became the region's first woman gynecologist. Boris Reinstein earned a degree in pharmacy in the United States. In 1905, the newly arrived Nahum, then thirty, met Nadina, seventeen, when he rented a room in the Reinstein's house. They married a year later; "18 years old and pregnant," Nadina began studying medicine at the University of Buffalo. In 1912, the two doctors moved to Southern California, seeking a climate in which Nahum could recover from tuberculosis.[10]

Despite economic success in the United States, neither the Kavinokys nor the Reinsteins abandoned their commitment to progressive, if not revolutionary causes. Nadina Kavinoky, a gynecologist, served as director of Mothers' Clinics sponsored by the Los Angeles County Health Department. In the 1930s, she was an outspoken advocate for married women's access to birth control.[11] Nahum Kavinoky combined philanthropic work related to a local tuberculosis sanatorium with support for communist-aligned causes. In addition to serving as president of the American-Russian Institute of Southern California, he was active in the American League for Peace and Democracy and ICOR, the Association for Jewish Colonization in the Soviet Union.[12]

Anna and Boris Reinstein were more radical than Nadina and Nahum Kavinoky, but still upstanding professionals in suburban Cheektowaga, New York. Both "became active as local organizers in the Socialist Labor Party." Anna was often the main Polish-language speaker at party rallies.[13] Boris traveled widely as a socialist activist able to rally workers in English, German, Polish, Russian, and Yiddish.[14] In 1917, he returned to the Russian Revolution, leaving Anna behind in Buffalo. Like

---

[10] Hermann Schott, "Nadina and Nahum in America," n.d., after 1991, [1], Schott Family Papers, Box 1, Folder 11.

[11] Newspaper clippings scrapbook, Schott Family papers, Box 3; Cathy Moran Hajo, *Birth Control on Main Street: Organizing Clinics in the United States, 1916–1939* (Urbana: University of Illinois Press, 2010), 40–43.

[12] "Southland Jewry Mourns Death of Dr. Kavinoky, J. C. R. A. Leader," *B'nai B'rith Messenger*, 12 August 1938; Doug Rossinow, "'The Model of a Model Fellow Traveler': Harry F. Ward, the American League for Peace and Democracy, and the 'Russian Question'" in American Politics, 1933–1956," *Peace & Change* 29 (April 2004): 177–220; Robert Weinberg, *Stalin's Forgotten Zion: Birobidzhan and the Making of a Soviet Jewish Homeland: An Illustrated History, 1928–1996* (Berkeley: University of California Press, 1998), 51–57.

[13] William G. Falkowski, Jr., "Reinstein, Anna," in Judy Barrett Litoff and Judith McDonnell, eds., *European Immigrant Women in the United States: A Biographical Dictionary* (New York: Garland, 1994), 244.

[14] Michael H. Ebner, "The Passaic Strike of 1912 and the Two IWW's," *Labor History* 11 (1970): 456; Zvi Gitelman, *Jewish Nationality and Soviet Politics: The Jewish Sections of the CPSU, 1917–1930* (Princeton, NJ: Princeton University Press, 1972), 120–21.

Gumberg, he helped Williams and Reed navigate the confusing political situation. But unlike Gumberg, who returned to his life as a New York businessman, Reinstein stayed. Initially sympathetic to the more moderate Mensheviks, he joined the Bolshevik party after the October Revolution. He soon became an important Comintern propagandist and liaison with foreign communists.[15] In 1922, Reinstein briefly returned to the United States. He came as an official Comintern representative to a secret Communist Party congress held in the Michigan woods. Law enforcement broke up the gathering and arrested many of the attendees, but Reinstein escaped.[16] Before returning to Soviet Russia, he managed to meet with Nadina, who covered her father's tracks by loading "the car with beach things" and then taking "him and the family up into the mountains."[17]

The daring trip ended up being Reinstein's last high-level Comintern assignment. In 1924, he became the director of the Comintern archive, a post he held in 1936 when he was expelled from the Party for "Trotskyite" affiliations and lack of "vigilance." In mid-1937, seemingly unaware of Reinstein's troubles, Williams tracked down his old friend to get his take on the confessions extracted from so many Old Bolsheviks at the recent show trials. Reinstein apparently replied that "not all had confessed." Williams took this to be the excuse of a "true believer" rather than an insight; he wanted a "rational" explanation.[18]

Rather surprisingly, Reinstein, unlike so many immigrants who returned to the Soviet Union, did not end up getting shot or sent to the gulag. In his own defense before the party, Reinstein emphasized that in 1918, when Trotsky and Bukharin had recommended him for membership, the "scoundrels" had occupied "very responsible positions in the leadership." He never imagined that "they were capable of betraying the party, even in the distant future" – a failure of imagination that, he added, offered "no consolation." For whatever reason, the appeal worked. In 1938, the Comintern's party committee reduced his punishment to a "strict reprimand" and finally to an "admonition." After his reinstatement, Reinstein edited the English-language magazine *Sovietland.*

---

[15] Williams, *Journey,* 46–47, 51–52, 168, 176–78, 207–208, 216–21.

[16] Branko Lazitch, *Biographical Dictionary of the Comintern: New, Revised, and Expanded Edition* (Stanford, CA: Hoover Institution Press, 1986), 392; "W. Z. Foster Seized in Radical Roundup," NYT, 24 August 1922.

[17] Schott, "Nadina and Nahum in America," [2]; Michelle Kerns, "Red Hero, Black Sheep: Family Secrets Leads Woman on Detective Quest to Learn More about Boris Reinstein," *Buffalo News,* 13 November 2011.

[18] Williams, *Journey,* 329.

He died in 1947 at the age of eighty-one and was buried in Moscow at Novodevichi Cemetery.[19]

Nahum Kavinoky likewise remained committed to the Soviet cause until the end. He died in August 1938, just as the purges that almost claimed his father-in-law were beginning to wind down. At his funeral, the power of the Popular Front message was palpable. The African American actor and singer Clarence Muse sang the Black spiritual "Steal Away" and "The International." To honor his memory, Kavinoky's friends contributed funds to purchase an ambulance for the Spanish Republic.[20]

Leaving Kavinoky out of *Low-Rise America*, Ilf and Petrov, consciously or not, advanced the Popular Front tactic of associating communist parties with "indigenous" radical traditions. They, like American communists, bridled at what they correctly identified as the American authorities' tactic of discrediting radicals by equating them with ethnic and racial Others, "dirty Mexicans, Slavs, and Negroes" – and also Jews. The stereotype of a largely immigrant and Jewish party was not wrong. In 1935, about 40 percent of the American party's members were American born and perhaps half were of Jewish descent. But during the period of the Popular Front, the party worked to "Americanize" its membership and its message. While praising Stalin, American communists promoted the slogan, "Communism is Twentieth Century Americanism."[21] In *Low-Rise America*, Ilf and Petrov similarly refuted the image of the "un-American" communist not by arguing against xenophobia and antisemitism but by turning immigrant Jewish radicals into unhyphenated American radicals – or excising them altogether.

Nonetheless, Nahum Kavinoky's story apparently pushed Ilf, at least, to acknowledge a problem the writers usually ignored: the complex identities of Jewish immigrants from the Russian empire. Petrov's letter reduced the meeting to Kavinoky's only-in-America insurance gambit.

---

[19] Information and quotations from Reinstein's Comintern personnel file (RGASPI f. 495, op. 65 a, d. 4542) as cited in Il'ia Alekseevich Suzdal'tsev, "Rol' I Kongressa Kominterna v sud'bakh ego inostrannykh delegatov," in O. S. Porshneva, ed., *Vremia Kominterna: materialy mezhdunarodnykh nauchnykh konferentsii k 100-letiiu Kommunisticheskogo Internatsionala* (Moscow: Gosudarstvennaia publichnaia istoricheskaia biblioteka Rossii, 2020), 74–75.

[20] "Southland Jewry"; Max Schott to Nahum Kavinoky Memorial Committee, 30 September 1938, Schott Family Papers, Box 1, Folder 3; Family news clippings, Box 1, Folder 13.

[21] James G. Ryan, "'Communism Is Twentieth Century Americanism': The Communist Party's Americanization Campaign," in J. Bret Bennington et al., eds., *The 1930s: The Realities and the Promise* (Newcastle upon Tyne: Cambridge Scholars Publishing, 2016), 112, 116; Tony Michels, "On Jews and Taboos in American Communist History," *American Communist History* 14 (2016): 249–55.

But Ilf's note, with its emphasis on the doctor's Soviet daughter, suggested the ambiguity of his status as an American. The uncertainty stemmed from Kavinoky's multifaceted self-presentation as a Russian political exile and successful Jewish immigrant, who presided over a Soviet-affiliated friendship organization, was fluent in both Russian and English, and nurtured family ties to the Russian intelligentsia and the Comintern. Clearly the doctor was hard to classify. But so, too, were Ilf and Petrov's other secular, Russified, Soviet-sympathizing Jewish American interlocutors, notably Trone and Gumberg, over whose hybrid identities the writers never puzzled. Perhaps the doctor's status as an official "friend" of the Soviet Union made his multiple identities more visible. Or perhaps the unexpected three degrees of separation between Ilf's wife and his host's daughter prompted him to consider Kavinoky's self-understanding.

The encounter in Pasadena suggested that powerful emotional bonds and cultural yearnings intensified, even underpinned, friendship with the Soviet Union. Ilf and Petrov grasped that the cultural and political upward mobility enjoyed by Soviet Jews likely appealed to immigrants with bitter memories of Russian antisemitism. In *The Little Golden Calf*, Ostap Bender informs a visiting American journalist inquiring about the "Jewish Question" that the Soviet Union had "Jews, but no question."[22] Still, that after thirty years in America the doctor felt this transformation so profoundly may have come as a surprise. The Soviet project offered immigrants like Kavinoky, who had joined Russian revolutionary movements in their youth, not only a road to the bright socialist future. It provided a path back to long-lost comrades and a return to "Pushkin Street," the Russian high culture to which they had aspired before they emigrated. For Jewish (former) revolutionaries, the Russian language remained, as the terrorist populist turned Siberian ethnographer Vladimir Jochelson put it, the language of "the striving for freedom."[23]

In their account of American radicals, Ilf and Petrov confronted an issue they faced throughout their travelogue: How to integrate immigrants from the Russian empire and the Soviet Union, who blurred the line between us and them, into a narrative structured around the difference

---

[22] Alice Nakhimovsky, "How the Soviets Solved the Jewish Question: The Il'f–Petrov Novels and Il'f's Jewish Stories," *Symposium* 53 (January 1999): 93.

[23] Jochelson (Iokhel'son) as characterized and quoted in Yuri Slezkine, *The Jewish Century*, new ed. (Princeton, NJ: Princeton University Press, 2019), 129, 135 (Pushkin); Daniel Soyer, "Soviet Travel and the Making of an American Jewish Communist: Moissaye Olgin's Trip to Russia in 1920–1921," *American Communist History* 4 (2005): 20; Tony Michels, "Toward a History of American Jews and the Russian Revolutionary Movement," in Nancy L. Green and Roger Waldinger, eds., *A Century of Transnationalism: Immigrants and Their Homeland Connections* (Urbana: University of Illinois Press, 2016), 145–62.

between the world of socialism and the land of capitalism. As we have seen, their strategies included cutting Jewish Russian Americans from the narrative; eliding their Russianness and Jewishness; or emphasizing their status as immigrants full of regret and yearning for home. The issue was particularly salient in the case of the American intelligentsia because so many radicals were immigrants who, like the Reinsteins and the Kavinokys, were both successful on American terms and friends of the Soviet Union. The problem of what to do with Russian (Jewish) Americans arose at least as acutely in Hollywood, where the writers simultaneously denounced the idiocy of American movies and admired the immigrant directors who made them.

25   Nothing Could Be More Hollywoody

> We serve our bosses and do everything that they order. You will ask me,
> how is it then that Hollywood turns out a few good pictures? They
> appear against the will of the boss.
>
> Unnamed American filmmaker in Ilf and Petrov, *Low-Rise America*

In early December 1935, Ilf and Petrov finally reached Hollywood.
During their two-week sojourn in the film capital, they immersed themselves more fully in American life than at any other point on their
journey. They also yearned more than ever to say goodbye to America.
As Ilf noted in a letter to his wife, in Los Angeles, the travelers were at
"the beginning of the return trip." He tried to cheer her and himself with
the reminder that from then on, every step the writers took brought them
closer to the Atlantic Ocean. Petrov, too, wrote excitedly of the pair's
plans for getting home.[1] All the same, they chose to prolong their stay in
Hollywood, where they moved from observing American culture to
participating in – and ideally profiting from – it.

At the suggestion of the director Lewis Milestone (born Leib Milstein
in the Russian empire), Ilf and Petrov spent nine days before Christmas
1935 holed up in their hotel writing a treatment of *The Twelve Chairs*.
In *Low-Rise America*, they did not tell the story of how they became bit
players in the American movie industry. Nor did they share the larger
realization that in Hollywood – as in the United States in general –
Russian Jewish immigrants created much "American" culture. Still, the
published work suggested bridges across the vast cultural divide.
Extravagantly criticizing Hollywood films as predictable and mindless,
Ilf and Petrov noted that they found many movie people who shared their
perspective. Their unpublished accounts and evidence from the
American side bring the central paradox of Ilf and Petrov's Hollywood
venture into sharper focus: Their brief and publicly unacknowledged

[1] PIA, Il'f, 10 December, Petrov, 10 December, 468, 469–70.

274

turn as Hollywood screenwriters solidified both their disdain and their respect for the American dream factory.

During their American adventures, Ilf and Petrov saw, by their own accounting, at least 100 films over the course of about eighty-five days. This extraordinary number is entirely plausible. In New York, they went to the movies "almost every evening." Their very first night in America, they "fought off the 'Crusaders,'" by which Ilf likely meant Cecil B. DeMille's 1935 film *The Crusades*, then in the last week of its eight-week run at the Astor Theater in Times Square. On the road to California, Ilf and Petrov reported that they went to double features "not almost, but simply every evening."[2] By the time of their journey, the bargain double bill, which included two features, newsreels, an animated short, and perhaps a serial, had become the dominant mode of film exhibition in the United States. The show played continuously, and viewers could walk in at any moment. If you arrived midway through the A-movie – the chief draw with a big budget and big stars – you had to sit through the shorts and the newsreels as well as the entire low-budget B-movie, before seeing the first half of the main attraction.[3]

Scorning most of the movies they saw as trash, Ilf and Petrov did not stop to consider what, given their limited English skills, they may have missed. Even at the start of their movie marathon, the titles hardly registered. Ilf's review of their night out in Dearborn, Michigan, five days into the road trip, was succinct: "Enormous cinema and bad pictures."[4] Some 75 percent of the 600 films American studios produced in 1935 were the B-features that filled the second slot on double bills. Many were shot in just a week.[5] If Ilf and Petrov really sat through 100 movies, they likely saw an awful lot of schlock. But their judgments rested on, at best, imperfect understandings of the dialogue. The weakness of their English as much as the power of their Soviet preconceptions may explain some of their judgments, such as the questionable conclusion that Hollywood's varied "social problem" pictures were all "vile fascist" concoctions.[6]

---

[2] OA, 304.
[3] Richard Maltby, "'Perhaps Everyone Has Forgotten Just How Pictures Are Shown to the Public': Continuous Performance and Double Billing in the 1930s," in Daniel Biltereyst, Richard Maltby, and Philippe Meers, eds., *The Routledge Companion to New Cinema History* (New York: Routledge, 2019), 159–61, 165–67; Iwan Morgan, "Introduction: Hollywood and the Great Depression," in Iwan Morgan and Philip John Davies, eds., *Hollywood and the Great Depression: American Film, Politics and Society in the 1930s* (Edinburgh: Edinburgh University Press, 2016), 6.
[4] ZK, 13 November, 446.   [5] Morgan, "Introduction," 14.
[6] OA, 308; Morgan, "Introduction," 11–13.

Ilf and Petrov reported that they kept seeing bad movies just as they kept eating allegedly bad steaks. Even before they left Moscow, where they had seen only the "best pictures of the best directors," they had "suspected" that average American movies would not be "treasures." Their suspicions were quickly confirmed. Yet every night they entered the theater with a "vestige of hope" that they might eventually encounter something palatable. Inevitably, they exited "with the feeling of having eaten in all its details the famous lunch No. 2, of which we were duly sick and tired."[7] Why, one wonders, did they keep going?

The writers attributed their persistence to the high technical polish of motion pictures "below the level of human dignity." By simply mentioning that they saw 100 films, Ilf and Petrov alerted readers to the advanced state of the American movie industry. In 1935–1936, Soviet studios turned out fifty features; in 1937, the year *Low-Rise America* was published, production was down to thirty-six. Ilf and Petrov sorted the Hollywood productions they saw into "four standard types": musical comedy, historical drama, gangster pictures, and films "featuring a famous opera singer."[8] The attentive Soviet reader could reasonably infer from this typology, with its emphasis on music and singing, that at a time when at least "two thirds of Soviet screens continued to be silent," American movies were primarily talkies, as indeed they had been since 1930.[9] Ilf and Petrov found that even a "nauseating" B-feature "slapped together in eight days," was so well produced that it exerted a powerful fascination.[10] They compared American movies that married incomparable technical achievements to idiotic characters and plots to the tiny monkey holding a baby that they saw in a pet store window. Tenderly caring for her "microscopic" child, the mama monkey at first glance seemed to be the "epitome of motherhood." But she was also, they decided, a "vicious caricature of mother love." Finding the scene inexplicably unpleasant, Ilf and Petrov also found it difficult to look away. The writers described themselves as standing transfixed with the rest of the crowd before a spectacle that, like the American motion picture, "seems like real art ... yet at the same time is unendurably disgusting."[11]

Once Ilf and Petrov got to Hollywood, they came to the realization that American directors, screenwriters, actors, and technicians shared their view that most of what the American film industry churned out was

---

[7] LGA, 224; OA, 304.   [8] OA, 304–305.
[9] Maria Belodubrovskaya, *Not According to Plan: Filmmaking under Stalin* (Ithaca, NY: Cornell University Press, 2017), 35, 30; William M. Drew, *The Last Silent Picture Show: Silent Films on American Screens in the 1930s* (Lanham, MD: Scarecrow Press, 2010), 13.
[10] LGA, 230; OA, 313.   [11] OA, 309.

dreck. In *Low-Rise America*, they recounted that an unnamed filmmaker giving the writers a tour of the "studio in which he works, literally poked fun at everything being shot." All the "sensible people" they met in Hollywood – and they met quite a few of them – "simply groaned at the defilement of art which goes on there every day and every hour." The actors, directors, and writers remained because "they have nowhere to go." The "bosses," who cared only about the box office, were the only Hollywoodites they found in "good spirits."[12]

Ilf and Petrov's account of Hollywood people mocking their own productions and desiring to make better films drew on a wealth of observation. They toured Fox Studios and the Warner Brothers back lot. While watching films being shot, they saw "good actors who were famous; bad actors who were famous; and actors famous for no longer being famous."[13] They spent time with Akim Tamiroff, a Russian-speaking Armenian veteran of the Moscow Art Theater, who had arrived in Hollywood in the 1920s and was making a good living playing ethnic characters with thick accents.[14]

Among Ilf and Petrov's key sources of information on Hollywood were two directors, Rouben Mamoulian and Lewis Milestone. Dapper portraits of Mamoulian in a bow tie and Milestone in a fedora and double-breasted jacket appeared in the "Hollywood" installment of "American Photographs." The caption identified Milestone as the director of the "excellent picture" *All Quiet on the Western Front* (1930) and a "bright spot" in the otherwise dark Hollywood landscape. As noted earlier, the photo essay described Mamoulian as a "remarkably talented and unusually successful" filmmaker, overstating his movies' box office draw. Ilf's correspondence makes clear that it was Mamoulian and Milestone who screened the "best" pictures for the visitors. Milestone showed them his 1931 screwball comedy *The Front Page*; Ilf deemed it "good but not great." He was more impressed by the "amazing" *The Informer* (1935), a drama about the 1922 Irish Rebellion that won four Academy Awards, including best director for John Ford. Milestone also screened *The Scoundrel* (1935), for which the writer/directors Ben Hecht and Charles MacArthur won the best original story Oscar. Mamoulian, who had invited the writers to see *Porgy and Bess* in New York, and who was now back in Los Angeles, showed Ilf and Petrov his 1931 film *Dr. Jekyll*

---

[12] OA, 314–15.   [13] PIA, Il'f, 13 December, 471.
[14] ZK, n.d., 463, 464; OA, 331–32.

and Mr. Hyde as well as his 1934 adaptation of Leo Tolstoy's 1899 novella *Resurrection*, titled *We Live Again.*[15]

In *Low-Rise America*, Ilf and Petrov represented "conversations with Milestone, Mamoulian, and other directors, among the ten best," as convincing them "that these excellent craftsmen are weary of the insignificant screenplays that they have to produce."[16] Petrov reported the same attitude in a letter home. Even as they exhibited their best work, the directors, like the actors, "complain," Petrov noted, that the "bosses don't let them breathe freely. They are insanely afraid that they'll end up on the street at any moment." He concluded, apparently repeating his informants' words, that "the cinema is in decline."[17]

What Ilf and Petrov did not know (or did not report) was that at the time of their visit, the directors were starting to stand up to the studios. In this endeavor, they were belatedly following the lead of the pioneering Screen Actors and Writers Guilds, established in 1933.[18] On 23 December 1935, thirteen directors, including Milestone, met "in great secrecy" at the home of King Vidor, the director of the politically engaged 1934 film *Our Daily Bread*, to lay the groundwork for the Screen Directors Guild. Vidor became the Guild's president and Milestone its vice president. Mamoulian is also sometimes counted among the participants in the secret meeting, but he was apparently in Mexico City at the time. In January 1936, Mamoulian attended the Guild's first public meeting, and became a member of its board.[19]

Representing professionals who could made salaries almost as big as the stars they directed, the SDG worked to protect creative workers' financial interests and, even more, their artistic autonomy. Recognized by the studios only in 1939, the Guild aimed, as director Frank Capra explained in a letter that year to the *New York Times*, to rectify the "sad situation" in which "80 percent of the directors today shoot scenes

[15] Il'ia Il'f and Evgenii Petrov, "Amerikanskie fotografii: VIII: Gollivud," *Ogonek*, no. 19–20 (20 July 1936): 20; PIA, Il'f, 13 December 1935, 470–71; The 8th Academy Awards: 1936, www.oscars.org/oscars/ceremonies/1936 (accessed 14 July 2022).

[16] OA, 331.   [17] PIA, Petrov, 14 December, 472.

[18] Ronny Regev, *Working in Hollywood: How the Studio System Turned Creativity into Labor* (Chapel Hill: University of North Carolina Press, 2018), 175–77.

[19] Quotation from "A Guild for Directors," NYT, 26 January 1936; David Luhrssen, *Mamoulian: Life on Stage and Screen* (Lexington: University Press of Kentucky, 2013), 91–92; Douglas W. Churchill, "Honor without Peace in Hollywood," NYT, 5 April 1936; Steven Pond, "A Guild is Born," *DGA Quarterly* (Winter 2006), www.dga.org/Craft/DGAQ/All-Articles/0604-Winter2006-07/Features-A-Guild-is-Born.aspx (accessed 16 July 2018); Diaries and diary notes, 1935, Manuscript Division, Library of Congress, Rouben Mamoulian Papers, Box 14, Folder 6; Diaries and diary notes, 1936, Box 14, Folder 18.

exactly as they are told to shoot them without any changes whatsoever."[20] The most prominent directors, such as Capra, Mamoulian, and Milestone, were among the minority who called their own shots. But even their authority was eroding, as studios announced that they would terminate the contract of any director who refused an assignment.[21]

Mentioning Milestone and Mamoulian as among their authoritative informants on the American film industry, Ilf and Petrov never revealed that the two had roots in the Russian empire and spoke Russian. Milestone, born in 1895 in Odesa, grew up in Kishinev (now Chişinău, Moldova), where as a child he experienced the 1903 pogrom. Sent to Germany to study engineering (or, he sometimes claimed, pharmacy), in 1913 he used the money that was meant to take him home for the winter holidays to emigrate to the United States.[22] Mamoulian emigrated to the United States in 1923 from Soviet Armenia via London. He liked to emphasize that he had not "fled from the Soviets," but had left with the innocent purpose of visiting his sister.[23] In his unfinished autobiography, Mamoulian described himself as "Armenian by nationality" and as thoroughly cosmopolitan. Before the age of six, he spoke "three languages with equal fluency": Russian at home, Armenian at one grandmother's, and Georgian at the other's. When he was seven, the family moved from Tiflis (now Tbilisi, Georgia) to Paris, where he quickly picked up French. Returning to the Russian empire, he briefly studied law and theater in Moscow. If, as he later claimed, he knew not "one word of English" when he arrived in London in 1920, he had apparently mastered the language by the time he left three years later to direct opera at the Eastman School of Music in Rochester, New York.[24]

In 1935, Milestone and Mamoulian remained deeply interested in Russian and Soviet culture and maintained connections to the large community of pre- and postrevolutionary Russian émigrés who worked in the motion picture industry.[25] They often cast immigrants in ethnic character roles. As Mamoulian told a reporter for a Russian-language

---

[20] "By Post from Mr. Capra," NYT, 2 April 1939.

[21] Virginia Wright Wexman, *Hollywood's Artists: The Directors Guild of America and the Construction of Authorship* (New York: Columbia University Press, 2020), 15–17.

[22] Harlow Robinson, *Lewis Milestone: Life and Films* (Lexington: University Press of Kentucky, 2019), 108–13.

[23] Daniel Lang and Russell Maloney, "The Other Armenian," *New Yorker*, 29 May 1943, 14.

[24] Rouben Mamoulian, "The Art of Gods and Monkeys," 1943–44, typescript, 36 (Armenian), 24 (English), 65 (French), Mamoulian Papers, Box 142, Folder 10.

[25] Harlow Robinson, *Russians in Hollywood, Hollywood's Russians: Biography of an Image* (Boston: Northeastern University Press, 2007), 18–21; Personal file, addresses, Mamoulian Papers, Box 5, Folders 3, 4.

San Francisco paper, in Hollywood a "hundred-percent Russian" could play a "hundred-percent Aztec."[26] Both were also interested in Russian-themed projects. In 1934, Mamoulian's lavish adaption of Tolstoy's *Resurrection* distilled the novella into a star-crossed love story between a prince (Fredric March) and a peasant (the Russian-born Anna Sten).[27] A year earlier, on the eve of the normalization of Soviet–American relations, Milestone had traveled to Moscow to do research for a film tentatively titled "Red Square" in collaboration with Ilya Ehrenburg. The Russian Jewish novelist remembered that during Milestone's stay in Moscow, he was "at once on the best of terms with our film-directors and kept saying: 'I'm no Lewis Milestone, I'm Lenya Milstein from Kishinev.'" The screenplay ended up being one of Milestone's many unrealized attempts to make a "Russia picture." According to Ehrenburg, Columbia's president nixed the film for having "too much social stuff and not enough sex." Milestone's recollection was that the studio "abandoned" the picture as too expensive. Whatever the case, the director made sure Ehrenburg got paid.[28]

Ilf and Petrov must have appreciated the opportunity to converse directly with the congenial and accomplished directors. Their translators, the Trones, took a well-deserved holiday in Ensenada, Mexico, while the writers hobnobbed in Hollywood.[29] Mamoulian's papers, which confirm several appointments with Ilf and Petrov in New York City, offer a glimpse of a relaxed meeting in Southern California. On the writers' second evening in Los Angeles, Mamoulian hosted them at his "bunga-low" in Beverly Hills. In a note in Mamoulian's autograph book dated 11 December 1935, "12 o'clock at night (the hour when it is time for guests to go home)," Ilf and Petrov commemorated their visit with a witticism that anticipated a passage in *Low-Rise America*: "Upon arrival here, we did our best to understand the soul of American cinema (*muvi pikchir* [movie picture]). We settled in the city of Hollywood, on Hollywood Boulevard, at the Hotel Hollywood." In the inscription, they

[26] "Istoriia odnoi kino-kar'ery," *Novaya Zarya*, 18 August 1936, Mamoulian Papers, Box 204, Folder 1.

[27] Luhrssen, *Mamoulian*, 75–77.

[28] Robinson, *Lewis Milestone*, 82–88; Il'ia Erenburg, *Memoirs: 1921–1941*, trans. Tatiana Shebunina (New York: Universal Library, 1966), 239–40; Brian D. Harvey, "Soviet-American 'Cinematic Diplomacy' in the 1930s: Could the Russians Have Really Infiltrated Hollywood?" *Screen* 46 (Winter 2005): 491–92; Harold F. Dodge, "Lewis Milestone," 11 May 1951, Federal Bureau of Investigation, Los Angeles, File no. 100-30825 (Milestone FBI); "Lewis Milestone: A Filmography," f-282 Biographical data, Lewis Milestone Papers, Margaret Herrick Library, Academy of Motion Picture Arts and Sciences.

[29] OA, 329–30; ZK, 25 December, 465.

asked, "What more can you ask of humble around-the-world travelers?" In *Low-Rise America*, the rhetorical question became the observation, "One surely could not think of anything more Hollywoody."[30]

Mamoulian was likely one of the "sensible Hollywood people" Ilf and Petrov heard lamenting the "defilement" of cinema art. That cinema *was* an art constituted a favorite Mamoulian refrain. At the time of the writers' visit, the director was promoting his most recent film, the first feature shot in Technicolor's new three-color process, *Becky Sharp*, as a technical and artistic triumph. In a September 1935 interview, in which he predicted "color is here to stay," Mamoulian likened directors to "men who have been condemned for life to draw in black and white, and who suddenly find ourselves painters with a palette and oil paints."[31] A year later, he proclaimed motion pictures "The World's Latest Fine Art."[32]

Ilf and Petrov agreed with both Mamoulian's contention that cinema could be art and his acknowledgment that at present there was much "bad art" on American movie screens. But, as their scathing reviews of American "trash" made clear, they rejected his recommendation that critics refrain from "impatience and harshness" at a time when "cinema has not yet come of age."[33] Nor did they share Mamoulian's expectation, expressed in a 1937 *New York Times* interview, that "with each new, progressive picture," the "mass production" motion picture industry was slowly, even "imperceptibly," nurturing the audience's appreciation of and demand for good films.[34] Privately, Mamoulian also blamed the preponderance of bad pictures on the executives, who made money catering to the lowest tastes. Writing in 1938 to Léopold Marchand, the French author whose play he had adapted in his 1932 feature *Love Me Tonight*, Mamoulian quoted "verbatim" a producer's reaction to his pitch for a film on St. Francis of Assisi: "if I had two million dollars to spend on a picture I wouldn't give you twenty-five cents for that idea." Still, he remained optimistic, noting, someday, "I hope I shall do this film."[35]

---

[30] Autograph book, p. 56, Box 206; 1935 Diary, Mamoulian Papers, Box 14, Folder 6; Diaries and Diary Notes 1935, Box 14, Folder 7; LGA, 227; OA, 308.

[31] Rouben Mamoulian as told to Jack Jamison, "What Do You Think of Color?" *The New Movie Magazine* 11 (September 1935): 45, Mamoulian Papers, Box 139, Folder 10; Kia Afra, "Becky Sharp, Technicolor, and the Historiography of Film Style," *Quarterly Review of Film and Video* 32 (2014): 108.

[32] Rouben Mamoulian, "The World's Latest Fine Art," *Cinema Arts* 1, no. 1 (September 1936): 21, Mamoulian Papers, Box 139, Folder 10.

[33] Mamoulian, "World's Latest Fine Art," 21.

[34] John T. McManus, "Defense of the Screen," NYT, 8 August 1937.

[35] Mamoulian to Marchand, 10 February 1938, Mamoulian Papers, Box 45, Folder 14.

Where Mamoulian imagined or hoped for a slowly emerging market for good films, Ilf and Petrov saw a system devoted to thwarting the artistic impulses of "the best" filmmakers. In *Low-Rise America*, they attributed this vision of the American movie industry to an unnamed American filmmaker with whom they spent an evening at a "small Hollywood café." In Hollywood, their informant explained, capitalists sought not "profit alone." The bosses dictated the production of "idiotic films" as a means of "systematically" training American spectators to stop thinking.[36] The writers perhaps took some liberties with their informant's monologue, which fills an entire chapter titled "Hollywood Serfs." It may have been Ilf and Petrov's Soviet frame of reference that prompted them to represent the filmmaker as railing not just against studio priorities, but against an apparent capitalist plot to "stupefy" Americans. Visiting the Soviet Union in 1933, Milestone had marveled, "They really believe that all Hollywood-made films are 'propaganda' made under direct instruction from the American government!"[37] Still, the unnamed filmmaker's stories sound remarkably like those that Milestone would have told to illustrate his struggle to make "'serious' films ... in a studio environment that valued efficiency, entertainment, and stars above all else."[38]

Among the stories Ilf and Petrov recounted was one about *All Quiet on the Western Front* that became Hollywood lore. Almost forty years after the writers' visit, an interviewer asked Milestone to confirm "the story that Universal wanted you to put a happy ending" on the film. The director was happy to oblige. In language more colorful than Ilf and Petrov's, he remembered countering the studio's fear that "with all the goddam war and what-not, you won't see a penny of your money back" with the threat that "'we'll have the Germans win the war! That will give them their happy ending.' The request ended there!"[39]

An incident that, according to Ilf and Petrov, the same filmmaker described as happening "only a few days ago," likewise sounds like a Milestone story: A "great and famous director" refused to direct a picture with Marlene Dietrich when she demanded changes to the screenplay. To cater to the star, the studio had only to turn to a lesser director, "who did not dare refuse anything for fear of losing his job altogether."[40] Milestone was, in fact, between pictures at the time of Ilf and Petrov's

---

[36] OA, 318, 319.   [37] As quoted in Robinson, *Milestone*, 84.
[38] Robinson, *Milestone*, 103.
[39] "Directors Go to Their Movies: Lewis Milestone," by Digby Diehl, *Action Magazine* [1972], pp. 15, 22, Milestone Papers, f-282; Erenburg, *Memoirs*, 127.
[40] LGA, 236; OA, 321.

visit. He had been slated to direct *Hotel Imperial*, starring Dietrich, but Henry Hathaway replaced him "at the last moment." As Milestone predicted, the movie, on which Dietrich "had approval of everything," was a disaster and never completed.[41]

Putting the criticism of the American film industry into the mouth of an American, Ilf and Petrov managed to suggest both the enormous differences between Soviet and American films and the shared sensibilities of Soviet and American artists. In a letter to his wife, Petrov highlighted the similarities, characterizing Milestone as "very Soviet-minded."[42] More circumspect in print, the writers refrained in *Low-Rise America* from specifying Milestone's Soviet sympathies. Still, their portrait of the "Hollywood serf" "tormented" by his complicity in producing "revolting, idiotic pictures, which little by little make the spectator dumber," suggested that the Other thought very much like us.[43]

Twelve years after Ilf and Petrov's visit, Milestone's alleged Soviet sympathies raised concerns on the American side of the ideological divide. In 1947, when the House Un-American Activities Committee subpoenaed forty-three actors, directors, and writers, Milestone was among the so-called Unfriendly Nineteen, the Hollywood witnesses hostile to the committee. He hosted strategy sessions at his Benedict Canyon mansion for the group, which included Bertolt Brecht, Ring Lardner, Jr., and Dalton Trumbo. The committee ultimately decided against calling Milestone to testify; thus, he was not among the Hollywood Ten convicted of contempt of Congress and blacklisted. In a 1951 interview with two FBI agents, he denied both "participation in or knowledge of Soviet espionage" and "membership in or sympathy with Communist Party." Nonetheless, Milestone ended up on the Hollywood "gray list," and spent most of the 1950s working in Europe.[44] In 1960, Milestone finally returned to the "Hollywood spotlight," filming what became his most profitable picture, the Rat Pack classic *Oceans 11*, a star vehicle at least as "empty and frivolous" as those he had complained about to Ilf and Petrov.[45]

While Ilf and Petrov emphasized the directors' gripes about the oppressive power of the studio bosses, they omitted from *Low-Rise America* any discussion of another grievance voiced by their Hollywood contacts: "brutal censorship (church and political)."[46] That in 1935, as

[41] Steven Bach, *Marlene Dietrich: Life and Legend* (Minneapolis: University of Minnesota Press, 2011), 209–11; Robinson, *Lewis Milestone*, 95–96.
[42] PIA, Petrov, 14 December 1935, 471.   [43] OA, 320.
[44] Robinson, *Lewis Milestone*, 178–84, 192–93; Dodge, "Lewis Milestone," Milestone FBI.
[45] Robinson, *Lewis Milestone*, 219.   [46] PIA, Petrov, 14 December 1935, 472.

Petrov's letter suggested, American filmmakers were complaining bit-terly about censorship is unsurprising. In 1930, as a means of warding off government intervention, studios had agreed to abide by a straitlaced Motion Picture Production Code (also known as the Hays Code, after Will Hays, who oversaw its promulgation). Only in 1934, however, did a newly established Production Code Administration (PCA) begin to rig-orously enforce its strictures.[47] Mamoulian and Milestone, early targets of the stepped up censorship regime, likely shared their woes with the visiting writers.

One of the pictures that precipitated more "brutal" censorship was Mamoulian's *Queen Christina*, a historical drama starring Greta Garbo. In December 1933, MGM premiered the film without the Production Code seal. Before the movie's wide release, the Hays Office warned the studio to "be careful to avoid anything which might be construed as lesbianism." The censors also advised keeping Garbo "away from the bed entirely" during a scene in which the incognito queen, mistaken for a boy, shares the only room at a snowbound inn with an attractive Spanish envoy. The producer, Walter Wanger, declined to make the requested cuts, and a jury of his peers, the Production Appeals Board, dismissed the violation. Joseph Breen, the new head of the PCA, was "apoplectic." By the summer of 1934, he had helped to rouse the public pressure that forced stricter enforcement of the code, including a $25,000 fine against any producer who released a picture without the PCA seal.[48] At the time, Mamoulian responded with the assertion that "There is nothing indecent about a real love story or an adult love story."[49] Fifteen years later, he still seemed perplexed and annoyed by the uproar. In his copy of the 1949 production code, the director scribbled a question mark alongside the prohibition on presenting "impure love" as "attractive and beauti-ful." "What," Mamoulian asked in the margin, "is 'impure love'? Needs definition."[50]

Milestone had a less publicized run-in with the censor over *Anything Goes*, a feature he completed in November 1935, about a month before

[47] Thomas Doherty, *Hollywood's Censor: Joseph I. Breen and the Production Code Administration* (New York: Columbia University Press, 2007), 45–47, 56–63; Sheri Chinen Biesen, *Film Censorship: Regulating America's Screens* (New York: Columbia University Press, 2018), 37–40.

[48] Luhrssen, *Mamoulian*, 73–74 (quotations); Marcia Landy and Amy Villarejo, "Queen Christina," in Edward Buscombe and Rob White, eds., *British Film Institute Film Classics*, vol. 1 (London: Fitzroy Dearborn, 2003), 225–26; Doherty, *Hollywood's Censor*, 63–69.

[49] Rouben Mamoulian, "Notes on Censorship," 26 July 1934, typescript, Mamoulian Papers, Box 170, Folder 9.

[50] Motion Picture Association of America, Inc., "A Code to Govern the Making of Motion and Talking Pictures," 1930–1949, Mamoulian Papers, Box 170, Folder 9.

Ilf and Petrov's arrival in Hollywood. An extravaganza with big stars (Ethel Mermen, Bing Crosby) and huge production numbers, the film was based on Cole Porter's hit Broadway musical. Milestone, who was "used to controlling all aspects of production," found himself "working like a cog in the industrial studio machine." The Hays Office, which objected to all the racy bits, starting with the title, further limited his freedom. In the end, the film retained only four songs from the Broadway show, and those were cleaned up; on screen, there was no more "sniffing cocaine" in "I Get a Kick Out of You."[51] And more censorship was in the offing. On 11 December 1935, *Variety* ran a story on the Catholic Legion of Decency's new film classification system – "not disapproved," "disapproved for children," and "disapproved for all" – that it planned to enforce with threatened boycotts.[52]

Ilf and Petrov's description of an unnamed American filmmaker forced to make films to the boss's specifications raises the question of how deeply they empathized with his dilemma. Did they, too, feel that the "boss" did not allow them to "breathe freely"? What should we make of the fact that Ilf and Petrov omitted from *Low-Rise America* the directors' concerns about "brutal censorship"? Their decision to exclude mention of censorship was perhaps intended to short-circuit unflattering, if implicit, comparisons with the Soviet Union. It is also possible that, in 1935, the writers along with their American interlocutors judged that capitalist America restricted filmmakers more effectively, if not more "brutally," than Stalin's Soviet Union. In his letter, Petrov seemed to genuinely pity the Hollywood actors and directors who, "despite their high salaries, live sadly."[53]

In the 1930s, Hollywood and Stalinist censorship followed two distinctive models. Film historian Maria Belodubrovskaya goes so far as to argue that filmmakers in "free-market capitalist Hollywood" faced "far more sophisticated censorship and content control" than their counterparts in the Soviet Union. Production Code censors vetted American films at every stage from preproduction (including scripts, song lyrics, and costumes) through shooting to the final cut. The process was intrusive but allowed some negotiation over sensitive material and made it possible for filmmakers to find workarounds before the final edit. The US scheme shaped movie content not by curtailing production, but by training filmmakers to regulate themselves.[54] By contrast, Soviet censors

---

[51] Robinson, *Lewis Milestone*, 93–94.   [52] Biesen, *Film Censorship*, 35–36.
[53] PIA, Petrov, 14 December 1935, 472.
[54] Biesen, *Film Censorship*, 37–42; Richard Ward, "Golden Age, Blue Pencils: The Hal Roach Studios and Three Case Studies of Censorship during Hollywood's Studio Era," *Media History* 8, no. 1 (2002): 103–19.

hardly interfered with directors as they worked. The state "delegated" content development, production, administration, and even the initial layer of censorship to the filmmakers themselves. The party censored not screenplays but finished films. After 1934, Stalin's growing interest in watching movies and "helping" filmmakers introduced a large dose of arbitrariness into the system. Unpredictable, "reactive," and inefficient, Stalinist censorship relied on the extreme measure of banning an "outsized number" of completed pictures.[55]

Milestone had censorship in mind when he commissioned the treatment of *The Twelve Chairs*. He proposed a "highly modified" version of the story set in the United States so as to avoid unnecessarily scaring the censors. As Ilf described it, "the action occurs in America, in a castle that a rich American bought in France and moved to his home state." To make good on their promise to the Trones to get back to New York by early January, Ilf and Petrov planned to work, in Petrov's words, "like wild beasts" and complete the project in nine days.[56] On 23 December, they delivered the final twenty-two-page product to Milestone. Both the director and the writers were pleased with the work.[57] Ilf and Petrov received an advance of about $600, and Milestone promised them a minimum of $3,000 if he succeeded in selling a screenplay based on their treatment.[58]

Milestone seems never to have followed through with the planned screenplay. I found no trace of it in his papers at the Motion Picture Academy archives. He had not spent much for the treatment. At a time when the lowest paid studio screenwriters got $250 per week, Milestone paid just $600 to two writers for nine days' work.[59] Actively looking for a new project, he soon found "The General Died at Dawn," a story set in contemporary China. He enlisted the playwright Clifford Odets to write the screenplay. Odets had never written for the movies, and, according to Milestone's biographer, the director "went about introducing Odets to Hollywood in a gentle and encouraging manner, taking him under his wing." One can imagine him behaving similarly with Ilf and Petrov. But he offered Odets $10,000 for ten weeks' work, arranged for him "to live

---

[55] Belodubrovskaya, *Not According to Plan*, 9, 7, 5, 176, 190; Sarah Davies, "Stalin as Patron of Cinema: Creating Soviet Mass Culture, 1932–1936," in Sarah Davies and James Harris, eds., *Stalin: A New History* (Cambridge: Cambridge University Press, 2005), 202–25.

[56] PIA, Il′f, 15 December; Petrov, 14 December, 471–72.

[57] PIA, Petrov, 23 December; Il′f, 26 December, 477–78.

[58] Il′f and Petrov's letters disagree on these figures. PIA, 26 December 1935, 478 (Il′f), 479 (Petrov).

[59] Regev, *Working in Hollywood*, 46.

in a comfortable house in Beverly Hills," provided a "studio car and driver," and ended up paying him the "enormous sum" of $27,500. Clearly, *The General Died at Dawn* was a higher priority than *The Twelve Chairs*. Released in September 1936, the picture starred Gary Cooper and Madeline Carroll, and earned Russian émigré actor Akim Tamiroff, who played the titular Chinese general, an Oscar nomination for best supporting actor.[60]

Their short stint as Hollywood screenwriters had greater significance for Ilf and Petrov, who harbored both commercial and artistic ambitions. They wrote ecstatically to their wives that the sale would make it possible to take "our trusty Ford" to Moscow. Petrov looked forward to buying a second Ford with the proceeds from the screenplay.[61] But their motivations, like those of their Hollywood peers, were not entirely mercenary. Ilf and Petrov were satisfied with their work, and seemed to think that in the right hands the scenario might turn out to be one of the (alas, few) good Hollywood pictures.[62]

It was precisely the relative success of their venture that likely dissuaded Ilf and Petrov from mentioning it in *Low-Rise America*. They were willing to include Americans who thought like "us." But it would not do to show two Soviet writers working contentedly, if frantically, in the land of the capitalists. Boris Pilnyak's 1933 travelogue turned a lengthy account of his 1931 misadventures as a Hollywood screenwriter into a condemnation of the American movie industry. He compared the process of writing a screenplay on the Soviet Union that met Hollywood's specifications to making "lemons ripen in Greenland."[63] Milestone sidestepped the tricky issue of how to represent the Soviet Union by having Ilf and Petrov set their story in the Hollywoody location of a castle brought stone-by-stone to the United States. Also, unlike Pilnyak, who worked for a month under a $500 per week contract with MGM, Ilf and Petrov reported only to Milestone. They respected him as an excellent director and apparently felt comfortable with him as a fellow former Odessan, whose Russian, as Ehrenburg recalled, retained "the colorful southern modes of speech."[64] Indeed, Ilf and Petrov seem to have preferred Milestone to the Soviet director Grigory Aleksandrov, who had made what they considered unconscionable changes to their

---

[60] Robinson, *Lewis Milestone*, 96–97 (quotation), 101; The 9th Academy Awards: 1937, www.oscars.org/oscars/ceremonies/1937 (accessed 15 July 2022).

[61] PIA, 26 December 1935, 478 (quotation), 479.

[62] PIA, Petrov, 22 December 1935, 475–76.

[63] Pil'nyak, *O'kei*, 65–85, 81 (lemons); Robinson, *Russians in Hollywood*, 52–58.

[64] Erenburg, *Memoirs*, 239.

screenplay for the American-themed movie *Circus*.[65] They felt valued in Hollywood, and were grateful for the comparatively paltry pay.

In the published work, Ilf and Petrov focused their ire on the place, not the people. From their perspective, Hollywood was an artificial city, full of "pretty" flowers that "for some reason have no scent" and oranges that they claimed, "don't taste very good."[66] The writers' letters confirm that by the time they completed their assignment for Milestone, they were, as Petrov expressed it "insanely fed up" with Hollywood.[67] This weariness was no doubt compounded by homesickness. In every letter they wrote, the writers longed for their families, whom they had not seen in three months. But they also seemed to feel particularly out of place in the dream world of Hollywood. Ilf described it as a "city of ominous provincial boredom"; although he also saw some of its appeal. The dazzling late December sun allowed them to sit "in a café with doors open to the street to allow in the summer warmth."[68] Petrov was less forgiving, declaring himself completely and irrevocably disgusted with Hollywood. He admitted that at first it was difficult to understand how one could be repulsed by a "clean city with one of the most invariable climates on earth." But finally he figured out that "everything here is somehow inanimate, like a film set," an impression strengthened by the "abundance of big palm trees." The hot winter sun cast "sharp" shadows. The city was filled with "a huge number of automobiles, gas pumps, and illuminated advertisements." Petrov experienced the "stench" of gasoline as overwhelming and had recurring headaches.[69]

In the published work, the film people Ilf and Petrov identified as Russian immigrants shared their alienation. The writers granted that the Russians working in Hollywood enjoyed comforts more alluring than the ferryboat comforts that cheered the Russian sailor in San Francisco. Nonetheless, they emphasized, the immigrants they met in Hollywood yearned for "home" and what might have been. The only exception was the absurd Captain Trefilev, a self-described former White Guard, who tracked the writers down at their hotel. He eagerly related what they took to be extravagantly exaggerated, if not fictive, wartime exploits. Asking that they keep his secret, the captain confided that his preternaturally smooth skin was the happy result of a face wound repaired with a skin graft "from my own backside." Ilf and Petrov provided more sympathetic portraits of Russians in the movie industry, who felt "guilty because they

[65] Rimgaila Salys, *The Musical Comedies of Grigorii Aleksandrov: Laughing Matters* (Bristol: Intellect, 2009), 124–32; Richard Taylor, "The Illusion of Happiness and the Happiness of Illusion: Grigorii Aleksandrov's 'The Circus,'" *Slavonic and East European Review* 74 (October 1996): 605.
[66] ART, 92.   [67] PIA, Petrov, 23 December, 477.
[68] PIA, Il'f, 22 December, 20 December, 475, 473–74.
[69] PIA, Petrov, 20 December, 473–74.

stick around here instead of being in Moscow." Although, they admitted, no one said "anything about this," they insisted that it was "evident by every indication."[70]

To support their claims, Ilf and Petrov recounted the story of an unnamed immigrant character actor. This was clearly Tamiroff, whom they described in print – just as Ilf did in a letter – as playing "foreigners," Mexicans, Spaniards, and Hungarians, "for whom an accent on screen is natural."[71] He worked constantly, had "a good American house with electric appliances, gas heat in the floor, and a silver Christmas tree," a "good American car with cigar lighter and radio," and a "good Russian wife with gray eyes," an unnamed Tamara Shayne. They reported that he made $500 a week, but had little security: The studio had the right to cancel his seven-year contract every six months. Most of all, Ilf and Petrov emphasized, the immigrant longed for artistic respect. (They did not seem to know that after their visit, Tamiroff was nominated for an Academy Award.) His "good" American life notwithstanding, the actor kept exclaiming a phrase that Ilf in his notebook attributed to Tamiroff: "It's a fact!" The "facts" became increasingly painful. He had so little time between pictures that he could scarcely learn his role! He had studied together with "now famous" actors from the Moscow Art Theater! And finally, late at night, walking "through the hushed Hollywood streets," he began to "curse everything": "Hollywood is a village! It's a fact! There is nothing to breathe here!"[72] The actor's outbursts echoed across the abyss between Soviet "art" and American "trash."

As Ilf and Petrov told the story in *Low-Rise America*, "the wailing in the night was the last thing we heard in Hollywood."[73] This was likely an exaggeration. According to Ilf's letter, they spent three hours on 21 December with Tamiroff and Shayne, who lived in Beverly Hills. This was four days before the writers left Los Angeles for San Diego, where they reunited with the Trones.[74] But the scene seems to have accurately reflected their mood as they took the train south and planned a quick dash "back to the Atlantic." They left Los Angeles on Christmas Day. On 11 January 1936, they were once again at the Shelton Hotel in New York City, from which they had set out two months earlier. On their last night on the road, Petrov ended his letter simply, "I will be home soon."[75]

---

[70] OA, 317–18; LGA, 244; OA, 331.

[71] PIA, Il'f, 22 December, 475; LGA, 244; OA, 332.

[72] LGA, 244–45; OA, 332–33; ZK, n.d., 463; Beth Holmgren, "Cossack Cowboys, Mad Russians: The Émigré Actor in Studio-Era Hollywood," *Russian Review* 64 (April 2005): 238n6; Robinson, *Russians in Hollywood*, 70–77: Regev, *Working in Hollywood*, 124.

[73] LGA, 245; OA, 333.   [74] PIA, Il'f, 22 December, 475.

[75] PIA, Petrov, 10 January 1936, 491.

Part V

Journey's End

When the Trones agreed to serve as Ilf and Petrov's guides, they set a firm two-month time limit on the cross-county trip. They had to be back in New York City by early January 1936. Thus, upon leaving San Diego on 26 December, the travelers resumed, even accelerated, the speed at which they had crossed the Midwest. They covered upwards of 300 miles per day, spending six hours or more in the car. They passed quickly through the desert just north of the Mexican border and then along the Gulf Coast. Ilf and Petrov sent letters from every stop along the route: Benson, Arizona; El Paso, Fort Stockton, and San Antonio, Texas; and Morgan City, Louisiana. Storms in Florida slowed their progress. From New Orleans, they traveled just over 200 miles to Pensacola, Florida, and then to Tallahassee. Once the weather cleared, they again picked up the pace, traveling from north Florida to Charleston, South Carolina, and Goldsboro, North Carolina, before reaching Washington, DC, on 9 January.[1]

Even as they sped home, neither the Trones nor Ilf and Petrov could bear to miss the sights along the way. Although they were eager to get back on the road, they spent several hours exploring San Diego.[2] They extended their stay in El Paso to see a bullfight in Juarez, Mexico. As Ilf explained in a letter, they "deviated slightly" from the main highway to San Antonio, backtracking into New Mexico to visit the "wonderful" Carlsbad Caverns.[3] They lingered two days in New Orleans, where they enjoyed "the kind of fillet that surely cannot be found anywhere else in America."[4] The writers and their guides parted ways in Washington, DC. The Trones drove back to New York City, leaving Ilf and Petrov to attend a presidential press conference and observe Congress in session before taking the train north. Only at the last moment did the writers decide to skip the tropical cruise and leave on the first available ship to

---

[1] PIA, Il'f and Petrov, 480–90; ZK, 491–92. [2] PIA, Petrov, 26 December 1935, 479.
[3] PIA, Il'f, 29 December, 30 December 1935, Petrov, 29 December 1935, 482, 483–84.
[4] LGA, 272; OA, 373.

Europe. On 22 January 1936, they sailed for Cherbourg, France on the *Majestic.* They arrived on 28 January and were back in Moscow by mid-February.[5]

Ilf and Petrov's rushed return to the East Coast solidified their vision of America as a land of scenic wonders and standardized technical marvels. Ilf described the entire city of El Paso, with a population of about 100,000, as "some kind of trick." The "huge buildings," the "men dressed exactly as they would be dressed in New York or Chicago," and the "fashionably made-up girls" seemed to deny and defy the barren desert that encircled them. A short walk across the bridge to the twin city of Juarez intensified the impression. There, the smells, sights, and sounds reminded Ilf more of the Moldavanka, Odesa's "crowded and dilapidated" old Jewish quarter, than the United States: "it smells of fried food and garlic; barefoot, swarthy young people walk around with guitars; cripples beg for alms; two hundred thousand microscopic boys run around with brushes and boxes to shine shoes."[6] The visitor center at Carlsbad Caverns National Park, with "absolutely New York elevators" that "quickly took us seventy feet below ground" to the enormous limestone caves, likewise appeared as an unexpected island of ultramodernity in the empty desert.[7] As the landscape changed, so did American tekhnika. Along the Gulf Coast, the writers found "lots of wonderful structures – bridges, dams, embankments – built to battle with water." The downside, Petrov observed, was that all these marvels cost money. They "sighed" and paid a fifty-cent or hefty dollar thirty-five toll each time they crossed a bridge.[8]

The new experience on this leg of the trip was the opportunity to observe American race relations in the "Negro states of the South." Driving through Louisiana, Mississippi, Alabama, Florida, Georgia, the Carolinas, and Virginia, Ilf and Petrov seemed genuinely shocked by the realities of Black poverty and powerlessness. At the same time, the Jim Crow South, with its segregated "cinemas, churches, and trams," was, Petrov asserted, something "we already know."[9] As the historian Meredith Roman argues, by the time of Ilf and Petrov's road trip, "exhibiting a superior 'Soviet' racial consciousness – relative to white Americans" – was a requirement of Soviet writing about the United States.[10] Rapidly traversing the South, Ilf and Petrov easily found what they expected.

---

[5] PIA, Il'f and Petrov, 486–96.

[6] PIA, Il'f, 29 December 1935, 482; Jarrod Tanny, *City of Rogues and Schnorrers: Russia's Jews and the Myth of Old Odessa* (Bloomington: Indiana University Press, 2011), 30.

[7] PIA, Il'f, 31 December, 485; LGA, 253; OA, 347.   [8] PIA, Petrov, 5 January, 488.

[9] PIA, Petrov, 5 January, 489.

[10] Meredith L. Roman, "Forging Soviet Racial Enlightenment: Soviet Writers Condemn American Racial Mores, 1926, 1936, 1946," *Historian* 74 (Fall 2012): 530.

In *Low-Rise America* and "American Photographs," Ilf and Petrov captured the words and images of a few of the "ordinary" Southerners with whom they interacted. But they provided no clues that might allow a historian to trace their informants' individual trajectories. To get a sense of the American side of these exchanges, I turned to the nearly contemporary photobooks in which teams of American photographers and authors documented the Depression-ravaged region. Comparing the "Negroes" installment of Ilf and Petrov's photo essay with these American productions, I was less interested in verifying or challenging the Soviet authors' conclusions than in better understanding their perspective. Traveling routes parallel to those taken by their American counterparts, did they notice the same people, places, and things? Did they explain them in similar ways?

Only at the end of the travelogue did Ilf and Petrov, usually so careful to avoid explicit comparisons with the Soviet Union, admit, as they did in their letter to Stalin, that they had been thinking about home the whole time. "It is necessary," they claimed, "to see the capitalist world in order to evaluate anew the world of socialism."[11] Their assertion invites us to consider the fundamental questions raised by their efforts to understand America and Americans. After 10,000 miles, did Ilf and Petrov's American road trip simply confirm their presuppositions? Or did it allow them to glimpse the United States, the Soviet Union, and perhaps themselves anew? Did they find ways to cross cultural, linguistic, and ideological divides?

By the time they returned to New York City, both writers, but, as Petrov wrote, "especially Ilf," were "brutally tired."[12] Diagnosed with tuberculosis in the 1920s, Ilf had become seriously ill in the United States. At the end of 1935, somewhere in the Sonoran Desert, Ilf recognized that he was dying. The strange saguaro cactuses that Ilf described as praying or embracing prompted a laconic note in his journal: "Sunset, sunset. The cactuses are standing, but life, it seems, is over." Still, he remained alive to his surroundings, in the next line reminding himself to describe a grocery store.[13] On New Year's Eve in San Antonio, after noting the general merriment, Ilf reflected, "Money is running out, and so, it seems, is life."[14] Four days later, he shared his fears with his partner. Petrov recalled that Ilf was "pale and thoughtful" on the "warm

---

[11] OA, 394.   [12] PIA, Petrov, 12 January 1936, 492.

[13] I have used the translation in Alice Nakhimovsky, "Death and Disillusion: Il′ia Il′f in the 1930s," in Katherine Bliss Eaton, ed., *Enemies of the People: The Destruction of Soviet Literary, Theater, and Film Arts in the 1930s* (Evanston, IL: Northwestern University Press, 2002), 217; ZK, 27 December, 466; PIA, Il′f, 27 December, 480.

[14] ZK, 31 December, 468.

and sunny January day," when the pair "strolled through a famous New Orleans cemetery." That evening at the hotel, Ilf told Petrov that for the last ten days he had been in constant pain. At the cemetery, he had "coughed and seen blood," and the bleeding had continued all day. Petrov remembered that Ilf then coughed and showed him the handkerchief. Ilf died fifteen months later, in April 1937, aged thirty-nine. *Low-Rise America* was published just days before his death.[15]

---

[15] Evgenii Petrov, "Iz vospominanii ob Il'fe," in V. D. Ostrogordskaia, ed., *Sbornik vospaminanii ob I. Il'fe i E. Petrove* (Moscow: Sovetskii pisatel', 1963), 12–13; ZK, 4 January, 470.

26   Racism and Democracy

> Each day when you see us black folk upon the dusty land of the farms or
> upon the hard pavement of the city streets, you usually take us for
> granted and think you know us, but our history is far stranger than
> you suspect, and we are not what we seem.
>
> Richard Wright, *12 Million Black Voices*, 1941

Ilf and Petrov's account of their trip through the "southern Negro states"
included no Black voices. Crossing Louisiana, Mississippi, and
Alabama in a single day, the writers saw many African Americans.
But they do not seem to have spoken to a single one. The only
American quoted in the "Negroes" installment of their photo essay is
a white hitchhiker they picked up in North Carolina. In *Low-Rise
America*, they emphasized that in Louisiana they had wanted to offer
a ride to an "old bent Negro woman," one of the many Black pedestrians "wandering along the highway." However, Mr. Adams dissuaded them. Asserting his own superior understanding of the
"nature of the Southern states," he explained that "she will never,
never believe that white people want to give her a lift. She will think
you are making fun of her."[1] Thus, Ilf and Petrov's portrait of the
Black South depended on the words of white people and relatively
long-range observations.

To interpret what they heard and saw in the South, Ilf and Petrov
relied on their own presuppositions – the same combination of Soviet
antiracism and romantic racialism that they brought to bear on their
adventures in Black New York. Comparing their photo essay and travelogue to the work of Americans who documented the region at roughly
the same time brings out the uniqueness, if not necessarily the
Sovietness, of their approach. Most of the images of the Depression
South captured by the US Department of Agriculture's Farm Security
Administration's (FSA) photographers took poor white people as their

---

[1] LGA, 269; OA, 369.

primary subjects.[2] In their 1937 collaboration *You Have Seen Their Faces*, the commercial photographer Margaret Bourke-White and the novelist Erskine Caldwell devoted a chapter to African Americans and included a substantial number of photographs depicting them. But it was the white sharecroppers and tenant farmers who emerged in the images and text as the "bearers of US national spirit."[3] By contrast, Ilf and Petrov emphasized that "the soul of the South," if not the nation as a whole, was "not its white people, but its black."[4] Placing the Black experience at the center of the American experience, they anticipated the 1941 collaboration between the novelist (and communist) Richard Wright and the German-born FSA photographer Edwin Rosskam. But unlike Wright, who insisted that "human nature is malleable," Ilf and Petrov perpetuated essentialized representations of African Americans as gifted primitives.[5] To challenge the oppression of Black people, they often drew more guidance from Harriet Beecher Stowe than Karl Marx.

As they drove through the South, Ilf and Petrov found what Soviet accounts of the "Negro Question" would have led them to expect: poverty and racism that reduced Black people to the status of "utter slaves."[6] Not bothering to recount what they – and presumably their readers – already knew, they provided only a brief and schematic description of Southern Black people's living conditions. In their letters and in print they emphasized the visibility of segregation in the South, where even churches were designated for "colored" only.[7] For the exhaustive depictions of impoverished Black farmers and Ku Klux Klan violence that the novelist Boris Pilnyak and the anthropologist Vladimir Bogoraz included in their early 1930s American travelogues, Ilf and Petrov substituted a photograph of the "wooden plank shacks of the Negro sharecroppers."[8] They were disturbed, but not surprised, to find among Southern Blacks the "lowest level" of "naked, hopeless poverty" alongside which "the poverty of the Indians would seem the height of

---

[2] Nicholas Natanson, "Politics, Culture, and the FSA Black Image," *Film & History* 17 (May 1987): 29–30, 40–41; Benjamin Balthaser, "Killing the Documentarian: Richard Wright and Documentary Modernity," *Criticism* 55 (Summer 2013): 363.

[3] Christian Ravela, "On the Weird Nostalgia of Whiteness: Poor Whites, White Death, and Black Suffering," *American Studies* 59 (2020): 40, 33 (spirit).

[4] LGA, 276; OA, 380.

[5] Richard Wright and Edwin Rosskam, *12 Million Black Voices: A Folk History of the Negro in the United States* (New York: Thunder's Mouth Press, [1941] 1988), 130.

[6] LGA, 278; OA, 382.   [7] OA, 376–77.

[8] Il'ia Il'f and Evgenii Petrov, "Amerikanskie fotografii: X: Negry," *Ogonek* 22 (10 August 1936): 14; ART, 114; Boris Pil'niak, *O'kei: An American Novel*, trans. Ronald D. LeBlanc, Faculty Publications, 926, University of New Hampshire, 2020, 95–98, 176–77; V. G. Tan-Bogoraz, *USA: Liudi i nravi Ameriki* (Moscow: Federatsiia, 1932), 63–64, 117–39.

prosperity, even luxury." The only thing that seemed to catch them off guard in the South was that "Georgia proved to be forest country." For a reason they judged "inexplicable," but that reflects their reliance on stereotype, they "had always imagined the Southern Negro states in the form of sheer cotton fields and tobacco plantations."[9]

Even as Ilf and Petrov encountered the well-known horrors of the South, they were captivated by Black Southerners, whom they imagined, like American Indians, as an atavistic, noble people managing to retain their sprit and their song in the face of oppression. A young Black girl, they saw in Charleston, South Carolina, whom they guessed was about twelve, embodied this romantic Other. Carrying a basket, she did not walk along the street, but, unaware of the Soviet spectators, danced "an unusually talented improvisation, a clear, rhythmic, almost completely polished dance." So musical was the dance, that the writers "felt we could hear the sounds of a banjo and a saxophone" in the deserted street.[10]

Racism became in Ilf and Petrov's telling not just something that limited Black people, but a feature of the "slave-owning psychology" that "infected" a large number of, if not all, Northern and Southern white people.[11] Rather than trying to explain the white racist mind, they allowed their unselfconscious white hitchhiker to speak for himself. By this point of their trip, the writers recognized the sixteen-year-old on his way home from a Civilian Conservation Corps camp as "a typical young American man: talkative, self-assured, and incurious." The hitchhiker was clearly down, but surprisingly not out. Although his father's "farm isn't doing too well," and he himself had been unable to afford college or find work, the "young American man," Ilf and Petrov reported, "doesn't think in the abstract": "He just knows he's young, he's healthy, he's got white skin, and he plays baseball." Those facts assured him that everything was "*ol-rait* [all right]" and that "he'll get by somehow"[12] (Figure 26.1).

Ilf and Petrov presented the young man as taking comfort in knowing that no matter how low he stood, Black people stood lower. As they drove past Black sharecroppers' cabins, he observed "You can tell right away which houses belong to Negroes and which to the white folks." This prompted Solomon Trone, who was no doubt undertaking his usual interrogation of the group's traveling companion, to ask, "You don't mean that all Negroes live that way?" To which the hitchhiker replied,

---

[9] Il'f and Petrov, "Negry," 14; ART, 115–16; LGA, 276; OA, 379.
[10] ART, 122; Il'f and Petrov, "Negry," 15; LGA, 277; OA, 380.
[11] LGA, 277; OA, 380.   [12] ART, 115; Il'f and Petrov, "Negry," 14; OA, 382.

Figure 26.1 Ilf and Petrov's hitchhiker may have resembled this "Civilian Conservation Corps boy returning to camp about thirty miles away after a weekend visit to his family in Los Angeles," 1940. Farm Security Administration, NACP 532088.

"Of course they do." Pushed to explain how it could be that he did not know "even one rich Negro," the youth could not. Granting that Black people "know how to work," that they are "good people," and that "some of them can play football well," he was unable to account for their poverty. Likewise, the hitchhiker could provide no reason why eating dinner with a Black person was laughably "impossible." That his interlocutor seemed to think otherwise he attributed to the fact that "you're from New York." Here, Ilf and Petrov quickly clarified that although Southerners regarded New York as "the far limit of free thought and radicalism," there, too, segregation prevailed, driven by the white person's need "to look down on the black one."[13]

If the young hitchhiker seemed to excuse segregation and Black poverty as unarguably natural, he also plainly understood and accepted that enforcing white supremacy required violence. Readily admitting that it might be possible to fall in love with a Black woman, he found the suggestion that he might marry a Black woman ridiculous; although again he could not articulate why. The questioner (presumably Trone) pressed further, asking, "what if a white girl fell in love with a Negro man and married him?" To which the uncomfortable hitchhiker could only reply, "you can tell right off you're from New York." Completing his cross-examination, the New Yorker asked one final leading question, "They'd probably hang a Negro like that, wouldn't they?" The youth agreed that "something like that would probably happen," and "laughed merrily for a long time." Underscoring the irony that the young man had effectively if unwittingly hanged himself, Ilf and Petrov ended the story by assuring their readers that they reproduced the conversation with "absolute accuracy."[14]

Revealing the laughing violence that underpinned white power, the Soviet authors did not question the fundamental assumption of Black difference. In *Low-Rise America*, rather than dismantling racist stereotypes, Ilf and Petrov, like earlier Soviet observers, simply revalued them. They implicitly agreed with Pilnyak, who pled ignorance as to "whether it's by way of race or history, whether it's on the basis of societal laws or biological ones, but Negroes really do possess some salient differences from White Americans." "Negroes," he proclaimed, "are distinguished from [white] Americans, of course, by their emotionality." And a few pages later: "Every Negro is, first of all, musical."[15] Ilf and Petrov provided a whole list of traits commonly attributed to Black people – artistic, impressionable, imaginative, contemplative, emotional, and inquisitive – that white Americans allegedly denigrated as qualities that impeded the operation of capitalism. They imagined a "Southern gentleman" finding in African Americans' love of nature evidence that they "are lazy and incapable of systematic labor." However, as Soviet people, Ilf and Petrov were able to appreciate such "Negro characteristics." They argued that "if Negroes were to be taken away from America, the country

[13] ART, 116, 121; Il'f and Petrov, "Negry," 14; OA, 383–84; Tan-Bogoraz, *USA*, 122.
[14] ART, 121; Il'f and Petrov, "Negry," 14; OA, 384.
[15] Pil'niak, *O'kei*, 101, 99; Tan-Bogoraz, *USA*, 60, 119.

would, of course, become somewhat whiter, but most certainly it would become at least twenty times duller."[16]

The two photographs of Black Southerners in "Negroes" likewise aligned the Soviet authors with the "traditional view of blacks as colorful, primitive, fundamentally contented figures."[17] Ilf and Petrov's caption identified a smiling, stiffly posed man as a "nice young Negro from Alabama, who works as something between a janitor and a lackey." The writers emphasized that the young man's true talents, unrewarded in the United States, would have received their proper due in the Soviet Union. He "dances so well," they observed, "that if he ever came to Moscow, he'd have it made." The caption does not suggest that Ilf and Petrov spoke with the young man or tell us how they knew he was a good dancer.[18] The description is remarkably similar to that of a janitor who tap-danced for the tourists at the Grand Canyon, and they perhaps simply moved the young man to Alabama to better fit the narrative of the "Negroes" photo essay.[19] As the art historian Christina Kiaer notes, "the combination of Ilf's amateur, snapshot style of photography with the descriptive text" had the effect of authorizing the racist stereotype of the "grinning, happy-go-lucky Negro."[20] At the same time, the writers applauded the racial enlightenment of Muscovites, who "know their dancing" and would elevate the Black janitor to the status of Black entertainer (Figure 26.2).

Ilf and Petrov based their claims to "know" Black people not on conversations with them, but on visual observation and familiarity with American literary representations. The caption above a photograph of a Black man in a fedora seated on an embankment, gazing at the Mississippi River, called the reader's attention to the river, not the man. Beginning with the statement that in New Orleans, the river is "wide and deserted," Ilf and Petrov contrasted the quiet scene they saw to the busy Mississippi River, where Stowe "introduced her readers to old Tom" and Huckleberry Finn "hid the Negro Jim from his pursuers." That river, they informed their readers, fell victim to modernization: "Transportation by waterway turned out to be too slow for the United States. Trains and trucks took over the river's loads." Framed by Ilf and Petrov's nostalgia for Stowe and Twain's Mississippi, the man watching

---

[16] LGA, 277–78; OA, 380–82.   [17] Natanson, "Politics, Culture," 28.

[18] ART, 122; Il'f and Petrov, "Negry," 15.

[19] OA, 221; Meredith L. Roman, *Opposing Jim Crow: African Americans and the Soviet Indictment of US Racism, 1928–1937* (Lincoln: University of Nebraska Press, 2012), 85.

[20] Christina Kiaer, "African Americans in Soviet Socialist Realism: The Case of Aleksandr Deineka," *Russian Review* 75 (July 2016): 431–32; Roman, *Opposing*, 85.

Figure 26.2 A page from the "Negroes" installment of "American Photographs" showing the smiling young dancer; a man on the banks of the Mississippi River in New Orleans; and the marquee of a segregated movie theater. *Ogonek*, no. 22 (10 August 1936): 15. Courtesy Library of Congress.

the steamers go by seems to be a character straight out of that slower world.[21]

Ilf and Petrov's failure to see beyond stereotype was hardly theirs alone. Critics have called attention to the "whiteness of the photographer's gaze" in numerous Depression-era American photodocumentaries.[22] In the summer of 1936, when Bourke-White and Caldwell traveled through the South to do research for their photobook, she captured an image 200 miles upriver from New Orleans that echoed Ilf's. Captioned with her subjects' imagined thoughts – "Just sitting in the sun watching the river go by" – her photograph of men obviously not working appeared, like Ilf's, "to support traditional notions of a black laziness–poverty nexus."[23] In the opening lines of *12 Million Black Voices*, Richard Wright engaged directly with such simplifications, common, he asserted, among "you," white readers, writers, and photographers, who "think you know us." In contrast to the Soviet writers, who flattered their readers with a caption anticipating a happy (if unlikely) future in the Soviet Union for the "nice young Negro" dancer from Alabama, Wright asked his readers to confront the long, sordid history behind Dorothea Lange's penetrating image of a thirteen-year-old sharecropper in Americus, Georgia. Above the photograph of a serious young man behind a plow, who has momentarily stopped working to look the photographer in the eye, Wright reflected, "We black men and women in America today, as we look back upon scenes of rapine, sacrifice, and death, seem to be children of a devilish aberration ... fledglings of a period of amnesia on the part of men who once dreamed a great dream and forgot."[24] Here, the issue was not some mystical Black musicality or love of nature, but white "forgetting" of the American founding principles (Figures 26.3 and 26.4).

Different as they are, Wright's *12 Million Black Voices* and Ilf and Petrov's photo essay and book can be understood as illuminating the complexities of Popular Front antiracism. Focused on creating broad

[21] ART, 122; Il'f and Petrov, "Negry," 15.   [22] Balthaser, "Killing," 362.

[23] Nicholas Natanson, *The Black Image in the New Deal: The Politics of FSA Photography* (Knoxville: University of Tennessee Press, 1992), 227; Erskine Caldwell and Margaret Bouke-White, *You Have Seen Their Faces* (Athens: University of Georgia Press, [1937] 1995), n.p.

[24] Wright, *12 Million*, 10–11, 27; Jeff Allred, "From Eye to We: Richard Wright's *12 Million Black Voices*, Documentary, and Pedagogy," *American Literature* 78 (September 2006): 553–54, 557; Jason Puskar, "Black and White and Read All Over: Photography and the Voices of Richard Wright," *Mosaic* 49 (June 2016): 167–83; Perry S. Moskowitz, "Many Dark Mirrors in Richard Wright's *12 Million Black Voices*," in Jane Anna Gordan and Cyrus Ernesto Zirakzadeh, eds., *The Politics of Richard Wright: Perspectives in Resistance* (Lexington: University Press of Kentucky, 2018), 250.

Figure 26.3 Margaret Bourke-White, "Just sitting in the sun watching the river go by," in the photobook *You Have Seen Their Faces* (1937). Margaret Bourke-White Papers, Special Collections Research Center, Syracuse University Libraries. © 2023 Estate of Margaret Bourke-White / Licensed by VAGA at Artists Rights Society (ARS), NY.

coalitions against fascism, the Popular Front seemed to require a "less militant" approach to antiracism. The shift is visible in Ilf and Petrov's decision to downplay, relative to earlier Soviet visitors, both white violence and African Americans' revolutionary potential. From this perspective, Wright, who had joined the American Communist Party in 1934, in its more militant phase, seemingly violated the "soft" Popular Front line: He included a graphic news photo of a lynching, precisely the sort of image that pre-Popular Front Soviet propaganda had deployed as a sensational means of unmasking "American 'democracy' as it really is."[25] But we can also understand *12 Million Black Voices*, published in 1941, as reflecting the high tide of Popular Front hopes for democratic inclusiveness.[26] In Wright's photobook, the group portrait of a crowd of

[25] Roman, *Opposing*, 10, 20, 83, 62–63 (democracy).
[26] Dan Shiffman, "Richard Wright's *12 Million Black Voices* and World War II Era Civic Nationalism," *African American Review* 41 (2007): 454–55.

Figure 26.4 Dorothea Lange, "Thirteen-year-old sharecropper boy near Americus, Georgia," July 1937. Farm Security Administration – Office of War Information Photograph Collection, Prints and Photographs Division, Library of Congress, LC-USF34-017915-C.

white men arrayed around the bloody body of a Black man hanging from a noose served not only to document the hypocrisy and brutality of American democracy. It aimed to reappropriate the photographs of lynchings that had long circulated "within a public sphere devoted to white supremacy." In the context of Wright's "folk history of the Negro in the United States," the photograph forced white readers to look at themselves acclaiming anti-Black violence.[27] Ilf and Petrov, whose métier was satire, not Wright's experimental "modernism that teaches," drew on their experiences in America to likewise reveal not (only) the fact of violence, but its central role in the creation of white community and identity.[28] Going beyond what they already "knew," Ilf and Petrov

[27] Allred, "From Eye," 559, 554; Balthaser, "Killing," 371.
[28] Allred, "From Eye," 551.

produced a devastating portrait of a poor, young white man merrily endorsing lynching.

What made Wright's photobook as much as Ilf and Petrov's travelogue an emblem of the Popular Front was the hope that if white Americans could be made to see themselves anew, America might yet remember and fulfill its promise. In the final pages of *12 Million Black Voices*, Wright asserted that "If we [Black folk] had been allowed to participate in the vital processes of American growth ... America would have been stronger and greater!" He called on white Americans to "Look at us and know us and you will know yourselves, for *we* are *you*, looking back at you from the dark mirror of our lives." This was more than a call for a strategic alliance between white and Black workers or even for transcendent proletarian solidarity.[29] Rather, Wright urged white Americans to see Black history as American history, to understand that "What we want, what we represent, what we endure is what America *is*. If we black folk perish, America will perish." Fighting for "the right to share in the upward march of American life," African Americans restored the "great dream" of America for all.[30]

Ilf and Petrov similarly hoped that white America might look into the dark mirror of the Other and see not only itself, but its better self. Because they approached the problem as Soviet people confident in their own racial enlightenment, their tone was at once more essentializing and more ironic than Wright's. Insisting on both Black difference and the possibility of human mutability, they reflected "Oh, if only the Southern gentlemen, the kindhearted spectator or the participant in a lynching suddenly understood that in order to attain one hundred percent humanity he needs what he lacks – namely, these very Negro characteristics which he derides!"[31] Ilf and Petrov did not specify how the Southern gentleman could be made to see or what would happen if he "suddenly understood." They did not expect Black people to challenge the white Bosses of the Buildings – to borrow Wright's homespun Marxist terminology. Even in New York, Ilf and Petrov asserted, Black people refrained from entering white establishments, because they "know only too well how such experiments might end." But they clearly believed that America would be better off if Black Americans had opportunities to "develop and grow" and to exercise their rights as "free citizens of the United States."[32]

---

[29] Joel Waller, "First-Person Plural: The Voices of the Masses in Farm Security Administration Documentary," *Journal of Narrative Theory* 29 (Fall 1999): 351; Shiffman, "Richard Wright's," 445; Moskowitz, "Many Dark Mirrors," 257.
[30] Wright, *12 Million*, 145, 146.   [31] LGA, 278; OA, 381.
[32] LGA, 278, 280; OA, 381, 384; Roman, *Opposing*, 86.

Ilf and Petrov's vision of white Southern gentlemen "suddenly" decid-
ing to learn from their Black compatriots perhaps owed something to
their own experience of unexpectedly finding something valuable in
American democracy. Their enthusiasm for Amerikanizm rested on Stalin's
authorization of the effort to harness American tekhnika to what he called
Russian revolutionary sweep. As we have seen, this borrowing assumed that
only in the Soviet Union could American know-how be put to humane use.
But in the final chapters of *Low-Rise America*, the authors made the startling
observation that the smooth, efficient, even humane functioning of American
production methods relied on American "democracy."

Of course, the Soviet writers offered all kinds of qualifiers and caveats,
reminding their readers that the grandiose "democracy" enshrined in
America's founding documents hardly existed in practice. The Southern
states effectively deprived African Americans of their right to vote. In the
nation's capital, the heart of American democracy, Jim Crow reigned.
A lone Black congressperson, Oscar De Priest of Chicago, fought unsuccessfully to end segregation in the House's dining room. Everywhere,
corrupt politicians fixed elections and failed "to protect the inviolability
of the personality" from the depredations of capitalists and gangsters.
Dismissing the Constitution as just a "beautiful parchment preserved in
the legislature's safe," Ilf and Petrov asserted that American democracy
"only masks the exploitation of human by human."[33]

Yet even as they noted the absence of truly free elections and equal
rights, Ilf and Petrov deemed the American democratization of daily life
"rather impressive."[34] They acknowledged that the "scrupulously" maintained "outer forms of democracy" often disguised inequality. While Henry
Ford and his employees might seem like "equals on the job," addressing
one another by first name, he remained ready to throw them out as soon as
they were no longer needed. Still, Ilf and Petrov recommended that Soviet
businesspeople adopt American-style democracy "in relations between
people." Their conclusion that such "outward forms" "help at work, strike
a blow against bureaucracy, and enhance human dignity" seemed to apply
to both the United States and the Soviet Union.[35]

While Ilf and Petrov carefully distinguished sham "constitutional"
democracy from dignity-enhancing "relational" democracy, promoting only
the latter as a model for Soviet people, their narrative often blurred the lines
between the two. Having taken in the main tourist sites in Washington, DC,
they decided that "Only the President remained to be seen." Getting access
to this final attraction turned out to be "not so difficult." On 10 January

---

[33] OA, 387, 401.   [34] LGA, 284; OA, 389.
[35] OA, 401; Nakhimovsky, "Death and Disillusion," 217.

1936, the two *Pravda* correspondents participated in the twice weekly "ritual" of the presidential press conference.[36] Back in 1932, when the US State Department advocated admitting Soviet journalists through a loophole in American visa regulations, the official who proposed the change noted that it might not be wise to allow them access to a White House press conference, although he did not specify his concerns.[37] Ilf and Petrov's adventure suggests that his worry was misplaced.

The writers' wide-eyed description of the press conference underscored the informality of the occasion. Before 10:30 in the morning, a crowd of almost 100 journalists gathered in a White House reception room. As seemed to be the case everywhere in America, there was no cloakroom, so the correspondents unceremoniously stowed their overcoats on a grand wood table, a "gift made to one of the former presidents" (actually, to FDR), and when that filled up, on the floor (Figure 26.5).[38] Waiting for the president, the journalists "smoked, talked loudly, and glanced impatiently at the small white door, behind which, apparently, the president of the United States was hiding." Advised to "stand as close as possible to the door" in order to secure a good view of the president, Ilf and Petrov gamely applied "the dexterity of experienced streetcar fighters" and "squeezed ahead." Only three "very respectable gentlemen" managed to get in front of the dauntless Soviet reporters.[39]

When twenty minutes after the appointed hour the president had still failed to appear, these three gentlemen, "quietly at first, and then more loudly," began to knock on the door. They knocked on the president of the United States's door, Ilf and Petrov observed, "just as some assistant director might rap on an actor's door to remind him of his entrance cue." Drawing no explicit comparisons to Soviet journalists' relationship with their leader, they emphasized that the waiting American reporters "knocked laughingly, but still they knocked."[40]

When the door finally opened, Ilf and Petrov sprinted ahead, easily overtaking the "panting grey-haired gentlemen," and gained prime spots for the press conference. They described it as taking place "in the depths of a circular private study." This was, of course, the Oval Office. When he became president in 1933, Franklin Roosevelt had begun the practice

---

[36] LGA, 284–85; OA, 390–91; PIA, Il'f, 10 January 1936, 490.
[37] Memorandum on visa case, 13 September 1932, NACP, RG, 59, 811.111 Firms-Amtorg-Mikhalski Pavel Ludvigovich.
[38] "Table for Roosevelt Is Gift of Aguinaldo," NYT, 11 January 1935; Federal Writers' Project, Works Progress Administration, *Washington: City and Capital* (Washington, DC: US Government Printing Office, 1937), 302.
[39] OA, 390; ZK, 489.   [40] LGA, 285; OA, 391; ZK, 489.

Figure 26.5 Journalists' hats and overcoats in the West Wing lobby.
The table, a 1934 gift from Filipino leader Emilio Aguinaldo, was too
big for the Cabinet Room. It was a cross-section of a giant red narra
tree, not, as Ilf and Petrov asserted, a sequoia. President Roosevelt's
Press Conference, 1937. Harris & Ewing Collection, Prints and
Photographs Division, Library of Congress, LC-H22-D-1265.

of holding frequent press conferences there.[41] FDR himself appeared "at
a medium-sized writing desk, a smoking cigarette in his hand and
Chekhovian pince-nez on his large handsome nose."[42]

The president won over the skeptical Soviet funnymen, much as he did
the American press corps. Ilf and Petrov particularly respected his ability
"twice a week to fob off a hundred pushy journalists with a joke."[43] At his
7 January 1936 press conference, Roosevelt had deflected attention from

---

[41] "The Press at the White House, 1933–1941," The White House Historical Association, www
.whitehousehistory.org/the-press-at-the-white-house-1933-1941 (accessed 30 July 2022).
[42] LGA, 285; OA, 391.
[43] OA, 391; B. H. Winfield, "Franklin D. Roosevelt's Efforts to Influence the News during
His First Term Press Conferences," *Presidential Studies Quarterly* 11 (Spring
1981): 189–99.

the Supreme Court's decision to declare the Agricultural Adjustment Act
(AAA) unconstitutional with the assertion, "I don't think there is any
news except that Charlie Michelson," the publicity director best known
for coining the damning term "Hooverville," "needs a haircut."
Responding, "Got to economize somewhere," Michelson got a big laugh
from the president and the press – and write-ups in *Time* magazine and
the *New York Times*.[44]

Three days later, at the press conference Ilf and Petrov attended,
Roosevelt began by inviting Michelson, who in the interim had gotten a
haircut, to take a bow. This set the tone for the friendly back-and-forth.
When he did not have a particular detail about the Gold Reserve Act, the
president told the reporters, "Frankly, I would have to look it up."
A question on agriculture elicited a lengthy explanation of the president's
responsibility to consider the problem "from the point of view of forty-
eight states."[45] After taking numerous follow-up questions, Roosevelt
ended the press conference with what Ilf and Petrov described as a
"quizzical" look. There "resounded a discordant *Gud-bai, mister prezi-
dent!*" and the journalists took their leave. The contrast with Stalin,
whom Soviet people lavished with "displays of public affection and
acclaim" and addressed as "father of the peoples" or "*vozhd* [supreme
leader] of the party," was implicit, but quite clear.[46] Tellingly, when Ilf
and Petrov published excerpts from this chapter in *Pravda* under the
headline "Journey to the Land of Bourgeois Democracy," they omitted
the press conference.[47]

From the White House, Ilf and Petrov trekked to Capitol Hill to watch
Senator Gerald P. Nye of North Dakota and the Senate Committee on
Investigation of the Munitions Industry question Wall Street titan
J. P. Morgan, Jr. The hearings aimed to uncover whether financiers
and bankers had dragged the United States into the Great War. On the
day Ilf and Petrov observed, the senators asked Morgan and his partners
whether they had tried to "force President [Woodrow] Wilson to alter
materially in favor of the Allies the neutrality policy of the United States."

---

[44] Press Conference #264, 7 January 1936, p. 1, Franklin D. Roosevelt Presidential Library
and Museum, Press Conferences of President Franklin D. Roosevelt, 1933–1945, www
.fdrlibrary.marist.edu/archives/collections/franklin/?p=collections/findingaid&id=508
(accessed 30 July 2022); "Quips & Cranks," *Time* 27 (20 January 1936): 11; "Economy
Quip Causes the President to Laugh," NYT, 8 January 1936.

[45] Press Conference #265, 10 January 1936, pp. 1, 2, 3, Press Conferences of President
Franklin D. Roosevelt.

[46] OA, 391; Sarah Davies and James R. Harris, *Stalin's World: Dictating the Soviet Order*
(New Haven, CT: Yale University Press, 2014), 144.

[47] Il'ia Il'f and Evgenii Petrov, "Puteshestvie v stranu burzhuaznoi demokratii," *Pravda*,
18 June 1936.

According to the *New York Times*, Morgan, showing "irritation" for the first time in the hearings, "indignantly denied" doing so.[48] Ilf and Petrov, by contrast, described Morgan as "calm." Knowing "nothing untoward would happen to him," he waited for his legion of lawyers to "dig frantically" through their files and books before offering an answer.[49]

Ilf and Petrov suggested that in the Senate Caucus Room, as at the White House press conference, the democracy of daily interactions promoted real democracy and equality. In the gallery, the writers joined a motley collection of spectators, depicted in *Time* magazine as including "inquisitive young men, professional peace lovers, retired businessmen, pretty maidens, frumpy matrons, distinguished-looking Negroes, [and] seedy individuals who frequent places of political excitement."[50] Ilf and Petrov may have had this crowd in mind when they noted, in a passage that can be read as both earnest and ironic, that "millions of people, old and young, who compose the great American people ... can do anything they like according to the Constitution, for they are the masters of the country." The American people, the writers emphasized, can even summon "John Pierpont Morgan himself, for questioning in a senatorial commission and ask him menacingly: 'Mr. Morgan, didn't you pull the United States into the World War because of the selfish interests of your personal enrichment?' The people can ask that." Ilf and Petrov doubted anything would come of the questioning: "It was not Morgan speaking; it was his billions. And when money talks in America, it always talks authoritatively." Nonetheless, they deemed the capitalist's public interrogation an "amazing scene."[51]

In *Low-Rise America*, the chapter in which Ilf and Petrov documented the wonders of "American Democracy" immediately followed their account of the Black South. This sequencing distinguished the "Negroes" chapter from the "Negroes" installment of Ilf and Petrov's photo essay, which included much of the same text. In the photo essay, Ilf and Petrov highlighted the "masking" function of American democracy. The caption that ran alongside a photograph of the marquee of the Palace movie theater in New Orleans asserted that African Americans "are free and enjoy their full rights before the law." However, their picture of the segregated cinema contradicted this claim. Ilf and Petrov exclaimed, "But just you let a Negro try and go into a movie theater, tram, or church where white people are sitting!" They emphasized that the cinema provided "grubby," substandard segregated accommodation,

[48] "J. P. Morgan Denies Letting Pound Slip to Force 1915 Loan," NYT, 11 January 1936.
[49] LGA, 286; OA, 392.   [50] "New History & Old," *Time* 27 (20 January 1936): 12.
[51] LGA, 286; OA, 391–93; ZK, 479.

ignoring the establishment's self-proclaimed status as the "South's finest theater for colored people."[52]

Despite Ilf's photo of the broadly smiling young man, the photo essay presented a picture of Black life as hopeless and stagnant. Like Wright's photobook, Ilf and Petrov's photo essay moved from South to North. But while Wright represented Black urbanites as "men in the making," newly class-conscious workers joining the struggle against the Bosses of the Buildings, Ilf and Petrov highlighted the persistence of racialized traits. They devoted the last two pages of the four-page photo essay to images of Black people marching, dancing, and singing in praise of Harlem's "god," Father Divine. Ostensibly a "demonstration against war and fascism," the parade appeared to be a display of credulous folk religion.[53] The pictured spectators are "respectable" women and "curious" children. Wright's "heroic male proletarian" capable of creating "disciplined class-conscious groups" and "new organs of action and expression" is nowhere to be seen.[54]

In *Low-Rise America*, Ilf and Petrov continued to ignore heroic (Black and white) proletarians. But slotting the "Negroes" chapter ahead of the "American Democracy" chapter, they constructed in the book a more optimistic and dynamic narrative than in the photo essay. Cutting all references to Father Divine and his followers, Ilf and Petrov added the transitional story of Oscar De Priest's effort to desegregate the House of Representative's restaurant. In the context of their discussion of American democracy, De Priest's failure can be read as a roadmap to victory. That the city of Chicago sent a Black representative to Congress disputed the writers' claim, made only a few sentences earlier, that Black people never challenged their de facto exclusion from white institutions.[55] When he was elected in 1929, De Priest was, as Ilf and Petrov may or may not have known, the first Black congressperson since the turn of the century and the first elected from a Northern state.[56]

In January 1934, De Priest made a public stand against the segregation of a House dining establishment that Ilf and Petrov simplified in telling ways. As a member of the House, De Priest had the right to eat in the

---

[52] ART, 122; Il'f and Petrov, "Negry," 15.   [53] Il'f and Petrov, "Negry," 16–17.
[54] Allred, "From Eye," 570 (heroic), 571; Wright, *12 Million*, 145.   [55] OA, 384–85.
[56] Information on De Priest from "'Every Right and Every Privilege': Oscar De Priest and Segregation in the House Restaurant," 12 February 2020, History, Art & Archives: United States House of Representatives, https://history.house.gov/Blog/2020/February/2-12-De_Priest_Restaurant/ (accessed 22 August 2023); Elliott M. Rudwick, "Oscar De Priest and the Jim Crow Restaurant in the U. S. House of Representatives," *Journal of Negro Education* 35 (Winter 1966): 77–82.

members-only dining room, and sometimes did so with his African American private secretary or his African American constituents. To avoid eating in the same room with a Black man, some House members took their meals in the Senate dining room instead. They did not, as Ilf and Petrov claimed, "close down the Congressional dining room entirely" in order prevent a Black man from dining with white people.[57] Indeed, the controversy was not over the members-only dining room, but over the House's public restaurant, where De Priest's private secretary Morris Lewis sometimes ate when he was not with his boss. In January 1934, the manager informed Lewis and his son that the restaurant was for whites only and asked them to leave. It was this exclusion that De Priest eloquently – and unsuccessfully – fought. The House's restaurant remained segregated at least until 1948.

It is understandable that Ilf and Petrov left out (or did not know) these details. The story they tell is a more dramatic moral tale. Unable to argue against democratic "relations between people," the white representatives' only option, in Ilf and Petrov's telling, was shutting down those relations altogether. Since clearly every restaurant could not be closed, the solution was hardly replicable or sustainable.[58] Ilf and Petrov's narrative did not rest on Black voices, but it illustrated how adherence to the "outward forms" of democracy could provide opportunities for African Americans, indeed all Americans, to make their voices heard.

Ilf and Petrov, like their imagined "Southern gentleman," suddenly (if only implicitly) seemed to understand that they needed to learn from people they derided. It turned out that a Black congressperson could use the mechanisms of American democracy to do what they claimed the "Negro will never do," that is, challenge white power. The idea that the "people are the masters of the country" would have been familiar to Ilf and Petrov and their Soviet readers. But when the Soviet media invoked the phrase, it authorized only recurrent campaigns targeting "'bureaucratic,' undemocratic practices among local party bosses."[59] The Stalin Constitution, promulgated with much fanfare in 1936 as the most democratic constitution in the world, promised freedom of speech, as long as it was exercised "with the aim of the struggle for the final victory of socialism."[60] The notion that the people could ask anything they liked of their national leaders, that a Soviet person could rap on Stalin's door,

---

[57] LGA, 280–81; OA, 385.   [58] OA, 384.

[59] David Priestland, "Soviet Democracy, 1917–1991," *European History Quarterly* 32 (2002): 120; Samantha Lomb, *Stalin's Constitution: Soviet Participatory Politics and the Discussion of the 1936 Draft Constitution* (London: Routledge, 2018), 117.

[60] Draft as quoted in Lomb, *Stalin's Constitution*, 24, 161 (Article 125).

or indeed on the door of any of the "little Stalins" who ran provincial party organizations, and laughingly request a hearing was simply unimaginable.[61] In Washington, DC, Ilf and Petrov saw how democratic "outward forms" could reshape personal and political relations. That knock on the president's door gave them a new perspective on American – and Soviet – life.

---

[61] Sheila Fitzpatrick, *Everyday Stalinism: Ordinary Life in Extraordinary Times: Soviet Russia in the 1930s* (New York: Oxford University Press, 1999), 30.

27   Anxious Life

> At the foundation of Soviet life lies the communist idea. ... That is why we, the people, by comparison with Americans – middle-class Americans – are now already much calmer and happier than they, in the land of Morgan and Ford, twenty-five million automobiles, a million and a half kilometers of ideal roads, the land of cold and hot water, bathrooms, and service.
>
> Ilf and Petrov, *Low-Rise America*

Returning to Moscow in February 1936 after five months abroad, Ilf and Petrov found a changed world. The relative openness of the period between 1932 and 1935, when it had been possible for Soviet authors to propose John Dos Passos's modernism as a model for Soviet literature, had passed. Two months before their homecoming, the newly established Committee on Arts Affairs began the process of consolidating control over "virtually every aspect of cultural life."[1] At the end of January 1936, an authoritative editorial in *Pravda*, "Muddle Instead of Music," marked out new limits on artistic production. The anonymous diatribe censured Dmitri Shostakovich's previously celebrated opera *Lady Macbeth of Mtsensk* as "a confused stream of noise" that was difficult to follow and "impossible to commit to memory." The brutal review came just two days after Stalin left a performance at the Bolshoi before the final curtain, apparently disgusted with the dissonant, openly sexual opera. Another editorial in early February, "Balletic Falsity," targeted *Limpid Stream*, which Shostakovich had scored, for failing to incorporate folk songs and folk dances. Soon came more attacks on so-called formalism, that is, Western-influenced modernism, in music, film, theater, literature, and the visual arts. Clearly people with clout had settled on a definition of "socialist realism" as traditional in form and accessible to the masses. Intimating the vicious and deadly denunciations to come, the

---

[1] Katerina Clark and Evgeny Dobrenko, *Soviet Culture and Power: A History in Documents, 1917–1953* (New Haven, CT: Yale University Press, 2007), 145.

314

editorial on *Lady Macbeth* ominously warned Soviet artists that formalism "is a game that can end very badly."[2]

Ilf and Petrov themselves had also changed. Petrov later recalled that they returned from their American road trip with a "maniacal desire to help, to do something, to make suggestions."[3] The fresh memory of American highways, American service, and American democracy made Soviet shortfalls more visible and more difficult to bear. In his journal, Ilf cataloged the annoyances and hazards encountered on a late evening drive to Kraskovo, the dacha suburb where he took a small house in the summer of 1936. Behind the wheel of the Fordchika, which the writers had managed to bring home, Ilf noticed the absence of everything they had admired in the United States.[4] He griped, "There's not a single sign on the road indicating where it's leading. Cars are riding without brake lights. ... A truck is stuck in the middle of the road with no flares to mark it." Ilf's notebook entries depicted a country of poor service, where a waiter in a "first class café," responded to a request for mineral water with "You'll wait." Ilf also described, as literary scholar Alice Nakhimovsky notes, a world "dominated by rank," which contradicted both "the Soviet ideal" and the American practice of democratic relations between people.[5]

In February 1936, Ilf and Petrov retained enough optimism, or perhaps naivete, to immediately sit down and write a letter to Stalin. As we have seen, their late February missive earnestly recommended sending local party secretaries to the United States so that they could see for themselves – and be inspired to imitate – the marvels of rational, efficient, smiling American service. Ilf and Petrov's note also intervened in the debate on the construction of a "Soviet Hollywood." The project's chief advocate was Boris Shumyatsky, the head of the Soviet film industry. He had traveled to the United States in 1935, just before Ilf and Petrov, and had met with many of the same filmmakers. Unlike Ilf and Petrov, he

---

[2] "Muddle Instead of Music: Concerning the Opera *Lady MacBeth of the Mtsensk District*," *Pravda*, 28 January 1936, as translated in Kevin M. F. Platt and David Brandenberger, eds., *Epic Revisionism: Russian History and Literature as Stalinist Propaganda* (Madison: University of Wisconsin Press, 2006), 136–37; Laurel Fay, *Shostakovich: A Life* (New York: Oxford University Press, 1999), 84; Hans Günther, "Soviet Literary Criticism and the Formulation of the Aesthetics of Socialist Realism, 1932–1940," in Evgeny Dobrenko and Galin Tihanov, eds., *A History of Russian Literary Theory and Criticism: The Soviet Age and Beyond* (Pittsburgh: University of Pittsburgh Press, 2011), 104–105.

[3] Evgenii Petrov, *Moi drug Il'f* (Moscow: Tekst, 2001), 200.

[4] "Spravka ob uplate poshliny za transportirovky 'Forda' Il'i Il'fa i Evgeniia Petrova iz Ameriki v Moskvu," 20 January 1936, Il'ia Il'f family archive. I thank Milla Fedorova for sharing this document.

[5] Nakhimovsky, "Death and Disillusion," 219–20.

returned enthusiastic about the Hollywood way. Touting the benefits of organizing Soviet moviemaking along American lines, he secured Stalin's initial approval for building a cinema city in the Soviet south. Ilf and Petrov had read about the project while they were in the United States. They did not address the most important aspect of Shumyatsky's proposal – introducing American-style producers, who would exercise more effective control over directors and their pictures. The humorists wrote to Stalin to debunk the idea that filmmakers needed sunny, southern locations. In the United States, they explained, directors had long since stopped shooting with natural light, preferring the predictability sound-stages offered. Why they felt the need to intervene in this discussion remains unclear. But the fact that they did so suggests they did not consider the risks to be dangerously high.[6]

Nonetheless, as the writers settled down to complete *Low-Rise America* in the summer of 1936, they clearly registered the increasingly "poison-ous" political atmosphere.[7] In his notebook, Ilf recorded a bitter response to the aftermath of the *Lady Macbeth* affair: "Composers have given up doing anything except writing denunciations of each other on sheets of music paper." With a seemingly random reference to prerevolutionary trials – "The gentlemen of the jury declared the accused innocent" – Ilf drew an implicit comparison to the August 1936 show trial of Stalin's opponents, Lenin's former comrades.[8] All sixteen confessed – we now know, under torture – to participation in farfetched, indeed fictive, conspiratorial networks that linked them to Lev Trotsky and foreign spy agencies. Declared guilty of treason and terrorism, the defendants were immediately executed.[9]

In the summer of 1936, Ilf and Petrov also faced a more personal challenge. As Petrov recalled, "we were so accustomed to thinking and writing together, that it was agonizing" to write separately. But Ilf was ill, and the partners' dachas were at opposite ends of Moscow. So they devised a plan. They would write a chapter together "for seed," and then divide up the remaining chapters. After a month working apart, they

---

[6] The letter was published in Iu. Murin, "Daesh Gollivud!" *Iskusstvo kino*, no. 11 (November 1992): 85–91; Maria Belodubrovskaya, "Soviet Hollywood: The Culture Industry That Wasn't," *Cinema Journal* 53 (Spring 2014): 100–122; Richard Taylor, "Ideology as Mass Entertainment: Boris Shumyatsky and Soviet Cinema in the 1930s," in Ian Christie and Richard Taylor, eds., *Inside the Film Factory: New Approaches to Russian and Soviet Cinema* (New York: Routledge, 1991), 193–216.

[7] Milne, *How They Laughed*, 241.   [8] Nakhimovsky, "Death and Disillusion," 222, 221.

[9] Wendy Z. Goldman, *Inventing the Enemy: Denunciation and Terror in Stalin's Russia* (New York: Cambridge University Press, 2011), 40–42; J. Arch Getty and Oleg V. Naumov, *The Road to Terror: Stalin and the Self-Destruction of the Bolsheviks, 1932–1939* (New Haven, CT: Yale University Press, 1999), 256–60.

would reconvene "with huge manuscripts." Petrov remembered he then spent "a whole day and a whole night, and then another whole day" unable to write anything. In desperation, he went to visit Ilf in Kraskova. Ilf was almost "unnaturally" happy to see Petrov. "You know, Zhenya," he confided, "I can't do anything." Petrov informed him that he had come "with the same sad news. We didn't even laugh. The situation was too serious." Finally, they decided that the problem was the scale of the task. They agreed that each would write one chapter, then they would meet, "correct the manuscript, discuss the next two chapters in detail, meet again, and so on, until the end of the book."[10]

On this personal front at least, their anguish quickly abated. Three days after their serious meeting, Petrov returned "very agitated" with his first chapter. Never, he recalled, had he so feared criticism. Petrov looked at Ilf's chapter first. Ilf, just as nervous as his coauthor, paced around the terrace, breathing with difficulty. Petrov "read and could not believe my eyes. Ilf's chapter was written exactly as if we had written in together." He told Ilf, "I like it." He had no changes to suggest. "You think so?" replied Ilf, unable to hide his joy. Now it was Petrov's turn to wait anxiously as Ilf reviewed his chapter. Ilf read slowly and attentively, finally saying, "I like it. I think it's good." Petrov concluded that after ten years, they had developed a "unified style," an "expression of both of our spiritual and physical peculiarities." They had also spent a great deal of time in hotels and the back seat of the Ford writing, thinking, and talking together about their impressions. So, "over the course of the summer, the book was written quickly and without much pain." They composed seven chapters together and divided the remaining forty between them. Literary critics largely agree with Petrov that the chapters of *Low-Rise America* that Ilf and Petrov wrote separately read as if the two wrote them together.[11]

The more difficult question is how or whether Ilf and Petrov responded to the unpredictable political climate in which they finished *Low-Rise America*. The only place where they hinted at the contemporary mood in the Soviet Union was in the title of the travelogue's penultimate chapter, "Anxious Life." This was also the only chapter that carried a different title, "They and We," in the English translation. I would argue that it was Ilf and Petrov themselves, not the translator, Charles Malamuth, who made the change. As we have seen in the case of John Dos Passos's appearance in the American edition, Malamuth was working with a version of the manuscript that did not reflect final,

---

[10] Petrov, *Moi drug*, 197, 199.
[11] Petrov, *Moi drug*, 199, 200; Milne, *How They Laughed*, 228n16.

perhaps last-minute edits. And indeed, in autumn 1936, Ilf and Petrov had published an excerpt under the title "We and They."[12] Perhaps wishing to avoid the confrontational connotations of the idiomatic "Us and Them," Malamuth apparently settled on "They and We" as more felicitous than "We and They." Ilf and Petrov eliminated the confrontation entirely with a phrase that might apply to us or them or both.

In "Anxious Life," Ilf and Petrov reflected on the end of their journey. They offered some sweeping and seemingly contradictory assessments of Americans – at once passive and businesslike, incurious and innovative, uncultured and committed to democratic relations among people – but no tidy summary of what they learned. By the time they returned to New York, rode the smooth and speedy elevators to the roof of the Empire State Building, and gazed at the "incredible city, winged with a comb of piers" spread out below them, they had seen a vast and varied American panorama and met an astonishing cast of characters. Ilf and Petrov quickly recapped their two-month, 10,000-mile road trip through "twenty-five states and several hundred towns": "we had breathed the dry air of deserts and prairies, and crossed the Rocky Mountains, had seen Indians, had talked with the young unemployed, with the old capitalists, with radical intellectuals, with revolutionary workers, with poets, with writers, with engineers. We had examined factories and parks, had admired roads and bridges, had climbed up the Sierra Nevada and descended into Carlsbad Caverns."[13] They also had adventures that they did not share with their readers: They had met Ilf's uncles in Hartford; seen Petrov's brother's play on Broadway; run into Paul Robeson at a Harlem nightclub; socialized with successful immigrant writers, artists, businesspeople, and former Russian revolutionaries; worked in Hollywood; and confronted the reality of Ilf's illness.

Anxiety provided an ambivalent and ironic framework for drawing conclusions from Ilf and Petrov's diverse experiences. Acknowledging that capitalism provided "ideal roads," running hot and cold water, bathrooms, and efficient service, they emphasized that it spawned an "entire population in a state of unrest."[14] The reasons were not far to seek. Where everything revolved around money, the dread of losing their meager allotment of America's riches consumed everyone: The unemployed feared never again finding a job; the employed feared losing theirs. Farmers feared a crop failure that would force them to pay more for bread, but they also feared a good harvest that would mean lower prices for their produce. The rich feared that bandits would kidnap their

---

[12] Il'ia Il'f and Evgenii Petrov, "My i oni," *Krasnoarmeets i Krasnoflotets*, no. 19 (1936).
[13] LGA, 296, 287; OA, 405, 393–94.   [14] LGA, 291; OA, 399.

children; the bandits feared the electric chair. Black people feared lynching. Politicians feared elections. The middle class feared illness, "because then the doctors will take everything." The American edition added one more anxiety: "Immigrants fear they will be deported from America." And both ended with a worry straight out of a gangster film: "The merchant fears that the racketeers will come and start shooting up his counter with a machine gun."[15] Clearly the apparent causes were absent in the Soviet Union. But what of the symptom?

In 1936, as Ilf and Petrov completed the manuscript and saw it serialized in the journal *Znamia* (nos. 10–11), Soviet life was quite obviously "in a state of unrest." The increasingly threatening international situation, including Japanese aggression in the Far East and Nazi aid to the rebels in the Spanish Civil War (1936–1939), ratcheted up (not entirely unfounded) fears of foreign espionage. These fears had animated the first Moscow show trial in August. The trial in turn generated a flood of denunciations as people rushed to protect themselves from charges of insufficient vigilance.[16] As *Low-Rise America* appeared in *Znamia*, Ilf confessed to Petrov his fear that "the brick is flying."[17] In late 1936, this was a not unreasonable premonition of the violent criticism and even violence that might be directed against the authors of a book that often praised the capitalist enemy.

"Anxious life" is a fitting epithet for 1937, a year that has become a shorthand for the Stalinist terror. The second Moscow show trial opened on 23 January 1937. Now seventeen defendants stood accused of treason, espionage, and terrorism. Again, convictions rested on (coerced) confessions; all but four of the defendants were shot. Newspapers fed the mood of fear and foreboding, emphasizing the dangers to ordinary citizens posed by internal opponents allied with fascists abroad.[18] Under these circumstances, *Izvestiya*'s March 1937 review of *Low-Rise America* was menacing. The reviewer, one V. Prosin, who had spent time in the United States as a journalist, charged that the book ignored the unemployed, struggling farmers, "millions of Negro sharecroppers," and the impoverished inhabitants of the Jewish Lower East Side and the

---

[15] OA, 399; LGA, 291.

[16] Goldman, *Inventing*, 29–42; William J. Chase, *Enemies with the Gates? The Comintern and the Stalinist Repression, 1934–1939* (New Haven, CT: Yale University Press, 2001), 146–91.

[17] Iakov Lur'e [A. A. Kurdiumov], *V kraiu nepuganykh idiotov: Kniga ob Il'fe i Petrove* (St. Petersburg: Izdatel'stvo Evropeiskogo universiteta v Sankt-Peterburge, [1983] 2005), 163; Milne, *How They Laughed*, 235.

[18] Goldman, *Inventing*, 45–47; Chase, *Enemies*, 192–201; Getty and Naumov, *The Road*, 331–63.

"Negro ghetto – Harlem." He questioned the authors' "racial division" in which only "Slavs, Jews, etc.," but not "real Americans" suffered.[19]

Ilf died less than a month after the review appeared, just as *Low-Rise America* reached Soviet book counters. On the day of his death, unwrapped copies lay in Petrov's dining room. When friends came to offer condolences, he gave each a book in memory of Ilf.[20] Petrov was left to navigate *Low-Rise America*'s publication in English on his own. In early June 1937, he wrote to Malamuth to thank him for his letter expressing sympathy for "poor Ilf." Petrov also requested a change in the Carmel chapter's account of Lucita Squier. For the phrase "after she visited [the Soviet Union] she came to hate everything American," he wanted to substitute the phrase (provided in English), "she has come to like everything Russian." (The Russian edition retained the hate.) In his translation, Malamuth changed the line to "she has come to prefer everything Russian."[21] At the end of the month, Petrov again wrote Malamuth, now underlining the absolute necessity of retaining the title *One-Story America* and criticizing the proposed *Little Golden America* as "unfortunate" and "nonsensical." Malamuth concurred, informing the publisher John Farrar that Petrov "insists on the original title" and "feels that 'Little Golden America' is far from a happy idea and utterly senseless in reference to the book's contents, point of view, theme, and purpose."[22] Farrar, apparently not grasping the anguish of Petrov's plea, did not agree.

In 1937 and 1938, Soviet people lived in a "world of rumor and diffuse anxiety" as arrests came ever closer to home.[23] Foreign émigrés and Comintern agents, along with diplomats and people with connections outside the Soviet Union, were particularly imperiled. But the mass arrests and executions struck all strata of Soviet society.[24] In mid-1937,

[19] V. Prosin, "Razvesistye neboskreby," *Izvestiia*, 21 March 1937; Milne, *How They Laughed*, 235.

[20] B. E. Galanov, "Kommentarii," in Il'ia Il'f and Evgenii Petrov, *Sobranie sochinenii v piati tomakh*, vol. 4, *Odnoetazhnaia Amerika* (Moscow: Goslitizdat, 1961), online version, n. p., https://traumlibrary.ru/book/ilfpetrov-ss05-04/ilfpetrov-ss05-04.html#s005 (accessed 19 August 2023).

[21] Evgenii Petrov to Charlz [Charles Malamuth], 4 June 1937, Columbia University Rare Books and Manuscript Library, Charles Malamuth Papers, Box 1; LGA, 218; OA, 297.

[22] Petrov to Charlz [Charles Malamuth], 25 June 1937; Malamuth to [John] Farrar, 7 July 1937, Malamuth Papers, Box 1.

[23] Karl Schlögel, *Moscow, 1937*, trans. Rodney Livingstone (Malden, MA: Polity, 2012), 355.

[24] Chase, *Enemies*, 4–7; Alastair Kocho-Williams, "The Soviet Diplomatic Corps and Stalin's Purges," *Slavonic and East European Review* 8 (January 2008): 90–110; J. Arch Getty, "'Excesses Are Not Permitted': Mass Terror and Stalinist Governance in the Late 1930s," *Russian Review* 61 (January 2002): 113–14.

the diplomats who had shown Ilf and Petrov around the United States, Jean Arens in New York and Mosei Galkovich in San Francisco, were recalled, arrested, and executed. Sergei Tretyakov, the pioneering author-photographer who had so impressed Berthold Brecht and Walter Benjamin, was arrested in July 1937, and shot that September. The novelist Boris Pilnyak, who in 1931 had taken his own American road trip and had traveled widely across Europe, East Asia, Central Asia, and the Middle East, was arrested in October 1937 and executed in April 1938. Boris Shumyatsky, the proponent of Soviet Hollywood, was arrested in January 1938 and shot in June.[25] Over the course of sixteen months in 1937 and 1938, the NKVD arrested more than 1.5 million people, convicting most, and executing about 700,000, most often by a bullet to the back of the head[26] (Figure 27.1).

Given this context, what should we make of Ilf and Petrov's claim that Soviet people, living in a state founded on the "communist idea," were calmer and happier than "they in the land of Morgan and Ford"?[27] There is no reason to doubt the sincerity of the declaration with which they end "Anxious Life": "We can say honestly, hand on heart, that we would not like to live in America."[28] The disgust with "American bourgeois empti-ness" that Ilf expressed in his notebook was if anything even harsher than the judgments the writers rendered in print.[29] Likewise, their claim that Americans, incurious and alienated from their country's achievements, could not appreciate what it truly meant to love one's homeland, seems heartfelt. True patriotism, they suggested, would require wanting to know "who built Boulder Dam and why, why Negroes are lynched in the Southern states, why [Americans] must eat frozen meat." Ilf and Petrov pitied the shallow and narrow-minded American, who "asks only one thing of his country – to let him alone, and not to interfere with his listening to the radio or going to the movies."[30]

---

[25] Data on purge victims from Memorial, "Zhertvy politicheskogo terrora v SSSR," https://lists.memo.ru/ (accessed 19 August 2023); Katerina Clark, *Moscow, the Fourth Rome: Stalinism, Cosmopolitanism, and the Evolution of Soviet Culture, 1931–1941* (Cambridge, MA: Harvard University Press, 2011), 274–75; Ben Hellman, "The Last Trip Abroad of a Soviet Russian Globetrotter: Boris Pil'njak's Northern Journey in 1934," *Russian Literature* 71 (2012): 198; Taylor, "Ideology," 216.

[26] J. Arch Getty, Gábor T. Rittersporn, and Viktor N. Zemskov, "Victims of the Soviet Penal System in the Pre-War Years: A First Approach on the Basis of Archival Evidence," *American Historical Review* 98 (October 1993): 1017–49; Nicolas Werth and Alain Blum, "La Grande Terreur des années 1937–1938," *Vingtième Siecle*, no. 107 (July–September 2010): 3–19.

[27] OA, 399.   [28] LGA, 293; OA, 401.

[29] Nakhimovsky, "Death and Disillusion," 219.   [30] LGA, 288; OA, 394–95.

Figure 27.1 Los Angeles Mayor Frank Shaw (left), Russian Consul General M. G. Galkovich, and Soviet Ambassador Alexander Troyanovsky, Los Angeles, 1935. In 1937, many of the diplomats who had shown Ilf and Petrov around the United States, including Mosei Galkovich in San Francisco, were recalled, arrested, and executed. The Soviet ambassador Alexander Troyanovsky remained in the United States until June 1938 and survived. Los Angeles Times Photographic Collection, UCLA Library Special Collections, ark:/21198/zz002cm148, CC BY 4.0.

Still, Ilf and Petrov allowed some space for irony, if not disillusionment. They may have genuinely concluded that the disengaged and self-
centered American could not possibly understand the Soviet person's
love of a "native land," where "he owns the soil, the factories, the stores,
the banks, the dreadnoughts, the airplanes, the theaters, and the books,
where he himself is the politician and master of all."[31] However earnest,
the claim echoed their earlier, ostensibly ironic, description of the
American people as the "masters" of their country. The repetition admitted the possibility that some of that irony might be at play in their
characterization of the Soviet Union. Or perhaps that the description of
the United States was not entirely ironic. Ultimately, Ilf and Petrov left
open the question, "What can be said about America, which simultaneously horrifies, delights, calls forth pity, and sets examples worthy
of emulation?"[32]

This openness hardly satisfied Soviet critics, who were at least as
interested in determining whether the book provided a successful illustration of already accepted truths as in assessing it as an exercise in cross-
cultural understanding. A. Mingulina, an expert on American literature,
praised the pair's "honest and truthful" illustrations of "American efficiency" and "everyday comfort." However, in Mingulina's estimation,
Low-Rise America had only limited "significance for our reader." The
problem was that the writers overplayed American comfort and underplayed the failures of capitalism. The book's "best pages" offered an
appropriately engaged description of American Indians, who "out of
hatred for the enslaver, stubbornly and with conviction, preserve their
traditional way of life." But overall, the critic deemed Ilf and Petrov
outsiders to the American "political atmosphere," who failed to reveal
what Soviet people already "know, not only from American writers'
books but from newspapers."[33]

The Americans who reviewed *Little Golden America* often started from
the opposite premise that Ilf and Petrov relied too much on what Soviet
people already "knew" about America. Kansas newspaperman William
Allen White, writing in the *Saturday Review*, compared the travelogue to
Mark Twain's *Tramp Abroad*, in which the writer "laughed at" Europe,
but did not teach his readers much about it. Likewise, he predicted that
Russians reading Ilf and Petrov's account "will learn ... little except

[31] LGA, 288; OA, 395.   [32] LGA, 293; OA, 401.
[33] Mingulina, "Ocherki," 114, 116. See also Lev Nikulin, "'Odnoetazhnaia Amerika' I. Il'fa
i E. Petrova," *Kniga i proletarskaia revoluitsiia*, no. 2 (1937): 121–22; Lev Gladkov,
Review of *Odnoetazhnaia Amerika*, *Novyi Mir*, no. 4 (1937): 278–80; Boris Grossman,
"Zametki o tvorchestve Il'fa i Petrova," *Znamia*, no. 9 (1937): 199–206.

surface things which intelligent Russians probably knew before their two bright young men landed on our shores." The book illuminated not America, but Russian "national ideas, set in a sort of mirror-like perspective." Americans, reading "between the lines," could discover "more about Russians – how they think, what they feel, and what they are trying to do." Unfortunately, White, who had visited the Soviet Union and apparently counted himself something of an expert on the communist Other, did not bother to specify the lines he was reading between to reach the conclusion that "the differences between the ruling classes in America and Russia, you can put in your eye." Still, he granted that on some matters Ilf and Petrov may have seen clearly: "Perhaps we are something like that – really!"[34]

The most skeptical American reviewers could not decide whether the Soviet writers were insulting them, engaging in communist propaganda, or criticizing the Soviet Union. Philip Rahv in the *Nation* noted that "of course" Ilf and Petrov found "our social system ... reprehensible, our movies boring, and cafeteria food tasteless." But in their hymn to the miracle of American laundering, which he quoted in full in his short review, he heard "elementary need and pathetic envy."[35] Robert Van Gelder in the *New York Times* likewise noted the writers' complaint that cafeteria and drugstore meals are "cheap enough, certainly, the helpings are generous, the preparation clean, but the taste of this food isn't exciting." However, Van Gelder seemed to take this complaint as an effort to deflect from the poor provisions at home. He imagined Soviet propagandists admonishing, "People should have black bread, herring, and vodka – not the tasteless stuff that capitalism forces on them." The *Times*'s reviewer was particularly annoyed by Ilf and Petrov's claim that the "average American" was "interested only in what is directly connected with his house, his automobile, or his nearest neighbors," and could not fathom the patriotism of the Soviet person who was the "master of all." Still, he granted that the writers "looked at the people and the country with more tolerance and with better humor than might be expected for a pair coming from a State so new as theirs." Like most of the American reviewers, he judged their satire "extremely mild."[36]

A less skeptical reviewer, Rose C. Feld writing in the *New York Herald Tribune*, treated the book as accurate reporting. Likening Ilf and Petrov to Lewis and Clark, she called their road trip a "voyage of discovery."

---

[34] William Allen White, "How Americans Look to Russians," *Saturday Review* 16 (2 October 1937): 10.

[35] Philip Rahv, "Golden Calves," *Nation* (25 September 1937): 326.

[36] Robert Van Gelder, "Two Soviet Humorists in America," NYT, 31 October 1937.

Feld surmised that far from seeing only themselves reflected in the travelogue, "Russians reading this book will probably get a good picture of the life we lead. They will learn about drugstore dining, cafeterias and automats, splendid highways, electrical gadgets, tourist camps, highballs, injustice to the Negro, rackets and the electric chair." Naturally, the explorers had some blind spots. Feld found their portrait of Mr. Adams especially off: "That Mr. Adams, in spite of his name, seems to have more kinship to Hyman Kaplan than to the founding fathers, Mr. Ilf and Mr. Petrov are unaware."[37] While the Soviet reviewer Prosin had asked suspiciously, "who speaks through Mr. Smith?" (he meant Adams), Feld recognized the writers' guide as a relative of the gregarious Jewish immigrant hero of Leo Rosten's *New Yorker* stories.[38] However, she did not guess that Ilf and Petrov, far from being "unaware" of Mr. Adams's kinship to a mythical Hyman Kaplan, had devised "Adams" as a disguise.

Uncovering the American side of Ilf and Petrov's journey makes it possible to shift our focus from judging the accuracy of their depiction to understanding the process of making – or missing – connections. The humorists' mix of rapturous evocations of American service and tekhnika, disdain for American vulgarity, condemnations of racism and poverty, and commitment to letting Americans speak for themselves allowed readers to find in *Low-Rise America* evidence that the travelers saw clearly and that they understood nothing. The book could be taken as a picture of the Soviet Union as reflected in the gaudy mirror of capitalism, a clear window on America, or an account distorted by the narrators' inordinate fondness for American service. Like all explorers, Ilf and Petrov could never entirely divest themselves of their frames of reference. Russian literary conventions, Soviet categories, and anti-capitalist assumptions guided their understandings of everything from burlesque to Boulder Dam. But carrying presuppositions does not preclude sharp observation. The question is, what happened when they turned their Soviet eyes on the American landscape?

The American traces of Ilf and Petrov's road trip suggest that they often misunderstood, misrepresented, mistranslated – or simply missed – what was before their eyes. Chaste Soviets abroad, they reduced the striptease to mechanical pornography, failing to notice, or perhaps suppressing, the show's winking, bawdy humor. Privately appreciating, but not publicly mentioning, cultural events such as *Porgy and Bess* and the

---

[37] Rose C. Feld, "Looking at Our Curious Land," *New York Herald Tribune*, 19 September 1937.

[38] Lur'e, *V kraiu*, 164; Leo Rosten, *The Education of H*Y*M*A*N K*A*P*L*A*N* (New York: Harcourt, Brace, 1937).

Museum of Modern Art's Van Gogh exhibition, they lost the opportunity to consider the possibility that Americans, no less than Soviet people, aspired to become cultured. Fixated on their own agenda or mired in their own preconceptions, they often failed to fully appreciate or engage with those they met. I would like to imagine that they talked to Witter Bynner, a true literary trickster, about more than Mark Twain and where to meet American Indians. But it seems unlikely. Condemning racism and imperialism, they perpetuated romantic, racialized images of musical, soulful, and curious African Americans and nobly savage American Indians. They camouflaged or omitted their interactions with complex immigrant hybrids such as Solomon Trone, the gracious and endlessly helpful Alexander Gumberg, Ilf's relatives in Hartford, Rouben Mamoulian and Lewis Milestone in Hollywood, and the Kavinokys in Pasadena.

Yet Ilf and Petrov's encounters could also destabilize Soviet expectations and produce new ways of seeing America. Overflowing with images of hell – from steam rising out of the New York subway to the mind-numbing standardization of small towns – *Low-Rise America* followed the template established by earlier Russian and Soviet travelers in America. Still, Ilf and Petrov's fragmented, dreamlike, boozy New York owed at least as much to John Dos Passos as to Maxim Gorky or Vladimir Mayakovsky. Their critique of capitalism was acute but, as the Soviet critics pointed out, hardly conventional. Fascinated by the power of capitalist publicity, Ilf and Petrov highlighted their American hitchhikers' willingness to explain misfortune as an unlucky break more likely to generate a heartwarming story of individual resilience than anger at social injustice. Their Soviet presuppositions did not prevent them from including memorable portraits of a kindhearted capitalist, the cowboy who ran the remarkable hostelry in the desert, and a truly humane missionary, the "man in the red shirt." Ilf's deadpan photographs, as Rodchenko caustically noted, conveyed no "special point of view," instead encouraging Soviet viewers, like the travelers themselves, to observe carefully.

Ilf and Petrov's extraordinary adventure produced not an anti-capitalist manifesto, but an unsettled story. Traveling through an archipelago of immigrant, exile, and fellow-traveler communities that stretched from New York to Los Angeles, the writers found many Americans who shared their Soviet sensibilities. While *Low-Rise America* omitted the complex hybrids who allowed the writers some measure of identification with the supposed Other, the book included many Americans who were like "us." Lincoln Steffens shared their aversion to idiotic American mirth. The young communist organizer in

Texas bore an uncanny resemblance to his comrade in Moscow. An American filmmaker voiced a thoroughly Soviet critique of American movies.

More than anything, Ilf and Petrov's laughter crossed and blurred, even as it marked, the divide between the world of capitalism and the socialist world. From the moment they tried to apply their newfound knowledge of when to doff their hats in a New York elevator, the writers mocked the strange land of the capitalists and their own efforts to make sense of it. Their penchant for deflating any authority too sure of itself made the Soviet humorists perceptive participant observers and gentle critics of America and (implicitly) the Soviet Union.

Although they could no longer turn their satirical gaze directly on their own society, Ilf and Petrov operated on the comic premise that from some angles, their truths, too, might look perplexing or ridiculous. To the end of their journey, they hesitated to proclaim that they had unraveled the riddle. Sailing out of New York Harbor, they passed Wall Street. As darkness fell and the skyscrapers lit up, their "windows gleamed with the gold of electricity, or perhaps it was real gold."[39] Low-rise America had vanished. Was this golden Wall Street an other-worldly illusion – created by technology, American publicity, or Soviet presuppositions? Or had Ilf and Petrov succeeded in catching a glimpse of the real America they sought?

[39] LGA, 296; OA, 406.

28   Coda

"Understanding," in all honesty, is a word pregnant with difficulties,
but also with hope.

Marc Bloch, *The Historian's Craft*, c. 1941

My own Soviet American road trip ended amid pandemic and war.
By the spring of 2020, when Covid-19 closed borders, not to mention
libraries and archives, I was, quite fortuitously, ready to settle down to
the task of writing. During the anxious months when I rarely ventured
more than a few blocks from home, I traveled vicariously with Ilf and
Petrov. Looking back, I can see that the unpleasant, often frightening
experience of adjusting to a new "normal" aided historical understanding.[1] In lockdown, I better appreciated the importance of travel literature
for people with little prospect of going anywhere. Dealing with long lines
at my local market and chatting via Zoom with family and friends
scattered across the continent, I felt acutely the desire for "service" and
the life-changing power of tekhnika. As the pandemic suddenly made
unimaginable things that I had taken for granted – from dinner out to
visiting my parents – it laid bare the presuppositions that so often impede
the historian's ability to understand the people of the past on their
own terms.

Then in February 2022, as Covid eased, the Russian invasion of
Ukraine revealed the precarity of Russian–American relations.
Journalists, diplomats, and even historians, usually so hesitant to draw
rash parallels, talked of the Cold War "reigniting."[2] Or perhaps it never
really ended, as after the collapse of the Soviet Union in 1991, the
conflict between capitalism and socialism morphed into a confrontation
driven on one side by "fever dreams of a limitless liberal order" and on
the other by dire prophecies of an "apocalyptic battle against evil forces

---

[1] Marc Bloch, *The Historian's Craft*, trans. Peter Putnam (New York: Alfred A. Knopf,
1959), 143. Bloch began writing *The Historian's Craft* after the defeat of France in 1940; in
1944, German forces executed him as a member of the Resistance.
[2] Anton Troianovski, "Reigniting Cold War despite Its Risks," NYT, 20 February 2022.

that have sought to destroy the God-given unity of Holy Russia."[3] Either way, in the face of a brutal, even genocidal war, Ilf and Petrov's road trip increasingly stood out as an urgent reminder that hostility is not preordained or inevitable. Even in the dark Stalinist night, transnational dialogues, however constrained and incomplete, retained some power to hold at bay the specter of the dangerous and subversive Other.

The circumstances in which I wrote pushed me to consider the value of history in dark times. Historians cannot mitigate pandemics or end wars. We certainly cannot predict the future. But we can tell stories that allow us to see the past, and therefore also our present, anew. Of course, historians often – and, some might argue, should – enshrine narratives that naturalize cultural, political, racial, or economic hierarchies. But our stories can also deflate triumphalism. Or, put a way that Ilf and Petrov might have appreciated, historical narratives can help us to laugh at ourselves. The Soviet writers' adventures demonstrate that people deeply embedded in specific cultural and political contexts can journey into strange lands and – at least sometimes – come away with a keener sense of the comical, ironic, absurd, or "savage" sides of themselves and their own society. Following Ilf and Petrov as they explored, understood, and misunderstood America, we, too, have an opportunity to see in the mirror of unknown lands a funhouse version of our own world. As we travel the byways of the past, the solid present melts into air, and we can begin to imagine a road to a changed future.

---

[3] Stephen Kotkin, "The Cold War Never Ended: Ukraine, the China Challenge, and the Revival of the West," *Foreign Affairs* 101 (May 2022): 64–78, EBSCOhost; Deborah Netburn, "Putin Ally Offering Up a Spiritual Defense of War," *Los Angeles Times*, 29 March 2022.

Select Bibliography

Archives

American Philosophical Society, Philadelphia
Franz Boas Papers
Bancroft Library, University of California, Berkeley
Ralph Reynolds Family Memoirs, BANC MSS 99/100 c
Boulder Dam Museum and Archive (BDMA), Boulder City, Nevada
Hoover Dam – Construction (1935–36)
Hoover Dam – Tourists and Tourism (1920s–1950s)
Thompson, CJ BF 6631
Center for Southwest Research, University of New Mexico
Frank Waters Papers, MSS-332-BC
Columbia University Rare Book and Manuscript Library
Charles Malamuth Papers
Albert Rhys Williams Papers
Federal Bureau of Investigation Files
Alexander Samuel Kaun, 100-SF-17879-889
Lewis Milestone 100-30825
Solomon Trone 100-NY-96127, 77-HQ-27252
Fray Angélico Chávez Library, Santa Fe, NM
E. Dana Johnson Papers, AC 116
Houghton Library, Harvard College Library
Witter Bynner Papers, MS Am 1891–1891.7, bMS Am 1891
Jewish Historical Society of Greater Hartford (JHSGH)
Oral History Collection
Library of Congress, Manuscript Division
Rouben Mamoulian Papers, MSS84949
National Academy of Motion Picture Arts and Sciences, Margaret Herrick Library
Lewis Milestone Papers
National Archives at College Park Maryland (NACP)
Record Group (RG) 59, Department of State
Harry Ransom Center, University of Texas, Austin
Walter Willard "Spud" Johnson Papers
San Francisco History Center, San Francisco Library
Paul Radin Papers, SFH 23

UC Santa Barbara Library, Department of Special Research Collections
Schott Family papers, SBHC Mss 112
Wisconsin State Historical Society, Division of Library, Archives, and Museum Collection
Alexander Gumberg Papers, New York Mss J; PH 3989

Select Published Sources

I have tried to include here books and articles that provide useful introductions to this book's main topics and arguments, focusing on work in English. Additional sources may be found in the footnotes. For the most important published primary sources, see "Abbreviations."

Allred, Jeff. *American Modernism and Depression Documentary*. Oxford: Oxford University Press, 2009.

Bailes, Kendall E. "The American Connection: Ideology and the Transfer of American Technology to the Soviet Union, 1917–41," *Comparative Studies in Society and History* 23 (January 1981): 421–48.

Ball, Alan M. *Imagining America: Influence and Images in Twentieth-Century Russia*. Lanham, MD: Rowman and Littlefield, 2003.

Brooks, Jeffrey. "The Press and Its Message: Images of America in the 1920s and 1930s." In *Russia in the Era of NEP: Explorations in Soviet Society and Culture*, edited by Sheila Fitzpatrick, Alexander Rabinowitch, and Richard Stites, 231–52. Bloomington: Indiana University Press, 1991.

Brown, Deming. "Dos Passos in Soviet Criticism," *Comparative Literature* 5 (Autumn 1953): 332–50.

Cassedy, Steven. *To the Other Shore: The Russian Jewish Intellectuals Who Came to America*. Princeton, NJ: Princeton University Press, 1997.

David-Fox, Michael. *Showcasing the Great Experiment: Cultural Diplomacy and Western Visitors to the Soviet Union, 1921–1941*. New York: Oxford University Press, 2012.

Dobrenko, Evgeny, and Galin Tihonov, eds. *A History of Russian Literary Theory and Criticism: The Soviet Age and Beyond*. Pittsburgh: University of Pittsburgh Press, 2011.

Denning, Michael. *The Cultural Front: The Laboring of American Culture in the Twentieth Century*. New York: Verso, 1997.

Etkind, Aleksandr. *Tolkovanie puteshestvii: Rossiia i Amerika v travelogakh i intertekstakh* Moscow: Novoe literaturnoe obozrenie, 2001.

Fedorova, Milla. *Yankees in Petrograd, Bolsheviks in New York: America and Americans in Russian Literary Perception*. DeKalb: Northern Illinois University Press, 2006.

Fischer, Nick. *Spider Web: The Birth of American Anticommunism*. Urbana: University of Illinois Press, 2016.

Fitzpatrick, Sheila. *Everyday Stalinism: Ordinary Life in Extraordinary Times: Soviet Russia in the 1930s*. New York: Oxford University Press, 2000.

Foglesong, David. "Rival and Parallel Missions: America and Soviet Russia, 1917–1943." In *A Companion to U.S. Foreign Relations: Colonial Era to the*

Present, Volume 1, edited by Christopher R. W. Dietrich, 446–66. New York: John Wiley, 2020.

Gage, Beverly. *The Day Wall Street Exploded: A Story of America in Its First Age of Terror*. New York: Oxford University Press, 2009.

Gal'tsova, E. D. "Zapadnye pisateli-modernisty v zhurnale 'Literaturnyi kritik': Prust [Proust], Dzhois [Joyce], Dos Passos." In *Postizhenie zapada: Inostronnaia kul'tura v sovetskoi literature, iskusstve i teorii, 1917–1941 gg.: Issledovaniia i arkhivnye materialy*, edited by E. D. Gal'tsova, 669–86. Moscow: IMLI RAN, 2015.

Graham, Malbone W. "Russian–American Relations, 1917–1933: An Interpretation," *American Political Science Review* 28 (June 1934): 387–409.

Haran, Barnaby. *Watching the Red Dawn: The American Avant-Garde and the Soviet Union*. Manchester: Manchester University Press, 2016.

Hasty, Olga Peters, and Susan Fusso. *America through Russian Eyes, 1874–1926*. New Haven, CT: Yale University Press, 1988.

Hessler, Julie. *A Social History of Soviet Trade: Trade Policy, Retail Practices, and Consumption, 1917–1953*. Princeton, NJ: Princeton University Press, 2004.

Hetherington, Philippa. "Dressing the Shop Window of Socialism: Gender and Consumption in the Soviet Union in the Era of 'Cultured Trade,' 1934–53," *Gender and History* 27 (August 2015): 417–45.

Hindus, Maurice. "Ford Conquers Russia," *Outlook* 147 (29 June 1927): 280–83.

Kennan, George F. *Russia Leaves the War: The Americans in Petrograd and the Bolshevik Revolution*. New York: W. W. Norton, [1958] 1984.

Kiaer, Christina. "African Americans in Soviet Socialist Realism: The Case of Aleksandr Deineka," *Russian Review* 75 (July 2016): 402–33.

Kupensky, Nicholas. "The Soviet Industrial Sublime: The Awe and Fear of Dneprostroi, 1927–1932. PhD diss., Yale University, 2017.

Levitana, Marina L. *"Russian Americans" in Soviet Film: Cinematic Dialogues between the US and the USSR*. London: I. B. Tauris, 2015.

Libbey, James K. *Alexander Gumberg and Soviet–American Relations: 1917–1933*. Lexington: University Press of Kentucky, 1977.

Liebling, A. J., and Harold Ross. "Soviet Funny Men," *New Yorker* (9 November 1935): 13–14.

Milne, Lesley. *How They Laughed: Zoshchenko and the Ilf–Petrov Partnership*. Birmingham: Centre for Russian and East European Studies, 2003.

Nakhimovsky, Alice. "Death and Disillusion: Il'ia Il'f in the 1930s." In *Enemies of the People: The Destruction of Soviet Literary, Theater, and Film Arts in the 1930s*, edited by Katherine Bliss Eaton, 205–28. Evanston, IL: Northwestern University Press, 2002.

"How the Soviets Solved the Jewish Question: The Il'f–Petrov Novels and Il'f's Jewish Stories," *Symposium* 53 (January 1999): 93–111.

Nesbet, Anne. "Skyscrapers, Consular Territory, and Hell: What Bulgakov and Eizenshtein Learned about Space from Il'f and Petrov's America," *Slavic Review* 69 (Summer 2010): 377–97.

Papazian, Elizabeth Astrid. *Manufacturing Truth: The Documentary Moment in Early Soviet Culture*. DeKalb: Northern Illinois University Press, 2009.

Pil'niak, Boris. *O'kei: An American Novel.* Translated by Ronald D. LeBlanc. Faculty Publications, 926, University of New Hampshire, 2020.

Phinney, Archie. "Racial Minorities in the Soviet Union," *Pacific Affairs* 8 (September 1935): 321–27.

Reischl, Katherine M. H. *Photographic Literacy: Cameras in the Hands of Russian Authors.* Ithaca, NY: Cornell University Press, 2018.

Rogger, Hans. "*Amerikanizm* and the Economic Development of Russia," *Comparative Studies in Society and History* 23 (July 1981): 382–40.

Roman, Meredith L. "Forging Soviet Racial Enlightenment: Soviet Writers Condemn American Racial Mores, 1926, 1936, 1946," *Historian* 74 (Fall 2012): 528–50.

Ryan, Karen L. "Imagining America: Il'f and Petrov's 'Odnoetazhnaia Amerika' and Ideological Alterity," *Canadian Slavonic Papers / Revue Canadienne des Slavistes* 44 (September–December 2002): 263–78.

Saul, Norman E. *Friends or Foes? The United States and Soviet Russia, 1921–1941.* Lawrence: University Press of Kansas, 2006.

Schmidt, Regin. *Red Scare: FBI and the Origins of Anticommunism in the United States, 1919–1943.* Copenhagen: Museum Tusculanum Press, University of Copenhagen, 2000.

Schrag, Peter. *Not Fit for Our Society: Immigration and Nativism in America.* Berkeley: University of California Press, 2010.

Shteir, Rachel. *Striptease: The Untold Story of the Girlie Show.* Oxford: Oxford University Press, 2004.

Soyer, Daniel. "Soviet Travel and the Making of an American Jewish Communist: Moissaye Olgin's Trip to Russia in 1920–1921," *American Communist History* 4 (2005): 1–20.

Stagl, Justin, and Christopher Pinney, "Introduction: From Travel Writing to Ethnography," *History and Anthropology* 9 (1996): 121–24.

Stites, Richard. *Revolutionary Dreams: Utopian Vision and Experimental Life in the Russian Revolution.* New York: Oxford University Press, 1989.

Tan-Bogoraz, V. G. *USA: Liudi i nravi Ameriki.* Moscow: Federatsii, 1932.

Wolf, Erika. "The Author as Photographer: Tret'iakov's, Erenburg's, and Il'f's Images of the West," *Configurations* 18 (2010): 383–403.

Youngblood, D. J. "Americanitis: The *Amerikanshchina* in Soviet Cinema," *Journal of Popular Film & Television* 19 (Winter 1992): 148–56.

Youngs, Tim. *The Cambridge Introduction to Travel Writing.* New York: Cambridge University Press, 2013.

Index